ADVANCE PRAISE FOR
PRISONERS OF HOPE

"Randall Woods's *Prisoners of Hope* offers us new and revealing insights into the remarkable history of Lyndon Johnson and the Great Society. He writes from the perspective of a scholar sympathetic to Johnson and his expansive goals, but well aware of the ways in which American history, culture, and politics constrained the activist government role that Johnson envisioned. Anyone who wants to understand our current political struggles should read this book."

—Dan Carter, Educational Foundation Emeritus Professor,
University of South Carolina

"In *Prisoners of Hope*, Randall Woods draws on his deep understanding of American political history and the southern populist tradition, bringing LBJ's vaulting ambition and his extraordinary political skill vividly to life. The Great Society emerges as a decisive moment in the forming of modern America—both for better and for ill."

—Gareth Davies, author of *See Government Grow:
Education Politics from Johnson to Reagan*

"Anyone wanting to understand the volatile mix that is American politics today needs to look no further than Randall Woods's penetrating analysis of LBJ's Great Society agenda, that set of ambitious economic, social, political, and cultural reforms of the mid-1960s that raised the hopes of the poor and dispossessed and transformed American society, yet, in these very successes, contained the seeds of a right-wing backlash aimed at dismantling its cherished accomplishments." —Richard Blackett

PRISONERS OF HOPE

Lyndon B. Johnson, the Great Society, and the Limits of Liberalism

RANDALL B. WOODS

BASIC BOOKS
A Member of the Perseus Books Group
New York

Books published by Basic Books are available at special discounts for bulk purchases in the United States by corporations, institutions, and other organizations. For more information, please contact the Special Markets Department at the Perseus Books Group, 2300 Chestnut Street, Suite 200, Philadelphia, PA 19103, or call (800) 810-4145, ext. 5000, or e-mail special .markets@perseusbooks.com.

Designed by Timm Bryson

Library of Congress Cataloging-in-Publication Data
Names: Woods, Randall Bennett, 1944–
Title: Prisoners of hope : Lyndon B. Johnson, the Great Society, and the limits of liberalism / Randall B. Woods.
Description: New York : Basic Books, 2016. | Includes bibliographical references and index.
Identifiers: LCCN 2015040042| ISBN 9780465050963 (hardback) | ISBN 9780465098712 (ebook)
Subjects: LCSH: United States--Politics and government--1963-1969. | Johnson, Lyndon B. (Lyndon Baines), 1908-1973. | United States--Economic policy--1961-1971. | Economic assistance, Domestic--United States--History--20th century. | Social legislation--United States--History--20th century. | Liberalism--United States--History--20th century. | United States--Social policy--20th century. | BISAC: BIOGRAPHY
& AUTOBIOGRAPHY / Presidents & Heads of State. | HISTORY / United States /
20th Century. | POLITICAL SCIENCE / Public Policy / Social Services & Welfare.

Classification: LCC E846 .W66 2016 | DDC 973.923--dc23 LC record available at http://lccn.loc.gov/2015040042

10 9 8 7 6 5 4 3 2 1

For Rhoda and Patricia

CONTENTS

"Return to your stronghold, O prisoners of hope;
Today I declare that I will restore to you double."
—ZECHARIAH 9:12

THE PARADOX
OF REFORM

THE PRESIDENTIAL ADMINISTRATION OF LYNDON JOHNSON IS remembered primarily for two matters: civil rights, considered a success, and the war in Vietnam, viewed almost universally as a disastrous mistake. Except for the Civil Rights Acts of 1964 and 1965, Johnson's domestic program—the Great Society—has largely been ignored. Yet it was perhaps the most comprehensive and ambitious effort to change the political, social, and economic landscape of the United States in all of the country's history. It established new policies and bureaucracies to deal not only with race relations but also federal aid to education, medical aid for the poor and elderly, immigration, environmental pollution and conservation, urban decay, and the federal role in arts and humanities. Those policies and bureaucracies have, for the most part, survived, but many of the issues with which they dealt remain unresolved. Indeed, they dominate today's headlines and public forums. The cover of the May 2015 issue of *TIME* magazine featured a photograph of Baltimore police in riot gear chasing a black protester; the title was "America, 1968 (2015)." Currently, Democrats and Republicans are deadlocked over immigration reform, limits on carbon emissions, Obamacare, education reform, and the proper role of the federal government in the nation's cultural life. For those who would understand the issues of today, it is imperative to begin with a reexamination—or, rather, examination—of Lyndon Johnson's sweeping domestic program.

Volumes have been written on the mainsprings of other great American reform efforts, such as the Populist and Progressive movements and the New Deal, but next to nothing on the forces and factors responsible for the Great Society. Those few liberals who have chosen to write about the reforms of the 1960s have portrayed them as the culmination of JFK's idealism, the fulfillment of the New Frontier, ignoring the fact that Kennedy's program remained stalled in Congress at the time of his death and that Johnson's vision transcended that of his predecessor. Vietnam has been an albatross that the historical LBJ has been unable to shed. Most academics of my generation were fervently committed to the antiwar movement and have never been willing to forgive the Texan for thrusting the republic more deeply into the Vietnam quagmire. For Franklin Delano Roosevelt, US participation in World War II enhanced his moral credibility and, in the process, the reputation of the New Deal. For LBJ, escalation of the conflict in Vietnam bankrupted him morally, casting a dark shadow over his domestic reform initiatives. Then, there is the enduring cultural and political power of Camelot. The Kennedys detested LBJ as a usurper, a man who through no merit of his own became president and reaped the harvest that JFK had sowed. Finally, some veterans of the civil rights movement see accolades heaped on Johnson as somehow diminishing Martin Luther King Jr. Thus, the extremely faint praise of LBJ in the motion picture *Selma*. Until Hillary Clinton in 2008, no Democratic presidential candidate had dared invoke Johnson's name. Her husband's Oval Office contained busts of every twentieth-century Democratic president except LBJ. For conservatives, the reform initiatives of the 1960s were and are anathema. During the 1980s, the Great Society became the perfect whipping boy for Ronald Reagan and the New Right, a classic example of the evils of "government overreach" and the "welfare state." Those who have been willing to defend the Great Society, even to speak to its historical significance, have been few and far between indeed.

ON SEPTEMBER 7, 1964, LYNDON BAINES JOHNSON ROSE BEFORE A large audience gathered in Detroit's Cadillac Square and delivered a speech as visionary and utopian as any ever given to the American people. "Man has never lived in a more exciting time," the president declared. "The world is changing before your eyes." The nation must rise to meet the challenges of the present and future, he said, or be relegated to history's dustbin:

> I remember the men who captured my native soil from the wilderness. They endured much so that others might have much. Their dream was for the children; mine too is for the child, even now struggling toward birth.
>
> I want all the ages of man to yield him their promise, the child will find all knowledge open to him; the growing boy will shape his spirit in a house of God and his ways in the house of his family. The young man will find reward for his work and feel pride in the product of his skills.
>
> The man will find leisure and occasion for the closeness of family, and an opportunity for the enrichment of life. The citizen will enrich the nation, sharing its rule, walking its streets, adding his views to its counsel, secure always from the unjust and the arbitrary power of his fellows.
>
> The least among us will find contentment, and the best among us will find greatness, and all of us will respect the dignity of the one and admire the achievements of the other.
>
> At the end of the journey, he will look back and say, "I have done all that a man could do, built all, shared all, experienced all."[1]

Extravagant language, especially from a Texas politician with a reputation for ruthlessness and opportunism. Under normal circumstances, a man like Johnson would have been laughed off the national stage, the butt of jokes by political cartoonists and ridicule by cynical political commentators. But this was not the case. His Isaiah-like rhetoric was generally hailed as that of an authentic man of the people. In the wake of the martyrdom of John F. Kennedy and LBJ's successful effort to push his predecessor's domestic program through Congress and in revulsion at the extremist rhetoric of Barry Goldwater, the arch-conservative senator from Arizona, and George Wallace, the race-baiting governor of Alabama, the vast majority of Americans looked to

Lyndon Johnson expectantly. The nation in 1964 was simultaneously confident and desperate enough to countenance talk of utopias. LBJ had given a name to his promise during his commencement address at the University of Michigan the previous spring—the Great Society.

ON THE AFTERNOON OF JFK'S ASSASSINATION, NOVEMBER 22, 1963, Johnson, newly sworn in as president, had flown back to Washington aboard Air Force One with his predecessor's body on board. The former first family and staff needed time to move out of the White House, so LBJ retired to the Elms, his vice-presidential residence. Instead of sleeping, President Johnson spent most of his first few nights as chief executive sitting up with his aides, filling yellow legal pads with legislative proposals. What followed during the next four years was the passage of more than one thousand pieces of legislation that, coupled with the edicts of the liberal Warren Court, would transform the American political and social landscape. First up was the Kennedy tax cut that would generate the prosperity that would make social and economic change possible. Then came the 1964 Equal Accommodations Act, the 1965 Voting Rights Act, Medicare and Medicaid, federal aid to education, the Job Corps, Model Cities, the 1965 Immigration Act, clean air and clean water legislation, the creation of public television and radio, and the Fair Housing Act of 1968. Some of the Great Society programs were more successful than others, but no reasonable observer can question their impact on most aspects of life in America.

What is exceptional about the myriad pieces of legislation that Congress passed during the Johnson presidency is that they were enacted not during a period of great moral outrage by the middle class at malefactors of great wealth or at a time when Americans feared that the country was about to be overwhelmed by alien, immigrant cultures or in the midst of a crushing depression that threatened the very foundations of capitalism. There seemed to be no sweeping mandate for change. JFK had barely defeated Richard Nixon in the election of 1960.

The two obvious power sources for the Great Society were the civil rights movement and the Cold War. Prior to the Montgomery Bus Boycott of 1954 and the emergence of Martin Luther King's Southern Christian Leadership Conference (SCLC), the black civil rights movement in the

United States had been largely a matter of elites attempting to use constitutional law to achieve civil equality and nondiscrimination. In the 1950s, however, civil rights became a mass movement, first drawing in working-class blacks through their churches and then spreading to younger, secular African Americans by means of the Student Nonviolent Coordinating Committee (SNCC) and the Congress of Racial Equality (CORE). The violence directed against blacks, especially children, during the 1963 protest marches in Birmingham seemed to dramatically alter racial perceptions.

In 1957 the United States was traumatized by the launching of *Sputnik*. The ability of the Soviet Union, America's archrival, to place a payload in earth orbit before the United States could do so came as a huge shock to the nation. A great hue and cry went up for education and cultural reform. John F. Kennedy and other Democrats blasted the Eisenhower administration for its complacency and superficiality. If the United States was not to be overwhelmed by the communist superpowers in the struggle for hearts and minds in the developing world, they declared, it must prove the superiority of liberal capitalism to Marxism-Leninism. And that meant not just more quantity but more quality—in education, in the arts, in technology, in national purpose.

Sputnik and the ongoing competition with the Soviet Union were calls to arms for the members of the Greatest Generation. The men and women who had survived the Great Depression and defeated the Axis powers had grown uneasy with the relatively comfortable days of the Eisenhower era. As John F. Kennedy would remind them in his inaugural speech, there were still frontiers to conquer in the form of domestic poverty, space exploration, and disease eradication. And, of course, there was the ongoing crusade to make the world safe for democracy. In many ways the Great Society, both imagined and real, would be the supreme achievement of the Greatest Generation. How fitting that those who had saved capitalism and defeated Hitler and Hirohito should secure freedom at home and abroad and establish a society in which each individual could realize his or her potential.

Tools were at hand. The crisis of confidence spawned by *Sputnik* was a bit illusory. In the years before and after World War II, thousands of European intellectuals, refugees from fascist persecution and the devastation and destruction of the war, had fled to the United States and joined with American scientists and social engineers to create a critical mass, producing such breakthroughs as the Salk vaccine to eradicate polio, solid-fuel rocket propulsion, and social engineering models that promised to solve problems ranging from entrenched poverty to juvenile delinquency to institutionalized racism.

Then there was the New Left, the creation of the children of the Greatest Generation. In an issue devoted to the baby boomers, *TIME* magazine estimated that by the end of the 1960s one-quarter of the population would be twenty-four years old and younger. Many working- and lower-middle-class youths continued about their business as usual, but college students at elite institutions created the Free Speech Movement and then the Students for a Democratic Society (SDS). With the Port Huron Statement in 1962, the manifesto of the SDS, the New Left was born. Joining with left-leaning faculty and public intellectuals, Tom Hayden, a radical student leader at the University of Michigan and coauthor of the Port Huron manifesto, and his cohort denounced Jim Crow, the military-industrial complex, and New Deal liberalism. The New Left called on its followers to mobilize in behalf of full citizenship for African Americans, to force disarmament on the Great Powers, and dismantle the military-industrial complex. "Participatory democracy" was its remedy for the racism, economic exploitation, and institutional oppression that plagued America.

The final, obvious power source was Lyndon Johnson himself. As a constellation of ideas, as a vision of America, the Great Society had been taking shape in Johnson's mind since he first heard on his parents' Victrola in Johnson City, Texas, the Great Commoner William Jennings Bryan orating in behalf of the downtrodden masses. From his father's fervent populism and his mother's liberal Baptist faith, from his experiences of racism at the Welhausen Elementary School in Cotulla, from Franklin Roosevelt and the New Deal, from his love for the American political process, from his own messianic aspirations for himself came a reform vision of massive proportions and the will to realize it.

Reform leadership, FDR had insisted, must combine principled rhetoric and solid accomplishments. "Theodore Roosevelt," Roosevelt commented to Ray Stannard Baker in 1935, "lacked Woodrow Wilson's appeal to the fundamental and failed to stir, as Wilson did, the truly profound moral and social convictions." But Wilson "failed where Theodore Roosevelt succeeded in stirring people to enthusiasm about individual events, even though these specific events may have been superficial in comparison with the fundamentals." As a rhetorician determined to tap into the wellsprings of American idealism, LBJ combined the best of both.[2]

In his effort to generate support for reform, Lyndon Johnson seized on Kennedy's martyrdom with a vengeance. How could Congress reject the 1964 Civil Rights Act, Medicare, and the War on Poverty without turning its back on the fallen hero? He was determined, LBJ said, to protect and extend JFK's legacy, and the country must follow his lead. In doing what Kennedy would have done, America would rediscover its national purpose. Though Johnson did not say it, he intended to interpret and if necessary manufacture JFK's legacy. Ironically, it was Johnson who made Jack Kennedy the great liberal that he is remembered as being by many Americans today.

Fortunately for LBJ and his campaign to arouse the public's conscience, the American people were in a God-fearing mood. The forces of conformity, so strong during the early postwar period, coupled with the anxieties of the Cold War, had led to a religious revival that was simultaneously intense and pervasive. Overall, church membership increased from 64.5 million (49 percent of the total population) in 1940 to 125 million (64 percent) in 1965. All religions and denominations gained, but leading the way were Roman Catholics, Baptists, and Southern Pentecostals. Americans, historian Richard Hofstadter has written, are prone "to fits of crusading" and "do not abide very quietly the evils of life." They are, political commentator Seymour Martin Lipset observed, "particularly inclined to support movements for the elimination of evil."[3] LBJ both participated in these perceptions and inclinations and manipulated them to achieve his policy objectives: "From our Jewish and Christian heritage, we draw the image of the God of all mankind, who will judge his children not by their prayers and by their pretensions," he told a group of newspaper editors, "but by their mercy to the poor and their understanding of the weak."[4] And these were hard-drinking, tough-minded journalists he was speaking to, not men and women of the cloth.

Though not initially significant, Vietnam would become another engine that drove the Great Society. The decisions to escalate the war made in the spring and summer of 1965 conflicted and depressed LBJ. Five days after approving General William Westmoreland's request for two additional combat divisions to be sent to Vietnam, Johnson called in Joe Califano, his chief domestic policy adviser, and gave him his marching orders for 1966—a new

department of transportation, model cities, fair housing, and new environmental initiatives. Guilt over the war led to a need to compensate; progress
in the fight against poverty, racism, ill health, and ignorance might be offered
in propitiation for the death and destruction being wrought in Southeast
Asia.

But what programs, legislative strategies, and political philosophies were
best suited to fulfill the promise of social and economic justice in America?
Most reform-minded individuals were and are well intended. The problem
was, as Lyndon Johnson and others observed, not a lack of willingness on the
part of men and women of affairs to do good but the ability to recognize
which actions and programs served the greater good and which did not.
Both those political philosophers, activists, public intellectuals, and politicians who proclaimed an abiding faith in human nature and those who did
not claimed to have virtue on their side—that is, a concern for the com-
monweal as a whole. But which ideologies, which social programs would
best coerce the mob or restrain the plutocracy and conserve a maximum of
freedom for the general polity?

Instinctively, LBJ and the architects of the Great Society drew on the past.
The liberal initiatives of the 1960s were descendants of a reform movement
that began with Populism and continued through the Progressive Era and
the New Deal. The War on Poverty could trace its roots back to the early
Progressive Era and the emergence of the Social Gospel as a force both in
the nation's religious and political life. In line with Progressivism, the reforms of the 1960s sought to restructure and reform the physical, social, and
political milieu in ways that enhanced equality, opportunity, and quality in
American life. The New Deal had promised to expand the rights guaranteed
to all Americans beyond "negative" rights—freedom of speech, religion,
association, and so forth—to include "positive" rights, such as the rights to
a basic education, equality of opportunity, and a degree of social security.
The Great Society moved not only to fulfill that promise—to expand the
definition of citizenship—but also to extend the rights of full citizenship to
those previously excluded.

IN THE WAKE OF HIS SWEEPING VICTORY OVER BARRY GOLDWATER IN
the 1964 election, Johnson told Bill Moyers, the young Texan who would

become one of LBJ's most trusted aides, that the administration had at most twenty-two months in which to bring the Great Society to fruition. He had a mandate from the public and a liberal Congress, LBJ said, but the window of opportunity was small, and it would begin to close by the mid-term elections in 1966. Johnson ticked off some of the forces that would be arrayed against the administration. The conservative coalition—the amalgam of southern Democrats and Republicans that had blocked reform since the days of Harry Truman—was down, but not out. The racial violence in Birmingham and other segregationist strongholds that had erupted as Martin Luther King and the SCLC launched their protests and practiced nonviolent civil disobedience had roused the consciences of whites outside the former Confederacy, but racism ran deep in American society, and there was the very real possibility of a backlash.

The citizenry was still profoundly conflicted about the causes and cures for poverty. Polls continued to indicate that half of all Americans believed that poverty was the result of individual failings, and half that it was due to forces beyond the control of the individual. And, of course, there was the political calculus, the law of diminishing returns. In the process of persuading Congress and the nation to embrace equal accommodations, voting rights, federal aid to education, Medicare, a war on poverty, sweeping environmental legislation, immigration reform, urban renewal, and the myriad other initiatives the president had in mind, the administration would have to expend all of its political capital. When its account was empty, the window of reform would close. And the Vietnam War loomed ominously on the horizon. In addition to these perceived roadblocks, forces also lurked in the shadows, forces beyond even the Texan's imagination, some of them offshoots of the engines driving reform in the 1960s, some unintended consequences of the Great Society programs themselves.

Indeed, in some areas the Great Society contained seeds of its own destruction. The administration seemed at times to be calling in artillery on its own position, pursuing policies that were antithetical to the moderate consensus it depended on.[5] Community action—that is, participation by the poor and underprivileged in the political, social, and economic decisions that affected their lives—was front and center in the Port Huron Statement, the manifesto of the Students for a Democratic Society. Maximum feasible participation sounded harmless to LBJ, and Community Action Programs

(CAPs)—the government-sponsored initiatives designed to institutionalize grassroots involvement in decision making—would be a lot less expensive than publicly financed works projects or a guaranteed income.

Very quickly, however, state and local authorities came to see the Community Action Programs as dangerously subversive, at worst a forum for criminals and at best a conduit through which the federal government and the inner-city poor could bypass the existing power structure. Johnson attempted to stem the tide, to rein in the Office of Economic Opportunity (OEO) as it set about sponsoring more than a thousand CAPs, but bureaucratic momentum proved too much for him. As a result, one of the lasting, if unintended, achievements of the Great Society was a vast network of local nonprofits that gave voice and opportunity to the nation's urban poor. But, at the same time, the CAPs upset the delicate political equation that Johnson depended upon to keep momentum for reform going. Among other things, maximum feasible participation spawned the National Welfare Rights Organization (NWRO), which used the courts to challenge restrictive welfare regulations and maximize welfare rolls. At a time when Johnson was telling conservatives and liberals alike that the object of the Great Society was to get people off welfare and into the workforce, the number of Americans on welfare, thanks in part to the efforts of the OEO, doubled.

The Great Society was predicated philosophically and politically on consensus. In the Johnsonian world, enemies were abstract—disease, ignorance, racism—not concrete—economic royalists, segregationists, doctors, the "Upper Ten," radical immigrants. Johnson as president abjured partisan politics, crossing the aisle repeatedly to secure votes for key legislation. To the dismay of the Democratic National Committee (DNC) and his personal political advisers, he virtually ignored party affiliation when making executive and judicial branch appointments. But rebellious youth, both conservative and liberal, decried consensus as the protector of an unjust status quo. The Free Speech Movement and the Students for a Democratic Society demanded that America's youth be liberated from the societal norms and institutional controls that had characterized the 1950s. The Port Huron Statement denounced the military-industrial complex, domestic racism, exploitive capitalism, and the liberal establishment. Consensus itself was something to be feared, a mechanism to perpetuate an unjust status quo and stifle individualism.

The Great Society's effort to address both quantity and quality-of-life issues produced a contradiction that would have profound consequences for minorities and women. A strong equity rationale ran through Great Society programs from the Civil Rights Acts of 1964, 1965, and 1968 to the Elementary and Secondary Education Act and the War on Poverty. But as many reformers were beginning to acknowledge, equity was not enough. Opportunity did not automatically translate into achievement. In his 1965 Howard University speech, LBJ seemed to be moving toward compensatory action. He cited the ravages of slavery and post–Civil War discrimination and called for "affirmative action" to level the playing field. But what Johnson and Kennedy before him had in mind was "soft" affirmative action—measures taken by federal, state, and local governments and private employers to ensure that all discrimination in hiring practices was eliminated.

Affirmative action, like so many other Great Society programs, took on a life of its own, however. By the time Johnson left office, representatives of disadvantaged groups were calling for hiring quotas and workforce configurations that mirrored local population percentages for race and gender. Conservatives and even some figures in the civil rights and women's movements denounced "hard" affirmative action as a threat to the equity rationale that had played such a fundamental role in the struggle for minority rights and women's liberation, but to no avail.

Yet another unforeseen and, as far as the coalition LBJ had crafted in support of the Great Society, subversive consequence of the reform program of the 1960s was the rising level of expectations and frustrations among northern blacks created by the successful campaign against Jim Crow. In 1961, the Urban League's Whitney Young warned of an impending urban crisis. Blacks might very well end up with "a mouthful of rights and an empty stomach," he declared.[6] For the most part there was no legally mandated segregation in the North, and black voters were not systematically disenfranchised. But informal segregation and discrimination were pervasive. Generally speaking, black voters were nothing more than powerless pawns in the machinations of big-city machines. Public policy, market practices, and racial prejudice confined African Americans to deteriorating neighborhoods, separate and unequal schools, and menial jobs. The result was a series of urban uprisings that shook the republic to its foundations. The Watts riot, beginning just five days after the signing of the Voting Rights Act of 1965,

marked a turning point in the history of the Great Society. As Lyndon Johnson and the architects of the Second Reconstruction (a name given to the
civil rights movement of the 1950s and 1960s, the First Reconstruction re-
ferring to the postemancipation civil rights regime in the 1860s and 1870s)
were soon to learn, they had built a political coalition to force equality of
opportunity and access on the South with northern constituencies that were
not themselves committed to those principles in their own backyard.

During the 1964 presidential campaign, LBJ, prodded by Goldwater's
charge that the Democratic administration was presiding over a massive
breakdown of law and order in the United States, touted the War on Poverty
as part of the War on Crime. In so doing he opened a Pandora's box that
threatened to overwhelm the entire Great Society. The commingling of
the two wars offered conservatives a rare opportunity to attack the Johnson
consensus. As the OEO and other agencies focused on the nation's inner
cities, ghetto violence only increased. By 1966, the mantra of the conservative coalition had become law and order. Critics of Johnson and the Great
Society proved increasingly successful in selling the American public on
three notions: first, that urban rioting and civil disorder grew out of the
civil rights movement, successfully conflating nonviolent civil disobedience
with looting and burning; second, that the Warren Court favored the rights
of criminals over the rights of victims; and third, that the Great Society, in
undermining individual initiative and self-reliance, was creating a comity
composed of individuals with no self-discipline and a deep-seated sense
of entitlement.[7] Thus did the War on Crime become a war on the War on
Poverty.

Still another irony that plagued the Johnson administration's ambitious
domestic programs was that, while Washington continually justified the Great
Society as an effective response to the putative utopia of Marxism-Leninism,
conservative Republicans and southern segregationists charged that many
of the organizations and initiatives spawned by the Johnsonian vision were
communist inspired and even controlled. Dixiecrats such as Georgia senator
Richard Russell and Mississippi senator James Eastland, in an effort to stave
off federally mandated civil rights programs, proclaimed that the civil rights
movement was nothing less than a communist conspiracy. States' righters
had long argued that social planning, intrusive federal programs, and big
government in general were heralds of a coming socialist state.[8] Indeed, for
decades not only segregationists but conservatives in general had been trying

to persuade the American people that liberalism equaled socialism and that socialism equaled communism. As they had during the 1930s, Dixiecrats were willing to tolerate programs that benefited poor white southerners, but they fought tooth and nail against the various 1960s civil rights acts as well as Medicare and federal aid to education, both of which were civil rights bills in themselves. For obvious reasons, segregationists were determined to paint the civil rights movement red, and in this they found a potent ally in J. Edgar Hoover's FBI.

Finally, the Vietnam War and the Great Society were inextricably intertwined, producing yet another brace of ironies. In the minds of many Cold War liberals—who were collectively the engine of reform in America from 1963 through 1965—the conflict in Vietnam was an extension of the effort to achieve social and economic justice abroad. For a year and a half following the Gulf of Tonkin incident, however, military considerations trumped nation building, and South Vietnam was treated to free-fire zones and indiscriminate sweeps by conventional military forces. Then, between late 1966 and early 1968, the White House presided over a shift in strategy in Vietnam from search-and-destroy to an emphasis on counterinsurgency and pacification, an approach more congenial to liberals. But it was too late. For many Americans, both hawks and doves, the 1968 communist Tet Offensive (a victory perceived as defeat) proved to be the last straw. Disillusionment with the war in Southeast Asia coupled with ongoing urban unrest eroded the consensus that LBJ had depended upon to enact the Great Society and fight the Second Indochina War.

Lyndon Johnson's pessimism concerning the time allotted to the administration to achieve its domestic goals was more than warranted. Credibility gaps were everywhere—unfulfilled promises in Southeast Asia, unredeemed expectations in the nation's ghettoes, and unmet pledges to restore law and order through antipoverty and civil rights initiatives. But as 1963 passed into 1964, these were clouds on the horizon. There was a window of opportunity; LBJ and his lieutenants were aching to take advantage of it.

CHAPTER I

"I AM A ROOSEVELT NEW DEALER": LIBERALISM ASCENDANT

THE BULLET THAT KILLED JOHN F. KENNEDY IN DALLAS ON NOVEMBER 22, 1963, ended Vice President Lyndon Johnson's two-and-a-half-year sojourn in the political wilderness. Scorned by the princes of Camelot, shut out of the decision-making process, left on the shelf as the administration tried to persuade Congress to implement the programs of the New Frontier, Johnson had spent the morning prior to the assassination wondering whether the Kennedys intended to drop him from the ticket in 1964. Then, suddenly, he was president of the United States. The day following Kennedy's murder, the new chief executive told an aide: "I am a Roosevelt New Dealer. As a matter of fact . . . Kennedy was a little too conservative to suit my taste."[1] Acting on a genuine commitment to help the poor of all colors and ages, and with an eye to the 1964 election, Johnson declared "unconditional war on poverty" and embraced a program that was rooted in the New Frontier but that vastly transcended it.

Influenced by Michael Harrington's *The Other America* and by the fact that the tax relief bill then pending in Congress reduced tariffs on upper- and middle-class incomes but provided no help to the poor who paid no income tax, Kennedy had asked the Council of Economic Advisers to make recommendations. Those proposals were presented to Lyndon John-son the day after he became president. He endorsed them enthusiastically. Indeed, unbeknownst to all but a few of his closest aides, Johnson, instead of sleeping, spent most of his first few nights sitting up with presidential aides and old political acquaintances filling yellow legal tablets with legis-lative proposals that would make a kindergarten-through-college education available to all; eradicate poverty in the nation's slums—both urban and rural; cleanse the environment of pollutants; enhance government bene-fits for the aged; guarantee equality under the law and equal opportunity for all Americans regardless of race, color, or national origin; rationalize the nation's discriminatory immigration policy; provide federal support to enhance the arts and humanities; and launch hundreds of other initiatives. Like Theodore Roosevelt, who had succeeded to the presidency following an assassination, LBJ was ready to take advantage of a national tragedy and the public's sense of vulnerability to affirm the union and advance the cause of social justice.[2]

On November 25, the day of JFK's funeral, Johnson delivered off-the-record remarks to the governors of several states:

> We have to do something to stop . . . hate and the way we have to do it is to meet the problem of injustice that exists in this land, meet the problem of inequality that exists in this land, meet the problem of poverty that exists in this land, and the unemployment that exists in this land. . . . I am going to be at it from daylight to midnight, and with your help and God's help we are going to make not only ourselves proud that we are Americans but we are going to make the rest of the world proud that there is an America in it.[3]

LBJ DECIDED TO RETAIN KENNEDY'S CABINET, BUT HE HAD HIS OWN brain trust, a group that he had assembled over the years, a collection of men whose pragmatic liberalism was tinged with the theological realism of Reinhold Niebuhr.

There was, of course, George Reedy, who would become LBJ's first White House press secretary in the spring of 1964. Since 1952, Reedy, the only member of the Johnson inner circle who was not a Texan, had been

LBJ's policy intellectual. The son of a *Chicago Tribune* crime reporter, Reedy was blessed with a phenomenal mind. As a student at the University of Chicago, he had consumed books by day and lived the Bohemian life by night, drinking, arguing, and fornicating. Following a stint in the Air Force as an intelligence officer during World War II, Reedy went to work for United Press International covering Capitol Hill. That is where LBJ discovered him.

No one did more to give substance to LBJ's liberalism than Reedy. At times, Johnson found his portly, shaggy-haired aide too ponderous, too philosophical. "You ask him what time it is," LBJ complained, "and he discusses the significance of time before he tells you it's eleven-thirty."[4] Nevertheless, it was inevitable that Pierre Salinger, Kennedy's White House spokesman, would leave, and Johnson felt that he owed the press secretary's job to Reedy. "I'm going to try to build you up," he told Reedy. "I want you to look real nice . . . put on your corset if you have to. . . . But look like a top-flight businessman. You look like a god-damned reporter."[5] Through it all, LBJ continued to take Reedy seriously. No one he knew was able to better combine the social gospel with political reality.

More important than Reedy, especially during the early months, was Horace Busby. "Buzz" had grown up in Fort Worth, the son of a Church of Christ minister. As a student at the University of Texas, Busby fell in love with the written word and had decided, not surprisingly, to focus on journalism. As a senior, he edited the student newspaper, the *Daily Texan,* and penned a series of stinging editorials in defense of UT president Homer Rainey, whom the reactionary board of regents was then in the process of firing. In these pieces, Busby's commitment to reform, to the social gospel, to freedom of inquiry and expression, to public figures committed to the welfare of the common man rather than special interests came to the fore.

In 1948, when LBJ had run for the US Senate as a New Dealer against Coke Stevenson, he had hired the twenty-five-year-old Busby as his speechwriter. Thus began an on-again, off-again relationship that would last the rest of the two men's lives. Like LBJ, Busby was not antibusiness—indeed, he had established and directed the American International Business Research Corporation—but he believed that government existed in main to be an agent of social justice. He had a sharp political eye, especially when it came to LBJ's future. But he was a sensitive, dignified man and, unlike Reedy, would not put up with Johnson's ridicule. Moreover, Johnson's sometimes coarseness repelled him. LBJ needed men like Reedy and Busby, exploited them, but frequently did not give them the respect they felt they were due. "Buzz is a very sound, solid, able, good boy," Johnson once remarked. The condescension infuriated his speechwriter. As a result, Busby moved in and out of the Johnson orbit, but he was a crucial figure during the early days of the presidency. The author of Johnson's powerful 1963 civil rights address at Gettysburg, Busby focused on domestic affairs and wrote most of LBJ's Rose Garden speeches.[6]

Throughout the transition the person who held things together was Walter Jenkins, LBJ's friend, confidant, and loyal factotum. Jenkins was far from the simple, one-dimensional man that he seemed to most. Born on a hardscrabble farm near Wichita Falls, Texas, Jenkins managed two years at the University of Texas before he ran out of money and went to work as de facto chief of staff for Lyndon Johnson. Between 1939 and 1964, Jenkins left the extended Johnson family only twice—to serve in the Army in North Africa and Italy during World War II, and to run unsuccessfully for Congress in 1951. Jenkins knew everything there was to know about Lyndon Johnson and his family—their dalliances, their business dealings, their friends, and the increasingly complicated social and political networks that grew up around the family. He was a quietly intense, mild-mannered man but would harden instantly when anyone or anything threatened his boss's reputation or interests. Jenkins was not ideological, was not well-read, and did not have a philosophical bent of mind. He was, as Eric Goldman, the Princeton historian who served for a time as White House intellectual, said, "an enormously decent human being . . . who sought fair play and kindliness in the dealings between men."[7]

A devout Catholic, Jenkins believed that to whom much was given, much was expected. It was incumbent upon America, a land blessed with genius and abundance, to help those who could not help themselves and to provide for the average hard-working person a degree of physical comfort and security and the means to provide food, shelter, health care, and education for his or her child. Moreover, for a "provincial," Jenkins was remarkably broad-minded, an important characteristic for the person who would determine who should have access to the president of the United States. Jenkins made sure that LBJ was exposed to persons and points of view across the political spectrum, even those whom and which he found personally abhorrent.[8]

Observers expected Jenkins, Busby, and Reedy to assume the prominent roles they did in White House affairs, but Jack Valenti was a total surprise. Valenti's father was the son of a Sicilian immigrant who earned $150 a month as a court clerk in Houston. Jack, a short, handsome, energetic youth with well-developed social skills, worked his way through the University of Houston as an office boy for Humble Oil. During World War II, he became a decorated bomber pilot who flew fifty-one missions over Germany and Italy. Out of uniform, he realized a lifelong dream by matriculating at Harvard Business School. Back in Houston, he and a friend established a successful public relations business. Like Busby, Valenti became a devoted wordsmith. He was an avid reader, but his education was uneven. He liked popular nonfiction and the nineteenth-century English historian Thomas Macaulay. He was also given to perusing anthologies of famous quotations. Valenti had caught Johnson's eye when he penned a worshipful portrait of him for the *Houston Post*. He worked in the 1960 election for the Kennedy-Johnson ticket and advanced the 1963 Texas trip. After the assassination, LBJ asked the sharp-dressing, ever-accommodating Valenti to accompany him on Air Force One to Washington. He subsequently lived at the Elms and then at the White House until he could move his wife, the former Mary Margaret Wiley, whom he had married off of LBJ's vice-presidential staff in 1963, to Washington.

Until he departed the White House in April 1966, Valenti was LBJ's constant companion. Unless dispatched as ambassador to some discontented legislator, or as emissary to an interest group that was being courted by the White House, Valenti was at the president's side, frequently staying up with him until the wee hours of the morning as LBJ unwound. Valenti, intelligent, sensitive, and diplomatic, proved skilled at assuaging hurt feelings and communicating the president's wishes. He was an uncritical admirer of LBJ. That and his belief in the efficacy of public relations sometimes worked to the detriment of his boss. At times, LBJ seemed like an overly exposed headline seeker rather than a thoughtful statesman. Washington insiders and gossip columnists marveled at Valenti's seeming indifference to rumors that an old affair between LBJ and Mary Margaret had started up again.[9]

Then there was Billy Don Moyers, the man who more than any other until his departure in 1966 was perceived as one person who could speak for the president. He had grown up during the Depression in Hugo, Oklahoma.

In search of a better life, Moyers's father moved the family to Marshall, an oil and gas town in east Texas that was heavily Baptist and that featured no fewer than four faith-based colleges. Bill was a star student at Marshall High and then earned degrees from North Texas State and UT. During the years that followed, he worked part-time for the Johnsons at KTBC, the family-owned radio station in Austin, and attended Southwestern Baptist Theological Seminary. At Southwestern, he studied under the liberal theologian Thomas Buford Matson. The son of a working-class family from east Tennessee, Matson had earned a PhD from Yale, where he studied under Reinhold Niebuhr, among others. During his half century as a teacher and pastor, Matson was an outspoken advocate of racial justice and a champion of labor unions. He and young Moyers talked as much politics as they did theology.

After working in the 1960 presidential campaign for the Kennedy-Johnson ticket, Moyers was selected to assist Sargent Shriver in directing the Peace Corps. He was the youngest person ever to be confirmed by the Senate. Moyers proved to be the perfect New Frontiersman—a hard-nosed idealist. He would point with pride to the Jeffersonian quotation hanging on his office wall: "The care of human life and happiness . . . is the first and only legitimate object of good government."[10] At the same time, he appreciated power and aspired to possess it. He was an instinctive bureaucratic politician. Exuding confidence and the promise of holding high office, he was able to attract other young men to him and, by 1965, commanded a network of supporters that spread throughout the top echelons of the federal government.

The constituency Moyers selected to represent was the offspring of the Greatest Generation. He addressed youth conventions as if they were labor gatherings, posing to them and to the outside world as their representative. LBJ loved a young man on the make, especially one who would work his guts out for him. Moyers was loyal, but he could also be diplomatically critical and was an independent voice within White House counsels. Reputedly, a father-son relationship developed between LBJ and Moyers, but that was more for show than for anything else. Johnson could trust Moyers not only to carry out his instructions but increasingly to make decisions. Moyers had received a Rotary scholarship and studied at Edinburgh University in Scotland, where he fell in love with Europe, with literature, with social sophistication. The crew from Camelot fascinated him, and he had managed to worm his way into its good graces. LBJ knew this and counted on Moyers to act as liaison with the Kennedys and those who frequented the Georgetown cocktail circuit. Moyers readily obliged, but although Johnson found this role useful, he would increasingly resent his protégé for playing it.[11]

ANYONE FAMILIAR WITH THE MIND-SET AND TRACK RECORD OF those that LBJ gathered around him during the closing days of 1963 could have predicted the Johnson administration's ensuing commitment to social justice. But he and his closest associates were largely a mystery, and LBJ knew it. He wanted there to be no mistake in Congress and the public's mind that he intended to take up not where JFK but where FDR had left off and so he moved to embrace several prominent New Dealers.

A week after the assassination, LBJ met with Jim Rowe and Tommy Corcoran, two veterans of the New Deal. He and Rowe had barely spoken since 1960, when they had had a falling out over campaign strategy. "I've been thinking back over 1960 and thinking of where I am now," LBJ said, "and I need friends. I need help and you have been a friend to me and one of the wisest advisors I know. And I let you and I drift apart and it was my fault and I was foolish and short-sighted and I'm sorry and I hope that you'll forgive me and be my friend and supporter." With tears in his eyes, Rowe said, "My God, Mr. President, it wasn't your fault." Johnson said, "Yes, it was. Don't argue with me. Just be content to be the first man to whom the 36th President of the United States has offered his apologies."[12]

And of course Abe Fortas and Clark Clifford composed a part of LBJ's inner circle from the very beginning.[13] Both were prominent attorneys and Washington insiders, but there was no comparing LBJ's relationships with the two. Clifford, who had been Truman's White House counsel and who remained a power in the Democratic Party, was loyal to no one but himself. He would keep his star hitched to the LBJ wagon only so long as it suited his interests to do so. For Johnson, he was a valuable tie to the Truman crowd, however. Fortas was Johnson's lawyer but also a person whom the president trusted to advise him on any and every issue.

The son of middle-class Jewish parents from Memphis, Fortas had attended Yale Law School, where he found himself in the midst of the great debate between "conceptualists," whose home base was Harvard, and "functionalists," increasingly centered at Yale. This great debate among legal scholars grew out of the Progressive Era and the revolt of jurists such as Louis Brandeis and Oliver Wendell Holmes against the notion that the practice of constitutional law lay in discovering and abiding by a group of unchanging principles that sprang from the minds of the Founding Fathers and that were embedded in the Constitution. Brandeis, one of the fathers of functionalism, argued that America had changed dramatically since the eighteenth century and that practitioners of jurisprudence ought to factor in current social and economic conditions in handing down their decisions. The law was something organic and changing, to be interpreted always to advance the common good.

At university as editor of the *Yale Law Journal,* Fortas embraced functionalism and after graduation moved to take advantage of the opportunities Roosevelt's Washington offered to young Catholic and Jewish lawyers. He spent his New Deal years justifying government regulation of big business and promoting the cause of social justice. He was the ultimate pragmatist who agreed with the New Deal official who told his aides, "I want to assure you that we are not afraid of exploring anything within the law and we have a lawyer who will declare anything you want to do legal."[14] Following the war, Fortas made a fortune representing the very corporations that he had once attacked. But he, like John Kenneth Galbraith, the famed economist, believed that the line between public and private in America was blurring. He saw himself as a member of an emerging body of disinterested experts who could simultaneously promote capitalism and advance the cause of civil liberties, civil rights, and economic justice.[15] In short, Abe Fortas was the perfect counselor to a pragmatic liberal like Lyndon Johnson.

All of Johnson's advisers agreed that it was imperative that the new president address Congress and through it the nation and the world. Throughout the two days following his return from Dallas, Johnson met with individuals in and out of government to gather ideas and to gauge the impact that his words would have on the near future. LBJ ordered Valenti, Busby, and Theodore Sorenson—Kennedy's house intellectual, speechwriter, and political adviser—to work on drafts; meanwhile, he consulted with Ken Galbraith, Kennedy's ambassador to India, who had already been lobbying Democratic liberals to forget the past and work to ensure Johnson's election in 1964.

Galbraith emphasized civil rights and the need to not become overextended in Indochina where US-supported regimes were battling communist insurgencies in Laos and Vietnam. Walter Heller, chairman of the Council of Economic Advisers, lobbied for a massive $11 billion tax cut that the administration had been considering.[16]

On Tuesday evening, the night before the speech, Johnson met at the Elms for more than six hours with Fortas, Senator Hubert Humphrey (D-MN), and others to go over drafts of the speech. Fortas remembered that one of those present urged Johnson not to give civil rights a high priority. Passage of the equal accommodations bill then before Congress looked pretty hopeless; the issue was as divisive as any ever faced by the nation, and it would be suicide to wage and lose such a battle. LBJ looked at the man and said, "Well, what the hell is the presidency for?"[17]

Amid the tension and high drama there was a moment of pathos. Jack Valenti remembered that, as he and Ted Sorenson rode with the president to Capitol Hill the next day, Sorenson clutched the final draft of the speech closely to his chest. Valenti asked to see it for a moment. Sorenson refused. When Valenti asked why, Sorenson said it was because he might change something else.[18] Only about 50 percent of his original draft remained. "But that's the best fifty percent," Johnson said soothingly.[19]

As Johnson stepped to the podium, Congress, the nation, and the world held its collective breath. Who was this man, now president of the most powerful nation in history? Few questioned his competence, but what did that matter?—Hitler had been competent. Would he be a front man for southern segregationists, as many white northern liberals believed, or a turncoat integrationist, as many white southerners suspected? Where would he stand on foreign policy? Many at home and abroad feared that he would turn out to be a simple Texas jingo, crying "Remember the Alamo," willing to bring the world to the brink of nuclear destruction at the drop of a hat. Most important, was LBJ a simple political fixer, or was he a man of principle with a value system that would promote the interests of peace, freedom, and social justice?

LBJ began quietly, so quietly that senators and representatives in the back rows had to strain to hear. To no one's surprise, he paid tribute to John F. Kennedy—"The greatest leader of our time"—and emphasized continuity. JFK had had a dream "of conquering the vastness of space . . . the dream of a Peace Corps in less developed nations . . . the dream of education for all of our children—the dream of jobs for all who seek them and need them—the dream of care for our elderly—the dream of an all-out attack on mental illness." President Kennedy had called to the nation, "'Let us begin.' . . . I would say to all my fellow Americans, let us continue."

After each dream was enunciated, Congress, the Supreme Court, the Joint Chiefs, foreign dignitaries, and the packed gallery broke into thunderous applause. Sensing that Johnson was about to address the issue of civil rights, southerners sat forward in their seats. "No memorial oration or eulogy could more eloquently honor President Kennedy's memory than the earliest possible passage of the civil rights bill for which he fought so long. We have talked long enough in this country about equal rights. We have talked for one hundred years or more. It is time now to write the next chapter, and to write it in the books of law." But civil rights was not only John F. Kennedy's cause, Johnson wanted to make clear; it was Lyndon Johnson's as well. "I urge you again, as I did in 1957 and again in 1960, to enact a civil rights law so that we can move forward to eliminate from this Nation every trace of discrimination and oppression that is based upon race or color." Again, applause, although this time arch-segregationist Senator Richard Russell (D-GA) and his followers sat silent. There was in their posture more a mood of resignation than defiance, however. Among black Americans, there was a collective sigh of relief. "You could hear 20,000 people unpacking their bags," comedian and civil rights activist Dick Gregory later joked.[20]

As to foreign affairs, there was to be peace through strength. "The Nation will keep its commitments from South Viet-Nam to Berlin," Johnson said, making a most significant linkage. And finally to the nation's and the world's most immediate concern, "Let us turn away from the fanatics of the far left and the far right, from the apostles of bitterness and bigotry, from those defiant of law, and those who pour venom into our Nation's bloodstream." The speech ended with the first stanza of "America the Beautiful," a maudlin touch under most circumstances, but somehow fitting coming from Lyndon Johnson's lips on November 27, 1963.[21]

The speech to the joint session of Congress was meant to evoke memories of JFK, but it was pure LBJ—military preparedness, peace through strength, holding the line against international communism, and advancing social justice at home. The phrase that Johnson's auditors should have paid the most attention to was: "We will carry on the fight against poverty and misery, and disease and ignorance, in other lands and in our own."[22]

Johnson's ascendancy to the presidency made demands and presented opportunities that enabled him to transcend mere pragmatism. In 1964, he would declare, "I do not accept Government as just the 'art of the practicable.' It is the business of deciding what is right and then finding the way to do it."[23] Johnson's self-acknowledged mentors are well known: Huey Long; Maury Maverick (the liberal mayor of San Antonio and New Deal congressman from Texas); Samuel Ealy Johnson, Lyndon's ardently Populist father; and his mother, Rebecca Baines Johnson, a Christian social activist. LBJ had been deeply moved by John Steinbeck's 1937 novel, *The Grapes of Wrath,* the story of a poor, hard-working Dust Bowl family crushed by a physical environment and socioeconomic system beyond their control. "I am not a theologian," he told members of the Southern Baptist Leadership Seminar in March 1964. "But in more than 3 decades of public life, I have seen first-hand how basic spiritual beliefs and deeds can shatter barriers of politics and bigotry. Great questions of war and peace, of civil rights and education, the elimination of poverty at home and abroad, are the concern of millions who see no difference in this regard between their beliefs and their social obligations."[24] In response to a genuine commitment to help the poor of all colors and ages and with an eye to the 1964 election, Johnson would declare "unconditional war on poverty."

LBJ WAS COMMITTED TO REFORM, BUT WAS THE COUNTRY HE PRESIDED over similarly committed? Was liberalism alive and well in the early winter of 1963, and if it was, what exactly did it stand for? What traditions and collective memories crowded the political stage as the Texan began to take command? What forces awaited his disposal, and what forces lay in wait to ambush him?

The New Deal was part of the American reform tradition that, along with Populism and Progressivism, sought to redefine the meaning of liberalism. Since the birth of the republic, liberalism had been associated with the

Jeffersonian principle of limited government, a notion growing out of natural rights philosophy.[25] The Progressive philosopher Hebert Croly had called
for using Hamiltonian means—government intervention in and regulation
of the economy—to achieve Jeffersonian ends: equality of opportunity and
realization of individual potential. During late 1929 and early 1930, John
Dewey, an American philosopher and psychologist, had published a six-
part series in the *New Republic* entitled "Individualism: Old and New." The
state, he declared, did not exist to protect rugged individualism and private
property but to guarantee the social and economic welfare of the general
population. Borrowing from Dewey, FDR termed his philosophy "liberalism," thereby meaning to convey the idea that the dignity of the democratic
individual required a stronger, more active federal government. Roosevelt
and his speechwriters wanted to do nothing less than legitimize advanced
Progressivism by presenting it as an expansion rather than a subversion of
the natural rights tradition.[26] In his Commonwealth Club address in 1932,
FDR declared that the task of modern government was "to assist in the development of an economic declaration of rights, an economic constitutional
order."[27] There was to be a new social contract in which the government
guaranteed individual men and women protection from the uncertainties
of the marketplace.

The New Deal introduced the concept of positive rights, the notion that
citizens of the United States were entitled to certain benefits, as opposed
to "negative rights," which protected them in the exercise of freedom of
speech, assembly, and religion, for example. In his 1936 acceptance speech
to the Democratic National Nominating Convention, FDR declared: "The
royalists of the new economic order have conceded that political freedom
was the business of government, but they have maintained that economic
slavery was nobody's business. They granted that the Government could
protect the citizen in his own right to vote, but they denied that Government could do anything to protect the citizen in his right to work and his
right to live. . . . If the average citizen is guaranteed equal opportunity in the
polling place, he must have equal opportunity in the marketplace."[28]

In his 1944 State of the Union address, FDR proclaimed a "Second Bill of
Rights": the right to a useful and remunerative job; the right to earn enough
to afford adequate food, clothing, and recreation; the right of every family
to a decent home; the right to adequate medical care and the opportunity

to achieve and enjoy good health; the right to adequate protection from the economic fears of old age, sickness, accident, and unemployment; and the right to a good education. Polls indicated that 79 percent of Democrats and Republicans alike believed that it was "the duty of the government to provide for the needy."[29]

Perhaps the most important achievement of the New Deal was its success in expanding the definition of citizenship. A minimum wage was guaranteed by the Fair Labor Standards Act; collective bargaining was institutionalized in the workplace under the National Labor Relations Act; aid to unemployed persons, older adults, and single mothers with children was guaranteed through the Social Security Act. All of these measures were passed between 1935 and 1938 during the Second New Deal, with congressional aide Lyndon Johnson looking on in approving awe.

Not all citizens were covered by the New Deal, however. Positive rights were extended to some, but not to others. Roosevelt and his lieutenants were concerned primarily with the plight of the "forgotten man," who had indeed been long neglected in laissez-faire America. Of the four major programs in the Social Security Act, Old Age Insurance (OAI) and Unemployment Insurance (UI) made eligibility for benefits contingent on each worker's previous employment status. The omission of employees in religious and nonprofit organizations put coverage off-limits to many women who worked as teachers, nurses, and social workers, and the exclusion of agricultural and domestic workers made coverage inaccessible to a majority of African American women as well as high proportions of Chicanos, Mexican Americans, and Asian Americans. Old Age Assistance (OAA) and Aid to Families with Dependent Children (AFDC) were separate from an individual's work history, and thus women were far more likely to qualify, but unlike OAI and UI, which were funded through contributory payroll taxes, they depended upon government appropriations and thus were more likely to become mired in partisan political wrangling. AFDC emerged as the program least able to extend rights of social citizenship to its beneficiaries. It was the most decentralized program in the Social Security Act. In determining client eligibility, state and local welfare offices employed "suitable home" rules that scrutinized the lives of potential beneficiaries, evaluating their child-rearing and housekeeping abilities and the school and church attendance of their children.[30]

The Fair Labor Standards Act (FLSA) excluded millions of working Americans from its purview, an injustice that the Kennedy administration had only limited success in remedying. FLSA coverage rested on occupational categories: those that came under the rubric of "interstate commerce" were included; those that did not were left high and dry. The exclusion of agricultural workers left 22.8 percent of the male workforce, a group in which nonwhite men figured disproportionately, unprotected in jobs characterized by very low wages and long hours. Nearly twice as large a proportion of the female workforce, 42.2 percent, worked in excluded occupations at wages below the minimum level, including those who were retail workers, waitresses, hotel employees, beauticians, and domestic servants.[31] The National Labor Relations Act did nothing to help those workers who were not union members, further disadvantaging women and minorities. When LBJ came to office, nearly 22 percent of all Americans lived below the government-defined poverty line.

During the New Deal, and especially during World War II, for one of the few times in their history, Americans came to see big spending by the federal government as a relatively beneficent force in their lives. The accomplishments of the New Deal were dramatic but paled in comparison with the social and economic progress of the war years.[32] The war economy "proved" that the government could engage in planning both production and consumption and that government debt could be used to finance economic expansion without bringing about the collapse of capitalism or creating runaway inflation.[33]

One of LBJ's principal concerns was to fill the yawning gap in the American reform tradition concerning racial justice. For a brief moment during the Populist uprising, reformers had envisioned a color-blind movement that pitted all working-class men and women against the robber baron capitalists who dominated the American power structure. When southern Bourbons (the regional aristocracy who had returned to power following Reconstruction) began voting black sharecroppers against Populist candidates and corporations employed African Americans as strikebreakers, however, the Populists became a moving force behind the passage of disfranchisement laws.

Progressives proved to be no different. Even as they labored diligently to bridge the gap between classes, the Progressives believed some social differences could not be erased for many years—if at all. They turned to segregation as a way to halt dangerous social conflict that could spin out of control. Physical separation might persuade hard-core racists to abjure lynching and other forms of violence. FDR had appointed a "Black Cabinet," Eleanor Roosevelt had campaigned vociferously for racial justice, and blacks benefited from various New Deal programs. But Roosevelt needed the Solid South. If the nation was to be preserved, white male heads of household would have to receive first priority. There was no room, then, in the New Deal for voting rights, equal accommodations, or school integration, much less affirmative action.[34]

The violence in Birmingham, Alabama, that took place during the civil rights marches of 1963, especially acts of brutality directed toward children, seemed to dramatically alter racial perceptions. Most whites during World War II had expressed the opinion that blacks were an inferior race, almost 70 percent favored separate schools, and only 45 percent thought that blacks were entitled to equal opportunity in the workforce. But after Birmingham and Kennedy's stirring speech on behalf of equal rights, pollsters found that citizens listed civil rights as the nation's number one problem, eclipsing even the Cold War. The affirmative response to the question "Do you think there should be separate sections for Negroes in streetcars and buses?" dropped in half from the 1950s to only 21 percent approving (with 79 percent disapproving). The percentage of northern whites who supported a law "which would give all persons—Negroes as well as whites—the right to be served in public places" rose from 55 percent in June 1963 to over 70 percent in January 1964, a time when Congress was debating the Civil Rights Act. In the summer of 1963, to the question "Do you think Negroes should have as good a chance as white people to get any kind of job?" a resounding 85 percent of respondents nationwide—as opposed to just those in the North—answered "yes."[35]

The exigencies of the Cold War seemed to mandate social and economic justice at home. In the 1950s, the focus of the East-West conflict had shifted from Europe and the Near East to the emerging Third World. Marxist-Leninists and liberal capitalists struggled to demonstrate the superiority of their respective systems. The Johnson administration would feel itself under constant pressure to prove that America truly was a land of freedom, justice, and opportunity for everyone. After all, wasn't that the message constantly being broadcast to the rest of the world by Radio Free Europe and the Voice of America? On one level, LBJ viewed domestic reform—the ongoing effort to fulfill the American promise of social and economic justice—as a safety valve to prevent revolution, a hedge against radicalism. "I think that democracy is constantly under challenge," LBJ told broadcaster Mel Stuart during an interview in the spring of 1968. "If we're unable to deal with these problems of poverty and ignorance and illiteracy and disease and discrimination, the people become disgusted and they despair—they're likely to do anything dangerous." He recalled the mood of the country after the Bonus Expeditionary March in 1932 and in the spring of 1945 before V-E Day in Europe and V-J Day in the Pacific. "Other philosophies competitive with ours . . . are rampant in the world," the president observed. "One of the things I'm very proud of . . . the Communist leaders of the world have annexed very little population and very little territory . . . during the last few years."[36]

The architects of the Great Society would also benefit from the fact that America was once again a nation of believers in a God committed to justice and compassion. The forces of conformity, so strong during the early postwar period, coupled with the anxieties of the Cold War, had led to a religious revival that was simultaneously intense and pervasive.[37] Led by Norman Vincent Peale, whose *Power of Positive Thinking* sold millions of copies, many contemporary religious figures, especially in the mainstream denominations, concentrated on quieting the American middle class's anxieties in the nuclear age. Confronted simultaneously with the omnipresent threat of "the bomb," the implacable competition with international communism, and the corrosive effects of a burgeoning materialism, the American people were in dire need of reassurance as they confronted the second half of the twentieth century. The Protestant Council of New York instructed its television and radio speakers to abjure condemnation, controversy, and guilt. Their task was to "sell" religion, and to that end, their message "should project love, joy, courage, hope, faith, trust in God, good will."[38]

There were, of course, serious alternatives to this syrupy, sin-free approach to religion. The 1950s witnessed a new interest in revivalism and fundamentalism. One of the most striking preachers of the period was a young, well-dressed Baptist evangelist named Billy Graham. In sermons that stressed the sovereignty of God and the absolute wisdom of the Bible, the charismatic

Graham drew hundreds of thousands of Americans to huge amphitheaters such as Yankee Stadium and Madison Square Garden. Graham and other fundamentalists offered clear moral and spiritual guidelines for middle-class Americans who craved substance and focus in their religion and for working-class Americans threatened by alcoholism, unemployment, and family disintegration.

Meanwhile, the intelligentsia was drawn to the preachments of Reinhold Niebuhr, a theologian who attacked the "feel-good" religion propounded by the dominant culture. Niebuhr, who taught and preached at Union Theological Seminary in New York, was the towering theological and philosophical figure in the movement known as Christian neo-orthodoxy. He attacked the materialism, complacency, and conformity that seemed to permeate postwar America. World War II and the advent of the atomic age had proved that sin and evil were real and permanent and that man could not perfect the universe through his own efforts. Human beings were called upon not to ensconce themselves in a cocoon but to love the world and assume some responsibility for its problems. True peace involved the endurance of pain; the root of sin, he reminded Christians, was self-love.

Theologically, Johnson and his advisers—Busby, Church of Christ; Moyers, Baptist; Valenti and Shriver, Catholic; and Harry McPherson, an Episcopalian Texan who would rise to the top of the aide pool after 1966—were Niebuhrians. Though LBJ and his advisers preached the politics of consensus, they were very much aware of the pervasive influence of evil in the world—racial prejudice, economic exploitation, political oppression, hunger, disease. Believers must do the best they could under the circumstances, but LBJ thought that they should do it with a vengeance. He was both motivated by feelings of Christian charity and compassion and determined to use religion in his quest to achieve some degree of social and economic justice in an imperfect world. His speeches in Appalachia during his 1964 tour to highlight rural poverty could only be described as "evangelical." He had met with the pope as vice president and would meet frequently with Billy Graham. "From the time of the ancient Hebrew prophets and the dispersal of the money changers," LBJ would tell a group of civil rights leaders in the spring of 1964, "men of God have taught us that social problems are moral problems on a huge scale. They have demonstrated that a religion which did not struggle to remove oppression from the world of men would not be able to create the world of spirit."[39] A devoted civil libertarian, Johnson was committed to the principle of separation of church and state, but that did not mean that men of state should separate themselves from faith and prayer or that people of faith should not apply their principles to their political decisions.[40]

CHANGE WAS IN THE AIR IN THE EARLY 1960S, BUT WHAT KIND OF change? Lyndon Johnson was a New Deal liberal, but at the time he entered the Oval Office, influential voices were questioning the relevancy of liberalism or, at the very least, trying to redefine it. For one, JFK considered the Roosevelt legacy the stuff of the past from which he and the Democratic Party needed to be liberated.[41] One of Camelot's resident intellectuals, Arthur Schlesinger Jr., argued that reformers needed to focus on "quality" more than "quantity." The New Deal had established the foundations of an economically just polity. In an increasingly bureaucratized mass society, government ought to work to help each individual reach his or her potential, he argued. Others were far more pessimistic. Profoundly affected by the Holocaust and the advent of nuclear weapons, historian C. Vann Woodward and theologian Reinhold Niebuhr expressed a deep distrust in the liberal ethos with its presumption that consensus and progress were always possible if not inevitable.[42]

Out of this general dissatisfaction with the liberal past sprang the New Left, the creation of the children of the Greatest Generation. In 1963, more than one-third of all high school students went away to college. There they found the hidden hand of their parents in the form of *in loco parentis*, a term meaning "in place of the parents." On most campuses, women had to be twenty-one years old before they could live off campus, dorms were strictly segregated by sex, and students were subjected to strict curfew. More important, perhaps, students had virtually no say in the rules and regulations of the institutions where they paid tuition. Administrators dictated course offerings, degree curricula, and extracurricular activities. In October 1964, students at the University of California, Berkeley, who ranged from liberal supporters of the civil rights movement to conservative champions of individual liberties, banded together to launch the Free Speech Movement, whose mission was to loosen regulations and democratize decision making on the nation's campuses.

The Students for a Democratic Society (SDS) was founded in 1960 as a successor to the Student League of Industrial Democracy (SLID). SLID traced its roots to several labor unions, most notably the International Ladies Garment Workers Union (ILGWU). The SDS rejected the post–World War II values of social conformity, consumerism, hierarchical power structures, centrism, and moral compromises in politics. The organization touted local-level, direct community participation in education, economics, and government; greater freedom of expression; an end to elitism and inequality; and respect for the uniqueness of each individual. "We would replace power rooted in possession, privilege, or circumstance by power and uniqueness rooted in love, reflectiveness, reason, and creativity," proclaimed an SDS manifesto.[43]

Then, with the enunciation of the Port Huron Statement in 1962, the New Left was born. Joining with left-leaning faculty and public intellectuals, Tom Hayden and his fellow proposed a new departure in American political life. The New Left denounced Jim Crow, the military-industrial complex, and New Deal liberalism. It called on its followers to mobilize to achieve full citizenship for African Americans, force disarmament on the Great Powers, and dismantle the military-industrial complex. "Participatory democracy" was the New Left's remedy for the problem of the poor and powerless in American society.

Though it was not readily apparent at the time, the New Left would serve as both an inspiration and a threat to the Great Society. According to sociologist Daniel Bell, centrist, bipartisan compromises had reduced sharp ideological and partisan differences by the end of the 1950s, as a mostly middle-class, relatively apolitical, increasingly homogeneous, bureaucratized, and mechanized "mass society" developed. In part, the Great Society was a rejection of Bell's analysis. Johnson and his advisers were acutely aware that 20 percent of Americans lived below the poverty line, that Jim Crow was still alive throughout the South, and that millions of Americans were being denied access to the positive rights that FDR had promised. At the same time, the type of mass society described by Bell was the inevitable by-product of consensus building that LBJ believed essential to achieving stalled domestic policy goals, such as Medicare, civil rights for blacks, and the fulfillment of American foreign and defense policy responsibilities in the Cold War.

The New Left would have none of it. C. Wright Mills, the radical sociologist whose iconoclastic ideas inspired many in the SDS, explicitly rejected consensus politics and, in doing so, undermined one of the main stratagems of Great Society planners. In his "Letter to the New Left," Mills, a Texan, wrote, "The end-of-ideology is a slogan of complacency. . . . If there is to be a politics of a New Left, what needs to be analyzed is the structure of institutions, the foundations of politics."[44] Hayden and his followers took that advice to heart. Throughout the 1960s, they analyzed and in most cases found existing institutions—even liberalism itself—wanting.

Finally, the conservative coalition consisting of right-wing Republicans and southern Democrats may have been knocked off balance by the revived liberalism that helped propel the JFK-LBJ ticket into office, but it remained a force to be reckoned with. Disciples of Senator Robert Taft (R-OH) continued to insist that liberalism was nothing more than creeping socialism that if not contained would morph into communism. Less government, less regulation, more free enterprise and more state and local autonomy, they insisted. Some southern Democrats shared these views; some did not. But virtually all saw in the Republican enthusiasm for states' rights and anticommunism powerful instruments to block the mounting assault on Jim Crow.

In 1964 hardline conservatives captured the GOP (Grand Old Party) and succeeded in nominating Barry Goldwater. Though most liberals and moderates dismissed the Arizona senator as an extremist and even a crackpot, New York Times columnist James Reston wrote that the Democrats had better take Goldwater seriously. He was asking some serious questions and tapping in to the predominantly conservative American political tradition. What sort of world was it when men so often aspired to do good but instead did evil? Was the individual and the family being swallowed up in an increasingly complex society? Big Government would strive ceaselessly to augment itself, and if individuals and local communities did not resist, tyranny was inevitable. What of morality and individual responsibility as guardians of liberty and justice rather than reliance on overweening federal power? Goldwater's questions resonated particularly with businesspeople and professionals who feared regulation and competition from public entities and with whites who feared integration and government-mandated antidiscrimination measures.[45]

In truth, Tom Hayden on the left and Barry Goldwater on the right were more in tune with the American political tradition than was Lyndon Johnson. All the basic tenets of the American Creed—equality, liberty, individualism, constitutionalism, democracy—are mainly antigovernment and antiauthority in character. Each of these values places limits on power and on the institutions of government. As historian Joseph Ellis has noted, Thomas Paine's ideas were designed to bring down a government, James Madison's to establish a limited one. A commitment to individualism led Madison to design a constitutional structure that would check and limit government authority. Paine's egalitarianism, in contrast, led him to question the very right of one individual to exercise authority over another.[46]

Of the forces arrayed against liberalism, some Johnson perceived clearly and some more dimly, or not at all. But he knew that he and the Great Society had but a brief window of opportunity and the champions of reform must act with alacrity. "He called me into the Yellow Room of the White House one late February or early March [1964] evening," Bill Moyers recalled. The president was holding a pad of white paper upon which he had written the years 1964, 1965, 1966, and 1967. Under the first two, he had listed measures that he intended to "P&P, propose and pass." Under 1967, it said "hold gains." "I really intend to finish Franklin Roosevelt's revolution," Johnson remarked to his aide. Ideally, he would have two full terms to accomplish his goals. "I'll never make it that far, of course," he said, "so let's assume that we have to do it all in 1965 and 1966, and probably in 1966 we'll lose our big margin in the Congress. That means in 1967 and 1968 there will be a hell of a fight."[47] If Johnson's plans were to come to fruition, the first two years of his administration would have to bear witness to the most productive executive-congressional collaboration in American history.

A HALF CENTURY EARLIER, PRESIDENTS THEODORE ROOSEVELT AND Woodrow Wilson had departed from the Gilded Age maxim that Congress should legislate and the executive administrate—period. Wilson, in particular, had transformed the American presidency. The author of *Congressional*

Government and an admirer of the British parliamentary system, Wilson argued that the president, although chief executive, was also leader of his party and the only official elected by the body politic as a whole. As such he should develop a legislative program and, through persuasion, coercion, cajolement, or whatever other means might be necessary, compel Congress to adopt it. Of all twentieth-century presidents, however, LBJ was the most ardent proponent and able practitioner of the art of presidential lawmaking. The Texan approached the daunting task he had set for himself with a political philosophy tailored, he believed, to suit the times.

Johnson's view of human nature was essentially positive, at least in the Jeffersonian sense that in a democracy free individuals will always vote their own self-interest and will recognize that their particular welfare is inextricably bound up with the welfare of the community as a whole. As a young high school teacher, under the influence of his uncle George Johnson, Lyndon had become an admirer of Andrew Jackson, or at least the Andrew Jackson as history then portrayed him. Old Hickory, as appreciated by Lyndon and George, was the hero of the common man, a devotee of the great republican principles of Thomas Jefferson. Politics was a continual battleground featuring contests between liberty and power, virtue and corruption. Public virtue, which required a willingness to subordinate private interests to the general welfare, was essential to preserving the precarious balance between freedom and order.

The Johnsons remembered Jackson as the man who had brought political power to the common man, expanding the franchise and democratizing politics.[48] "This old farmer that rides looking at the back end of the mule on the cultivator all day long," LBJ remarked to Roy Wilkins, head of the National Association for the Advancement of Colored People (NAACP), in 1965, " . . . he just sits there and thinks. It is his boy that is in Viet Nam, his sister that is out of a job, his brother-in-law that got his car repossessed—and somehow or other, they just add up and they will do what is right if you can get enough interest in them to vote."[49]

Subsequently, the Jefferson-Jackson principle had been filtered by two World Wars and the Great Depression. As a thoroughgoing New Dealer, LBJ had embraced the notion of positive rights. An active federal government was necessary to protect the common person from the vagaries of the marketplace and to ensure the fulfillment of each individual's potential. In a true democracy, enhanced federal power should augment, not restrict, liberty. "I would say that we believe there is a national answer to every national problem," Johnson told an interviewer in 1968, "and that we have tried to get the result of the greatest good for the greatest number of people."[50]

Political parties, anathema to the Founding Fathers, had emerged to represent differing interests and ideologies and to elect to office those individuals who would rule on behalf of those ideologies and interests. By the Gilded Age, however, party politics had become largely a contest to see who would control patronage. Neither the Democratic nor the Republican Party proved to be adequate political vehicles for the first two great reform movements of post–Civil War America: Populism and Progressivism. The agrarian radicals of the Gilded Age felt compelled to create the Populist Party and advanced Progressives to found the Progressive or Bull Moose Party. FDR was able to temporarily mold the Democrats into a vehicle for reform. There was the famous New Deal coalition consisting of labor, immigrant groups principally in the cities of the Northeast, African Americans, farmers hard hit by the Depression, and the Solid South. But the coalition was temporary, tenuous. FDR's strategy of bringing into the national political arena those who had previously been on the sidelines—Catholics, unskilled workers, and the mass of unemployed persons—proved in the end a threat to party unity. Anti-Catholic sentiment had threatened to destroy the party in 1924 and had driven a multitude of Democrats to vote Republican in 1928. The American Federation of Labor (AFL), the voice of organized, skilled labor, had declared itself adamantly opposed to the campaign to unionize unskilled workers launched by the Congress of Industrial Organizations (CIO).[51]

By the time he came to the presidency, LBJ had become one of the least partisan politicians in America. As majority leader in the 1950s, with a popular Republican president sitting in the White House, he had persuaded a reluctant Democratic Party to play the role of loyal opposition. To Johnson's way of thinking, a number of factors argued in favor of not only bipartisanship but also a suprapartisan consensus to effect reforms of the Great Society.

As he and his political advisers thought ahead to the presidential election of 1964, White House aide Horace Busby wrote the president a lengthy memo. Party leaders, including the Democratic National Committee, Busby wrote, were laboring under assumptions that were patently and dangerously false: that beginning in 1932 the political tide had set against the Republican

Party and was continuing to run against it; that the Democratic Party was in 1964 the majority party not only in congressional and local politics but also at the presidential level; that aside from their traditional base in the South, the Democrats were the party with the broader national appeal; that the Republican incumbency during the 1950s was an aberration attributable to Eisenhower's war hero appeal; that the Kennedy–Johnson victory was a party victory that validated the aforementioned assumptions.

Wrong, wrong, wrong! Only when FDR ran for the presidency did the Democrats command a majority of voters. The average for the four Democratic electoral victories in the twentieth century other than Roosevelt's had been 46.6 percent; indeed, the cumulative plurality for the GOP in the four postwar presidential votes, 1948 to 1960, stood at 13,934,000 votes. If the South was removed from those totals, the figure rose to 15,125,750 votes.[52] Johnson and his aides realized that prosperity breeds conservatism and that in 1963–1964, the vast majority of white Americans, who constituted a clear plurality, were relatively prosperous. The 1960s did not mark the high tide of liberalism during which the country came close to embracing European-style social democracy. The New Left, which evidenced a deep liberatarian streak, was a major cultural phenomenon attracting the attention of a number of public intellectuals, but it was electorally insignificant and evidenced a deep libertarian streak. The issue for LBJ and other Great Society proponents was what the president could get moderate Republicans to agree to, persuade increasingly conservative unions to agree to, get a middle class worried about maintaining its status and social stability to agree to. In short, how to achieve the full flowering of the Great Society in a fundamentally conservative polity.

In telephone conversations with Senate Minority Leader Everett Dirksen of Illinois and House Minority Leader Gerald R. Ford of Michigan after he succeeded to the presidency, LBJ referred to political scientist James Macgregor Burns's theory of "four party politics," in which the liberal Democratic "presidential party" was often frustrated in its legislative efforts by the often obstructionist, conservative Democratic "congressional party," and the moderate, presidential branch of the GOP was hamstrung by the more conservative congressional wing. The temptation for Johnson was to try to make the Democratic Party *the* progressive party in America. FDR had attempted that in 1938 with his attempted purge of reactionary southern

Democrats, however, and had failed. Instead of envisioning a political system characterized by strong, disciplined party leadership in which each of the two major political organizations was distinct and unified in its ideology and policy agenda, LBJ opted to work through a suprapartisan consensus. In his scheme, the Democrats and Republicans within Congress, and the executive and Congress as separate branches, should agree on broad national policy goals and then productively negotiate and compromise their differences to achieve these objectives.[53] "I hope we could have the relationship that I had with Eisenhower," Johnson told Congressman Ford in January 1965, "that you could support me when you thought I was right . . . and be proud of it and I think it'll get you more Republican seats than anything else. . . . I don't believe in Taft's philosophy that it is the duty of the opposition to oppose; it's the duty of the opposition to analyze and do what's best for the country."[54]

During his presidency, Johnson would give the cold shoulder to the Democratic National Committee (DNC) and neglect state and local party organizations. LBJ perceived a strong, national party organization with regular publicity and activities emphasizing partisan differences to be a threat to the suprapartisan, centrist consensus that he needed to underpin the Great Society and his policies in Vietnam.[55] In the summer of 1965, the president would bypass DNC chairman John Bailey entirely, naming Clifton Carter, a longtime political aide from Texas, to serve as his liaison with committee headquarters and facilitate his plan to reduce the expenses, staff, and activities of the group. Crippling the DNC would also keep it from becoming a base of operations for Robert F. Kennedy if he chose to challenge Johnson for the presidency.[56]

From late 1963 through 1966, Lyndon Johnson interacted with senators and congressmen on a daily and even hourly basis. He became personally familiar with the details of the more than one thousand major bills Congress considered during this period. His memory banks were still full of information concerning the political characteristics of the various congressional and senatorial districts and of the personal peccadilloes of those men and women who served them. "There is but one way for a President to deal with the Congress," Johnson would observe to an interviewer "and that is continuously, incessantly, and without interruption. If it's really going to work, the relationship between the President and the Congress has got to be almost incestuous. He's got to know them even better than they know themselves."[57] Drew Pearson noted admiringly of Johnson, "He phones them, writes them notes, draws them aside at receptions to ask their opinions, seeks them out to thank them for political favors."[58] As LBJ labored to build congressional, press, and public support for one revolutionary piece of domestic legislation after another, the pressure on those involved became almost unbearable. "Don't assume anything," he told himself and his aides. "Make sure every possible weapon is brought to bear . . . ; keep everybody involved; don't let them slacken."[59]

LBJ DISTRUSTED MUCH OF KENNEDY'S WHITE HOUSE STAFF, BUT Larry O'Brien, a public relations expert who had joined Kennedy's staff in 1952, was a delightful surprise. A gravelly voiced, amiable man with a good sense of humor, O'Brien was a traditional New Deal Democrat. Though the Kennedy legislative program was mired in gridlock by the time JFK was gunned down, that was no fault of O'Brien and his very capable assistant, Henry Wilson. O'Brien and Johnson seemed to hit it off immediately. The Irishman had fallen in love with congressional politics, and like his new boss, he took a can-do, art-of-the-possible approach to the House and Senate. Perhaps most important to LBJ, O'Brien was tenacious and tireless. In turn, O'Brien was impressed with Johnson's openness, his commitment to social justice, and his knowledge of congressional politics.

O'Brien, and to an extent during the first year Bill Moyers, oversaw and coordinated the Johnson administration's legislative activities, but the president himself was the real manager. Moreover, he expected every cabinet member, his staff, and lobbyists for the interests they represented to become actively involved with Congress on bills that were pertinent and pending. The true instrument of the Johnson legislative will, however, was the telephone. Given his other duties as president, LBJ could not possibly have the same amount of face time with senators and congressmen as he did when he headed the Senate. Thus, the telephone, always important in the Johnson scheme of things, became crucial after he assumed the presidency.

During his first two-and-a-half years in office, LBJ had most of his conversations taped and then transcribed by his secretaries. The purpose was not, as the tapes have subsequently revealed, to gather dirt on his former colleagues or to trick them into saying things or making commitments that could be used against them with others but rather to keep track of the incredibly complex political math that underlay the hundreds of pieces of legislation that were enacted during these intense early years. What happened on an urban transit bill would have an impact on civil rights; that year's farm bill might be used to buy southern silence on certain aspects of civil rights legislation; a conservative might not be able to support both Medicare and federal aid to education and survive the next election, but he or she might be able to withstand voting for one if federal funds were forthcoming to help build a new hospital or vocational school. Individual congressmen and senators had only to keep up with the part of the web that affected them directly; LBJ had to keep up with the whole. He was extremely intelligent, but given the complexity of the legislation and the perceived need for speed, the president needed a record.

CHAPTER 2

FUNDING THE GREAT SOCIETY AND THE WAR ON POVERTY

THE FIRST ITEM ON LBJ'S LEGISLATIVE AGENDA WAS AN $11 BILLION tax cut proposal he inherited from the Kennedy administration. Although popular memory of the 1950s sees the decade as bathed in prosperity, the economy Kennedy inherited from Eisenhower had obvious problems. There had been three recessions in Ike's eight-year tenure (the last of which was still in progress when Kennedy took office), inflation had slowly but surely reared its ugly head, and annual growth rates had decreased significantly during the second half of the decade. For the Keynesian economists who had acted as an informal network of advisers for Kennedy's presidential candidacy, the economy was suffering from persistent stagnation and chronic slack because it could no longer deliver full employment at the peak of the business cycle. That was the message Kennedy received from the trio of economists he appointed to his Council of Economic Advisers (CEA)—Walter Heller of the University of Minnesota as chair, James Tobin of Yale, and Kermit Gordon of Williams College.[1]

Kennedy's CEA economists had entered the academy during the Great Depression. They had absorbed Keynesian doctrine during their stint in graduate school and, like the famous Briton, considered economics a tool of public policy rather than just an academic discipline. John Maynard Keynes was a man much misunderstood in the United States, most often used by conservatives to discredit New Dealers specifically and liberals in general. He was portrayed as a rigid ideologue, a virtual socialist who would use big government to regulate every aspect of the economic life of a nation. Nothing could have been further from the truth. Though he started out firmly rooted within traditional, classical economics, Keynes moved away from it because of what he perceived to be its often erroneous economic assumptions and policies and its antisocial consequences. Laissez-faire theory would work only under conditions of full employment, but in a truly free, capitalist society there would always be unemployment. He devoted a good part of his time to proving that governmental acceptance of more responsibility for the smooth working of the economy could increase human freedom and choice.[2]

To combat the Great Depression, Keynes advocated countercyclical deficit spending, that is, during periods of recession the national government should stimulate the economy by funding public works and subsidizing business and agriculture. The temporary deficits that resulted over time would be eliminated by increased tax revenue from a recovered economy. FDR had reluctantly accepted countercyclical deficit spending but had rushed to restore a balanced budget in 1938. During World War II, the federal government had cast caution to the winds and run up huge deficits. The war economy demonstrated that the government could engage in planning, production, and consumption and that national debt could be used to finance economic expansion without bringing about the collapse of capitalism or creating runaway inflation, Keynesians argued.[3] The conservative coalition and "classical economists" held sway beginning in 1946, however; Truman and Eisenhower, during his second term, would not go beyond the countercyclical model.

Heller and his colleagues wanted to transcend temporary stimuli to combat downturns and use the budgetary power of the federal government to maximize prosperity when the economy was not in recession. This was the essence of the "new economics." Instead of responding to fluctuations in the business cycle, the members of Kennedy's CEA sought the continuous expansion of productive output and the closing of the gap between productive output and the economy's expanding potential. They estimated a performance gap of almost $50 billion between potential gross domestic product (GDP) at full employment and actual output in the economy that Kennedy inherited.[4] "What we seek," declared Heller, "is an increase in the total demand in the economy, a removal as it were of the fiscal drag on spending in the country." The chief source of the fiscal drag was taxation— as the economy emerged from recession, its potential growth was hindered by the automatic rise of tax receipts that took away a growing portion of private income before the economy was operating at full employment. To the Kennedy economists, a tax cut would turn the fiscal drag into a fiscal dividend and would be a far more efficient, fast-acting stimulant than public-spending increases. In early 1961, therefore, they urged the president to propose a temporary personal income tax cut of $9.5 billion in the belief that this would deliver a further $20 billion in GDP growth.

For a number of reasons, JFK was initially resistant to a tax cut. There was the prevailing notion that unbalanced budgets inevitably led to inflation. A tax cut seemed to contradict the president's inaugural call for sacrifice in the national interest. Strongly pro-business at the outset of his administration, JFK feared that an unbalanced budget would undermine business confidence and send the economy into a spiral.[5] Over time, however, the president changed his mind. Heller and his colleagues proceeded to update his economic education and repair the damage from a major falling out with the business community. By the summer of 1962, JFK was publicly extolling the virtues of a tax cut. The administration introduced legislation to enact an across-the-board reduction, but it became entangled with various vested interests in the House Ways and Means Committee, and Kennedy was assassinated before Congress could act.

Heller was aboard a plane carrying various cabinet members to Japan when Kennedy was paying his ill-fated visit to Dallas. Upon hearing news of the assassination, the delegation immediately turned the aircraft around and headed back to Washington. When they landed at midnight, Heller went directly to his office where he and his lieutenants drafted a memo for LBJ on the tax cut and its projected impact on the budget. Tax relief was not needed, they argued, to prevent disaster or to rescue a nation poised for an economic tailspin. Rather, it was needed to prolong prosperity. The United States was entering its eleventh consecutive quarter of expansion. Wages were moving upward and prices appeared stable. Nevertheless, the unemployment rate stood at 5.5 percent, and the outmoded tax structure left over from the Korean War would eventually drag the economy down. If Congress passed the tax bill, it would produce an immediate $12 billion increase in the gross national product (GNP) and $30 billion the year following. The economic activity generated would so increase the tax base that revenues collected by the Treasury would actually increase rather than decrease.[6]

On November 25, LBJ met with the "Troika," the economic team that Kennedy had relied on to develop policy—Heller, Secretary of the Treasury Douglas Dillon, and Budget Director Kermit Gordon—to discuss the tax bill and budgetary matters in general. The first thing Johnson did was to tell Heller to call off his liberal friends who were already proposing new or expanded programs that could be funded by tax revenues expected from a full-employment economy: "Tell them to lay off, Walter. Tell them to quit lobbying. I'm for them. I know they have good programs, and that the economy needs to have that money pumped in. I want an expanding economy. The budget should be $108 billion." But an increase in expenditures would have to wait until 1965. Dillon, more conservative than Heller, had been talking with Senator Harry F. Byrd, the hoary-headed reactionary from Virginia who chaired the Finance Committee, and had told the president that the administration could not expect approval of a budget for fiscal year 1964 of more than $100.6 or $100.7 billion.[7] The conservative coalition was not going to accept a tax cut without cuts in federal expenditures. It had flatly rejected Heller's argument that the object of federal fiscal policy should be to balance the economy, not the budget. Johnson observed that if they expected to get the tax cut, the budget could not be a cent above $100 billion. If it is, he said, "You won't pee one drop." Dillon observed that they would have to pay the price for the tax bill, but "then when you have it, you can do what you want." Right, said Johnson, "like Ike did—talked economy and then spent."[8]

In the days that followed, LBJ met with leaders of organized labor and big business, lobbying for a tax cut. He closeted himself with individuals and groups. He telephoned Wall Street bankers and agribusinessmen. And he met almost continuously with Byrd. The Virginian remained adamantly opposed to a reduction in taxes. It would unbalance the budget and lead to economic and financial chaos, he protested. At the same time the president conferred with Budget Director Gordon. At first, Gordon recalled, he thought his mission was to get the budget down to $100 billion, which would not be difficult, but then Johnson began to press for more cuts. And more cuts. Farm programs suffered; so did education and space. Gordon and Heller became worried, concerned that they were dealing with a Herbert Hoover in Roosevelt clothing.

Orville Freeman, Kennedy's liberal secretary of agriculture who had agreed to stay and serve LBJ, encountered Gordon at a January 1964 cocktail party and found him beaten down and depressed. They decided that they would have to have faith for the time being, but only for the time being. "I agreed," Freeman wrote in his diary, "that if a year from now we were going through the same thing after a successful election, I for my part would be happy to go back to practicing law. He said he would be happy to go back to the University."[9]

The president's principal ally in his budget-cutting campaign was, surprisingly enough, Secretary of Defense Robert McNamara. In various meetings McNamara insisted that the United States possessed two-and-a-half to three times the number of missiles, submarines, and airplanes as the Soviets and that the Soviets would never catch up.[10] With McNamara's blessing, the president sent letters to seventy-five hundred defense contractors demanding economies and cost reductions. And, in fact, despite the fears of liberals, most of the reductions came in Defense ($1 billion), in Space ($600 million), and in Atomic Energy ($300 million).[11] "I am not going to produce atomic bombs as a WPA project," LBJ declared.[12]

At the crucial moment, LBJ invited Byrd to a private luncheon at the White House. Jack Valenti remembers it as the only time LBJ ever ate in the small room off the Oval Office. Johnson "personally . . . supervised the setting and the menu."[13] If he could get the budget below $100 billion, would Byrd let the tax bill out of his committee? "We might be able to do some business," the Virginian replied. Johnson subsequently called Byrd and told him that the administration would come in with a $97.9 billion budget. Byrd congratulated the president on his frugality: "I'm going to have to vote against the bill, [which he did both in committee and on the floor of the Senate] but I'll be working for you behind the scenes."[14] As the dates for the decisive votes approached, Johnson pulled out all the stops, personally calling every congressional waverer. "It looks like to me that you are not being very wise in your southern strategy," LBJ told Richard Russell, a member of the Senate Finance Committee. "It is not up to me to tell you how smart you are, for the son to tell the father. But looks like you and Harry Byrd and Albert Gore [D-TN] ought to let that damn tax bill come on out. . . . What you will do is you will have every businessman in the country messing with your civil rights."[15]

Students of the Johnson presidency have speculated why the president proposed a $97.9 billion budget rather than the $100 billion that Byrd apparently would have been satisfied with. Competition with Kennedy, some said. Johnson noted in his memoirs, "A recent poll had indicated that the most unpopular aspect of the Kennedy administration was what the public considered fiscal irresponsibility. I knew that we had to turn that feeling around."[16] No doubt, Johnson was looking ahead to the 1964 presidential contest and was determined to prove to fiscal conservatives that they could trust him. Talking to George Brown, the Houston construction tycoon and LBJ supporter, after reaching the $97.9 billion figure, LBJ exulted that "Eisenhower and Oveta [Culp Hobby, publisher of the conservative *Houston Post*] are going to have to vote for me now."[17] LBJ believed that Bobby Kennedy would probably challenge him for the Democratic nomination. RFK might be able to attract the support of the left wing of the labor movement and liberal intellectuals. As had so often been the case in Texas politics, the business community, nominally Republican, might hold the balance of power.

LBJ spent his first six weeks in office courting big business, primarily by cultivating members of the Business Advisory Council, the private body established in 1933 to help ensure that the policies of federal agencies were acceptable to Wall Street and large manufacturers. In early January 1964 he had the entire membership—which included W. B. (Bev) Murphy of Campbell Soup Company, Albert Nickerson of Mobil Oil, and Frederick Kappel of AT&T—to the White House for dinner. "It's the first time in our history," one executive remarked, "that we've been invited to dine at the White House—it didn't even happen under Ike."[18] At that dinner LBJ told his audience of executives that he was going to cut future federal spending far below the levels projected by the Kennedy administration. One by one, cabinet officers rose to tell the corporate leaders exactly where the cuts were going to be made.[19] He also hinted at the moves he was going to make in the areas of civil rights, education, medical insurance, poverty, and area redevelopment. "President Johnson really gave the business guys the treatment," Orville Freeman recalled approvingly in his diary.

> He emphasized more than anything else Civil Rights and told the story of his Negro cook. Later on in the week Bob McNamara said to me it was an amazing performance—then he kinda grinned and said, can you imagine John F. Kennedy telling these businessmen that the Negro cook had to stop along the road to relieve herself because there was no place to go to the bathroom, and yet he said, and he knew many of these people, that they were much more enthusiastic and much more convinced by Lyndon Johnson than they would have been by John Kennedy.[20]

Addressing the five thousand delegates to the national Chambers of Commerce convention in May 1964, LBJ declared, "If you don't remember anything else that I tell you here today, I want you to remember this: 'If peaceful change is impossible . . . then a violent change is inevitable.'" He accused them of having "a martyr complex." And he told them that they had a bigger stake than any other group in fighting poverty and ignorance. His talk was punctuated with waves of applause.[21] "Your mixture of dedicated concern for the nation's welfare and the welfare of human beings," John T. Connor of Merck and Company subsequently cabled LBJ, "coupled with your realistic appraisal of the federal government's fiscal responsibilities seemed just about right to me and many others with whom I talked. In spite of the difficulties ahead you will certainly receive strong support for your program in the business community."[22] "Understanding businessmen, their problems and their role in our economy," editorialized the conservative *Dallas Morning News,* "he seeks their aid and support and treats them as valued partners in the task of building a better America."[23]

Economically, the tax cut of 1964 was a stroke of genius. Month after month, quarter after quarter, the major indices of growth moved upward. Gross national product rose from $569.7 billion in the first quarter of 1964 to $631.2 billion in the last quarter of 1965. Disposable personal income shot up from $423 billion in the first quarter of 1964 to $486.1 billion in the last three months of 1965. The number of poor families in America, defined as earning less than $3,000 per year in 1965 dollars, dropped from 8.5 million in 1963 to 8 million in 1965. The number of people out of work fell sharply from 4.1 million in January 1964 to 3.1 million in December 1965. Moreover, by the first half of 1965 government revenues had actually increased $7.5 billion over the last pre-tax-cut year. "If we continue to advance at a rate of 4.1% for the remainder of this decade," the CEA reported to the president in April 1965, "our real output in 1970 will be 51% above 1960."[24] It was a president's dream—lower taxes and additional funds for new and existing domestic programs. The primary goal of the Kennedy-Johnson tax program was not ingratiation with the well-to-do, per se, but creation of the political and economic capital to fund measures of health, education, and welfare.

The prosperity created by the tax cut of 1964 would have a profound impact on Lyndon Johnson and his crusade to create an American Utopia. By 1964, John Kenneth Galbraith, who like Walter Heller was an interpreter and exponent of Keynesian thought, was hard at work on a new book, *The New Industrial State*. Taking up where he had left off in his *The Affluent Society*, Galbraith discussed the evolution of the modern corporation, demonstrating how in cooperation with government and labor, it had acted effectively to minimize risk, protect itself from the vagaries of the free market system, and ensure its survival. What had resulted was not stagnation but greater efficiency and productivity so that it had become possible to use the energies of the economy for nonindustrial purposes—"the expansion of public services, the assertion of the aesthetic dimension of life, widened choice as between income and leisure, the emancipation of education." What Galbraith proposed was that the emerging science and education elite be harnessed to this purpose by the will of the federal government.[25]

The scientists, engineers, and social scientists who had played such an important role in the development of American industry and finance were more than ready to oblige. "The universities, the academies, the think tanks, . . . had a sense that there were important problems to which there could be solutions," recalled Charles Haar, White House adviser on urban development and the environment, "that resources could be applied to them, that they were capable of being handled."[26] Galbraith's ideas were echoed by other public intellectuals, such as Walter Lippmann. "An affluent society is not simply a rich society," he wrote, "it is one which has mastered the new art of controlling and stimulating its own economic growth . . . we have a sufficiently promising start to justify our thinking that we have seen a break-through—that we are escaping from the immemorial human predicament of the haves and the have-nots."[27]

LBJ had known and respected Galbraith for years. He read Lippmann's columns religiously, had had him to the Texas ranch when he was vice president, and consulted with him shortly after the assassination.[28] Although he was largely on the outside looking in during the Kennedy presidency, Johnson had become aware of the present and future significance of the emerging science-education elite during the vice-presidential years. Shortly after he assumed office, LBJ instructed Bill Moyers and Eric Goldman to go out into the highways and byways of academe and assemble task forces that would address the great social and economic problems of the day and suggest policies to remedy them.[29] Johnson then embraced the "politics of productivity," to use historian Charles Maier's phrase. Given the affluence and technical expertise then existing in America, the federal government could care for those who could not care for themselves, provide education and opportunity to the disadvantaged, and ensure social justice for all without taking from one group of citizens and giving to another. All could be invited to the table and all could be served. For Johnson, the class-based politics of the 1930s that had given way to the interest-based politics of the 1940s were now about to give way to the consensus-based politics of the 1960s. A reformer's dream was about to come true—justice and equity without conflict.

LBJ REALIZED THAT HE NEEDED A SLOGAN FOR THE BROAD PROGRAM that was then germinating in the federal agencies and task forces under his command. In early 1964 he began badgering Richard Goodwin, a Kennedy aide who had decided to stay on and write speeches for Johnson, to come up with a catchy phrase like New Deal or New Frontier. Although only thirty-two years old, Goodwin was already a prominent prowler of the halls of power. A Bostonian, Goodwin had graduated first in his class at Tufts and Harvard Law School and then clerked for Supreme Court Justice Felix Frankfurter. He was a brilliant and arrogant youth with wide-ranging interests and tastes, a self-proclaimed Renaissance man who already knew many of the leading artists and writers of his day. Devoted to John and Robert Kennedy, he had dabbled in Latin American affairs, the Peace Corps, and various cultural activities. A regular on the Georgetown cocktail circuit, Goodwin had by the time he succeeded to the Johnson staff acquired a reputation for ruthlessness and an ability to subsume means to ends.

Realizing that he was too close to the Kennedys to ever completely win LBJ's trust, Goodwin seduced Bill Moyers and used him as a bridge. Moyers, still in his mind very much the naïf from Marshall, Texas, found Goodwin irresistible. "Here was a former aide to the illustrious Felix Frankfurter," Eric Goldman wrote in his White House memoir, "a connoisseur of the latest in literature and art, who, at the age of thirty-two, last week's soup stain on his suit, puffing his cigar and twirling his gold chain enigmatically, talked of power and policy with a faintly weary smile."[30] Goodwin would spend his nights ridiculing LBJ and his days working to shape the policies of the man who had usurped JFK.

In February 1964 LBJ summoned Goodwin and Moyers to the White House pool. As was his custom, the president was swimming in the buff. Goodwin was struck by the scene and, with the knights and ladies of Camelot in mind, subsequently described it: "We entered the pool area to see the massive presidential flesh, a sun bleached atoll breaching the placid sea, passing gently, sidestroke, the deep-cleft buttocks moving slowly past our unstartled gaze. Moby Dick, I thought. . . . 'It's like going swimming with a polar bear,' Moyers whispered."[31] The president had the two young men strip and join him. Johnson suddenly stopped and began talking as if to some invisible audience in the distance. He wanted to build on Kennedy's accomplishments and dreams but go beyond them. America could be a land of plenty but also one with a social conscience and an eye to excellence in all things public: education, conservation, beautification, cultural activities, and technological innovation. Despite himself, Goodwin was inspired. LBJ assigned his two assistants the task of drafting a speech that would outline his vision and, more important, inspire the nation to support that vision.

Goodwin met with Eric Goldman, who had taken up the post of resident intellectual at the White House following Arthur Schlesinger's departure. Goldman had come to the White House's attention through an aide to Moyers, Hayes Redmon, a former Goldman student. Goldman had reinforced Johnson's commitment to consensus politics, social justice at home, competitive coexistence abroad, and an emphasis on improving the quality of life for all human beings. In his first interview with the president, the Princeton academic, overcoming initial nervousness, had dared to outline his vision of the future. Confronted with death and division, Goldman declared, past presidents had drawn the country together by invoking the national interest. Avoiding partisanship and ideology, they had thrown their weight behind a broad domestic and diplomatic program that represented what a variety of significant groups could agree upon or could be persuaded to agree upon. Theodore Roosevelt had brought the country out of the divisiveness of the 1890s by posing as the "steward" of the needs and aspirations of the general population. A too-sharply divided nation was an immobile and potentially self-destructive one. Domestically, the president could clean up essential, unfinished business, such as action directed toward education needs, the legitimate restiveness of the African American community, and the dangerously mounting costs of medical care. Johnson, Goldman recalled, was entranced. "His long face was fixed on me and he would interject an occasional 'Yes.'"[32]

Throughout March and April, Goodwin worked on a speech, focusing particularly on a title for the Johnson program. Goldman suggested "The Good Society," the title of a book written by Walter Lippmann some years earlier. Eventually, after consulting with Moyers, Valenti, and the president, Goodwin came up with "The Great Society," the title of a 1919 book penned by Graham Wallas, who, not coincidentally, had been one of Lippmann's mentors.[33] Wallas, a London School of Economics professor and Fabian socialist, used the term "Great" to refer to large and complex. He was a pioneering social psychologist writing about human nature, intelligence, and the tasks of organizing modern industrial societies in ways that contributed to the greater good. (Lippmann's book—he was trying to impress Wallas—was mostly psycho-socio babble.) Despite its socialist origins, "the great society" was also an expression that had been used by conservative publishing magnate Henry R. Luce in a 1939 speech to the Economic Club of Detroit. Similar in tone and theme to FDR's Commonwealth Club address of 1932, Luce's speech urged his fellow businessmen to assume greater social responsibilities and "take part in the creation of the Great Society."[34]

Goodwin recalled that he wanted the speech to go beyond the unfulfilled promises of the New Deal and reflect the burgeoning movements of the sixties. "My objective—my mandate as I understood it—was not to produce a catalogue of specific projects, but a concept, an assertion of purpose, a vision . . . that went beyond the liberal tradition of the New Deal," Goodwin observed in his memoirs.[35] The speechwriter claimed that he read manifestos of the civil rights movement such as Martin Luther King's "Letter from a Birmingham Jail" as well as Betty Friedan's *The Feminine Mystique,* Ralph Nader's indictment of the auto industry, *Unsafe at Any Speed,* and the Port Huron Statement—the manifesto of the New Left—in preparation. (*Unsafe,* however, was not published until 1965.)

There was in truth a ghost coauthor of the Goodwin version of the Great Society speech—Arthur Schlesinger Jr. In 1956, the historian had written an essay in *The Reporter* titled "The Future of Liberalism," which anticipated the Great Society. Schlesinger had been one of the cofounders of the Americans for Democratic Action (ADA), an organization composed of political liberals who were at the same time Cold War hawks. During the McCarthy era, Schlesinger and the ADA had waged an ongoing battle against Republican charges that Truman and the Democratic Party as a whole were "soft on communism." Government loyalty investigations, both federal and state, had put those suspected of communist sympathies on public display and helped conservatives portray all collectivist theories calling for a larger, more active government as "socialist" or, worse, "communist." This became the political mantra used to indict one liberal program after another, from national health insurance to public housing proposals.[36]

"Liberalism in an age of abundance must begin shifting its emphasis," Schlesinger wrote in his *Reporter* article. "Instead of the quantitative liberalism of the 1930s, rightly dedicated to the struggle to secure the economic basis of life, we need now a 'qualitative liberalism' dedicated to bettering the quality of people's lives." The battle for the necessities of life had been won, and it was time for liberals to "move on to the more subtle and complicated problem of fighting for individual dignity, identity, and fulfillment in a mass society."[37] Hopefully, Schlesinger's call for a new individualism would both appeal to the various movements of the sixties and blunt the ongoing campaign to portray liberals, in general, and Democrats, in particular, as advocates for a collectivist, mass society.

When Valenti, Busby, and George Reedy read Goodwin's draft, they were appalled. How were these "quality-of-life" issues to be achieved? How exactly was the federal government going to enable individual Americans to realize their potential beyond providing them with Roosevelt's positive rights? What did "individual dignity, identity, and fulfillment in a mass society" mean? It would be like legislating transcendentalism. These were men of the New Deal: environmental concerns, consumer protection, women's liberation, and the youth rebellion had not yet appeared on their radar screen. The president should stick to bread-and-butter issues, they insisted, and Valenti rewrote Goodwin's draft to that end. Instead of the Great Society, Busby suggested "A Confederacy of Excellence."[38]

Moyers and Goodwin fought back. In mid-May the two wrote to Johnson, urging him to resuscitate the original version of the speech, appealing to the president's ambition and his desire to be taken as seriously as had been John Kennedy—to be anointed a man of ideas. The bold version of the address, Moyers and Goodwin declared, was "designed to make people like Reston and Lippmann . . . sit up and say: 'This President is really thinking about the future problems of America.'"[39] Johnson agreed.

The venue selected for the Great Society's coming out party was the commencement exercises at the University of Michigan scheduled for May 22, 1964. On the appointed day, LBJ rose to the appreciative applause of the eighty thousand who filled the Michigan football stadium at Ann Arbor. It was sunny and mild, and those in attendance were in a festive mood. "For a century," Johnson began,

> we labored to settle and to subdue a continent. For half a century we called upon unbounded invention and untiring industry to create an order of plenty for all of our people. The challenge of the next half-century is whether we have the wisdom to use that wealth to enrich and elevate our national life, and to advance the quality of our American civilization. Your imagination, your initiative, and your indignation will determine whether we build a society where progress is the servant of our needs, or a society where old values and new visions are buried under unbridled growth. . . . For in your time we have the opportunity to move not only toward the rich society and the powerful society, but upward to the Great Society.

An end to poverty and racial injustice was only the beginning. The search for a more perfect civilization would require a massive effort in behalf of slum clearance and urban renewal, new and improved systems of mass transit, and the creation and preservation of urban green spaces. In the countryside, the federal government would have to join with state and local polities to conserve, preserve, and enhance: "The water we drink, the food we eat, the very air that we breathe, are threatened with pollution. Our parks are overcrowded, our seashores overburdened. Green fields and dense forests are disappearing." Quoting Aristotle—"Men come together in cities in order to live, but they remain together to live the good life"—the president declared that increasingly that was proving impossible. The central cities were in decay, the suburbs "despoiled," and there was a severe shortage of housing and transportation. Noting that eight million adult Americans had no more than a fifth-grade education and that a hundred thousand qualified high school graduates annually were barred from college for financial reasons, LBJ hinted at a massive federal effort to support education at every level.

"There are those timid souls who say this battle cannot be won," the president concluded, "that we are condemned to a soulless wealth. I do not agree. We have the power to shape the civilization that we want. But we need your will, your labor, your hearts, if we are to build that kind of society."[40]

The Great Society speech was interrupted by applause twenty-nine times. Those in attendance were, of course, euphoric at the prospect of graduation, but there was more to it than that. LBJ had offered an inspiring vision of the future, had reassured the nation that it still harbored the seeds of greatness, had asserted that in the future lay more than assassination, racial turmoil, and the possibility of a nuclear holocaust. One of the reasons JFK had been elected, albeit by the narrowest of margins, was that he had issued a call to arms, had promised especially young people sacrifice and hard work on behalf of a noble cause, a breath of fresh air after the complacency of the Eisenhower years. The Great Society speech recaptured that mood and re-kindled those fires.

Americans did not necessarily take LBJ literally. When a Gallup poll sub-sequently asked whether people thought poverty would ever be eliminated from American society, only 9 percent answered in the affirmative.[41] Nevertheless, the new president's idealism, his competence and impatience to do the right thing, and his faith in the nation were balm to postassassination America. Johnson himself was caught up in the euphoria of the moment.

"When we got back on the plane," Charles Roberts, a member of the press pool, remembered, "he was sweating and exuberant. He violated his old rule and had himself a drink, a Scotch highball, and came back to our press pool. . . . Then he took the script from Jack Valenti and read, with emphasis, portions of the speech to us. He wanted to make sure we got the story. He'd say, 'Now did you get this?'"[42]

Arthur Schlesinger, the men around Kennedy, and a number of public intellectuals were anxious to attribute the speech to Richard Goodwin and hence to the Kennedys. In a speech delivered to the eighteenth annual convention of the ADA in the spring of 1965, Schlesinger would attribute the concept of the Great Society entirely to New Frontiersman Richard Goodwin. All of LBJ's men—Valenti, Busby, Reedy—were against the idea, arguing that the "dreamy vague proposals would be interpreted as a hangover from the Soviet Union's series of unsuccessful five-year plans." Warming to his audience, Schlesinger hailed the triumph of Goodwin's proposals as "a clear victory of the liberal cause of American politics over the messianic conservative complex of the President's Texas mafia."[43] In an interview with journalist Hugh Sidey, LBJ insisted that Barbara Ward's *The Rich Nations and the Poor Nations,* which he kept on the nightstand by his bed, had been the chief inspiration for the Great Society address.[44]

There were those who would argue that Johnson was creating a political order in which he did not fit, that he, like Reedy and Valenti, were men of the thirties and forties, of a time of class-based politics and meat-and-potato legislation like the minimum wage measure, social security, and federally supervised collective bargaining. The women's movement, consumer protection, the environmental movement, the youth movement were phenomena that transcended party and were beyond the reach of traditional politics, unsuited to horse trading. But Johnson would stick to his guns, at least for the time being. As the president subsequently remarked to the 1964 convention of the Communications Workers of America, "In Franklin Roosevelt's time there was a sense of crisis, of desperate danger, of threatening disaster. The need for action was plain." In contrast, LBJ warned, the Great Society summoned the country to address problems that were virtually invisible—"like some giant iceberg." The government's most important task during the 1960s was not to close the gap between rich and poor, to prevent class warfare; the greatest challenge was to alert an "indifferent" nation that ignored subterranean but potentially fatal social ills tied to excessive self-absorption. The contest today, Johnson declared, was not "so much between the oppressed and the privileged, as between the farsighted and those without any vision."[45] This semimystical call to utopian community was Camelot and Port Huron, but it was also Johnson. One could almost hear the mystical voices of Charles Marsh, the wealthy Texas newspaperman who had advised LBJ during the first part of his career, and Henry Wallace, FDR's left-leaning vice president.

IF THE TAX CUT OF 1964 WAS THE FIRST BUILDING BLOCK IN JOHN-son's utopia, the second was the War on Poverty. Intertwined as it was with issues of race, public morality, and the proper role of government in society, it would come to define the administration in the minds of the public and press as much as civil rights and Vietnam.

The notion that civil society was responsible for those of its members who could not or would not care for themselves was a relatively new concept in Anglo-America. Britain in the mid-nineteenth century, in the midst of industrialization and the enclosure movement, was home to a burgeoning population of chronically poor people. In 1849 journalist Henry Mayhew began chronicling their lives collectively and individually, and in the process pricked the consciences of the middle class. Hard upon his heels came novelist Charles Dickens, who in *Oliver Twist, Hard Times,* and *Our Mutual Friend* brought to life the pickpockets, street children, and prostitutes of Britain's underworld. Gradually, the British were sensitized to the deep division in their land between the haves and have-nots.

In the United States, mass awareness of the existence of a more or less permanent underclass grew out of the Progressive movement of the early twentieth century. Jacob Riis, himself a Danish immigrant, produced a score of books and articles, the most notable of which was *How the Other Half Lives,* describing the plight of those New Yorkers who struggled to eke out an existence in the city's tenements and sweatshops. Meanwhile, Jane Addams and other social activists were attempting to mobilize local governments and political parties as well as philanthropists in a movement to alleviate not only the material but also the spiritual plight of the poor. Persons of faith like LBJ's mother, Rebekah Baines Johnson, were reading C. M. Sheldon's *In His Steps,* which argued that if Christians would live the lives to which

Christ had called them, it would be impossible for millions to walk the streets in search of food and for thousands of children to die each year from lack of adequate health care.

The coming of the Great Depression spawned a new wave of revelatory and reform literature. John Steinbeck, LBJ's favorite author, stirred the souls of millions with his *Grapes of Wrath*. The photographic record of rural poverty produced by the Farm Security Administration during the Dust Bowl years reinforced Steinbeck's literary images. The 1940s and 1950s witnessed a mass migration of some three million blacks from the rural South into northern, southern, midwestern, and West Coast cities, where they were segregated into slum-infested ghettoes. From the day in 1944 when the first mechanical cotton pickers were tested in Mississippi, African American farm workers were doomed to move or starve. Birmingham, Atlanta, and Houston in the South, New York, Philadelphia, and Newark in the North, Chicago in the Midwest, and Los Angeles and Oakland in the West became the homes of a new urban underclass. Jobs were scarce to nonexistent, city services such as water and sewage were substandard, education was strictly segregated, and escape, virtually impossible.

In 1961 anthropologist Oscar Lewis published *The Children of Sanchez,* a study of a fictional Mexico City slum-dwelling family. He found a "culture of poverty" characterized by high rates of alcoholism, suicide, and violence; female-headed, fatherless families; high levels of drug use; and high rates of infant mortality. Members of the underclass were cynical about the church, fatalistic, superstitious, and distrustful of authority. Not only were they under-educated, they lacked respect for education. What Lewis found was that families born to urban poverty passed on their beliefs, characteristics, and habits from generation to generation. In 1962 Michael Harrington, a Catholic idealist and socialist, popularized Lewis's ideas and Americanized his book's images in *The Other America*. That same year CBS ran Edward R. Murrow's "Harvest of Shame," a powerful indictment of poverty among migrant farm workers in America. And Harry M. Caudill published *Night Comes to the Cumberlands,* depicting the abject poverty of the half million whites who lived on the Cumberland Plateau in the Appalachian Mountains.[46]

Liberal economists like Galbraith and Heller believed that the economic boom of the 1950s and 1960s had produced the largesse to alleviate poverty in America, but they worried that there did not exist the mechanisms of distribution necessary to do the job. Although Heller had been instrumental in selling Kennedy on the tax cut, stressing growth and efficiency as the objectives of economic policy, he had been trained in the Economics Department of the University of Wisconsin, which, since the days of John R. Commons, had been concerned with distributional objectives, namely, social justice and economic equity.[47] Using Social Security Administration data, Heller posited the conservative figure of $3,000 for a family of four as the poverty line. He found that although those in poverty had declined in number by 10 percent from 1947 through 1956, that figure had dropped to only 2 percent between 1956 and 1961. As of 1962, thirty-three million to thirty-five million Americans—one-fifth of the entire population—were living in poverty.[48] JFK was aware of the problem and sympathetic to Heller's pleas that something needed to be done. Among other things, how could capitalism argue convincingly to the inhabitants of the Third World that it was superior to communism when one-fifth of America's citizens lived in poverty? Under Heller's direction, the Council of Economic Advisers set to work eliciting and coordinating plans from Health, Education, and Welfare as well as Labor and other departments.

Economists, sociologists, and psychologists studying poverty during the 1950s advanced three basic solutions. First, Keynesian aggregationists emphasized the productive capacity of the postwar economy, and these economists exhibited a boundless confidence in the ability of the federal government to manage that growth in such a way that it would offer ever larger slices of the American pie to all citizens, reducing poverty in an absolute sense and eliminating class conflict over scarce resources. Heller and his colleagues proposed dealing with poverty by altering tax policies to ensure that actual productivity increased to match potential productivity. The result would be perpetual full employment.

Second, structuralists noted the limits of economic growth, as evidenced by people left behind during the period of economic boom during the 1950s and early 1960s. Social scientists emphasizing this view, such as sociologist Gunnar Myrdal and economist John Kenneth Galbraith, perceived persistent structural limits in the economy that were based on race, place ("depressed areas" such as Appalachia), or vocational education deficits. Structuralists proposed government programs to deal with unemployment, low wages, racial integration, job training, and local and regional economic development. Income redistribution was also a structuralist goal, to be secured through social welfare spending and progressive taxation.

Third was the culture of poverty thesis advanced by Lewis, Harrington, and others. The environments that bred and perpetuated poverty had to be altered in ways that countered the social disorganization and self-defeating ethos of those families who had known nothing but poverty for generations.[49] Eventually, culture of poverty advocates would shy away from the extreme social engineering schemes that their analysis implied and embrace income supplements and mandatory wealth redistribution.

The trigger for poverty planning in the Kennedy administration had been mounting public concern with the problem of juvenile delinquency. In May 1961, JFK established the President's Commission on Juvenile Delinquency and Youth Crime (PCJD). The commission subsequently submitted a report that predicted a coming juvenile crime wave and proposed solutions that grew primarily from a 1960 book, *Delinquency and Opportunity,* written by Lloyd Ohlin and Richard Cloward of the Columbia School of Social Work. Their approach was labeled "opportunity theory." Delinquency was admittedly a separate subculture, but the two social theorists maintained that delinquents held mainstream values and aspirations; they simply lacked the means to attain them. Frustration and despair mounted, Ohlin and Cloward argued, when the decline of urban institutions such as public schools, political machines, and organized crime eroded social controls and blocked legitimate as well as illegitimate avenues of advancement. Violence and delinquency thus resulted when middle-class goals collided with lower-class reality. The commission employed the two as consultants and made opportunity theory its guiding intellectual premise. "We cannot control delinquency by building new institutions," the PCJD proclaimed. "We must prevent it by building new opportunities for underprivileged young people to find a useful place in the mainstream."[50] This relic of Progressivism with its emphasis on environmental engineering would become a conceptual mainstay of the Great Society. It should be noted that by 1963 the Justice Department's delinquency program had begun to view delinquency as shorthand for urban poverty and, by extension, racial discrimination.[51]

Several days following the Kennedy assassination, Johnson invited two of his oldest friends from his New Deal days, social worker Elizabeth Wickenden and her husband, Arthur Goldschmidt, to the Elms for Sunday supper.

"I have a very difficult problem," Johnson confided. "I feel a moral obligation to carry on the things that Kennedy proposed, but I have to have issues
I can take on as my own. I have to get reelected in a year." Johnson told
them that he was considering making poverty his headliner.[52]

Plans to eradicate poverty excited Johnson's imagination, but he knew
that government programs dedicated to closing the inequality gap would
be controversial. As Sargent Shriver, whom LBJ would select to command
the antipoverty effort, later observed, LBJ was attempting something revolutionary: "the only national effort ever conducted by the majority for the
benefit of the minority."[53] The Roosevelt revolution had taken place during
a time when a huge proportion of middle-class white people were in dire
straits and race was not conspicuously involved. The Johnson administration
would be attempting to use the federal government and taxpayer money to
eradicate poverty during a period of rising prosperity and growing racial
tension.

Heller understood this, and at the LBJ ranch during the Christmas holi-
days he, the president, Kermit Gordon, Moyers, and Valenti discussed ways
and means. The administration's commitment to the cause would have to
be loud and clear. "One thing I did know," LBJ later told journalist Douglas
Cater. "When I got through, no one in this country would be able to ignore
the poverty in our midst."[54] Johnson and Heller also agreed that if white
middle-class Americans were going to join the war, they would have to be
assured that the campaign would destroy—not subsidize and perpetuate—
the culture of poverty. Heller's argument that "poverty was not only wrong,
it was something we could not afford" was music to Johnson's ears.[55] His
goal, as the president subsequently told conservatives such as Richard Russell, Harry Byrd, and Everett Dirksen, was to "make tax payers rather than
tax eaters" out of the disadvantaged.[56]

"This administration today, here and now, declares unconditional war
on poverty in America," LBJ proclaimed in his State of the Union address
on January 8, 1964. The tax cut would create jobs, but the federal government must go beyond mere monetary policy. "Very often a lack of jobs and
money is not the cause of poverty, but the symptom," he said. "The cause
may lie deeper—in our failure to give our fellow citizens a fair chance to
develop their own capacities, in a lack of education and training, in a lack of
medical care and housing, in a lack of decent communities in which to live

and bring up their children." He envisioned area redevelopment programs, youth employment legislation, a National Service Corps paralleling at home what the Peace Corps was doing abroad, a broader food stamp program, Medicare for the elderly, and special education for children living in the most depressed areas.[57]

Like those crusaders against poverty who preceded him, LBJ would be swimming against a strong tide of individualism in American society, an ethos that prized self-reliance and condemned government largesse to the poor as counterproductive. Classical economists such as the Reverend Thomas Malthus, who in 1798 had penned a scathing indictment of the English Poor Laws, insisted that the best antidote to poverty and unemployment was an unregulated free market system. Only the pain of poverty coupled with visibility of wealth and the possibility of gain, however slight, could motivate the masses to work. Americans from the Puritans of New England to the robber baron capitalists of the Gilded Age insisted that aid to the poor was morally corrupting, reinforcing the selfish and sinful aspects of human nature. Well into the twentieth century, many Americans accepted the conservative truism that poverty was the fault of the poor themselves, the product of character flaws beyond the reach of legislative remedy. Of course, even the most hardened disciples of laissez faire admitted that there were in society those who could not care for themselves. The sick, the lame, widows with dependent children could not work and must be supported—they were the "deserving poor"—but the undeserving, the lazy, the venal, the improvident, could not claim support by right and must rely on private charity. Even after World War II, the idea that poverty was the penalty for people who had not tried hard enough remained strong. Those who had framed the New Deal's chief welfare program, Aid to Families with Dependent Children (AFDC), had had in mind a mother and wife of a West Virginia coal miner killed in an accident.[58]

Poverty was primarily a Democratic issue, one that Republicans were more than willing to let them have. Welfare was of great benefit to the GOP in its never-ending struggle to taint the Democratic Party and liberalism in general as soft, emotional, and even anti-American. Campaigning for president in West Virginia in 1960, Richard Nixon denounced his Democratic opponent's assertion that seventeen million people went to bed hungry every night. Such assertions only provided "grist for the Communist propaganda mill," he said, and he repeated Eisenhower's reaction to Kennedy's claim: "Now look, I go to bed hungry every night, but that's because I'm on a diet."[59]

WHEN LBJ ADDRESSED THE NATION AND ISSUED HIS CALL TO ARMS in the War on Poverty, neither he nor his advisers had a clear picture of the strategy and specific programs that would constitute the campaign. Johnson's mind turned first to the selection of a person who would supply the energy and vision to make an antipoverty program work. Robert Kennedy, who as attorney general had taken a special interest in juvenile delinquency, let it be known that he would like such an assignment, but Johnson had no intention of giving aid to an enemy who was already trying to position himself to be the Democratic Party's vice-presidential candidate in 1964. Galbraith suggested Moyers, but he was too young and inexperienced. Besides, Johnson needed him to be available for a variety of assignments. But Moyers's former boss in the Peace Corps, Sargent Shriver, would be perfect.[60] Shriver, the husband of Eunice Kennedy, was associated with the Kennedys but was not a member of the tribe. Following the assassination, he had let the White House know that he was his own man and would very much like to be considered for the vice presidency. Though Shriver was financially secure himself, his family had suffered during the Depression, and that experience had made an indelible impression on him. A Catholic, he had worked with the poor as part of the Catholic Worker Movement in New York. Shriver was a disciple of Saint Francis of Assisi and an active member of the Saint Vincent de Paul Society in Chicago. As president of the school board there, he had concentrated on improving ghetto schools.[61]

RFK's brother-in-law had made the Peace Corps into one of the most successful of the New Frontier initiatives. Looking back on the program, Shriver observed that in the beginning, "many were worried that it would be a tutti-frutti organization, a lot of kids bouncing around the world in Bermuda shorts."[62] But it was hardly that. The students who volunteered went out into the highways and byways of the Third World, exposing themselves to hunger, disease, tribal conflict, and political oppression. They taught English, hygiene, modern farming techniques, civil administration, and a hundred other subjects without expecting anything in return, in hopes of shielding the program from communist charges of Yankee imperialism. And Shriver proved to be a shrewd politician. He and the Peace Corps were perhaps the only two aspects of the New Frontier that were genuinely popular on the Hill.

Johnson recruited Shriver in typical whirlwind fashion. On the morning of February 1, 1964, the phone rang at Sarge and Eunice's home in Washington. Shriver had just returned from a Peace Corps trip to Europe.

"Sarge?" the president said.

"Good morning, Mr. President. How are you?"

"I'm gonna announce your appointment at that press conference."

"What press conference?"

"This afternoon."

"Could you just say that you have asked me to study this?"

"Hell no. They've studied and studied. They [the press] want to know who in the hell is going to do this."

Shriver asked for a week's delay so that he could put some plan together. It would serve neither his, the president, nor the program's interests if it appeared that he did not know what he was talking about. No, said Johnson, we'll announce you as head and tell newspeople that you are putting together a team that will devise a workable program in the immediate future. Breathless, resigned, Shriver gave in.[63]

In the weeks that followed, Johnson made it clear that the administration's antipoverty program would encompass neither welfare in the form of direct relief nor a government jobs program that would compete with the private sector. During a cabinet meeting in February, Secretary of Labor Willard Wirtz had proposed a massive jobs program similar to the Work Projects Administration (WPA), costing $3 billion to $5 billion and financed by an increased tax on tobacco. Johnson wanted none of it. "I have never seen a colder reception from the president," a staffer in attendance said. "He just—absolute blank stare—implied without even opening his mouth that Shriver should move on to the next proposal."[64] Nor was LBJ interested in direct relief. "Smith [House Rules Committee Chairman Howard Smith, a reactionary] has got to understand that I want these people taken off relief and trained to do something," he told Congressman Carl Albert [D-OK] . . . we're spending $8 billion on relief now. . . . But I'm gonna cut down that $8 billion, if he'll let me, and put 'em to work."[65] Indeed, Johnson's War on Poverty might have accurately been termed a war on welfare. "Our American answer to poverty is not to make the poor more secure in their poverty," Johnson would say later that year, "but to reach down and to help them lift themselves out of the ruts of poverty and move with the large majority along the high road of hope and prosperity. . . . The days of the dole in our country are numbered."[66]

It was not that LBJ was opposed to government jobs programs or direct relief; he had supported both vigorously during the Depression. But the economic and political climate was far different in the 1960s than it had been in the 1930s. The vast white middle class was prosperous, not impoverished. Keynesianism, specifically the tax cut, would create additional space in the private sector, but the disadvantaged must be educated and trained to take advantage of the resulting opportunity. In addition to the political problems that relief and public sector jobs would create, Johnson sensed that they were not the answer to the culture of poverty that had taken root in the rural South, Appalachia, and the nation's urban centers.

Despite his protestations to the contrary, Johnson saw the poverty bill very much as civil rights legislation. Moyers recalled that shortly after he assumed the presidency, LBJ had one of his secretaries dig up a flyer published widely in Mississippi, Alabama, east Texas, and northern Georgia in 1959 by the White Citizens Council. "We intend to see that no Negro who believes in equality has a job, gets credit, or is able to exist in our communities," it read. He kept it in his desk in the small office adjoining the Oval Office throughout the first year of his presidency. During the spring of 1964, the White House was bombarded with statistics showing that poverty was concentrated disproportionately among blacks. There was discrimination in hiring and discrimination in pay for those who were hired. In December 1963, Johnson met with Roy Wilkins, head of the NAACP, and convinced him that the poverty program was a civil rights bill and a necessary complement to the pending public accommodations and voting rights legislation.[67]

Hammering out the specific programs that would comprise the administration's poverty bill proved a painful process. There was hardly a department or agency in the federal government that did not have an interest in or program bearing on the struggle to eliminate poverty: Labor; Health, Education, and Welfare (HEW); Agriculture; the CEA; Bureau of the Budget; even the Pentagon, which worried about the tens of thousands of young men who could not qualify for military service; and the Department of Justice, which faced the task of combating juvenile delinquency. At first, "the walls dripped with blood as the empire-builders clashed with the empire-wreckers," as one participant put it.[68] To Shriver's credit, he was able to impart to the 137-person task force he had convened a sense of mission and purpose that transcended their parochial bureaucratic objectives. There was chaos, but it was exhilarating, "a beautiful hysteria," as one participant described it.

Frank Mankiewicz, Peace Corps director in Peru, introduced Shriver to Michael Harrington and took six weeks off to work on the poverty bill. But Shriver's chief comrade-in-arms was Adam Yarmolinsky, a special assistant to Secretary of Defense Robert McNamara. He was, as Eric Goldman has observed, one of those activist intellectuals tailor-made to raise the hackles of conservatives, especially southern conservatives. He was brilliant and arrogant, short, dark, Jewish, and a native New Yorker. Yarmolinsky, a Harvard academic, was one of those aggressively liberal Charles River intellectuals who had come to Washington as a member of the Kennedy entourage. As a high school student he had attended several Young Communist League meetings, but the totalitarian, statist aspects of Soviet-style communism repelled him. At the Pentagon he had organized a commission to investigate racial discrimination in the armed forces and then headed the effort to implement its recommendations.[69] According to the scenario that Shriver envisioned, Yarmolinsky would draft the poverty bill, and he, Shriver, would maneuver it through Congress. Yarmolinsky would then head whatever administrative agency Congress approved to administer the poverty program. LBJ was enthusiastic about the Harvard academic's participation, but he sounded a warning: "I think he's very able," he told Shriver, "and very fine . . . wonderful fellow . . . he's a good friend of mine . . . you want to watch that background on the Hill though. . . . I'd be worried a little bit about that."[70]

THE ECONOMIC OPPORTUNITY ACT (EOA) THAT THE ADMINISTRATION sent to Congress in March 1964 combined several different approaches and philosophies. It proposed to spend $962 million, less than 9 percent of the estimated cost of eliminating poverty for one year. But Shriver and his lieutenants saw the EOA as a beginning, not the be-all and end-all. Title I appropriated $190 million to fund a youth jobs training program. The Job Corps would establish rural residential camps where trainees would receive basic and vocational training. In the cities, a Neighborhood Youth Corps would hire the same eighteen- to twenty-one-year-olds to work on minimum wage jobs for the city, county, or a nonprofit agency. In the process they would learn a skill—carpentry, bookkeeping, or welding, for example. The budget for it was $150 million. For students, there was a work-study program that would employ youths at an educational or other public institution for a maximum of fifteen hours a week. Title II established a community action program, Yarmolinsky's favorite, and what would prove to be the most controversial of the administration's poverty programs. The idea was for those who were caught in the culture of poverty to meet and design programs in education, employment, vocational rehabilitation, welfare, housing, and other fields that were particularly suited to their community. They would then apply to a new federal agency, the Office of Economic Opportunity (OEO), for funding. Community action would receive $315 million. In calling for "maximum feasible participation," community action was supposed to benefit the disadvantaged materially but also psychologically by giving them a sense of empowerment.

Elizabeth Wickenden, a social welfare consultant who participated in the poverty task force, warned that community action would be controversial because local political machines would see it as an attempt to undercut them. Mayors and city councils would complain to their representatives in Congress that they should be given control of the funds.[71] Yarmolinsky insisted it was a nonissue: "My conception of what it meant was that you involved poor people in the process, not put them in charge."[72] Apparently, that was how LBJ viewed community action as well. "Get your planning and development people busy right now to see what you can do for the crummiest place in town," he told Chicago mayor Richard Daley, "the lowest, the bottom—and see what we can do about it and we'll get our dough and then you'll have your plan ready and we'll move."[73]

After the poverty bill passed, Moyers and Shriver suggested using some of the money to subsidize nongovernmental organizations (NGOs). "I'm going to re-write your poverty program," Johnson exploded. "You boys got together and wrote these things and I thought we were just going to have the NYA [National Youth Administration]. . . . Do you know what I think about the poverty program? What I thought we were going to do? I thought we were going to have CCC [Civilian Conservation Corps] camps and I thought we were going to have community action where a city or a county or a school district or some government agency could sponsor projects. . . .

I am against subsidizing any private organization. . . . I would prefer Dick Daley do it than the Urban League. . . . I just think it makes us wide open and I don't want anybody to get any grants."[74]

Because LBJ was by experience sympathetic to rural poverty, and because a number of congressmen and senators who would be voting on EOA represented farming areas, the administration's bill contained something for the country-dwelling poor. Secretary of Agriculture Orville Freeman and his principal assistant for the poverty program, James Sundquist, were particularly worried about the disappearance of small farms. They wanted a provision "where significant quantities of land could be bought up, broken into family size farms, and sold at low interest on long term sales to Negroes, former sharecroppers and others, to rebuild these rural communities, and thus try and reverse the very damaging trend of people buying up big chunks of land and then operating it partly for pleasure, only partly for agriculture with hired labor, making virtually peons out of the displaced sharecroppers who have been driven North to the city slums."[75] As a result, Title III provided low-interest loans of up to $2,500 to low-income families to purchase or improve small farms. The EOA would establish the Office of Economic Opportunity to review and fund proposals. Shriver was also authorized to recruit citizens to Volunteers in Service to America, or VISTA, whose participants would work with Native Americans, migratory workers, persons with mental illness, and those with developmental disabilities.[76]

As LBJ, Shriver, and congressional liaison Larry O'Brien turned their attention to Congress and the struggle to see the EOA passed, they were daunted. Republicans under Senate Minority Leader Everett Dirksen and House Minority Leader Charles Halleck (he was not replaced by Gerald Ford until after the 1964 elections) were determined to depict the War on Poverty as the hare-brained idea of soft-headed liberals sure to bankrupt the nation. Southerners viewed the program as a civil rights Trojan horse, a federal program to empower blacks and further the cause of integration. When an administration official presented Arkansas congressman Wilbur Mills, the chair of the House Ways and Means Committee, with materials in support of the EOA, Mills threw it back at him, "said a few choice words about how he was not going to be involved in any program to help a bunch of niggers and threw me out of the office."[77] Moreover, working-class whites everywhere were liable to buy in to the argument that the EOA was a mechanism to aid the unemployed in competing with them for their jobs.[78] Walter Heller of the Council of Economic Advisers remembered being taught at Wisconsin that unionists generally regarded the poor as competitive menaces.[79]

The administration did not want the House and Senate to enter into extended debates on the merits or demerits of the components of the EOA. Rather, its strategy was to focus on the plight of the poor in order to arouse a wave of public sympathy that would overwhelm Congress. Most of the sixty witnesses who testified before the House committee that held hearings on the poverty bill talked about the moral depravity of a society as affluent as America permitting children to go hungry, bed down with rats, and suffer from diseases that could easily be prevented. To highlight the plight of America's poor and to demonstrate that the EOA was intended to help whites as well as blacks, LBJ, accompanied by his wife Lady Bird, made two conspicuous tours of Appalachia in April and May.[80] He met with the governors of seven states and, with print and broadcast journalists in tow, visited some of the most depressed areas in the United States. One of Johnson's secretaries recalled a particular appalling slum in Tennessee: "The stench was so unbelievable; it was like standing in the middle of a human feces pool . . . everyone was gagging. The President insisted on walking into a house of ill repute."[81]

In speeches on those trips and in other venues, LBJ played the role of evangelist in the cause of the social gospel. "It is almost insulting to urge you to enlist in this war for just economic motivations," he told the Advertising Council. "This is a moral challenge that goes to the very root of our civilization, and asks if we are willing to make public, personal sacrifices for the public good."[82] Never mind that the EOA would not require anyone to give up anything. "We are determined that this Nation is going to be strong enough to secure the peace," he remarked to another audience. "This Nation is going to be prudent enough to be solvent . . . but strength and solvency alone don't quicken the heartbeat. The thing that really makes a great nation is compassion. We are going to have strength and solvency and compassion, love for thy neighbor, compassion and understanding for those who are less fortunate."[83]

The Appalachian trip, or "Poverty Tour," as the press dubbed it, offered Secretary of Agriculture Orville Freeman—a sophisticated, cultured, but unpretentious man—his first opportunity to experience the new president up close and personal. He initially found him brusque and insensitive. Chiding Freeman for not yet having guided the administration's food stamp bill through Congress, the president walked away while the Minnesotan tried to explain. Freeman subsequently found himself excluded from picture taking with administration officials and the rural poor. And yet there was the president's obvious commitment to the cause:

> We went into town [in North Carolina], and I must say that he [LBJ] performed magnificently . . . he made inside the Courthouse a rather impassioned and most effective plea which was repeated in substance out in the street to maybe 20,000 or 30,000 people. . . . I must say honestly that during the day a feeling for the people and effort to improve the lot of people, a dedication to the principles of the New Deal and Franklin Roosevelt. . . . He came through with strength and a sincerity and intentness of purpose that was really quite stimulating. And so, here we have it on the one hand you ride a lightning rod of intemperate, thoughtless, mean, hypercritical kind of insensitive un-informed criticism and on the other an enormous energy, a demand for action, and a humanitarian feeling . . . which makes one feel that whatever the personal abuse you might be subject to . . . the goals are worth taking it if you can contribute to doing something which needs to be done.[84]

White House strategists perceived that in votes on the EOA, northern liberals and Republicans would cancel each other out. The balance would be held by southern Democrats. The outlook looked gloomy. When LBJ pressed Roy Wilkins of the NAACP to go up on the Hill and lobby for the poverty bill, he at first refused. "Mr. President," he said, "going up there is like going to a KKK rally."[85] That the chair of the House Committee on Education and Labor and the Subcommittee on the War on Poverty Program that would conduct hearings on the EOA was black—Congressman Adam Clayton Powell, the handsome, dapper, dissolute cleric who represented Harlem—did not help matters. In what Yarmolinsky considered "a great stroke," LBJ persuaded conservative Georgia congressman Phillip Landrum, coauthor of the antiunion Landrum-Griffin labor bill, to sponsor the EOA in the House. The president convinced the Georgian that poor whites as well as blacks in his district would benefit.[86]

Republicans were convinced that the race issue could be depended upon to sink the administration's antipoverty program. When that possibility began to fade, they turned to religion. The GOP encouraged an amendment to the EOA ensuring that a portion of the funds made available would go to parochial schools. Sponsored by Congressman Hugh Carey (D-NY), the addendum provided for money to be given not only to local school boards but also directly to private institutions to conduct remedial reading and arithmetic courses. The National Education Association let the administration know that if it accepted the Carey amendment, it would "scuttle the bill."[87] "[House Minority Leader] Halleck has got it going," LBJ complained to Shriver. "He's outsmarted you. . . . He tried the Negro thing and that didn't get off the ground and now he's got the religious thing."[88]

But there was yet another complication. Carey and Congressman Thomas P. "Tip" O'Neill (D-MA) were up in arms because, as part of the administration's economy drive, McNamara had scheduled a shutdown of the Brooklyn and Boston Naval Yards. Johnson refused to be blackmailed, but he was willing to give O'Neill some space. "I see O'Neill is giving out interviews about closing the base in his District and he's got to answer all these letters so he hasn't got time to work on the Administration team," he remarked to House Speaker John McCormack (D-MA). "He oughtn' to threaten me. . . . I can't operate a WPA Navy Yard but I can put it [the closure] off until next year."[89]

On the parochial school issue, Johnson assured Catholics that Shriver, who would administer the program and who was a coreligionist, would not discriminate against parochial schools. To Protestants, he declared that as long as Bill Moyers, "a Baptist preacher," was on the White House staff, the Catholic Church would not take over the poverty program, or as he put it, "we've got Moyers in on this program and he's not going to turn it over to the Pope."[90] Still, LBJ was far from confident. He asked Larry O'Brien, anxiously, if the bill were going to pass. "Yeah, I think so," O'Brien replied, "if we can just keep the boys that should be sober, sober, and the ones that should be drinking, drinking."[91]

On July 16, Shriver predicted to LBJ that the poverty bill would pass the Senate by a two-to-one margin, but the House would prove more difficult. A group of southern red-baiters headed by Congressman Harold Cooley (D-NC) had decided to compel the administration to sacrifice Adam Yarmolinsky as their price for voting for the measure. By 1964, Yarmolinsky had become something of an antihero to true-believing anticommunists and southern segregationists who had decided to use each other's movements to further their own cause. General Edwin Walker, who had been forced to retire from the military for distributing John Birch Society material to his troops and who was the heart and soul of the right wing in Dallas, had been lambasting Yarmolinsky as nothing less than a communist mole in the Defense Department. His mother had been "a communist poet," conservatives charged, and Yarmolinsky himself had been active in the communist youth movement. This was music to the ears of southerners who blamed him for the Defense Department's drive to desegregate off-base facilities that catered to the military.

On August 6, Speaker McCormack summoned Shriver to a meeting in his office. Cooley and several other southern congressmen were there. Cooley informed him that if Yarmolinsky was given any role in administering the poverty program, he and his seven Carolina colleagues would not vote for the EOA. Shriver said that Yarmolinsky was extremely competent and his friend to boot, and he would not abandon him, but the decision was the president's. After several painful phone calls to the White House, Johnson persuaded Shriver to relent. It was all a plot by the National Association of Manufacturers, LBJ observed: "it is all a lie" and you should not be expected to "denounce the man because somebody is starting to lie on him," but keeping Yarmolinsky in Defense was a small price to pay for passage of the poverty bill.[92] The president would not recommend Yarmolinsky for a position in the poverty program, Shriver assured Cooley. Subsequently, when conservative Congressman W. H. Ayres (R–OH) rose on the floor of the House to declare that Yarmolinsky, not Shriver, would be the real power in the poverty program, Phil Landrum cut him off: "So far as I am concerned, this gentleman, Mr. Yarmolinsky, will have absolutely nothing to do with the program." Shriver later recalled: "That was the most unpleasant experience I ever had in the government of the United States. . . . I felt . . . as if I ought to just go out and vomit."[93]

But opponents of the poverty bill were not through. The conservative coalition offered an amendment to the measure requiring recipients to sign a loyalty oath: a pledge of allegiance to the United States and a promise that the beneficiary had never belonged to a "subversive organization." The Senate had not included such an amendment, and if the House adopted it, the measure would have to go to conference. But to be referred to conference, the measure would have to have a rule from Congressman Howard Smith's committee. LBJ did not intend for his pride and joy to fall into the hands of the House's number one reactionary. Moyers and Shriver were opposed to the loyalty oath and wanted it to go to conference if the House adopted it. Johnson was determined that his advisers squelch their liberal impulses; if the bill that went to the Senate had to include a loyalty oath, so be it. "We'll handle the communist thing," he told his lieutenants. "We don't give a damn about that, that's professional liberals . . . but we'll kill the whole bill if we have to rely on Smith for another rule." Gradually, he worked himself up to near hysteria. Calling Moyers and Shriver "children" and "school kids," he told them "learn this for all time to come so nobody'll ever have to teach it to any of you again; you can never get a bill into conference without a rule or unanimous consent. . . . These amendments don't amount to a tinker's dam . . . everybody that goes on the payroll . . . says I'm not a communist."[94]

The loyalty oath amendment did not pass the House, and in the subsequent vote on the EOA, the administration won by a margin of 226 to 185. Southerners voted 60 to 40 against, but those 40, together with 22 Republicans, were enough to carry the day. In a signing ceremony at the White House, Johnson declared that "for the first time in all the history of the human race, a great nation . . . is willing to make a commitment to eradicate poverty among its people."[95]

LBJ UNDERSTOOD THAT THE POVERTY PROGRAM WAS A BEGINNING, that its architects were not at all sure where it was going or what the consequences of the policies it implemented would be. But it was a beginning. Hopefully, it would produce new instruments of social justice like Social Security, the minimum wage, and the Tennessee Valley Authority (TVA). Once in place, programs and agencies tended to develop a life and constituency of their own. One thing was certain: if something was not done to raise America's consciousness concerning the problems of the nation's inner-city poor, the nation would explode, and in the white backlash that followed, any hope that the civil rights movement might succeed would evaporate.

CHAPTER 3

THE SECOND RECONSTRUCTION

AS FAR AS LBJ WAS CONCERNED, THE KEY TO REALIZING THE GREAT Society, the issue that if not resolved could prevent progress on all other fronts, was civil rights. Because the legislative process was what he knew best, because Congress was the cockpit where democracy and social justice would and must be conjoined, LBJ's mind in the spring of 1964 was never far from the bill then pending before Congress.

The civil rights measure the Kennedy administration had introduced was sweeping. It would make completion of the sixth grade prima facie proof of literacy for the right to vote in federal elections; compel access to hotels, motels, places of entertainment, stores, restaurants, and other public facilities without regard to race, religion, or national origin; empower the commissioner of education to establish programs to desegregate public schools and the attorney general to file suit against school boards that did not participate; establish a Community Relations Service to mediate disputes over segregation and discrimination; require federal agencies to withhold funds from state and local entities and programs that discriminated in hiring; and establish a permanent Commission on Equal Employment Opportunity.[1]

Early in his administration, JFK, with the help of House Speaker Sam Rayburn (D-TX), had won a key civil rights victory in the House. Among that chamber's foes of the Second Reconstruction, none was more

determined or well positioned than Congressman Howard Smith, chairman
of the Rules Committee. Born in 1883 in the family farmhouse in Farquier
County, Virginia, Smith was a genuine relic of the Confederacy. An honors
graduate of the University of Virginia Law School, Smith was brilliant, dil-
igent, gracious, soft-spoken, and thoroughly reactionary. Democrat Carl Albert, the former Rhodes Scholar who represented Oklahoma in the House,
summed him up:

> By birth and by choice Judge Smith, as we knew him around the
> Capitol, was an unreconstructed nineteenth-century Virginian. He
> spent his entire legislative life trying to ward off federal encroach-
> ments into the world in which he was born. He had all the attributes,
> including all the prejudices, of his native state. He distrusted all in-
> fluences outside of his own area. He was brought up believing that
> Yankees, carpetbaggers, Republicans, and foreigners were enemies
> of his people and of the way of life they enjoyed. He was a white
> supremacist who fought racial integration to the bitter end. He op-
> posed nearly all federal social reforms, including health, education,
> and welfare bills. He believed in the Constitution "as written." He
> was a strict constructionist and states' righter.[2]

As chair of the Rules Committee, "Judge" Smith was in a position to prevent any legislation of which he did not approve from coming to the floor
of the House for a vote. During the debate over the 1957 Civil Rights Act,
Smith had shut down his committee for a week. He had to go home, he told
reporters, because his barn had burned down, prompting the Speaker, Sam
Rayburn, to observe, "I knew Howard Smith would do almost anything to
block a civil rights bill but I never knew he would resort to arson."[3] Shortly
after Kennedy's inauguration, Rayburn succeeded by the barest of margins
in enlarging Smith's committee from twelve to fifteen members, which
gave liberals and moderates at least a chance of an eight to seven majority.
Despite this breakthrough, progressive measures such as the 1963 civil rights
bill would still have to have Republican support to pass.[4]

Events in Birmingham, Alabama, and Oxford, Mississippi, had pricked
the consciences of many white middle-class Americans and galvanized the
black working class. The Student Nonviolent Coordinating Committee

(SNCC) and Congress of Racial Equality (CORE) continued to campaign to integrate public facilities and secure the right to vote for their brethren in the South. Frustrated, angry, paranoid southern segregationists struck back. Cross burnings, night ridings, and bombings multiplied at a frightening rate during 1963. In June, Medgar Evers, NAACP field representative in Mississippi, was shot dead by a sniper outside his home in Jackson.

On August 28, 1963, two hundred thousand Americans, black and white, descended on Washington to express their support for the civil rights measure then pending in Congress. The march on Washington marked the culmination of a long-held dream of A. Philip Randolph, the legendary head of the Brotherhood of Sleeping Car Porters, the first all-black union. Not until after Birmingham was he able to persuade the Southern Christian Leadership Conference (SCLC), NAACP, and National Urban League to support his "radical" idea. The participants, who included hundreds of nationally prominent church and civic leaders, marched peacefully from the Washington Monument to the Lincoln Memorial. There they heard pledges of support from politicians; the folk music of Peter, Paul, and Mary; and the gospel songs of Mahalia Jackson. The culmination of the March on Washington was Martin Luther King Jr.'s incomparable "I Have a Dream" speech.

Lyndon Johnson's decision to secure passage of the Kennedy civil rights bill pending in Congress no matter what the cost was fraught with danger. His advisers told him that he could not afford to lose and he could not afford to compromise. "The Negroes have seen two significant bills [1957 and 1960, although their significance is debatable] on civil rights become law," George Reedy told him. "From here on out, they will regard any measure which does not pass as a cynical gesture."[5] And there was good reason to believe that the measure would not pass. "It must be realized that the proper groundwork has not been laid," Reedy said. "Negroes are not convinced that the Administration is really on their side. Southern whites still believe that the turmoil is a combination of 'ward politics' and 'outside agitators.' Republicans believe that the issue is a matter of partisanship."[6] When Johnson subsequently asked Hubert Humphrey to spearhead the civil rights bill in the Senate, he told him, "This is your test. But I predict it will not go through."[7]

And what if it did pass? Southerners would be so embittered that there was a real possibility that white voters south of the Mason-Dixon line would

abandon the Democratic Party, and Johnson would be ignominiously defeated in the forthcoming presidential election. Moreover, the defection
might prove permanent. There was certainly no reason to believe the die-
hards were ready to let up. When the Kennedy administration had submitted
its civil rights bill in 1963, Richard Russell rose on the floor of the Senate to
charge JFK with threatening "mass violence" so he could trample on "property rights" and create a "special right for Negroes."[8] Thus, in attempting to
serve the cause of social justice, there was a very real possibility that Johnson
would destroy the one party that he believed was genuinely committed to
social justice.

Despite these negatives, there were compelling reasons to support the
Kennedy civil rights bill, and Johnson never hesitated. There was, first, the
very nature of the man. His parents, his upbringing, his psyche impelled
him to embrace the politics of unity and nurture. Second, LBJ believed that
the continued existence of the Union depended upon the guarantee of full
citizenship and equality of opportunity for all Americans. In taking the lead
in compelling adherence to the Constitution, he as president and the federal
government might be risking turmoil and even bloodshed in the short run,
but if they did not, there was sure to be a revolution that would end either in
equality or further repression. Indeed, this was the very signal the NAACP,
SCLC, CORE, and SNCC were attempting to send. "The message these
groups have been preaching to the Negro in his discontent is that there is
hope for justice within our social and political system," political columnist
Anthony Lewis wrote in the *New York Times*. That system was now on trial;
it was time to put up or shut up. In the face of the Birmingham bombings,
the murder of Medgar Evers, continuing police brutality, and ongoing segregationist intransigence, one could not expect the Negro to be "realistic"
about the difficulties of getting legislation through Congress.[9]

And then there was the South. Race had been a burden that Dixie had
carried since the Civil War, and it had barred the region from full participation in the life of the Republic. The end of segregation and discrimination
would bring the South finally and firmly into the national mainstream,
with all the economic prosperity and political influence that that would
mean. Racial justice was just as much in the interest of southern whites as
southern blacks. In fact, Johnson and those around him were convinced
that if racial harmony was to come to America, it would come first to the

South. Once white southerners realized that integration and equal opportunity for blacks did not mean miscegenation or even social mixing but a
right to travel freely, live and work where they wanted, compete for jobs
on an equal basis, and enjoy the comforts of public accommodation and
the benefits of truly equal education, animosity would quickly subside. "If
the Southerners understand this, they will solve the problem much easier
than the North because Southerners have lived with Negroes longer than
Northerners and really like them better," George Reedy had observed to
his boss.[10] This came not only from LBJ's white advisers but also from his
black aides. "There's something in the folklore of Negro life that a recon-
structed southerner is really far more liberal than a liberal Yankee," Louis
Martin observed.[11]

Finally, Johnson believed that passage of a sweeping civil rights bill had
at last become politically possible. Because President Kennedy had proposed the civil rights legislation Congress was then considering, because
he had gone on national television to condemn the 1963 church bombing
in Birmingham in which four young black girls were killed, JFK's name
had become associated with the Second Reconstruction. In the wake of
his assassination, the fallen president became a martyr to the cause. What
John Kennedy failed to do in life—make civil rights a compelling moral
issue—he could do, or be made to do, in death. Polls taken from the fall of
1963 through the spring of 1964 were revealing. As of June 1963, 49 percent of those queried indicated they favored a public accommodations law,
while 42 percent opposed. In January 1964, the approval rating stood at 61
percent. There was even some movement in the South, where opposition
shrank from 82 to 72 percent.[12] Most important, perhaps, polls revealed
that southerners were becoming fatalistic about civil rights. Although the
vast majority remained opposed to integration, some 83 percent of those
questioned indicated they believed racial integration to be inevitable; 49
percent indicated they thought it would come about in the South within
five years.[13] It was Johnson's particular achievement to realize that the time
had come, and to act on that realization.

LBJ's role in civil rights reminded White House aide Harry McPherson
of a quote from Sir Robert Peel, the eminent nineteenth-century English
statesman:"Public opinion, as it is said, rules, and public opinion is the opinion of the average man. [Charles James] Fox used to say of [Edmund] Burke,

'Burke is a wise man, but he is wise too soon.' The average man will not bear this. Politicians, as has been said, live in the repute of the commonality. They may appeal to posterity, but of what use is posterity?"[14]

JOHNSON AND HIS CHIEF POLITICAL STRATEGISTS ON THE CIVIL rights bill—Larry O'Brien and Deputy Attorney General Nicholas de B. Katzenbach—began huddling within days of JFK's assassination. The keys to passage would be the civil rights organizations, labor, business, the churches, and the Republican Party.

The first order of business, Johnson perceived, was to reassure black leaders that he was and would continue to be their unwavering ally. Some reassurance was called for. As vice president, Johnson had pressed the White House to allow him to take the lead on the civil rights bill, but the president and his brother, Robert, counting on the Texan to help carry southern and border states in the 1964 election, had insisted that he stay in the background. On November 24, two days after the assassination, LBJ talked with Whitney Young of the Urban League, asking his advice on congressional strategy. He also secured invitations to Kennedy's funeral for Young and other civil rights leaders.[15] Five days later the president met with Roy Wilkins, the head of the NAACP, and assured him that passage of the civil rights bill was the primary objective of the administration in the domestic field.[16] During the next six months, the president talked and met regularly with Wilkins, urging him to remind Republicans in Congress that the GOP was the "party of Lincoln" and to persuade hotheads in the movement to hold their fire until the fate of the civil rights measure became clear.

Johnson also spoke with Martin Luther King; James Farmer, a founder of the Congress of Racial Equality; and A. Philip Randolph. He explained that the poverty bill was basically a civil rights bill and that he wanted to secure its passage before the great battle over the accommodations and employment measure began. Don't go off half-cocked, he pled. "I don't want to stir up the folks on the Hill until we get ready to see the whites of their eyes," he told Randolph.[17] All had or would issue public statements expressing confidence in the new president, but they were still somewhat wary—not of LBJ's visceral commitment to civil rights but of his fondness for pragmatism and compromise. Johnson might indeed become "another Hugo Black [the former Alabama senator and current Supreme Court justice who had turned his back on his racist past]," civil rights activist Bayard Rustin observed. He might "be able to control the South better than Mr. Kennedy did. . . . SNCC must help Mr. Johnson—but to help Mr. Johnson means to create an atmosphere in which he is pushed even further."[18]

On his way to the office on the morning of December 4—the Johnsons were still living at the Elms—LBJ had his driver swing by and pick up American Federation of Labor and Congress of Industrial Organizations (AFL-CIO) head George Meany, who lived nearby. During the ride, Meany promised that he would do everything possible to secure support for the civil rights bill from leaders of the AFL-CIO—no mean task because the measure covered apprenticeship programs. A day later, LBJ stopped by to give a ride to House Republican Minority Leader Charles Halleck on the way downtown. Halleck was wary, but Johnson made it plain that he was going to hold the GOP's feet to the fire on civil rights. He told Halleck what he would tell other Republicans: "I'm going to lay it on the line . . . now you're either for civil rights or you're not . . . you're either the party of Lincoln or you're not . . . by God, put up or shut up."[19] The Brownell (Herbert, Eisenhower's attorney general)-Nixon-Dirksen strategy of using the race issue to divide the Democratic Party might work, but Republicans could not have that and their conservative cake, too. He invited Hallek and the Republicans to join wholeheartedly with the administration in support-ing a robust civil rights bill, and their party would receive full credit.

In January 1965, Johnson spoke to business and corporate leaders who had agreed to participate in Plans for Progress, the Kennedy administration's initiative to promote nondiscriminatory hiring in the private sector. Urging them to take "affirmative action" to eliminate discrimination in hiring, he declared, "And I can just almost guarantee each of you men that when your retirement time comes and you sit on your front porch in that rocking chair with your white Panama pulled down over your eyes and in retrospect look back over your days as a leader in your company, I can almost guarantee that one of your proudest moments and one of your greatest achievements will be the day that you took the leadership to destroy bigotry and bias and prejudice from the atmosphere of your own company."[20] At the same time, the president was not above appealing to conservative fears. "There's all this stuff [bombings, beatings, killings] going on," he told Robert Anderson, a wealthy Texas businessman and Eisenhower confidante, "and we've been talking about this for 100 years . . . and I just think that we're going to have them out in the streets again if we don't make some little progress."[21] Johnson did not have to lobby the churches and synagogues. In the wake of the killing of four black girls in Birmingham, Catholic, mainline Protestant, and Jewish organizations instructed their representatives in Washington to go all out in behalf of the civil rights bill.

Having rallied the troops, Johnson and Larry O'Brien turned their attention to the House, Judge Smith, and the Rules Committee. Of the fifteen members on Rules, ten were Democrats and five Republicans, but four of the Democrats were from the Deep South. To Smith's intense satisfaction, the conservative majority had been blocking measures of social and economic justice for years. The most attractive option for bypassing the Rules Committee was a petition of discharge. If a majority of the House—218 members—so voted, a measure could be removed from the purview of the committee and introduced directly on the floor. Because it would appear to the public to be democracy in action, the president favored this option.

Ninety of those sitting in the lower house were from the South; as a result, fifty-plus Republicans would be required to achieve a majority. Because a petition of discharge would open the door to direct consideration of other liberal measures that the GOP opposed, Halleck told the White House to forget a petition. It was, as LBJ had intuited, Abraham Lincoln who saved the day. Two Republican members, William McCulloch and Clarence Brown—both of Ohio—were conservative on every issue but civil rights. They treasured their party's linkage to the Great Emancipator. Moreover, Wilberforce and Central, two predominantly black colleges, were located in Brown's district.[22] The Ohio congressmen indicated to Smith that if he did not release the civil rights bill, they would lead a revolt. "I know something about the facts of life around here," Smith confided to a friend, "and I know that many members want this bill considered. They could take it away from me and they can do it any minute they want to."[23] Consequently, the chairman announced hearings on the bill to begin January 9, 1964; it was subsequently reported out with a positive recommendation on January 30.[24]

The version of the Civil Rights Act that Johnson submitted to Congress in February 1964 went beyond Kennedy's and contained within it the roots of affirmative action. Title II aimed to integrate all public facilities, including private businesses that marketed to the public such as motels, restaurants, theaters, stores, and gas stations. Title VII committed the government to ending discrimination in employment in all firms with twenty-five or more employees, a proposal that had aroused so much ire among conservatives and businesspeople that it was not in the Kennedy bill. Yet another provision would establish the Equal Employment Opportunity Commission.[25]

During the hearings on the 1964 Civil Rights measure, a number of questions arose concerning the notion of affirmative action. If two job applicants were basically equal in terms of qualifications, which one should get the nod? The idea of preferences was rare but not new in American history. During Reconstruction, the federal government had singled out freedmen for "preferential treatment." The Social Security Act of 1935 privileged citizens older than age sixty-five years. The GI Bill of Rights provided payments to attend college, federally guaranteed low-interest home loans, and other benefits to 15 million veterans out of a total population of 140 million.[26]

In 1962 the Congress of Racial Equality had begun demanding that employers hire a specific percentage of blacks and adopt a set of preferential employment guidelines. President Kennedy was opposed. During a press conference, he admitted that "there is some compensation due but [I] don't think quotas are a good idea. . . . I think it is a mistake to begin to assign quotas on the basis of religion, or race, or color, or nationality. I think we'd get into a good deal of trouble."[27] Despite Title VII, the Johnson administration seemed to agree. During the Senate debate over the Civil Rights Act, the floor manager, Hubert Humphrey, declared, "Contrary to the allegations of some opponents of this title there is nothing in it that will give any power to the Commission or to any court to require hiring, firing, or promotion of employees in order to meet a racial 'quota' or to achieve a certain racial balance." His declaration swayed many pro-business Republicans.[28]

In a last-ditch effort to cripple or defeat the 1964 civil rights bill, Howard Smith proposed the addition of one word to Title VII that prohibited discrimination on the basis of national origin, race, and religion. That word was "sex." As the Virginian well knew, many conservatives, men as well as women, were opposed to legislation mandating gender equality. He also knew that the women's movement itself was deeply divided on the issue. In response to the exploitation of women in the workplace during the industrial revolution, Progressive-era reformers had thrown their support behind a series of protective measures that would establish minimum wages, maximum hours, and regulated conditions for women in the workplace. In other words, women would be singled out for special treatment. Woodrow Wilson had been lukewarm about such protective measures, but FDR was enthusiastic and made them centerpieces of the New Deal. Meanwhile, Alice Paul, the famous suffragist, formed the National Woman's Party and succeeded in having an equal rights amendment (ERA) to the Constitution introduced in Congress in 1923. Paul and her associates were upper-middle-class women, mostly Republicans, who wanted to protect women in the professions and business. Equality of opportunity, not special treatment, was their watchword.

The idea to add sex to the 1964 Civil Rights Act was the work of Martha Griffiths, the liberal Democratic congresswoman from Michigan, who had tried to bring the two feminist groups together. "It would be incredible," she declared, "that white men would be willing to place white women at such a disadvantage." Without adding "sex" to the act, she continued, "you are going to have white men in one bracket, you're going to try to take colored men and colored women and give them equal employment rights, and down at the bottom of the list is going to be white women with no rights at all." Conservatives argued that among the consequences of a non-discrimination provision for women would be compulsory military service, elimination of laws against rape, and destruction of the family.[29] But to no avail. As Griffiths put it, "I used Smith." Of course, Smith was trying to use Griffiths to block the civil rights bill. The congresswoman had the best of it—or at least that was the take at the time. Actually, Smith and Paul were friends. The Judge had no qualms about equal treatment for women—as long as they were white. The House added the gender amendment by a teller vote of 168 to 133.[30] On February 10, the House passed the civil rights bill of 1964 by a vote of 290 to 110.

Johnson was jubilant. No sooner had the final tally been taken than one of the phones in the House cloakroom rang. It was LBJ looking for Joe Rauh, then vice president of the Americans for Democratic Action, and Clarence Mitchell, he of the Washington, DC, chapter of the NAACP. "I don't know how he ever managed to get us on that phone," Mitchell later recalled, "but he was calling to say, 'All right, you fellows, get over there to the Senate and get busy because we got it through the House and now we've got the big job of getting it through the Senate.'" At two o'clock the following morning, Johnson telephoned Congressman Jake Pickle, who represented

LBJ's old congressional district and was one of only six southerners to have voted for the bill, to congratulate him. LBJ noted that he, Johnson, had not displayed the same courage when he had been in the House.[31]

On February 11, the president convened a meeting comprising Katzenbach; Burke Marshall, an assistant attorney general for civil rights; Larry O'Brien; Bobby Kennedy; and Pierre Salinger. "I'll do . . . just what you think is best to do on the bill. We'll follow what you say," the president told Kennedy. He subsequently instructed Majority Leader Mike Mansfield and Hubert Humphrey, whom he had selected to manage the bill in the Senate, to clear every move they made with the attorney general. Bobby was cynical concerning Johnson's motives. "He didn't think we'd get the bill," Kennedy later observed. "If I worked out the strategy, if he did what the Department of Justice recommended . . . —and particularly me—then . . . he could always say that he did what we suggested and didn't go off on his own."[32] Perhaps, but both Katzenbach and O'Brien would later observe that no one was more ardent or genuine in their espousal of civil rights than Lyndon Johnson.[33]

As a former colleague, Johnson felt close enough to several southern senators to appeal to them to moderate their opposition to the civil rights bill. He called Robert Byrd, the young Democratic senator from West Virginia, and asked him to allow the accommodations and employment bill to come to the floor for a vote. "No. . . . No. . . . No sir, I wouldn't make them vote on it because I know if they vote on it, they're going to get it," Byrd replied. "And if a man starts to coming to my house if I can't beat him with my fist . . . I'm going to take a poker to him . . . the only way we can win here is to not let them vote."[34] Johnson gave up. It was clear that the Dixie Association, the coterie of Deep South senators committed to maintaining Jim Crow, was going to filibuster, to "fight to the last ditch," as Richard Russell subsequently declared. "You can't do anything with the Southern Democrats," the president told Joe Rauh, "there ain't nobody that can get [Strom] Thurmond or Olin Johnston, Dick Russell, or [Herman] Talmadge."[35]

Thus it seemed that civil rights advocates were back to square one, where they had been in 1957 and 1960. But Johnson was now president of the United States, not a senior senator from Texas. Bill Moyers recalled that during a press conference in the midst of the fight over the civil rights measure, Jim Deakin, a reporter for the *St. Louis Post-Dispatch,* asked LBJ a pointed question: "Mr. President, I don't understand. You didn't have a very sterling progressive record on civil rights either in the House or in the Senate, and yet here you have thrown the full weight of your presidency behind the civil rights movement. Would you, please, sir, explain the contradiction?" Johnson paused a full thirty seconds before answering. Resisting the temptation to rationalize, to defend his past actions, he said, "Well, Jim, some people get a chance late in life to correct the sins of their youth and very few get a chance as big as the White House."[36]

Now that he was free, Johnson wanted everyone to know where he stood. On New Year's Eve, some five weeks after he had succeeded to the presidency, LBJ attended a party in honor of Horace Busby at the Forty Acres Club on the campus of the University of Texas at Austin. The club had been, since its inception, strictly segregated. Johnson swept in at the head of a small entourage. On his arm was his new, attractive black secretary, Gerry Whittington. Before they went in, Whittington asked, "Mr. President, do you know what you are doing?" LBJ replied, "I sure do. Half of them are going to think you're my wife, and that's just fine with me."[37] From that point on, the Forty Acres Club accepted black members.

Subsequently, after the civil rights bill was transferred from the House to the Senate on March 30, 1964, LBJ let it be known that he would not compromise, not even if the filibuster lasted the rest of the year. Shortly after the fight over the measure began, LBJ asked his old friend Dick Russell to the White House for a frank talk. "The President sat in a wing chair," Jack Valenti recalled. "The Senator sat at one end of a small couch. Their knees almost touched. . . . 'Dick, you've got to get out of my way. I'm going to run over you. I don't intend to . . . compromise.' 'You may do that,'" Valenti remembered Russell replying, "'but by God, it's going to cost you the South and cost you the election.'" So be it, LBJ responded.[38]

Johnson was determined to be the public face of the civil rights forces in the Senate, but he would leave tactics and day-to-day operations to the senators themselves and the lobbyists for labor, the civil rights organizations, and the churches. "A President cannot ask the Congress to take a risk he will not take himself," he later observed. "He must be the combat general in the front lines, constantly exposing his flanks. . . . I gave to this fight everything I had in prestige, power, and commitment. At the same time, I deliberately tried to tone down my personal involvement in the daily struggle so that my colleagues on the Hill could take tactical responsibility."[39] Chief among those colleagues were Mike Mansfield and Hubert Humphrey.

THE ADMINISTRATION UNDERSTOOD THAT IT HAD THE VOTES TO PASS the civil rights bill if it was ever allowed to be considered by the full Senate. There existed a clear majority in behalf of a discharge petition, and so Jim Eastland's Judiciary Committee could be bypassed. The issue was the southern filibuster. Two methods were available for defeating Russell and his troops. The first consisted of exhausting the talkers, a stratagem LBJ had employed previously and one he still favored. The rules of the Senate limited members to two speeches per calendar day. Once debate on a measure began, the calendar day lasted as long as the debate—a week, a month. LBJ wanted to keep the Senate in continuous, twenty-four-hour-a-day session, thus finally exhausting the filibusterers.

Mansfield, a self-made man who fancied himself something of an intellectual, was opposed. The strategy had not worked in the past. Opponents of the filibuster had become just as fatigued as the participants, and the result had been no measure or one so weakened as to be almost meaningless.[40] Mansfield favored a petition of cloture, which, if approved by two-thirds of the Senate, would shut off further debate after an additional one hundred hours. The problem was that of the eleven cloture petitions dealing with civil rights ever voted on, all had been defeated, including two in 1962 on a bill that Kennedy had submitted dealing with literacy tests.

LBJ resisted the cloture approach throughout the February 11 meeting at the White House, which finally adjourned so that the participants could attend a reception for foreign diplomats. In the middle of the festivities, Johnson and Nick Katzenbach pulled two chairs together and continued the argument. "I think we've got fifty-eight votes for cloture," Katzenbach said. "Well, where are you going to get the others?" Johnson asked. Katzenbach pulled out a copy of the Senate roster and identified fourteen possibles; "we get nine of those we'll get our sixty-seven votes." Finally, Johnson acceded.[41]

The key to obtaining cloture and thus passage of the civil rights bill was the Republican contingent in the Senate. Of the sixty-seven Democrats in the Senate, twenty-one of them came from states of the former Confederacy. Unless twenty-three to twenty-five Republicans deserted the conservative coalition, there would be no breakthrough in public accommodations and employment. That meant winning over Minority Leader Everett Dirksen. At the legislative leader's meeting on February 18, Johnson took Humphrey, who had just been designated to manage the bill, aside and said,

> This bill can't pass unless you get Ev Dirksen. You and I are going to get Ev; it is going to take time. You make up your mind now that you've got to spend time with Ev Dirksen. You've got to let him have a piece of the action. He's got to look good all the time. Now don't let those bomb throwers [Paul Douglas, Joe Clark, and other liberal Democrats] talk you out of seeing Dirksen. You get in there to see Dirksen; you drink with Dirksen, you talk with Dirksen, you listen to Dirksen.[42]

Before 1954 most northern Republicans had been willing to support modest federal intervention to protect voting rights and equal protection of the law. Republican leaders such as Richard Nixon and Herbert Brownell saw GOP support for racial justice as a powerful political wedge to divide northern and southern Democrats. Following the 1954 *Brown v. Board* decision in which the Supreme Court declared school segregation unconstitutional, northern Republicans increasingly split. Barry Goldwater and William F. Buckley's *National Review* both joined Dixiecrats in denouncing the ruling and opposing federal desegregation efforts generally. Other voices, such as the editors of the *Chicago Tribune* and Nixon, continued to call for support of federal intervention on behalf of black civil rights.[43]

The sixty-eight-year-old minority leader was one of those politicians who shielded a shrewd, agile mind with a veneer of buffoonery. Heavyset with wavy silver hair, a mellifluous speaking voice, and a broad face folded in wrinkles, Dirksen was a man who delighted in his own oratory. He was given to unusual words like "baleful" and "felicitous." His speeches were often studies in digression. An avid gardener, he rose on the floor of the Senate every spring to propose that the marigold be selected as "the national floral emblem of our country."[44] His rhetoric was that of Robert Taft, but Dirksen epitomized pragmatism. "He will be the ideal Republican [minority leader]," one Democrat told Harry McPherson. "The Republican Party is the party of special interests. Most of them represent one or two. Dirksen represents them all."[45] He could be partisan, but he was jealous of his place in history, and thus presidents could appeal to his patriotism. As a result, there was little consistency in his voting patterns: for foreign aid one day, against it the next. Like Johnson, Dirksen was a shrewd calculator of men and counter of votes. He liked to deal with other men and he could be dealt with—Johnson's kind of politician. Friends worried about his health. Although he suffered from a peptic ulcer, Dirksen drank moderately but almost continuously. "Champagne is Mrs. Dirksen's favorite vegetable . . . and I prefer a fellow by the name of Johnathan Daniels," he told a reporter.[46] After he was elected minority leader, Dirksen cordoned off part of his office and named it the Twilight Lodge. All of the numerals on the clock that hung there were fives.[47]

Humphrey proved true to the courtship. "I would have kissed Dirksen's ass on the Capitol steps" to secure his support for cloture, Humphrey later said, and he virtually did.[48] Appearing on *Meet the Press,* Humphrey responded to a question concerning Dirksen's stated reservations about the civil rights bill: "Senator Dirksen is not only a great senator, he is a great American, and he is going to see the necessity of this legislation. I predict that before this bill is through Senator Dirksen will be its champion."[49]

On February 26, the Senate adopted a Mansfield motion to bypass the Judiciary Committee and consider the bill directly. On March 9, 1964, the longest filibuster in the history of the US Senate began. The debate over whether to take up the bill continued through March 26, when the Senate finally voted to make it the next order of business. Formal debate began on March 30 and continued for nine straight weeks.[50]

During the filibuster, LBJ worked assiduously to wrap white America in a moral straightjacket. How could individuals who fervently identified themselves with a merciful and just God continue to condone racial discrimination, police brutality, and segregation in education and public accommodations? "Now you get your Bible coming back tonight," he told Bill Moyers, presidential aide, speechwriter, and Baptist minister, "and get in one of those hotels . . . and get us some good quotations on equality, all of God's children."[51] Johnson's language was not the kind traditionally wielded by liberal intellectuals, the reasoned Jeffersonian phrases rooted in a deep faith in progress and reason, but those of the believer who has encountered profound evil, Lincolnesque words of suffering and sacrifice.[52] Where in the Judeo-Christian ethic was there justification for killing young girls, denying an equal education to black children, barring fathers and mothers from competing for jobs that would feed and clothe their families? Was Jim Crow to be America's response to "Godless Communism"?

Addressing business executives who had committed to Plans for Progress, LBJ asked rhetorically, "I don't know why you can't say, 'Except for the grace of God, I might be in his place and he might be in mine.'" Capitalism did not guarantee social and economic justice; only the consciences of God-fearing men and women could do that. The only way America could lay claim to world leadership would be "because of our moral standards and not because of our economic power."[53] To the Interreligious Convocation on Civil Rights, Johnson pointed out that the story that Christ chose to illustrate the meaning of love was that of the Good Samaritan: "the Samaritan's attitude was one of good will born of a recognition of the fatherhood of God and the brotherhood of men—an attitude that expressed itself in action on the behalf of another's needs."[54] Even so conservative a newspaper as the *Fort Worth Star-Telegram* was moved by Johnson's sacred logic. "Now I knew that as President I couldn't make people want to integrate their schools or open their doors to blacks," he later said, "but I could make them feel guilty for not doing it and I believed it was my moral responsibility to do precisely that—to use the moral suasion of my office to make people feel that segregation was a curse they'd carry with them to their graves."[55]

Johnson's decision to define civil rights as a moral issue, and to wield the nation's self-professed Judeo-Christian ethic as a sword in its behalf, constituted something of a minor watershed in twentieth-century political history. All presidents were more or less fond of invoking the deity, and some conservatives, such as Dwight Eisenhower, had flirted with employing Judeo-Christian teachings to justify their actions or lack thereof, but modern-day liberals, both politicians and the intellectuals who challenged and nourished them, had stayed away from spiritual witness. Most liberal intellectuals were secular humanists. Academics in particular have historically been deeply distrustful of organized religion, which they identified with small-mindedness, bigotry, and anti-intellectualism. Liberals were more at home with the worldly vocabulary of law, education, and politics than with the language of sin and redemption.[56] Johnson distrusted organized religion to an extent, but not Judeo-Christian teachings, particularly those in Isaiah and the New Testament. Indeed, in them were to be found, he believed, the Western world's most compelling call to social justice. He did seem to foresee that to employ Christian moral philosophy might open the door—à la John Brown and William Lloyd Garrison—to invocation of a higher law. But he believed the United States Constitution to be the highest expression of the Judeo-Christian ethic. Others, of course, did not agree. Out of the admixture of religion and civil rights would come non-violent civil disobedience, a tactic that transcended established institutions and procedures and that ironically aroused a great deal of angst in the thirty-sixth president.

During the second week in May, LBJ electrified the nation by stumping Georgia in behalf of the pending civil rights bill. On May 8, he addressed a breakfast attended by members of the Georgia legislature in Atlanta, the city that General William Tecumseh Sherman had burned to the ground a century earlier. Governor and Mrs. Carl Sanders appeared on the dais with him, as did Senator Herman Tallmadge and his wife. He declared that the motto of the state of Georgia—"Wisdom, Justice, Moderation"—should be the motto of the nation in its time of trouble. Johnson quoted Atticus Haygood, president of Emory College, who in 1880 declared: "We in the South have no divine call to stand eternal guard by the grave of dead issues." How Georgia went, so would go America, the president proclaimed. "Heed not those who would come waving the tattered and discredited banners of the past, who seek to stir old hostilities and kindle old hatreds, who preach battle between neighbors and bitterness between States."[57] At Franklin D. Roosevelt Square in Gainesville, he declared, "Full participation in our society can no longer be denied to men because of their race or their religion or the region in which they live."[58]

As remarkable as his words was the reception that he and his message received. The crowds that lined the streets in Atlanta to greet LBJ numbered at least a half million. "I've never seen anything like it in my 18 years in Atlanta, even for 'Gone with the Wind' and Franklin Roosevelt," the police chief remarked. The presidential motorcade took almost two hours to cover the fifteen miles in from the airport. Johnson stopped twenty-five times to address the cheering throng. The crowd in Gainesville, a town of eighteen thousand, was estimated at over fifty thousand.[59]

Members of the Dixie Association sensed that they faced probable defeat unless somehow public opinion in the North turned against the civil rights bill. So, its leader, the redoubtable Richard Russell, who had refused to join LBJ on the dais during his southern tour, played for time. He sensed that there was a growing backlash fueled by the SCLC, CORE, and SNCC's constant protests and demonstrations. If George Wallace, the racist governor of Alabama who was running for the Democratic presidential nomination, were to make a good showing in the Wisconsin, Indiana, and Maryland primaries, and if Goldwater were to best Nelson Rockefeller in the Republican contests, then Russell hoped a number of Republicans in the Senate would rally behind the Arizonian and oppose passage.[60]

Roy Wilkins and Clarence Mitchell of the NAACP wanted the civil rights groups to focus on lobbying Congress, as Johnson had requested, holding demonstrations in reserve as a threat if Congress did not act. But the SCLC, SNCC, and CORE refused to cooperate. Indeed, Martin Luther King felt so strongly about the 1964 bill that he considered going on a hunger strike until the filibuster ended. He would issue a public statement, he told his associates: "Either you stop the filibuster and pass the Civil Rights Bill. . . . Or let me die."[61] In an effort to intensify pressure on Congress and the president, King—with lieutenants Andrew Young and Hosea Williams—led a nighttime march of four hundred demonstrators in St. Augustine, Florida, a deeply divided community and a Ku Klux Klan hotbed. They were set upon by a howling mob of some 250 Klansmen and Klan sympathizers and beaten with chains, tire irons, and fists.[62]

Civil rights protests not only intensified in the spring of 1964 but began spreading to the North as blacks' protests against de facto school segregation in New York, Chicago, Philadelphia, and other northern cities—as well as against segregated housing and employment discrimination—heated up. William McCulloch, a key Republican civil rights advocate in the House, warned Senate colleagues that he had lost the support of 25 percent of the Republican congressmen who had voted for the bill six weeks earlier.[63]

By mid-April, Dirksen was ready to move. On the afternoon of the twenty-first, Humphrey sat down beside the minority leader. As the southerners droned on, Dirksen murmured that the administration's bill was a good one and he was ready to support it. He wished, however, to avoid a cloture vote; in fact, he did not think he could muster a sufficient number of his colleagues to shut off debate. Humphrey replied that he would have to. The White House had promised Rauh, Mitchell, and the liberals that it would not stand for a watered-down bill. Besides, if he lost a cloture vote, Russell could claim to his segregationist supporters that he had fought to the last but in the end had been overwhelmed by sheer numbers. Dirksen conceded the point. "The jig is up," Russell remarked privately when he heard the news.[64]

Dirksen proceeded to play out his self-scripted drama as the latter-day Abraham Lincoln. The minority leader requested a meeting with the president for April 29 and was granted it. The day before, he told Republican leaders at lunch that he intended to give the Dixie Association one week to end its filibuster; if by then it had not, he would file a cloture petition. Before he went in to see Johnson, Dirksen held a press conference. He announced that he was about to tell his friend in the White House that he was not going to get his bill without making serious concessions to conservatives. "In my humble opinion, you are not going to get it," he said. "Now it's your play. What do you have to say?" He also criticized Johnson's handling of his dogs. The president had been photographed picking up one of his beagles by its ears. The president was not pleased. "I don't know what is happening to him here lately. He's acting like a shit-ass," he complained to Mike Mansfield. "He said he wouldn't treat his dog like I treated mine. . . . It's none of his damned business how I treat my dog. And I'm a hell of a lot better to dogs—and humans too—than he is."[65]

When he met with Dirksen, LBJ did not budge.[66] Johnson felt he could not even give the appearance of compromising, lest Democratic liberals rebel. But that was not true of Humphrey and Mansfield. Over the next two weeks, they and Nick Katzenbach met almost daily with Dirksen and in essence let him write the bill. There was no change in substance, but the language was Dirksen's, and he could proudly claim to be the coauthor, an honorific the Democrats were more than willing to bestow.[67] Johnson called the minority leader: "You're worthy of the Land of Lincoln. And the Man from Illinois is going to pass the bill, and I'll see that you get proper attention and credit."[68]

Meanwhile, the filibuster wore on. Rhetoric from the Dixie Association was as fiery as ever, but close observers sensed an air of resignation. Russell, already suffering from the emphysema that would eventually kill him, seemed deflated. In December 1963, before the battle in Congress over civil rights really got under way, the Georgian had visited with Orville Freeman. "He said that Lyndon Johnson was the most amazingly resourceful fellow," Freeman recalled, "that he was a man who really understood power and how to use it. . . . He said that man will twist your arm off at the shoulder and beat your head in with it, and then he said, you know we could have beaten John Kennedy on civil rights, but not Lyndon Johnson."[69] After the filibuster began, Russell ran into Bill Moyers. "Now you tell Lyndon," he said, "that I've been expecting the rod for a long time, and I'm sorry that it's from his hand the rod must be wielded, but I'd rather it be his hand than anybody else's I know. Tell him to cry a little when he uses it."[70]

As the drama's climax neared, the president opened his pork barrel to ensure success. He arranged for Secretary of Interior Stewart Udall to meet with Carl Hayden of Arizona. Representing a small state that was jealous of minority rights, Hayden had never voted for cloture and was loath to do so in 1964. When Udall promised administration support for the Central Arizona Water Project, a massive scheme to divert waters from the Colorado River to Tucson and Phoenix, Hayden promised his vote for cloture if it were needed.[71] To soften the blow for southerners, Johnson arranged for northern urban votes for the cotton and wheat bill.[72] The farm bill passed on April 9 by a vote of 211 to 103. "We just whipped the living hell out of your friend Charlie Halleck [Republicans had opposed the farm subsidy bill]," Johnson chortled to Russell, "and we had to do it with Yankees."[73] There were those in the Senate as well as the House who could be swayed by federal largesse. LBJ pressured a reluctant Budget Director Kermit Gordon to approve $263 million for the Tennessee River–Tombigbee project, a federally funded project to improve river navigation from Tennessee to the Gulf of Mexico.[74]

On June 10, following seventy-five days of debate, the Senate voted on cloture. Dirksen had the last, dramatic word. Relishing the moment, he quoted Victor Hugo: "Stronger than all the armies is an idea whose time has come. The time has come for equality . . . in education and in employment. It will not be stayed or denied. It is here."[75] Humphrey, who had predicted sixty-nine aye votes, and Johnson followed the proceedings intently. Upstaging Dirksen was Senator Clair Engle of California who, dying of a brain tumor, appeared on the floor of the Senate in a wheelchair. Unable to speak, he pointed to his eye when it came his turn to vote.[76] The final tally was seventy-one for cloture and twenty-nine against, four more than needed and two more than Humphrey had predicted. The cloture vote, of course, ensured passage of the civil rights bill. The rules permitted a final one hundred hours of debate. Russell was the last to speak and had to suffer the ignominy of being cut off in midsentence by the president pro tem who happened that day to be Senator Edward Kennedy of Massachusetts. On June 19, the Senate passed the civil rights bill of 1964 by a vote of 73 to 27.

An observer noted that Russell had tears in his eyes as he sat down. But were they tears of frustration and disappointment, or tears of joy? Why would a man of Russell's intelligence and will support the political career of a man—LBJ—whom he knew was thoroughly committed to the Second Reconstruction and capable of bringing it to fruition? On April 20, in the midst of the debate, he had declared to the Senate, "This is mere socialism. . . . Every Socialist and Communist in this country has been supporting the proposed legislation." But then, shortly thereafter, Russell instructed the Democratic Senate Campaign Committee to take $25,000 earmarked for his reelection campaign and give it to Hubert Humphrey. Russell told Senator Gaylord Nelson over lunch in the Senate dining room, "I did something yesterday that my people would throw me out if they knew. Humphrey is good for the institution."[77] In the wake of the passage of the Civil Rights Act of 1964, the leader of the Dixie Association, rather than invoking massive resistance, would counsel his constituents to remain calm and obey the law. It could very well have been that the Georgian was a conservative, not a reactionary, a man committed to slowing change. For better or worse, his beloved South was entering the twentieth century, joining the political mainstream. Ambivalence, an awareness and even an appreciation of paradox, is the fate of all introspective individuals, and Russell certainly numbered among that group.

A jubilant Johnson scheduled a televised signing ceremony for July 2.[78] But before the president could count his coup, the murder of three young civil rights workers in Mississippi threatened to touch off a cycle of violence that would undermine all of the president's plans for peaceful change in American race relations.

Although African Americans constituted 42 percent of Mississippi's population, only 5 percent were registered to vote. The median income for black families was under $1,500 a year, less than one-third of that for white families. Like its economy, Mississippi's politics were dominated by a tiny white elite that had for a century manipulated white working-class prejudices to keep blacks "in their place."

Early in 1964, Robert Moses of SNCC and David Dennis of CORE had come up with the concept of Freedom Summer. Black and white college students, carefully trained in the techniques of nonviolent resistance and political activism, would spread out across rural Mississippi, encouraging African Americans to register to vote, teaching in "freedom schools," and organizing a "freedom party" to challenge the all-white Mississippi Democratic Party. That spring, flyers appeared on college campuses across the North that read, "A Domestic Freedom Corps will be working in Mississippi this summer. Its only weapons will be youth and courage."[79] In June, students from over two hundred universities and colleges met with representatives of the Council of Federated Organizations in Oxford, Ohio. Most of the students were from affluent families and the best universities. They came for different reasons, but most held the view that segregation was morally wrong. "There is a moral wave building among today's youth," one declared, "and I intend to catch it!"[80]

Over the objections of some of SNCC's other black staffers, Bob Moses, named director of the Mississippi Summer Project, had argued successfully for bringing hundreds of white student volunteers into the state. A dedicated pacifist and believer in the Gandhian tactic of nonviolent civil disobedience, Moses envisioned blacks and whites working together to achieve a more just society. But Moses was a hard-headed strategist as well; he made no secret of the fact that he wanted to involve idealistic white youth in the bloody southern struggle in order to produce a confrontation between federal and state authorities. "No administration in this country is going to commit political suicide over the rights of Negroes," he had told a group of student volunteers. That meant putting their white coworkers in harm's way. Along with Dennis, director of CORE in Mississippi, Moses assigned white volunteers to Meridian, the first they had dared station outside Jackson.[81]

On June 21, reports reached Moses and Dennis that three young project workers—Andrew Goodman, Michael Schwerner, and James Chaney—had disappeared near Philadelphia, Mississippi. Goodman and Schwerner were white, Chaney black. Six weeks later, the three were discovered buried in an earthen dam. Goodman and Schwerner had been shot in the heart and Chaney beaten to death. An FBI investigation subsequently uncovered a conspiracy to murder them involving local law enforcement officers and members of the Ku Klux Klan. Before the summer was out, three more civil rights workers would die violently. A volunteer from the Mississippi Summer Freedom Project wrote home in July 1964: "Yesterday while the Mississippi River was being dragged looking for the three missing civil rights workers, two bodies of Negroes were found. Mississippi is the only state where you can drag a river any time and find bodies you were not expecting."[82] In Macomb, there were seventeen bombings in three months, and white extremists burned thirty-seven black churches to the ground.

ON THE EVENING OF JULY 2, MORE THAN ONE HUNDRED PERSONS— members of Congress, Justice Department officials, civil rights leaders, representatives of the AFL-CIO and religious organizations—gathered in the elegant East Room of the White House for the signing of the 1964 Civil Rights Act. "We believe all men are entitled to the blessings of liberty," LBJ declared to the assemblage and a national television audience. "Yet millions are being deprived of those blessings—not because of their own failures, but because of the color of their skin. The reasons are deeply imbedded in history and tradition and the nature of man. We can understand—without rancor or hatred—how this happened, but it cannot continue. . . . Our Constitution, the foundation of our Republic, forbids it. The principles of our freedom forbid it. Morality forbids it. And the law I will sign tonight forbids it."[83] And it was an historic bill. The measure not only desegregated public parks, swimming pools, libraries, restaurants, hotels, and places of amusement but also expanded the authority of the Congress to enforce the Supreme Court's 1954 *Brown* decision. The president also announced that he was appointing former Florida governor LeRoy Collins to head the Community Relations Service, a government agency whose task it would be to mediate between civil rights activists and local businesses.[84] A week earlier, Johnson had consulted Eastland about selecting his fellow southerner. "He's a damned cheap double-crosser and a liar," Senator Eastland said. "I called him a goddamned lying son of a bitch out there [at the 1960 Democratic convention in Los Angeles]."[85] For Johnson, that confirmed that he had selected the right person for the job.

In the wake of his civil rights triumph, LBJ was characteristically conflicted. He had worked his will on Congress in an historic manner and won a place of honor for himself in the American social justice movement. But he empathized with the white people of the South, people he had grown up with and loved. He appealed to LeRoy Collins, Buford Ellington, Luther Hodges, and other southern moderates to tell the governors, legislators, and their segregationist constituents that he had not abandoned them. "I moved a bunch of FBI people into Mississippi last night," Johnson said during the Schwerner-Goodman-Chaney crisis, "but I'm not going to send troops on my people if I can avoid it, and they got to help me avoid it."[86] He still hoped that when the scales of prejudice dropped from the eyes of poor whites in the South, they would make common political cause with poor blacks within the context of the Democratic Party. "I can't make people integrate," he told Richard Goodwin, "but maybe we can make them feel guilty if they don't. And once that happens, and they find out the jaws of hell don't open, and fire and brimstone doesn't flood down on them, then maybe they'll see just how they've been taken advantage of."[87] At the same time, Johnson was aware that the accommodations, employment, and education bill just passed was not the end of the struggle for racial justice in America. "He used to tell me," Humphrey wrote in his memoirs, "'Yes, yes, Hubert, I want all those other things—buses, restaurants, all of that—but the right to vote with no ifs, ands, or buts, that's the key. When the Negroes get that, they'll have every politician, north and south, east and west, kissing their ass, begging for their support.'" Within days of passage of the 1964 act, he was badgering Nicholas Katzenbach "to write me the goddamndest, toughest voting rights act that you can devise."[88]

Johnson was afraid that the more militant members of the civil rights movement would become intoxicated by their success in passing the civil rights bill and press too hard. The president had great faith in the Federal Mediation and Conciliation Service he was in the process of putting together, an agency headed by moderate white southerners that would quietly negotiate racial accommodation before violence erupted. "If trouble breaks out . . . you've always got a break," he told Texas governor John Connally, "and a cushion, and a sponge to absorb it if you take a good man with a religious background . . . nine times out of ten they can work it out."[89]

Immediately after the signing ceremony, Johnson had met with Wilkins, Whitney Young, Randolph, and other civil rights leaders and asked them to hold off on further demonstrations lest they provoke a white backlash and prevent enforcement of the measure just signed.[90] Young promised to help: "I know you are working on the southern governors and southern businessmen and . . . I don't want to see King and Farmer and everyone else talking about how they're going to insist on immediate compliance. . . . If you can keep the southerners—as you are—from issuing defiance orders then we ought not to be talking about how we're going to test 'em."[91] But Johnson sensed—correctly as it turned out—that the movement was moving beyond the control of Young and the conservatives. And then there was the political situation. The evening of the signing, Bill Moyers visited the president in his bedroom and found him deflated. Why so down? Moyers asked. "Because, Bill," he replied, "I think we just delivered the South to the Republican Party for a long time to come."[92]

Unlike the *Brown* decision, the Civil Rights Act did not bring in its wake a wave of violence or calls for massive resistance; defections from the Democratic Party there were, but Johnson would go on that November to carry half of the states of the former Confederacy. The Republicanization of the South would have to wait for the massive influx of white northerners into the region seeking economic opportunity and an escape from the extreme racial tensions that came to grip northern cities. Richard Russell believed that the contrast was due to *Brown* being an edict of the court and the second of a series of laws enacted by a duly elected majority. As Johnson's remarkable reception in Georgia had revealed, the relative calm was also the result of the president being a southerner and his determination to make integration and nondiscrimination a gift to the nation from the South, not something that was imposed on the region from the outside.

CHAPTER 4

THE MANDATE: THE ELECTION OF 1964

"IT IS INCREASINGLY DIFFICULT TO WORK WITH THIS FELLOW LYNDON Johnson," Orville Freeman, the Kennedy-appointed secretary of agriculture LBJ had kept on, recorded in his diary in mid-1964.

> Actually, I guess he is doing a great job. He's certainly enjoying every minute of it. But one never knows what to expect. There are about a half a dozen people in the White House, any of them are apt to call at any time on any thing, and seldom does one know what the other is doing. [Johnson] lays out in all directions, you can't be sure when he really means it. He is quite a kidder but with a bite, and of course, a complete ham, grandstander, political par excellent [sic]. He reminds one very much of Humphrey without Humphrey's sensitivities really, but with all of Humphrey's ego drive and demand to grab and hold the limelight. . . . He sure loves being President. . . . On the other hand, in all fairness, a real human side comes out. It was interesting that before we went to church [LBJ had invited the Freemans to attend services at the National City Christian Church] when we were sitting up in the lounge on the second floor of the White House drinking coffee he remarked that Connally, the Governor of Texas,

and one of the Congressmen, I believe Jim Wright, was not our kind
of person. They are fine, intelligent, decent, able men, but they were
conservative and not liberals like we were. . . . . I have the feeling that
this is genuine.[1]

After witnessing LBJ's efforts to convince reporters that he was physically
robust enough to be president by leading them on breakneck walks around
the White House grounds, Freeman observed, "He is doing this kind of
thing constantly. His whole life is involved in his job. His family, his recreation, his avocations—everything revolves around this and every person
seems to be a target to be shot at, hit, and then consumed."[2]

IT SEEMED A FOREGONE CONCLUSION WITHIN THE LEADERSHIP OF
the Democratic Party and among political pundits that LBJ would be a
candidate for president in his own right in 1964, and that he would win.
While JFK's blood was still clotting in his veins, John Kenneth Galbraith,
the economist, was urging members of the old regime to do nothing to
embarrass Johnson and imperil the Democratic Party's chances for holding
on to the White House. And yet, as LBJ's friend Ed Weisl observed, "The
real liberals—never truly accepted Johnson. I don't know why, because he
was more liberal than the most liberal of them. . . . It's partly style, partly the
fact that he's from Texas. . . . They would tell you, 'He's good and he's wise
and he's effective, but well, he just isn't our kind of a guy.'"[3]

Commenting on the photo of LBJ in the president's 1964 campaign
volume, *My Hope for America,* journalist Murray Kempton wrote: "There is
on this face both the effort to believe everything and to believe nothing. It
is a low face of high aspiration. . . . Being the king's face, it is innocent in a
way in which General Eisenhower could not imagine being innocent; being
also the minister's face, it is devious to a degree that Everett Dirksen would
find serpentine. Of course, it lies to itself, and that is proper. Hervey said to
Walpole: 'All princes must now and then be deceived by their ministers.'"[4]

In short, LBJ in the view of most liberal intellectuals was a man devoid of
integrity. Weisl remembered a conversation he had with Art Buchwald, the
famed political cartoonist, at an election-night party after Johnson had defeated Barry Goldwater. "Boy, now we're going to get this son-of-a-bitch."

Weisl asked, "What do you mean, Art?" And he said, "Well, we were nice to this fellow while he was running against Goldwater because we were scared of Goldwater, but now we're going to get him because he's just a Texas clown."[5] The hypersensitive Johnson sensed this disdain, of course, and it deeply embittered him. "What's the difference between a cannibal and a liberal?" he would ask. "A cannibal doesn't eat his friends."[6]

Johnson knew that he could do the job, and he was determined to prove his critics absolutely wrong. He consulted with a wide variety of people concerning strategy before the 1964 election—James Rowe, Clark Clifford, Abe Fortas, Richard Russell, Robert Anderson, Larry O'Brien, and many others—but his principal adviser was Horace Busby. The messages that Busby continually sent to his boss during the spring and summer of 1964 were that the Democratic Party was not the majority party in the United States and that Lyndon Johnson could lose the election. Only when FDR ran for the presidency had the Democrats commanded a majority of voters, he pointed out.[7] The Republicans, especially the Goldwater wing of the party, were posing as reformers. What they proposed to change was bloated government that, acting in the name of special interests such as big labor, minorities, and the welfare community, was allegedly taxing average Americans into penury and trampling on their liberties.[8] Finally, Busby was blunt in assessing LBJ's liabilities as a campaigner—the president was perceived as a mere tactician rather than a person of vision; he was given to exaggeration and excessive enthusiasm; everything seemed of pressing, immediate urgency, implying that Johnson had no sense of judgment or proportion; he was prone to sloganeering and building straw men to knock down; he pandered to the press; and he was vulgar.[9]

What then was to be done? Philosophically, LBJ could not abandon the notion that the federal government was an instrument to be wielded for the good of the people. White House support for the poverty bill and the civil rights measures as well as the Great Society speech delivered at the University of Michigan underlined the president's commitment to the notion of positive government action to end discrimination, guarantee equal opportunity, regulate the marketplace, and aid the disadvantaged. Busby argued that the campaign should point out that not only would these goals be obtained without revolution but also they were an alternative to revolution. Princeton historian Eric Goldman urged the president to emphasize that positive action by the federal government actually enhanced individualism in America rather than detracted from it. The effect of antitrust legislation, worker safety laws, hours and wages legislation, a commitment to civil rights by the federal government, financial and occupational aid to the disadvantaged "has actually been to create much more opportunity for the American to be a genuine individual, with much more chance to express his individual self in both the practical and non-practical sense of living," he wrote LBJ.[10]

Tactically, of course, LBJ had to reach out to traditional Republicans and whittle away at the GOP base. Given the possible, even likely defection of the South, such an effort was crucial. In an economic climate of a growing GNP, increasing wages and prices, and ever-rising family incomes, Johnson could practice the politics of productivity. "Until recently it had been assumed there was only so much pie," influential columnist Walter Lippmann had observed, and the social question was how to divide it. But in the current generation a revolutionary idea had taken hold: you could make the pie bigger with fiscal policies "and then a whole society, not just a part of it will grow richer."[11] With this promise in hand, LBJ could appeal to the social consciences of businesspeople, he could avoid the language of class warfare, he could call forth a corporate state in which a rising tide would lift all boats. All the while, LBJ should continue to pose as the "can-do" statesman, a prudent man of vision who could tease progressive legislation from the bureaucratic and political jungle in Washington.[12]

April brought the perfect opportunity for LBJ to showcase his own talents as political mediator and the virtues of the corporate state philosophy. For five years the nation had been confronted with the possibility of a nationwide railway strike. By the spring of 1964, no progress had been made, and the railroad brotherhoods announced that they were going to walk out. Shortly before they declared their intentions, unknown agents had dynamited a section of track, blowing up a locomotive and derailing twenty-seven cars.[13] A prolonged work stoppage would wreak havoc with the economy, shutting down industries starved for raw materials and businesses begging for finished product. Johnson summoned negotiators from both sides to the White House in a last-ditch effort to stop the walkout.

Aware that the public had JFK's success in settling the 1962 steel strike on their minds and fearful of the political consequences for his prestige and the prestige of his office if he intervened and failed, LBJ was at his most intense.

What Johnson wanted was for both sides to agree to give him fifteen days to work out a settlement before they inflicted a strike on the nation. He subsequently described the negotiations to Marshall McNeil, his journalist friend from Texas:

> I told them that this country couldn't stand this. . . . And that I wanted them to give me twenty days to see what I could do about it and for them to go off . . . and come back and tell me. They came back. And the carriers said, "We accept your proposal." The labor people said, "We do not accept your proposal. . . . We've been at this four years and Presidents have asked us to postpone time and time again . . . and we just lost our ass every time. . . . " I said . . . I'm not going to take that kind of no. I'm supposed to be a great healer and a great pleader. You go in the President's private office by yourselves. Talk it over and see if you want to tell the people of this country that you said no to their President when he hasn't had a chance. . . . So . . . they came back and the old boy said . . . " We're going to go with you."[14]

LBJ subsequently brought the Illinois Central president and the head of the Brotherhood of Locomotive Engineers into the Fish Room, where he announced his achievement on national television.[15] Eric Goldman, who was present throughout, remembered the call to patriotism. "I want all of you to recognize," he remembered the president saying, "that we are in high focus throughout the world tonight. Please give me this opportunity to show that our system of free enterprise really works. As patriotic Americans, I tell you you must delay." As Roy Davidson, head of the International Brotherhood of Locomotive Engineers, later said, "What else do you do if the President looks you straight in the face and tells you that it is your duty as an American?"[16]

During the next two weeks, Johnson oversaw negotiations that were held in the Executive Office Building next door to the White House. The issues involved overtime pay and featherbedding. For example, the union wanted a full day's pay for every 100 miles traveled, while the owners wanted to up the mileage to 150. Twice a day Johnson would stick his head in, warning of the dire consequences of a strike and appealing to the participants' patriotism. "Every night Lyndon and I talk about what's happening to the railroad negotiators," Lady Bird recorded in her diary, "and I know how much is hanging in the balance for him."[17]

In the end, management accepted most of the union's demands in return for concessions from the government. LBJ promised to press Congress to grant the railroads greater leeway in setting rates, and he intervened with Attorney General Kennedy, asking that Justice stretch the letter of antitrust laws and approve rail mergers whenever possible.[18] On April 22, over coffee, the two sides indicated to LBJ that they were ready to sign an agreement. Overjoyed, he swept up the four negotiators, stuffed them into the presidential limousine, and with police sirens screaming, drove directly to the local CBS affiliate, WTOP, where his friend CBS president Frank Stanton had arranged for a three-network broadcast.[19] Jubilant, LBJ hailed the settlement as a triumph for American industrial democracy. The press reaction was more than LBJ's campaign staff could have hoped for. "The President scored a great coup—a 'miracle' some called it—in helping to settle the five-year-old railroad dispute that had defied all previous efforts at solution," announced a *New York Times* editorial. Scotty Reston declared "the tireless negotiating skill" of the president "one of the vital natural resources of this country."[20]

THE END OF APRIL SAW LBJ RIDING HIGH IN THE POLLS. A POLITICAL cartoon reflected the strength of the president's position. It showed LBJ seated at a card table with a deck before him and "tax cut" cards tucked in the brim of his Stetson, "R.R. Settlement" and "Boom Times" cards coming out of his sleeves, and "Common Touch" and "Poverty Fight" cards protruding from the cuffs of his pants. A smiling Johnson asks, "Now Who'd Like to Play?"[21] Johnson was the only presidential candidate in history, complained the chairman of the Republican National Committee, to have both poverty and prosperity going for him. There even seemed some hope of capturing the South. In January no less a Dixiecrat than Strom Thurmond had declared in Houston that LBJ had a much greater chance of carrying the South than JFK would have had. "Today we have in the White House a Texan with whom I have also had the honor of serving in the United States Senate," he told his audience, "a man with whom I have often disagreed on legislative matters, but a man whom I respect as one of the most capable and experienced men to ascend to the White House."[22] In July southern moderates, three former southern governors—Luther Hodges of North Carolina, LeRoy Collins of Florida, and Buford Ellington of Tennessee— embarked on a trip through the South, meeting with every governor except George Wallace of Alabama and Paul Johnson of Mississippi to lobby for LBJ.[23] "You tell 'em," LBJ instructed his lieutenants, "it's a hell of a lot easier to sit beside a Negro in a restaurant than to fight beside him with a gun overseas."[24]

One of the problems facing LBJ and his campaign strategists as spring gave way to summer was that they were not at all sure who the GOP nominee would be. Former vice president Richard Nixon was threatening to throw his hat in the ring once again, and Governors William Scranton and Nelson Rockefeller had already tossed in theirs. Ambassador Henry Cabot Lodge had returned from Vietnam hoping to be embraced as a heroic proconsul. Of these, Rockefeller seemed the strongest; JFK had believed that if the GOP had run him instead of Nixon in 1960, it would have won.[25] Fortunately for LBJ and the Democratic Party, the Republicans were in no mood for moderation and reason in 1964. Contorted by internal bickering and frustrated by the Democratic resurgence of the late 1950s and early 1960s, the GOP abandoned the moderate course it had been following since 1940 and succumbed to the siren song of militant conservatism.

The darling of the New Right was Senator Barry M. Goldwater of Arizona, the heir to a department store fortune and a reserve Air Force general who had first been elected to Congress in 1952. There seemed to be two Goldwaters, columnist Richard Rovere noted; one was the easygoing, affable southwesterner most senators knew personally, and the other was the humorless, ideologically rigid author of *The Conscience of a Conservative*. That book, ghostwritten by Goldwater's handlers as a campaign tract, called for reduced government expenditures, elimination of government bureaucracies, an end to "forced integration, reassertion of states' rights, an end to farm subsidies, and welfare payments, and additional curbs on labor unions." Above all, Goldwater called for "total victory" over communism both at home and abroad. Negative in domestic policy and aggressive in foreign, Goldwater, who had never authored a bill, declared, "My aim is not to pass laws but to repeal them." Containment was too defensive a foreign policy, "like a boxer who refuses to throw a punch."[26] At the Republican National

Convention held in San Francisco in July, delegates rejected the path of moderation and nominated the senator from Arizona.

Goldwater's selection was stunning. Johnson and other observers believed it signaled the demise of the Republican Party. The New Right was "a pretty intense, fanatical group," he told newspaper publisher Houston Harte, "a bunch of screwballs . . . the Birch Societies. . . . I think it [will] probably mean the death of the Republican party. . . . He wants to drop atomic bombs on everybody. I don't believe the people will stand for that."[27] But the demise of the GOP did not necessarily translate into a victory for LBJ in November. The country seemed in a mood for extremism. Orville Freeman observed in his diary that "Goldwater has capitalized on a general frustrated feeling of people in a complex society, . . . [it seems] that he has picked up the backlash on the racial question, that he is capitalizing on the general fear of bigness and anti-big government attitudes, that he is emphasizing the individual in his efforts to maintain his identity in an increasingly large and collectivized society both publicly and privately."[28] Goldwater may have been raising complex questions, but he was offering simple answers, declared journalist I. F. Stone. He and his ilk seemed "to see the world with the pristine purity of *Wagon Train,* where good and evil are sharply and unmistakably juxtaposed and the hero's six-shooter brings the triumph of justice at the end of each episode."[29]

But Barry Goldwater was not the only figure in American politics in 1964 seeking to gnaw away the edges of the vital center. On May 19, George Corley Wallace won 43 percent of the vote in the Maryland Democratic primary against Senator Daniel Brewster, a stand-in for LBJ. In June 1963, the Alabama governor had become segregation's newest hero by standing in the door of the University of Alabama admissions building in an attempt to bar the registration of two black students, James Hood and Vivian Malone. Though he was forced to withdraw, Wallace used the incident to whip the white backlash into a fury and to become a factor in presidential politics. When, on August 28, Martin Luther King led the famous March on Washington, Wallace made a point of announcing to reporters that he had better things to do than "waste my time" watching a march led by "communists and sex perverts."[30] When he subsequently announced that he was going to be a candidate for president on the Democratic ticket, pundits scoffed; the Dixiecrat card had been played and discarded in 1948. Others were not so sure. "Wallaceism is bigger than Wallace," King had warned CBS television reporter Dan Rather following the schoolhouse door incident.[31] The Alabama governor was, one of his contemporaries observed, "emotional, energetic, single-minded, rough-hewn, strong and appealing to the masses," a kind of redneck Ivanhoe "astride a great white charger, doing battle for the white people of Alabama and the South."[32]

Millions of working-class whites in the North and Midwest felt socially and economically threatened by the civil rights movement. In July 1964, rioting erupted in Harlem after an off-duty police officer shot a black teenager. Amid arson, looting, and violent clashes between the police and black youths, one person died and more than one hundred were injured.[33] Reporting from his heavily Polish district in Illinois, Democratic congressman Dan Rostenkowski told Jack Valenti that there was a definite white backlash among voters. A recent poll showed 78 percent opposed to the civil rights bill. Fear of job competition and declining real estate values had overridden the Catholic Church's strong stand in behalf of civil rights.[34] Wallace subsequently dropped out of the race, but he had mobilized a potent constituency that would presumably switch their support to Goldwater. "It is time someone said to the President what apparently no one has yet said to him," a White House staffer memoed Bill Moyers, "that he could lose this election and that he could lose it despite having lined up all the press and the television networks, all the top labor leaders, most of the top business leaders, all of the Negro vote, and perhaps even Lodge and Rockefeller." A Goldwater campaign based on "three potent commodities: Race prejudice . . . Chauvinism . . . [and] simple answers to complicated questions" could produce an upset.[35]

The president's advisers need not have worried about their man. Johnson fought every campaign as if it were in doubt, as if every vote against him would be taken as a personal affront. He would leave no stone unturned in his search for support, no effort unexpended in campaigning. From his first run for Congress through the 1964 presidential campaign, he had always run scared. But even when the polls showed him far ahead and a sure winner, he worked intensely. Johnson coveted a landslide for his own personal gratification but also as a mandate in behalf of the Great Society.

LBJ's biggest decision during the campaign was selection of a running mate. Early in the spring of 1964, Schlesinger, Kenny O'Donnell, and their allies in the press started a Kennedy-for-vice-president boom. It worked. National polls indicated that the people preferred Bobby to his nearest rival, Hubert Humphrey, by a four-to-one margin. Syndicated columnist Stewart Alsop observed that it would be virtually impossible for LBJ to reject the attorney general as his running mate. To do so would risk losing Catholics, blacks, and the labor vote in the large industrial states of the East and Midwest.[36]

Three weeks after JFK's death, Johnson had told O'Donnell, "I don't want history to say I was elected to this office because I had Bobby on the ticket with me. But I'll take him if I need him." But he also said, "If I don't need him, I'm not going to take him." But how to get Bobby out of the unofficial race for the vice presidency without appearing to be mean and vindictive? Johnson consulted Clark Clifford and Abe Fortas about "the Bobby problem." Aside from their personal differences, LBJ observed, Bobby would be the wrong choice because as a person and as attorney general he was identified in the collective mind of the South with federally enforced integration. After much pulling and hauling, Clifford suggested that LBJ announce that no one currently sitting in the cabinet would be considered for the second spot on the ticket—it would be too great a diversion from the work of the people.[37]

On Wednesday, July 9, Johnson met with RFK in the Oval Office. The conversation was dignified and to the point. LBJ told him that he had decided not to consider any sitting cabinet member. Kennedy flushed slightly and then asked if he had settled on anyone. LBJ said no, but that he was faced with the same issues of geographical and philosophical balance that had confronted JFK in 1960. He told Bobby that he had a very bright future in the party and that he would do whatever he could to advance his career. He asked RFK to stay on as attorney general, but the latter refused, recommending Nick Katzenbach as his replacement.[38] Humiliated, RFK privately declared personal and political war on the Texan.

The approach of the Democratic convention in Atlantic City brought forth LBJ's paranoia and control tendencies in full force. Upon learning that Jackie and Bobby Kennedy were planning a giant tribute to JFK, Johnson became convinced that the Kennedys were going to stampede the delegates and force a draft of Bobby for the second place on the ticket. To their enragement, he managed to have the tribute moved to the last day of the convention. Furthermore, prior to the convention LBJ asked J. Edgar Hoover to send a secret team of agents under the direction of Cartha "Deke" DeLoach to Atlantic City to gather intelligence on potentially disruptive elements, including the Kennedys. In other words, Johnson was asking the FBI director to spy on his immediate superior, the attorney general of the United States.[39]

The director was happy to do so, for he hated the younger Kennedy. Their rivalry dated back to the 1950s, when as special counsel to the Mc-Clellan Committee (the Senate committee that investigated the penetration of labor unions by organized crime) Bobby stole Hoover's and the FBI's thunder as the nation's number one crusader against organized crime. At the 1960 Democratic convention, Hoover had made no secret of his preference for LBJ as the nominee. The Kennedys knew that the FBI had compiled a thick dossier on Jack's sexual exploits, and Jack had made Bobby attorney general in no small part to keep a tight rein on Hoover. The one point on which the director and attorney general were able to agree was the need to wiretap Martin Luther King's phones. Bobby wanted to be forewarned of possible disruptive civil rights demonstrations, and the director hoped to get the goods on King, whom he detested, as a communist stooge. Any possibility of reconciliation had gone by the boards when Bobby let it be known that the administration would not lift a finger to exempt the director when he reached mandatory retirement age in January 1965. No sooner had JFK's body been interred at Arlington National Cemetery than Hoover began reporting directly to LBJ, bypassing RFK, his boss.[40]

The Hoover-Johnson relationship stretched back twenty years. The two men's homes in Washington were both on 30th Street, directly across from each other. The Johnsons would occasionally ask Hoover over for a drink, and Lyndon encouraged daughters Lynda and Lucy to call him "Uncle Edgar." Privately, Johnson considered Hoover, who never married and lived alone in the same house with his deputy, Clyde Tolson, to be a hypocritical "queer."[41] But as FBI Deputy Director Deke DeLoach recalled, the two men found each other useful. "President Johnson," he said, "knew of Mr. Hoover's image in the United States, particularly among the middle-of-the-road to conservative elements, and he knew it was vast. He knew of the potential strength of the FBI—insofar as being of assistance to the government and the White House is concerned."[42] There was an irony, also. By having Hoover and the FBI head investigations of abuses of civil rights activists by white supremacists, by involving the bureau as deeply as possible in the movement, the president could give the Second Reconstruction some cover from segregationist charges that it was communist inspired and dominated. Hoover could not resist the White House's call to take on the Klan, although he was determined to continue his private war with King, because he and the agency could once again bask in the public limelight. To seal the deal, Johnson assured Hoover that he would be able to stay on as director well beyond the mandatory federal retirement age.[43] But typically, LBJ never let the FBI chief forget who was boss. During one of their early conversations after Johnson had become president, he said, "Edgar, I can't hear you well. What's the matter, you got this phone tapped?" Hoover had laughed nervously.[44]

Johnson had a reason for dispatching a team of FBI agents to Atlantic City other than subverting a possible Kennedy coup. The all-white Mississippi delegation was being challenged for its spot on the floor by the mixed-race Mississippi Freedom Democratic Party. The looming conflict, if allowed to get out of hand, might very well split the Democratic Party and lead to a Dixiecrat walkout or the disaffection of the party's increasingly important black constituency.

By the summer of 1964, Mississippi had once again become the principal battleground in the struggle over civil rights. Mississippi, as reporter Juan Williams put it, "led the nation in beatings, lynching, and mysterious disappearances." The black population was the most disfranchised in the nation. Only 5 percent of black Mississippians (who made up 45 percent of the state's population) were registered to vote, the lowest rate in the United States. With majorities in many counties, blacks might well have controlled local politics through the ballot box. But segregationists were not about to let blacks vote; many would sooner kill them.[45]

During the "Freedom Summer" of 1964, local activists joined with volunteers from CORE and SNCC to try to register blacks to vote. Rebuffed at every turn, they announced a "freedom registration" campaign. In April, delegates assembled and voted to establish the Mississippi Freedom Democratic Party (MFDP).[46] On August 6, twenty-five hundred people jammed into the Masonic Temple in Jackson for the MFDP state convention. There they selected sixty-four blacks and four whites to compose the MFDP delegation to the Democratic convention in Atlantic City. The plan was for the MFDP to challenge the regular all-white Mississippi delegation on two grounds: that it had racially discriminated and that its members would refuse to sign a loyalty oath pledging that they would support the Democratic presidential nominee, whoever that might be. After LBJ's nomination, the segregationist delegation would be sure to bolt the party for Barry Goldwater and the GOP.

Joe Rauh, labor lawyer and ADA activist, who had agreed to serve as legal counsel to the MFDP, told the cheering Freedom Party delegates that he had commitments from a number of northern delegations to support the challenge. The MFDP would present its case to the credentials committee. If only 10 percent of that 108-person body voted to uphold the challenge, there would have to be a minority report. With the issue on the floor, there would be a roll-call vote. With the nation watching, delegations from the East, Midwest, and West would have to vote against the white supremacist regular Mississippi delegation.[47]

The revolt among Mississippi's black voters frightened Johnson. "I don't know how anybody can stop what they're doing on the Freedom Party," he told John Connally.

> I think it's very bad and I wish that I could stop it. . . . It may very well be that Bobby has started it. . . . Joe Rauh and Martin Luther King and folks that normally run with that crowd [the Kennedys] are leading 'em. On the other hand, I don't see how a fellow like Dick Hughes [governor of Iowa] . . . and Dick Daley [Chicago mayor Richard Daley] . . . can possibly go back to their states and say that they were for seating the Alabama group and the Mississippi group when they won't say they'll support their nominees. . . . So it looks like you just pretty well split the party. . . . Worse than Goldwater and Rockefeller even.[48]

LBJ felt he had to win Georgia and that with the support of Governor Carl Sanders he had a good chance of doing so. He certainly did not want to lose Tennessee and the border states, Kentucky and Maryland. There was a chance, however, if the regular Mississippi delegation was forced out and replaced by an overwhelmingly black group, that all of the southern delegations would bolt. Mississippi and Alabama were probably going to rebel anyway over the loyalty oath issue. "I think what they ought to do is to put Mississippi and Alabama near the nearest exit," Johnson told Speaker McCormack, "so that if they want to walk out, let them walk out . . . but [do] not let us throw them out."[49] In a telephone conversation with Roy Wilkins on August 15, LBJ declared, "If I were the Negro . . . I'd just let Mississippi [the all-white delegation] sit up on the platform, if they wanted to, and I'd stand at attention and salute the son of a bitch. Then I'd nominate Johnson for president . . . and I'd go out and elect my Congressman. . . . And the next four years, I'd see the promised land."[50]

Unfortunately for Johnson, the principal civil rights organizations— CORE, SNCC, the SCLC, and even the NAACP—were mobilizing in behalf of the MFDP. Martin Luther King had staged a march from Jackson in hopes of bringing national attention to the issue. On July 17, Bishop Stephen Gill Spottswood, chair of the NAACP board of directors, had sent a telegram to LBJ demanding that he take over administration of the state of Mississippi under Article IV, Section 4 of the United States Constitution, which declared, "The Citizens of each State shall be entitled to all Privileges and Immunities of Citizens in the several States."[51]

On August 19, LBJ met with a delegation from the MFDP as well as representatives of CORE and SNCC. He pled with them to listen to reason. The poverty bill, which was essentially a civil rights measure, was pending before Congress. If the MFDP tried and failed to be seated at the convention, there were liable to be massive and probably violent demonstrations across the country. The ensuing white backlash could well undermine what he was trying to do in the area of civil rights. Law and order would be part of the fall campaign; it would be the base upon which the administration would build its case in the South for obedience to the civil rights act. If nothing else, he pled, CORE and SNCC must keep their demonstrations focused on specific objectives "to prevent them from becoming leaderless riots with attendant looting and violence."[52]

Wilkins, Young, Randolph, and Rustin supported the president with James Farmer of CORE and John Lewis of SNCC vigorously dissenting. "Demonstrations are CORE's only weapons," declared Farmer. "If we talk to wrongdoers and ask them to change their ways, they'll laugh at us if they know we've given up our weapon. If we try to negotiate, we become an amateur Urban League. If we file suit, we become an amateur NAACP or Legal Defense and Education Fund. For CORE to give up demonstrations, even for six months, would be to give up its genius, its raison d'être. It might sound our death knell."[53] King reluctantly sided with the establishment figures, but no one was in favor of abandoning the MFDP. Voting rights—representation in the American democracy—was a floor below which no civil rights leader was willing to sink.

Suddenly, Johnson was confronted with the possibility that the Democratic convention might blow up in his face and the presidency slip from his grasp. As his protégé, Governor Connally, indelicately put it to LBJ, "If you seat those black jigaboos, the whole South will walk out."[54] Governor Sanders of Georgia echoed Connally's warning. Whereas Mississippi and Alabama were probably going to withdraw anyway if a loyalty oath was required, this was not likely to precipitate a bolt by the entire South. But seating the MFDP would. The stakes were considerable: Texas and Georgia alone accounted for thirty-seven electoral votes. And then there were the border states. "I know this," LBJ told Hubert Humphrey, his running-mate-to-be. "If we mess with the group of Negros . . . who said we want you to recognize us and throw out the governor and the elected officials of the state . . . we will lose 15 states without campaigning. . . . I don't want to do anything in Mississippi to lose Oklahoma for me and I don't want to do anything in Mississippi to lose Kentucky for me."[55]

THE MFDP DELEGATION ARRIVED BY BUS IN ATLANTIC CITY ON AUgust 21. The group included a handful of experienced local politicos; most were professional people but there was a smattering of farmers, sharecroppers, and domestic workers. After settling in the tiny, run-down Gem Hotel, they began fanning out to lobby members of the credentials committee. On the twenty-second, David Lawrence gaveled the credentials committee to order, and spokespersons for the MFDP and the regular, all-white delegation proceeded to make their cases in front of a bank of television cameras. Heading the regular contingent was Governor Paul Johnson, who had once joked that NAACP stood for "niggers, alligators, apes, coons, and possums."[56] The regulars cited the long history of Mississippi as an integral part of the Democratic Party and denied that blacks had been barred from voting in their state. Speaking for the MFDP was Mrs. Fannie Lou Hamer, a black sharecropper from Ruleville who had been ejected from her farm, jailed, and finally beaten for trying to vote. Before the credentials committee and a rapt television audience, she described her travails and asked, "Is this America, the land of the free and the home of the brave, where we have to sleep with our telephones off the hooks because our lives be threatened daily, because we want to live as decent human beings, in America?"[57] Privately, Paul Johnson dismissed Hamer as a rum runner and a prostitute. "She, of course, had been a convicted bootlegger and operator of a house for women there in the Delta around Louisville," he said.[58]

At this point Joe Rauh was still confident that he had seventeen committee members pledged to sign a minority report supporting the MFDP and ten states pledged to ask for a roll call on the convention floor. That evening, black delegates to the convention gathered at the Deauville Hotel. Although not invited, a number of MFDP members attended. Prominent conservatives from around the country made speeches declaring that all good Democrats must respect the wishes of the president. At the meeting, a black congressman close to the White House persuaded Bob Moses to give him a list of the names of those on the credentials committee who had committed to Rauh and the MFDP.

In truth, LBJ knew what the MFDP was going to do before it did it. So agitated had he become over the issue that in late July he had authorized the FBI to install illegal wiretaps and bugs to monitor the MFDP in an effort to protect his presidential candidacy. On August 1, Johnson had had his aide Walter Jenkins call Deke DeLoach, the FBI's liaison to the White House. "Deke," Jenkins said, "the President is very concerned about his personal safety and that of his staff while they're at the convention. Would you head a team to keep us advised of any potential threats?"[59] Jenkins subsequently spelled out exactly what the White House expected, namely, all the information the FBI could gather about the MFDP, its sixty-eight delegates to Atlantic City, and its allies in SNCC, CORE, and the SCLC. The president wanted to know every detail of the Freedom Democrats' strategy and tactics as they presented their case to the convention's credentials committee. "Lyndon is way out of line," Hoover commented when DeLoach told him. Nonetheless, he instructed his assistant to "tell Walter [Jenkins] we will give him whatever help he wants."[60]

Over dinner at the White House on August 20, the night before the MFDP delegation arrived at the convention center in Atlantic City, Johnson complained to his close friend, Senator Richard Russell of Georgia, that it took him "hours each night" to read all the wiretap reports he was receiving, including those of Martin Luther King speaking with Joseph Rauh, the

MFDP's chief counsel. "Hoover apparently has been turned loose and is tapping everything," Russell noted in his diary.[61]

As the president became more anxious about his ability to control the outcome of the Mississippi imbroglio, he became depressed, pessimistic, and paranoid. For months Hoover had been bombarding the White House with raw data allegedly proving that Martin Luther King was in bed with the Communist Party USA. "Those communists are moving in on King, and King's moving in on Rauh," Johnson complained to Secretary of Labor Willard Wirtz.[62] When Mayor Richard Daley of Chicago questioned whether there was "someone behind" the MFDP challenge, Johnson replied, "Oh, yes, Dick. The Communist party is the leader."[63]

The credentials committee was divided, but Rauh had enough votes to lead a floor fight. If the dispute went to the convention as a whole, the deep schism in the party would be revealed on television for all to see. The president was as frustrated by the regular all-white Mississippi delegation—which refused to compromise even on a loyalty oath—as he was with the MFDP. He demanded of Senator James Eastland to know whether the Mississippi regulars had come to the convention "as traitors to the party—or are they going to try to be helpful?" On Sunday evening he warned Eastland that he "might cut out your goddamn [agricultural] subsidies and cut out your $6 billion cotton program."[64]

On the morning of August 25, Johnson, mired in depression, called his Texas friend and business partner A. W. Moursund. He informed Moursund that he was leaning toward announcing later in the day that he was withdrawing as a candidate for the Democratic presidential nomination and retiring to Texas.[65] "I am absolutely positive that I cannot lead the South and the North," he told George Reedy later in the day. "And I don't want to lead the nation without my own state and without my own section. I am very convinced that the Negros will not listen to me. They're not going to follow a white southerner."[66]

Johnson then called Richard Russell at his home in Winder, Georgia. He was going to Atlantic City at about seven thirty that night, and there he would serve notice that he had incurred "too many scars and could not unite the country." He would tell the convention "to get some fresh figure to nominate and elect." Russell listened patiently until his friend exclaimed that he had "only accepted the vice presidential nomination in 1960 to avoid dropping dead on the Senate floor as majority leader," and he was "looking for the peace and quiet of the vice president's job." That was too much for Russell, who had endured Johnson's overweening ambition for sixteen years. He told the president that he was "speaking like a child—and a spoiled one at that." He advised him to "take a tranquilizer and get a few hours' sleep."[67]

With the credentials committee deadlocked, the White House proposed a compromise on the afternoon of the twenty-fifth: two MFDP delegates would be seated as delegates-at-large; only those members of the regular Mississippi contingent who signed a loyalty oath would be seated; and the Democratic Party would prohibit racial discrimination in the selection of delegates to all future conventions. The committee was deeply divided, but in the end announced at a televised press conference that it had voted to accept the two-seat compromise. Despite the pleadings of Bayard Rustin, Martin Luther King, and others, the MFDP would have none of it. "We didn't come all this way for no two seats," Fannie Lou Hamer famously exclaimed.[68] The all-white Mississippi delegation, most of whose members immediately departed Atlantic City, were just as disgruntled. On Tuesday evening, twenty-one MFDP delegates, furnished credentials by friendly delegates from other states, pushed their way into the seats vacated by the regular delegation. After an unsuccessful effort to evict Hamer and her colleagues, the sergeant-at-arms and his men simply ignored them, and the convention proceeded with its business.[69]

The MFDP brouhaha marked a watershed in the history of the civil rights movement. It pushed SNCC and CORE into a more radical posture and contributed to a growing image among many younger blacks of King, Young, Rustin, and Randolph as Uncle Toms. Civil rights activists in general became increasingly dubious about working within the Democratic Party, rejecting the notion, so dear to Lyndon Johnson's heart, that it was the political instrument of the social justice movement in America. For many people, observed SNCC's Joyce Ladner, "Atlantic City was the end of innocence."[70]

Civil rights activists and liberals in general were confusing appearance with substance, privileging the present over the future. During the dustup with MFDP, LBJ had told Walter Reuther, "We don't want to cut off our nose to spite our face. If they [MFDP protesters] give us four years, I'll guarantee the Freedom delegation somebody representing views like [theirs] will be seated four years from now." The president was as good as his word: he championed a fundamental reform of convention rules that would have enormous long-term consequences for the Democratic Party. Previously, state parties had sole authority to establish delegate selection procedures. Henceforth, the national party agencies not only would decide how many votes each state delegation got at the national convention but also enforce uniform rules on what kinds of persons could be selected.[71]

But perhaps most significant for the Johnson presidency, the MFDP episode made LBJ and J. Edgar Hoover allies whether the president wanted it or not. The director knew that the White House had authorized illegal wiretaps on the Kennedys and the MFDP, and Johnson knew that he knew. The knowledge would give Hoover leverage in his ongoing campaign to portray both the civil rights and antiwar movements as part of the international communist conspiracy.

Except for the tribute to JFK, the rest of the proceedings at Atlantic City were somewhat anticlimactic. On the evening of Wednesday, August 26, Johnson's name was put in nomination by John Connally and Governor Pat Brown of California. There were no challengers. He was quickly and unanimously elected. The candidate stood in the wings and listened to the cheering and demonstrations for what seemed to many to be an interminable period. Finally, with Carol Channing singing "Hello, Lyndon" to the tune of the Broadway musical *Hello, Dolly!* in which she had starred, the president made his way to the podium, took the gavel from Speaker McCormack, who was presiding, and announced that his choice for the second place on the ticket was Hubert Humphrey.

The following evening, the last of the convention, LBJ's and Humphrey's acceptance speeches were sandwiched in between gala celebrations of the president's fifty-sixth birthday. "The end of the Convention Hall is decked with five pictures," Orville Freeman noted in his diary. "Three small pictures across the top—Roosevelt, Kennedy, Truman—and on the side enormous Johnson pictures dominate the hall. This has been a Johnson show from beginning to end with the complete dominance of the man evident at every hand."[72]

THERE WAS NEVER ANY CHANCE THAT BARRY GOLDWATER WOULD win in 1964. As political commentator Theodore White put it, "No man ever began a Presidential effort more deeply wounded by his own nomination, suffering more insurmountable handicaps. And then . . . he made the worst of them."[73] During the campaign, he stumped in Florida, home to the nation's largest elderly population, and warned against "the outright hoax of this administration's Medicare scheme."[74] Instead of trying to shed or modify his image as a trigger-happy, heartless extremist, Goldwater embraced it. Although physicians as a whole indicated that they were going to vote for the GOP nominee, a survey of psychiatrists indicated that they were against him ten-to-one.[75] In the middle of September, Gallup found that Johnson had fashioned an astounding 69 to 31 percent lead.[76]

But the campaign was still important. Some of Johnson's advisers came to the conclusion that the purpose of the Goldwater crusade was not to win—the polls showed that to be impossible—but to damage LBJ as much as it could so as to cripple him and his agenda during the next four years. "Although Goldwater will almost certainly be beaten overwhelmingly," campaign adviser Fred Dutton observed to Bill Moyers, "our opposition will likely use October to try to blemish the President's long-term public standing as much as possible—the wheeler-dealer charge will almost surely be the main underlying theme to which they will keep returning."[77]

"The aim is not your defeat in November," Horace Busby advised LBJ, "but your compromise after January. Your Texas enemies and others failed to deny you the Presidency—a goal they long feared you would reach. But, having failed that, they now are driving for a final goal—to deny you a place either in the hearts of your countrymen or in history."[78] Consequently, Johnson's political brain trust concluded, what was important was how the campaign was waged. The rhetoric that Johnson employed, the interests he attracted to his political coalition, the hopes and expectations that he aroused would have a profound impact on the remainder of his presidency and on the country as a whole. LBJ fought the campaign as if the outcome were in doubt because that is what good politicians do but also because he fantasized about exceeding Warren Harding's 60.3 percent of the vote garnered in 1920 and even FDR's total of 60.8 percent in 1936. He would be able to shed the JFK albatross once and for all, be president in his own right, and use his popular mandate to push through Congress a revolutionary legislative program.

LBJ had no intention of conceding the South to the Goldwaterites. He had been encouraged by his reception in Georgia and in Virginia and Tennessee during a subsequent trip. The Georgia delegation to the Atlantic City convention had included four blacks. "We've had a tremendous registration last year in our Negro vote," Governor Carl Sanders, a rising spokesman for the New South, reported to LBJ, "and we [are] still registering those every day."[79] On the surface, however, the situation in the South looked bleak. Opinion polls taken in July indicated that the Democrats would not carry a single state from the former Confederacy.

The person Johnson selected to get his message across to southern governors, congressmen, and state legislators was John Connally. At the same time that polls indicated a total Democratic washout, southern governors and legislators were telling the president that they would not support the national ticket if RFK were the vice-presidential nominee and that they disliked Humphrey only a little less. You tell them, LBJ instructed Connally, that there were only three possible nominees available to Democrats: Johnson, Humphrey, and Kennedy. If they did not straighten up and get behind him, he would withdraw. In which case Bobby would get the nomination, would most certainly become president, and then the South would really be in a pickle.[80]

There was more than politics behind LBJ's southern strategy, however. He wanted to be president to all the people. He sympathized with those whites in the South who were being asked to leave their hallowed traditions behind and enter unknown territory. "I think it is a mistake not to help them and leave them out in the cold," he told Senator John Sparkman (D-AL). "I don't expect to carry them. I owe more obligation to those that I'm not going to carry than I do the ones I will."[81]

Whereas Connally was LBJ's private ambassador to the South, his public emissary was Lady Bird. In early October the first lady would embark on a four-day, 1,628-mile train trip through eight southern states. Her message would be clear: the Civil War was over; blacks and whites were fellow human beings and fellow countrymen; segregation and discrimination were unpatriotic and un-Christian. Once again Johnson would be placing the South in a bind. Arguably, as of 1964 Lady Bird was the nation's most visible southern belle. Long known for its chivalry toward women, the region would either treat Texas's native daughter with kindness and respect, or it would betray one of its most hallowed traditions.

As preparations for the trip got under way, Lady Bird contacted southern senators, congressmen, and governors, asking if they or their wives would appear with her at one or more stops in their respective states. Russell, Eastland, Tallmadge, Senator John Stennis of Mississippi, Senator Allen Ellender of Louisiana, and Senator Willis Robertson of Virginia all at first refused.[82] The only enthusiasts were Louisiana congressman Hale Boggs and his wife, Lindy, who was one of the chief organizers of the campaign and who would accompany the first lady throughout. After the FBI received word that hate groups might blow up the train, the Secret Service arranged for a separate locomotive to travel fifteen minutes ahead of the first lady in order to detonate a bomb if there turned out to be one. Accompanied by a coterie of female campaign workers decked out in red-white-and-blue outfits and her twenty-year-old daughter, Lynda, Lady Bird set out on the morning of October 6. She was particularly drawn to small towns and added them to the itinerary whenever possible. The citizens of Ahoskie, North Carolina, population five thousand, cabled her, "Nobody important has been through here since Buffalo Bill came through in 1916. Please have your train stop here."[83] She did, and ten thousand North Carolinians came out to welcome her.

The Lady Bird Special first encountered real opposition on October 7 at Columbia, South Carolina. As the train pulled into the station, a large crowd began to chant, "We Want Barry!" When Lady Bird began to speak, the crowd drowned her out with boos. South Carolina governor Donald Russell appealed to the "good manners and hospitality" of his constituents. A tight-lipped first lady pressed ahead. Finally, she stopped in midsentence, held up a white-gloved hand, and said, "This is a country of many viewpoints. I respect your right to express your own. Now it is my turn to express mine. Thank you." The crowd quieted.[84]

Plans called for the southern tour to end in New Orleans. Lyndon flew down from Louisville to meet the train. When the Lady Bird Special pulled in at 8:16 in the evening, the president bounded up the steps of the last car and embraced his wife and daughter. Exhausted, Lady Bird momentarily broke down in tears. She then turned to address the huge throng that had gathered, mostly black in the depot itself and mostly white in the plaza that opened out from it. "I was on the station platform when they arrived," Katherine Graham recalled. "It was a tremendously dramatic moment. It was a hot and steamy night, and we all watched the President greet Lady Bird with a big hug and kiss. Then Lady Bird talked in such a moving way about how the South had to turn away from hatred."[85]

Later that evening at a Democratic fund-raiser attended by Senator Allan Ellender and Russell Long and Louisiana governor John McKeithen, LBJ delivered one of the most memorable speeches of his career. "If we are to heal our history and make this Nation whole," he declared, "prosperity must know no Mason-Dixon line and opportunity must know no color line. . . . Robert E. Lee counseled us well when he told us to cast off our animosities, and raise our sons to be Americans. . . . Whatever your views are, we have a Constitution and we have a Bill of Rights, and we have the law of the land, and two-thirds of the Democrats in the Senate voted for it [the Civil Rights Act of 1964] and three-fourths of the Republicans. I signed it, and I am going to enforce it." He then quoted Sam Rayburn: "I would like to go back down there [to an unnamed state of the Deep South] and make them one more Democratic speech. . . . The poor old State, they haven't heard a Democratic speech in 30 years. All you ever hear at election time is 'Nigger, Nigger, Nigger!'"[86] After a stunned silence, the racially mixed audience rose and gave the president a thunderous ovation.

Southern newspapers delivered mixed reviews, while publications outside the region were almost unanimous in their praise. It was the "most moving speech of the campaign," wrote Mary McGrory in the *Washington Star*. "The New Orleans speech was courageous," Horace Busby reported in summing up press opinion, "and, most especially courageous politics." He noted a sudden shift in the attitudes of the press contingent covering the Johnson campaign. Many of the older hands were explaining to the less experienced: "This is the real Johnson."[87]

What LBJ was doing during the 1964 campaign, of course, was attempting to cover the Confederate flag with the Stars and Stripes. Only the South had at one time been a separate nation, and as such it was the only part of the country where the Confederate flag, a symbol of rebellion and disunion, could be waved enthusiastically by individuals considering themselves as genuinely patriotic Americans.[88] "I say when you divide your country, that is wrong," Johnson proclaimed. "The new South is here in America. What Americans want today is a new politics, a politics of national unity, a politics concerned with progress and peace for the Nation, a politics of honor, and a politics for decency for all. . . . It is the sons of Georgia that have carried that flag to every corner of this globe, and they have brought her back without a tarnish on it. They know there is only one Nation, one people, one flag, one Constitution, united and indivisible under God."[89]

LBJ was not at all sure that his stratagem would work. Talking with Secretary of State Dean Rusk, a native Georgian, after the New Orleans speech, he recalled the story about the brilliant young attorney who defended a

Negro against a rape charge. How did it go, asked his friend? It was the greatest speech of his life, the lawyer said; the jury was in tears when he finished. What about the verdict? "He said, well, they hung the son of a bitch. That's the way I [LBJ] feel."[90]

Even if he lost the South, however, the trip was worth it, Johnson believed. He was going to win, and he wanted to be president of all the people. "We didn't want those people to think we didn't care," he told a Texas friend. "We didn't want them to think they were left out. When a child gets to feel like he's hurt and mistreated he goes on home and don't come back and we don't want that to happen. We love those people and we thought the only thing to do was go tell 'em we loved 'em."[91] James Madison once argued that so long as there is no "nation of philosophers," the "most rational government will not find it a superfluous advantage to have the prejudices of the community on its side."[92] In the matter of race, however, in 1964 LBJ was convinced that if the community were to survive, prejudices had to be changed, not enlisted, or the community would not survive at all.

THERE WAS NEVER ANY QUESTION THAT CIVIL RIGHTS LEADERS FAvored a Johnson victory, but there were initial concerns that because of Goldwater's extremism, LBJ might be tempted to take the black community for granted. "I think we've got to extract a little more concessions from the Federal Government [before openly and unequivocally declaring for Johnson]," Clarence Jones, Martin Luther King's personal counsel, advised his boss in July, "while at the same time maintain a little more degree of, shall we say, maneuverability."[93] But then, following the Jenkins scandal—Walter Jenkins had been arrested in October by the police and accused of engaging in a homosexual act in the bathroom of the Washington YMCA—Harry Wachtel, a New York civil rights lawyer, advised King and his lieutenants to cast caution to the winds and launch a "get out the vote" campaign in behalf of Johnson.[94] King agreed. On October 20, he confided to an associate that in order to ensure LBJ's election, the SCLC must discourage any further demonstrations for the present.[95]

The outcome of the general election exceeded LBJ's expectations if not his dreams. Goldwater won but six states, five in the South plus Arizona. The Texan won 486 electoral votes to his opponent's 52; only Roosevelt's

523 to 8 margin in 1936 was larger. Most important, however, Johnson's 43,129,484 popular votes against Goldwater's 27,178,188 represented the largest vote ever cast for a winning candidate, and his 61 percent margin of victory was the widest in American history to date.[96] LBJ's fears that he would lose the South were not borne out. Although southern support for Johnson was 14 percent less than that given to the party by voters in all other regions combined, he carried 51 percent of the popular vote in eleven ex-Confederate states, up from 49 percent for Kennedy. He also won Arkansas, Florida, North Carolina, Tennessee, Texas, and Virginia.[97] The Republicans lost more than five hundred seats in state legislatures, thirty-seven in the House, and two in the Senate.[98]

It would seem that Johnson at last had the validation that he had so long craved. He could claim that he had a clear mandate for the poverty program, Medicare, and the other components of the Great Society, some already envisioned and some not yet dreamed of. The election, too, seemed a mandate for patient firmness in foreign policy, a referendum on the policy of containment. All this had been done without a Kennedy on the ticket. As one Republican senator put it: "That damn Lyndon Johnson hasn't just grabbed the middle of the road. He's a bit to the Right of center, as well as a bit to the Left of center. And with Johnson hogging the whole road, Right, Left and center, where the devil can we go except the ditch?"[99] Or as Jim Rowe put it, "How are you going to beat Franklin Delano Hoover?"[100]

CHAPTER 5

LIBERAL NATIONALISM VERSUS THE AMERICAN CREED: THE GREAT SOCIETY FROM SCHOOLROOM TO HOSPITAL

THE INAUGURATION OF LYNDON JOHNSON IN JANUARY 1965 WAS most important, perhaps, as the precipitate for the Great Society, the details of which the president and his advisers had been mulling over since that sunny afternoon the previous May in Ann Arbor when the term was first brandished by LBJ. Two weeks after that Michigan commencement address, Johnson had dispatched Bill Moyers and Richard Goodwin to Cambridge, where at lunch at John Kenneth Galbraith's house they met with some thirty academics from Harvard, the Massachusetts Institute of Technology, and other area institutions. Out of this and subsequent meetings came some fourteen task forces comprising academics, government officials, and prominent citizens, with instructions to recommend policy initiatives in the following fields: transportation, natural resources, education, health, urban problems, pollution of the environment, preservation of natural beauty, intergovernmental fiscal cooperation, efficiency and economy, anti-recession policy, agriculture, civil rights, foreign economic policy, and income maintenance policy. Johnson insisted that the task forces operate in secret so that debate on the issues would not start prematurely in the media and in Congress. He wanted the members to be able, he said, to make recommendations free of political considerations and without regard to cost. When the reports were duly received at the White House on November 10, 1964, White House aides Goodwin, Moyers, Douglass Cater, and Myer Feldman sifted through them to see which were workable from a political and fiscal point of view. "If we had adopted all their ideas," said one bemused assistant, "we would have had to come up with a budget of over $300 billion."[1] There was, for example, $3 billion for a 200-mile-per-hour, tube-encased, rocket-powered railroad line linking Boston to Washington.

Moyers and his team delivered a 1,200-page, sifted-down list of programs to Johnson, who read it during his stay at his Texas ranch in November and December. As he lay in his hammock soaking up the sun, the aides made their presentation. "I thought I was being especially articulate," Moyers recalled, "but when I looked over at the hammock, the President appeared to be asleep. So I stopped speaking, and for five minutes we sat in silence. Then bang, bang, bang, the President spoke—he had obviously heard everything that had been said—and he told us precisely why the recommendation would not work and how it should be repackaged."[2] Some of the programs envisioned for the Great Society such as federal aid to education and Medicare were going to have a price tag—potentially an enormous one—but others, such as a voting rights bill and immigration reform, would not, although their impact on American society promised to be just as great. Johnson was, as usual, in a hurry. "I was just elected president by the biggest popular margin in the history of the country, fifteen million votes," he told his aides. "Just by the natural way people think and because Barry Goldwater scared the hell out of them, I have already lost about two of these fifteen and am probably getting down to thirteen. If I get in any fight with Congress, I will lose another couple of million, and if I have to send any more of our boys into Vietnam, I may be down to eight million by the end of the summer."[3]

The State of the Union address—delivered at night for the first time since 1936—to a joint session of Congress on January 4, 1965, was an inspirational rally in behalf of the Great Society rather than a detailed outline of programs. Not surprisingly, the speech emphasized both change and continuity. The

Great Society would mean a new day for the eight million American children who had never finished the fifth grade and the fifty-four million who had not finished high school, the president declared. It would mean a new day for the millions of elderly Americans who had no health insurance. It would mean a new day for those black Americans so long denied the right to vote.[4] What was envisioned was a fulfillment of dreams dreamed since the Puritans came to the New World. "A President does not shape a new and personal vision of America," he told the senators and representatives, the Supreme Court justices and ambassadorial corps. "He collects it from the scattered hopes of the American past. It existed when the first settlers saw the coast of a new world, and when the first pioneers moved westward. . . . It shall lead us as we enter the third century of the search for 'a more perfect union.'"[5]

Like Populism, Progressivism, and the New Deal, the Great Society would be an attempt to change a status quo that had embedded within it racial discrimination, insensitivity to social and economic injustice, and a self-serving attachment to laissez faire. LBJ would be flying in the face of the American Creed. All of its basic tenets—equality, liberty, individualism, constitutionalism, and democracy—were basically antigovernment and antiauthority in character, calling for the placing of limits on the institutions of government. Individualism stresses freedom from government control, and egalitarianism emphasizes the right of one individual to be free from control by another.[6] Thus could all of those with a vested or emotional interest in the status quo invoke hallowed American principles: segregationists who saw the Great Society as a conspiracy to foist integration on the South, manufacturers who saw the poverty program as a conspiracy to rob America of its cheap labor force, physicians who perceived Medicare as a government plot to prevent them from charging all the traffic would bear, employers who feared having to pay for a national health care system, and Catholic and other faith-based groups that viewed federal aid to education as a scheme to crush parochial schools.

Johnson's stratagem for combating conservatives wielding the American Creed was to clothe his mandate in a dress of consensus—a profoundly conservative word. "'Consensus' is a word designed to conceal," British political commentator Henry Fairlie noted in the *New Republic*. "What it tries to imply is that nothing exceptional is happening: that what has been achieved by precise (possibly new; possibly revolutionary) political methods, has, instead, 'just growed'—out of the goodness of heart, one is left to suppose, of big business and labor, of the cities and the countryside, of rich and poor."[7]

But the Great Society did not just appear; it was not the inevitable product of prosperity. The brilliantly managed economy of France's Fourth Republic had produced only "the rather grand but irrelevant designs of Charles De Gaulle," to quote Fairlie. West Germany's vision as its economy soared was simply more prosperity. The Great Society was the product of complex social forces, history, and circumstance. And suprapartisan consensus notwithstanding, the promised programs of the Great Society dealt with first principles and promised fundamental change. Johnson and the other architects of the Great Society could not tackle the problem of poverty without becoming involved in profound social and moral questions about race, which in turn raised even more questions concerning the nature of republican government and political community. They could not address the problem of education without encountering issues of race and religion, and of the function of public education in a democracy. America's cities were complex entities, also involving matters of race, religion, socioeconomic status, and overlapping political jurisdictions. Daunted though he was at times, LBJ, the newly, overwhelmingly elected popular sovereign, intended to move the nation more quickly and more dramatically down the road of reform and social justice than it had ever been moved before.

IF, AS JOHNSON BELIEVED, HE HAD APPROXIMATELY TWENTY MONTHS to pass Medicare and a voting rights bill, reform the immigration laws, dramatically expand the federal nature conservancy, and do approximately nine hundred other things that had or would come to mind, Congress would have to be a lean, mean, bill-passing machine, not the stifling logjam it had so often been since the halcyon days of the Second New Deal. At first glance, Congress would have seemed to pose little or no problem. The Democrats enjoyed two-to-one majorities in both houses. As soon as the Eighty-Ninth Congress convened, the House Democratic Caucus stripped Representatives John Bell Williams of Mississippi and Albert W. Watson of South Carolina of their seniority rights for failing to vote for the ticket in the presidential election just past. Not since 1911 had a Democratic representative been disciplined for political disloyalty.[8]

Despite his sixteen-million-vote mandate, LBJ insisted that the Great Society was hardly home free. "I've watched the Congress from either the inside or the outside, man and boy, for more than forty years," he remarked shortly after the election, "and I've never seen a Congress that didn't eventually take the measure of the President it was dealing with."[9] And he was right. During the first session of the 89th Congress, during which more than one hundred administration-backed bills passed, the average margin of victory in the House was only 235 to 200. The bulk of the support was provided by 213 Democrats who supported the president at least 70 percent of the time, and 22 Republicans who supported him at least 55 percent of the time. "A shift of a mere 18 votes—just half of the Democrats' net gain in 1964—would have meant the failure of much of the program," Doug Cater later noted.[10]

LBJ realized that if he approached Congress with a mandate on his hip—threatening, talking tough, showing up congressmen and -women and senators—he would get exactly nowhere. In his State of the Union address, Johnson was almost obsequious. "I am proud to be among my colleagues of the Congress whose legacy to their trust is their loyalty to their Nation," he declared.[11] After outlining one proposal, he ad-libbed the words "and I welcome the recommendations and constructive efforts of the Congress." Democratic senator Vance Hartke (D-IN) noted the passage approvingly and observed, "He told us in effect that there was room for difference without difference of principle."[12] Every cabinet department, every agency was to have its own liaison team to work with Congress, the overall effort to be coordinated by Larry O'Brien and his staff.

Johnson insisted that the liaison personnel get to know members as thoroughly as he had during his congressional heyday. And they did. "It's not something that you can put in a computer and get out an answer," said Wilbur Cohen, who headed the Social Security Administration and who was one of the administration's most effective lobbyists. "Every man is different and every woman is different. . . . Again, a man is very different if he's the bottom man of a committee or he's the chairman . . . [if] he wants to run for the United States Senate in five years—he's obviously going to do different things than if he isn't . . . you've got to understand that Wilbur D. Mills comes from a little town of 2,500, which is a small, rural town but he nevertheless is a Harvard Law School graduate."[13] LBJ would court members of Congress, flatter them, drink with them, above all pay attention to them—it was not unusual, for example, during the crucial stages of the battle over a major component of the Great Society, for the president to talk to twenty members in a single day. There was also a subtle warning to the House and Senate in his State of the Union message: "You will soon learn that you are among men whose first love is their country, men who try each day to do as best they can what they believe is right."[14]

In late February, LBJ presided over a meeting of key members of the House and Senate in the State Dining Room. He singled out the effective for praise and chided the recalcitrant. "There was this great range of emotions displayed," D. B. Hardeman recalled, "from near anger to ribald humor, to history—appeals to history; it was a very fascinating intellectual and dramatic display. . . . It was an evening that held you on the edge of your seat."[15] "In some ways," Johnson confided to a friend, "Congress is like a dangerous animal that you're trying to make work for you. You push him a little bit and he may go just as you want but you push him too much and he may balk and turn on you. You've got to sense just how much he'll take and what kind of mood he's in every day. For if you don't have a feel for him, he's liable to turn around and go wild."[16]

The order in which the components of the Great Society were presented to Congress would be extremely important. Federal aid to education, the antipoverty program, voting rights, Medicare, welfare reform, area redevelopment, and aid to urban areas would all be voted on by the same representatives and senators who were politically, emotionally, or ideologically attracted to or repelled by a particular proposal. The task, as Johnson viewed it, was to prevent the coalescing of Republicans and southern Democrats into the force that—acting on the states' rights–private property–individual liberty philosophy of Thomas Jefferson, John C. Calhoun, and Robert Taft—had blocked the advance of social justice throughout the post–World War II period.

Labor constituted an absolutely crucial element of the Great Society coalition. Since the passage of the Taft-Hartley Bill in 1947, an anti–organized labor bill, unions and their lobbyists had been obsessed with securing repeal of Section 14b, the provision authorizing states to pass right-to-work laws that undermined the unions' power to organize and bargain collectively. LBJ told United Auto Workers chief Walter Reuther, however, that if labor insisted on forcing an early congressional showdown on 14b, "that will wreck everything. We oughtta do it but the first thing we ought to try to put through, if we can, is medical care. The second thing is the excise taxes to put a little soup in this economy. The third thing is unemployment insurance. The fourth thing and simultaneously if we can ought to be Appalachia and maybe some ARA [area redevelopment] to end these distressed areas. . . . If we bring that other thing up first that'll drive the South and the Republicans together in an old bloc again."[17] Reuther was persuaded and, during the first year of the Great Society, organized labor worked strenuously for Medicare, voting rights, and area redevelopment while waiting patiently for revision of Taft-Hartley.

A number of the issues LBJ intended to address had been pending before Congress for up to twenty years. The arguments were well known; the lines clearly drawn. It was time to decide. Two crucial reforms were enacted at the outset of the 89th Congress, reforms that heavily greased the legislative wheels. In its first substantive action, the House adopted new criteria for appointment to committees, thus enabling administration supporters to place more liberals on the Appropriations and Ways and Means Committees. "This change means that half the battle of enacting the Johnson program is over," Larry O'Brien exulted.[18] In addition, the House adopted a rule that allowed the speaker to force a bill out of the Rules Committee after twenty-one days. Thus was the reactionary Howard Smith effectively bypassed. The House had the power to send a measure to a House-Senate conference without approval by the Rules Committee.[19] "Mr. [Speaker of the House Sam] Rayburn used to say, 'The body has got to be able to work its will,'" LBJ told John McCormack. "Now, we've got to work our will and you can't work your will when Howard Smith can keep a bill from going to conference. . . . These people in the 44 [sic] states and the District of Columbia didn't vote for Howard Smith. He's an able man . . . but he's representing another century."[20] The results were immediately evident. "So far," *Newsweek* reported the second week in February:

> committee hearings on many major bills have been held with breath-
> taking dispatch. The House Banking Committee held only one day
> of hearings on President Johnson's request to ease the 25 per cent
> gold-cover requirements [legislation that required the Treasury to
> keep on hand in gold one-quarter of the value of paper currency

issued]—and didn't even bother to schedule any time for opposition witnesses. The Senate Public Works Committee held just two days of hearings on the Appalachia bill . . . and in the House Ways and Means Committee Chairman Wilbur Mills, hitherto an unrelenting roadblock for the measure, scheduled closed-door consideration to accelerate the medicare legislation which he has now decided to support.[21]

THE TEXANS WITH WHOM LYNDON JOHNSON GREW UP WORSHIPPED at the shrine of education. The Germans who settled the Hill Country emanated from a culture known for its expertise in science, philosophy, and music. For Rebecca Baines Johnson, education was one of the joys she had shared with her beloved father and the key to her elevated social status, real and imagined, in Johnson City. One of the reasons Lyndon was so rebellious in school, a notorious truant at times, was that his home was a school. Lessons, recitations, discussions of public affairs were never ending. South Central Texas was a breeding ground for teachers; Southwest Texas State, Johnson's alma mater, was a teachers college. "I came from a family that is interested in public life and in education," LBJ told the National Conference on Educational Legislation in 1965. "My mother was a teacher and my father was a teacher. My great grandfather, my mother's grandfather, was the second president of Baylor University when it was located down at Washington on the Brazos."[22] And LBJ himself was a teacher, the only profession he had ever known except politics.

But there was more than the Hill Country's respect for education, more than the American pragmatist's belief that education was the gateway to a better material life for one's self and humankind in general. LBJ was a man who was acutely aware of the vastness of the American republic and the centripetal forces—race, religion, region, class, ideology, national origin—that continually threatened to tear it apart. When nation-states formed in the thirteenth and fourteenth centuries, rulers frequently insisted that subjects take on the religion of their ruler. General education was provided by a church that taught not only godliness but also patriotism. Nationalism, religion, and a unifying education emerged with and reinforced the development of nation-states.

In an extensive republic like the United States, without an established religion and flooded periodically with immigrants, an integrating education system was not important—it was crucial. It was not surprising that the "common school" envisioned and championed by Horace Mann originated during the 1830s and 1840s in the midst of one of these influxes.[23] Systems of public education could not eliminate prejudices, eradicate differences— indeed, racial and ethnic minorities traditionally received unfair, even brutal treatment at the hands of textbook authors who not so subtly held up white Christianity as the ideal—but the teaching of mathematics, science, logic, and rhetoric, which were universal, together with respect for the Constitution, democracy, republicanism, and the other tenets of American political culture would unify and integrate.[24]

Johnson, the democratic nationalist, the prophet of pluralism, shared Mann's faith, stripped of its New England prejudices. Like Senator Robert Taft, LBJ believed that education was the key to achieving the virtuous republic; he voted for federal aid to education in 1949 and supported it at every opportunity thereafter.[25] As president, LBJ was determined to elevate education to one of the fundamental positive rights to which all Americans were entitled. During a "state of education" address in February 1968, Johnson would declare that "on January 6, 1941, President Franklin D. Roosevelt set forth to Congress and the people four essential freedoms for which America stands. . . . Today, wealthier, more powerful, and more able than ever before in our history, our nation can declare another essential freedom—the fifth freedom is freedom from ignorance."[26]

Education gained new prominence in America after World War II as high school completion became the norm, and the GI Bill prompted a dramatic increase in college enrollment. The Warren Court's compelling statement on the importance of equal education opportunities together with the civil rights struggles that followed reinforced the notion that education was the birthright of a free citizenry. *Sputnik* highlighted the importance of quality education to national security. The National Defense Education Act (NDEA) of 1958 provided categorical aid to states to improve math, science, and foreign language instruction in American schools. Yet even as of 1960, national support for education remained small in absolute terms (less than $1 billion) and as a percentage of total education spending (around 2 percent).[27]

A large body of social science research released in the early 1960s—James Conant's *Slums and Suburbs,* for example—documented the terrible education conditions facing poor children and the dire consequences that these conditions held for their life prospects. Nevertheless, political opposition to an expanded federal role in education remained strong. Federal "intrusion" into an area that had traditionally been the preserve of state and local governments and private institutions would take the administration into a political minefield. The issue of federal education pitted Democrat against Republican, liberal against conservative, Catholic against Protestant and Jew, federal power against states' rights, white against black, and rich constituency against poor.[28]

By 1964, elementary and secondary education for both public and parochial students was in a woeful state and getting worse. There was a shortage of teachers, salaries were abysmally low, classrooms overcrowded, many school buildings run-down and dilapidated, and textbooks worn and outmoded. The postwar baby boom had flooded public and private institutions with students that they simply did not have the resources to handle. It was worse in some areas than others—much worse. Mississippi spent $241 per student per year in 1963–1964 compared to New York's $705.[29] Because nearly all monies for public education came from local property taxes and state subsidies—the federal government as of 1964 provided only 3.5 percent of the monies spent on elementary and secondary education—children who grew up in the rural South or Appalachia or in inner-city ghettoes received educations grossly inferior to that of those who were lucky enough to be born and raised in suburbia, the towns and cities of the Midwest, West, and Northeast. "Millions of students," social historian Irving Bernstein wrote, "were denied a proper education because they lived in states too poor to provide one, or in central cities in which the schools were beggared, or suffered from physical or emotional handicaps in localities which offered no or, at best, inadequate special education."[30]

Federal aid to education, championed by both Robert Taft and Harry Truman, had foundered on a number of rocks. Segregationists had fought it tooth and nail, seeing it as a weapon wielded by an overweening federal authority to force integration on the South. Passage of the Civil Rights Act of 1964, however, had undercut opposition to federal aid to education on racial grounds. Title IV authorized the US Office of Education, upon the request of local school boards, to assist in the planning or implementation of racial desegregation policies, and Title VI prohibited racial discrimination in the conduct of federally financed programs.[31] Conservatives like Howard Smith shifted to states' rights, denouncing the concept as an unwarranted interference with local control that would lead to federal dictation of everything from dress to curricula.

But the real sticking point for federal aid to education was religion. Protestants and Jews were enthusiastic supporters of federal aid to education, but only to public school systems. They viewed the constitutional stipulation that "Congress shall make no law respecting an establishment of religion, or prohibiting the free exercise thereof" as sacrosanct. Surely this meant that public funds should not go to support private, faith-based schools. If Catholics, and for that matter fundamentalist Christians and orthodox Jews, wanted to send their children to private schools, let them and their churches pay the extra tariff. Over the years the National Education Association, the powerful teachers union, the National Council of Churches, which included the major Protestant denominations, and the principal Jewish organizations had adamantly opposed federal aid if any was to go to parochial schools.[32] Conversely, Catholics, who operated 85 percent of the nation's parochial schools totaling some five million pupils, insisted that the "free exercise" of religion guaranteed by the Constitution included the right to religious education and that it was unfair for Catholic parents to pay taxes to support schools that their children would not attend. Speaking for the parochial school forces on the federal aid to education issue was the National Catholic Welfare Conference (NCWC).[33]

The Kennedy administration had submitted a federal aid to education bill to Congress that provided funding to public but not private schools under a formula weighted to give disproportionate help to systems in the poorest states and in inner-city ghettoes. As a Catholic, JFK felt he could not afford to champion aid to private institutions. Parochial school forces in the House led by James Delaney, a Catholic congressman from New York, managed to block passage.[34] Thus did it fall to LBJ's task force on education to find a way around the impasse. Leading the charge were John Gardner, a research psychologist and head of the Carnegie Foundation, and Francis Keppel, the dean of Harvard's College of Education whom Kennedy had made commissioner of education.[35] It was obvious to all concerned that there would be no federal aid to education bill if parochial students were not somehow included. Johnson had no compunction at all about including private institutions. He and his family were products of both Southwest Texas (public) and Baylor (private). Nor was he unaware of the growing political power of Catholic voters; church membership had grown to some forty million by 1965, and for the first time Catholics (107) outnumbered Methodists (98) in the House of Representatives.

The key, the task force realized, was to focus on the child and not the institution. In 1947 in *Everson v. Board of Education,* the Supreme Court had approved the use of state funds to provide bus transportation to parochial schoolchildren; the benefit was going to the individual pupil, not the institution, the court ruled. In addition, the education aspects of the poverty bill had focused on the child. Title II of the Equal Opportunity Act provided for "special remedial and other non-curricular educational assistance for the benefit of low-income individuals and families," presumably for both public and parochial school students.[36] In 1965 the Office of Economic Opportunity would offer a community action preschool program called Head Start that would be open to all.

The Elementary and Secondary Education Act (ESEA) that would be introduced into Congress in January 1965 was based on a rather simple formula: the federal government would allocate funds to each state according to the number of children in the state from low-income families (less than $2,000 a year) multiplied by 50 percent of the state's average expenditure per pupil.[37] Title I of the ESEA provided funds to public institutions to help the children of low-income families, but services in these institutions would be available to public and parochial students alike. Title II funded textbooks and library materials that state agencies could distribute to both private and public institutions. Title III would create supplementary education centers to provide physical education, music, languages, advanced science, remedial reading, television equipment, and teaching innovations for both public and private schools.[38] Keppel estimated that private school children would receive between 10.1 and 13.5 percent of the dollars appropriated under ESEA, slightly less than their per capita ratio.[39]

It was time for Johnson the evangelist. "Nothing matters more to the future of our country," he declared. If Congress did not act, of the 30 million boys and girls slated to enter the job force during the forthcoming decade,

2.5 million would never see the inside of a high school, 8 million would never earn a high school diploma, and more than a million qualified to attend college would never go.[40] He envisioned, he said, a doubling of federal spending on education from $4 billion to $8 billion, with $1 billion going to elementary and secondary students. Eric Goldman with Horace Busby was assigned to draft the president's special message to Congress on education.[41]

In his quest to pass a landmark education bill, LBJ was able to count on a number of assets. As noted previously, passage of the 1964 Civil Rights Act had drawn some of the venom from the segregationists. The energy mobilized in behalf of the poverty bill would spill over into the fight for ESEA. It was framed in part as an antipoverty measure, and who could be in favor of poverty? Moreover, some of the anti-Catholic prejudice that had at one time been as strong as anti-Semitism in the United States was waning. There were signs that both public- and private-school advocates were coming to the conclusion that if they did not compromise, the very thing they professed to be serving would continue to deteriorate. That is, Catholics, by demanding equal treatment for parochial schools, were getting no help at all; by insisting on nothing for religious schools, non-Catholics were getting nothing for themselves.

The Elementary and Secondary Education Act was introduced in the House on January 12, 1965, by Carl Perkins (D-KY), chair of the General Education Subcommittee, and in the Senate at the same time by Wayne Morse (D-OR), chair of the Education Subcommittee. The Senate had always been more favorably inclined toward federal aid to education than the House, and so O'Brien, Cater, and their forces concentrated on the lower house. All seemed well when the measure was referred to the House Labor and Education Committee chaired by Adam Clayton Powell of New York. A cleric and a fiery crusader for civil rights, Powell had previously insisted that any federal aid to education measure include a compulsory school desegregation proviso. With passage of the equal accommodations sections of the 1964 Civil Rights Act, there was no longer any need to single out education.

Powell was certainly a supporter of public funding for schools, but he had personal needs that had to be met. A strikingly handsome and charismatic man, Powell was a notorious playboy, taking frequent trips to the Caribbean with one beauty or another. "He headed the Abyssinian Baptist Church, the biggest organization and the largest black church in the country," black journalist-politician Louis Martin remembered. "Adam was absolutely as handsome as a man could be."[42] Such a lifestyle required money, and when the House refused to increase his committee's expense account from $225,000 to $440,000, Powell retired to Puerto Rico and refused to take phone calls. Holding his nose, LBJ lobbied key members of Congress to give the reverend his money.[43] Pointing out that Powell had been key to passage of the poverty bill, Johnson noted that the chair of Labor and Education was like Oklahoma's Democratic senator Robert Kerr—"he always took something out of every pot but he by God put more into it than he took out."[44] His coffers now overflowing, Powell returned from self-imposed exile to lead the charge for the education bill. He announced that the committee would meet all day, every day, including Saturday, until the bill was passed.

Edith Green, the ambitious congresswoman from Oregon, was the fourth-ranking Democrat on Labor and Education and the voice of the National Education Association, an increasingly powerful union and lobby for public school teachers. Green wanted to ensure adequate local control of federal funds appropriated for education and wanted to make certain that the mostly Catholic parochial schools would not financially (and un-constitutionally) benefit from the bill. Above all, she intended to leave her mark on ESEA. A devoted Protestant, she tried to play the religious card but to no avail. The congresswoman was more successful in arguing that under the bill's funding formula, rich states would get richer and poor states proportionately poorer. For example, New Jersey under the administration's proposal would receive $283 per child, and Mississippi $120. Why not give each child found to be impoverished a flat $200? It was more expensive to educate children in the Northeast than in the South, supporters of the mea-sure replied, but Congresswoman Green had equity going for her, and the Republicans adopted her flat rate as their alternative education bill.

Johnson would prove flexible, even malleable, on other pieces of Great Society legislation, but not on federal aid to education. His orders to his troops were to get ESEA through Congress as quickly as possible and with-out changing a comma. To those who would cry that they were being steamrollered, O'Brien and company would say that this historic opportu-nity to establish the principle of federal aid to education was too important to be missed. Faults in the legislation could be corrected in the future.[45] When Adam Powell suggested three courses of action in dealing with Mrs.

Green—strip her of her jurisdiction over vocational education, fire her sister from the staff of the Education and Labor Committee, or exclude her from any future Democratic deliberations on the bill and thus any credit for it, LBJ jokingly suggested "All three."[46] Johnson placed a call to Vice President Humphrey and lashed him to greater effort. "You've got Old Lady Green," he said. "I've had her down here. I've bragged on her. But she is just a mean woman, and she's going to whup you. . . . We just cain't [let the bill be defeated]! We're smarter than they are. We've got more energy. We can work faster. We've got all the machinery of the government."[47] On March 26, 1965, the House passed ESEA by a vote of 263 to 153. Approximately 98 percent of the nonsouthern Democrats, 43 percent of the southern Democrats, and 27 percent of the Republicans in the House voted for the bill.[48]

In the Senate Wayne Morse drove the measure through in a matter of days. He saw to it that there were no amendments, thus obviating the need for a potentially contentious conference committee with the House. There were cries of "railroad" and allusions to the Force Acts of Reconstruction days. Senator Winston Prouty of Vermont declared, "The principal issue facing the nation today is not education. It is the future of the Senate as a co-equal partner in the legislative process." As the final vote was taken, Republican senator Peter H. Dominick of Colorado stood, pounding his desk, and shouted, "I resent the whole procedure." The final count was 73 to 18.[49] All but four Democrats and a majority of Republicans voted for it.[50] In a mere eighty-seven days, Congress had acted on legislation that had been pending for twenty years, establishing a federal-state partnership in one of society's fundamental activities.

LBJ decided to hold the signing ceremony in Texas in front of the one-room schoolhouse at Junction, a mile and a half down the road from the Ranch. He picked the Junction schoolhouse to represent all one-room schoolhouses, an emblem of the original common school system. He chose it because it was a reminder of his own origins and journey; hopefully, in the public perception, Junction School would be to LBJ what the log cabin was to Abraham Lincoln.[51] Back in Washington, he presided over a more formal ceremony attended by a virtual who's who in education and politics. "I will never do anything in my entire life," LBJ said, "now or in the future, that excites me more, or benefits the Nation I serve more, or makes the land and all of its people better and wiser and stronger, or anything that I think means more to freedom and justice in the world than what we have done with this education bill."[52] He quoted Thomas Jefferson: "'Preach, my dear sir, a crusade against ignorance; establish and improve the law for educating the common people.'"[53]

The Elementary and Secondary Education Act was both an antipoverty measure and a civil rights bill. "We decided," LBJ remarked to a group of legislators, "that our first job was to help the schools serving the children from the very lowest income groups. . . . We know that they cannot bear their share of the taxes to help pay for their education. And unless those children get a good education we know that they become dropouts and they become delinquents and they become taxeaters instead of taxpayers."[54]

Everyone was well aware that the overwhelming majority of low-income families were nonwhite. During the remainder of the Johnson administration, the ESEA, coupled with Title VI of the 1964 Civil Rights Act and two federal court rulings, transformed school integration in the South from theory to reality. The Department of Health, Education, and Welfare (HEW) developed annual "Guidelines" for the enforcement of Title VI that imposed specific numerical goals on southern school districts, focusing on the percentage of black children who had to be enrolled in schools with whites. The guidelines presumed that school districts had a legal obligation not merely to stop segregating students but to achieve racial integration in schools.

In *United States v. Jefferson County Board of Education,* in 1967, the US Court of Appeals for the Fifth Circuit, the court with the largest number of school desegregation cases, endorsed the requirements of and the philosophy behind the HEW Guidelines. In a landmark decision handed down by the Supreme Court in 1968—*Green v. County School Board of New Kent County, Virginia*—the court ruled that the ultimate test of compliance with *Brown* was the actual achievement of racial integration in schools.[55] The ESEA provided Title VI enforcers with a big carrot—more than $1.3 billion in federal aid distributed according to a formula weighted to favor chronically distressed areas, which included most of the rural South.[56]

ESEA WAS ONLY THE FIRST OF A TWO-PRONGED ATTACK ON THE NA-
tion's education problems. The second was the Higher Education Act of 1965.

During the New Deal, the federal government had assisted higher education in three direct and two indirect ways: the direct ways were campus construction, work-study aid, and land-grant spending. Campus construction was mostly the handiwork of the Public Works Administration, which built several hundred libraries, dormitories, laboratories, and classrooms. The Federal Emergency Relief Administration launched the student work program, designed to prevent students from dropping out of school and swelling the unemployment rolls. The Department of Agriculture provided millions of dollars to boost the country's land-grant colleges, which enrolled approximately 20 percent of all students during this period.[57]

Roosevelt and Harry Hopkins, his aide and alter ego, both thought that making high culture available to the masses would democratize American life, and Hopkins spent liberally, subsidizing individual artists, dramatists, writers, and musicians. They did not embrace the "Wisconsin idea," however, in which a major university took the lead in intellectual and cultural life. That was not the model in the East. There, cultural workers were largely independent and cultural production largely commercial.[58] During the New Deal, however, academics—particularly in law, history, and the social sciences—were called upon in unprecedented numbers to play a role in policy making and administering. Intellectuals were important in Washington in a way that they had not been since the days of Thomas Jefferson and John Adams. In turn, repelled by the materialism of the Roaring Twenties and then by the failure of capitalism, and flattered by the New Deal's attention, the intelligentsia, including professors, became overwhelmingly liberal and predominantly Democratic for the first time in history.[59] Nevertheless, with the exception of land-grant colleges, Washington played no direct role in higher education, and FDR never demanded one.

The *Brown* decision, specifically, and the civil rights movement, generally, stirred the waters of higher education to a degree, but it was the Cold War that really prompted the nation to see colleges and universities as vital to the country's mission. The primary goal of the post-*Sputnik* education campaign was to increase the number of experts—engineers, scientists, social scientists—which in turn would better enable the United States to compete with the USSR. Johnson was all for this, but he was also very aware of the battle between Marxism-Leninism and liberal capitalism at another level—competition for the loyalty of the Third World. Liberal capitalism had to prove that it was no less a catalyst for economic and social justice than

Marxism–Leninism. This meant that US education policy must stress equity and inclusiveness.

When Johnson assumed the presidency, the nation's twenty-three hundred institutions of higher education were straining to accommodate the children of the World War II generation. Libraries at half of the four-year and 82 percent of the two-year institutions failed to meet minimum standards of books per student. Qualified students from poor families could not afford to apply to college, or if they did and were admitted, they could not stay in school. As of 1960, 78 percent of high school graduates from families with incomes over $12,000 attended college; only 33 percent from families with incomes under $3,000 did so. Twenty-two percent of college students dropped out during their first year; the overriding reason was financial distress. There would be no public–parochial debate during deliberations on the higher education bill. Most of the nation's colleges and universities had begun as private, faith-based entities. In 1960, 41 percent still were. It would make no sense at all to starve one and feed the other when all were bulging at the seams, and the United States was involved in a cold war with the forces of international communism.

The Higher Education Act of 1965 provided funds to colleges and universities to develop education programs focusing on housing, poverty, health, and other public interest areas. It proposed to pump millions of dollars into long-neglected libraries. The heart of the bill, however, included scholarships, reduced-interest loans, and work-study programs to encourage lower-income students to go to college and to enable them to stay there. In addition, any student enrolled full-time in an accredited postsecondary institution would be eligible to borrow without regard to need up to $1,500 per academic year to a limit of $7,500. President Johnson signed the Higher Education Act in the Strahan Gymnasium at Southwest Texas State College in San Marcos on November 8, 1965. "I shall never forget the faces of the boys and girls . . . [at that] little Welhausen Mexican school [where LBJ had practice taught, and served as principal] . . . and the pain of knowing then that college was closed to practically every one of those children because they were too poor," he told those who had assembled.[60]

ESEA and the Higher Education Act did not do all that LBJ had hoped. He viewed the measures as both civil rights and poverty measures. "It's the Negroes," he had exclaimed to Hubert Humphrey. "Now, by God, they can't work in a filling station and put water in a radiator unless they can read and write. Because they've got to go and punch their cash register, and they don't know which one to punch. They've got to take a check, and they don't know which one to cash. They've got to take a credit card, and they can't pull the numbers."[61] But of course federal aid to education did not end poverty, and it did not prove to be the escape route for children born in inner-city ghettoes. The culture of poverty was too complex. The ESEA did not end up helping poor students exclusively or even overwhelmingly. Historian and Great Society critic Allen Matusow quotes a 1977 study showing that nearly two-thirds of the students in programs funded by Title I were not poor; more than half were not even low achievers; and 40 percent were neither poor nor low achieving.[62]

Nevertheless, ESEA was an historic piece of legislation and of monumental importance to the nation. Other than as stratagems to fight poverty and achieve school integration, the ESEA and the Higher Education Act did not make much sense as education policy. They did not address questions of pedagogy, testing, pupil placement, and other issues. But education took its place alongside national defense as an overriding concern of the federal government. And the measures were exemplars of creative federalism. They facilitated desegregation and, most important, led to a general improvement in school buildings, libraries, textbooks, and quality of education in the nation's public and parochial schools. The Higher Education Act helped make America's colleges and universities the envy of the world and its population the most educated in history. By 1970, one out of every four college students in the United States was receiving some form of financial assistance provided by HEA.[63] As of 1993, 36 percent of Americans between the ages of 25 and 64 years held college degrees.[64] In his classic study of federal aid to education, James Sundquist observed that with enactment of ESEA "the national 'concern' for education had become a national 'responsibility.' . . . The question would be, henceforth, not whether the national government should give aid but how much it should give, for what purposes—and with how much federal control."[65]

THE NEXT JEWEL IN THE GREAT SOCIETY DIADEM WOULD BE MEDI-care, a system of health insurance for elderly Americans. Of all the advanced industrial democracies extant in the 1960s, only the United States did not have in place a government program to protect the elderly from the often catastrophic costs of health care. Indeed, Britain, France, Sweden, and Denmark all boasted either a nationalized health system or national health insurance. There were in the United States no federally or state-supported nursing homes, no help for aged Americans afflicted with cancer, diabetes, heart disease, and stroke who did not have private means. In 1934, FDR had suggested including a program of national health insurance in the Social Security Act but had backed off in the face of opposition from the American Medical Association (AMA), which represented the nation's physicians. In 1939, liberal Democrats had sponsored legislation to create a system of national health insurance, but it had gotten nowhere. Harry Truman included plans for a national health insurance program in his Fair Deal, but Robert Taft and the conservative coalition sided with the AMA and private insurance companies, and the man from Missouri was stymied.[66]

Since his New Deal days, Lyndon Johnson had supported the concept of federally subsidized health care for those who could not afford it. During the 1940s, he had championed the Hill-Burton Act, a measure that provided federal funds to the states to aid in the construction of hospitals. He had played a key role during the Eisenhower years in expanding social security benefits for the disabled. In 1959 George Reedy warned his boss that the absence of government-supported health care for the aged was a national disgrace and would only get worse. "In 1900," he noted, "there were three million people in this country over sixty-five. Today, the number is close to fifteen million, and in ten years there will be about twenty-one million. . . . Somehow, the problem must be dramatized in some way so that Americans will know that the problem of the aging amounts to a collective responsibility. America is no longer a nation of simple pioneer folk in which grandmother and grandfather can spend their declining years in a log cabin doing odd jobs and taking care of the grandchildren."[67]

LBJ was innately empathetic with the afflicted, particularly those who were dependent. Memories of his paralyzed and wheelchair-ridden grandmother who had to live with him and his family still haunted him. Arthur Schlesinger Jr. recalled that LBJ, early in his presidency, expressed his passion for Medicare in a particularly Johnsonian way. Complaining about the draft of a speech on his plan for a dental care program, LBJ told his speechwriters:

"That draft of yours is no good. It doesn't have any—what is that intellectual word?—empathy. Empathy—that's what I want. When I give that speech, I want you to make that l'l old lady in the front row—the one without a tooth in her mouth—feel my hand under her skirt."[68]

For Johnson the issue of health care was not just about affordability and access to medical treatment, it was also about fighting disease and disability itself. Johnson was very much a member of the Greatest Generation and shared its cresting optimism. There was no world that could go unexplored, no wrong that could not be righted, no disease that could not be eradicated. LBJ was particularly sympathetic to the need to fund medical research and preventative care. Early in his administration he declared "war" on the major maladies of the day—heart disease, cancer, and strokes. (He had had a heart attack, his grandmother a stroke, and his mother cancer.) In April 1964 he assembled a blue-ribbon commission of medical experts to advise him. At its initial meeting, he declared:

> The point is, we must conquer heart disease, we must conquer can-
> cer, and we must conquer strokes. This Nation and the whole world
> cries out for this victory. I am firmly convinced that the accumulated
> brains and determination of this Commission and of the scientific
> community . . . will, before the end of this decade, come forward
> with some answers and cures that we need so very much. When this
> occurs—not "if" but "when," and I emphasize "when"—we will face
> a new challenge and that will be what to do within our economy to
> adjust ourselves to a life span and work span for the average man or
> woman of 100 years.[69]

In his Special Message to Congress on the Nation's Health, his recommendations included not only Medicare but also a five-year program of project grants to fight the big three. In November 1965 LBJ added tuberculosis, measles, and whooping cough to the list.[70]

LBJ wanted to define health care—as well as education, a healthy diet, and adequate shelter—as basic rights. He once recalled discussing education and the Constitution in a college essay. He received an F. The Constitution said nothing about education—or health care—but they were implied; like trial by jury and freedom of speech, he told an aide, adequate health care ought to be a federal guarantee: "A person who comes into birth in this country ought to have those rights, whatever the price is."[71] In November 1964, on the eve of the election, when a reporter asked if a health insurance bill for the aged would be a priority if he were elected, LBJ replied, "Just top of the list."[72]

In 1961, JFK had asked Wilbur Cohen, longtime administrator of the original Social Security system, then teaching at the University of Michigan, to head his task force on Health and Social Security. In 1951, Cohen had coauthored the first Medicare bill. In 1957, the Eisenhower administration supported a bill for the federal subsidization of private health care plans, but the AMA opposed even that limited step as a sure segue to socialized medicine. Democrats, including Jack Kennedy, had taken up the issue in the 1960 election, and it figured prominently in the Nixon-Kennedy televised debates.

What Cohen and the task force came up with was a scheme of contributory medical insurance for the nearly 14.8 million Americans receiving Old-Age, Survivors and Disability Insurance—OASDI, otherwise known as Social Security. The federally administered benefits were to cover hospital care, skilled nursing home care, and home health care visits. Carefully excluded were doctors' bills. Thus did Cohen and his associates hope to placate the AMA and its private practice membership.

It proved an exercise in futility. Three major obstacles stood in the path of the Kennedy administration's drive to enact a Medicare bill: the AMA, a philosophy of conservatism that was opposed to anything that smacked of "welfare," and Congressman Wilbur Mills (D-AR). To prevent any and all federal subsidization or regulation of the health industry, the AMA had launched the biggest and costliest lobbying campaign ever seen in the United States. Seventy publicists toiled away at the organization's Chicago office, while no less then twenty-three lobbyists patrolled Capitol Hill. The physicians organization spent more than $50 million to defeat the Kennedy Medicare proposal. Eyeing their incomes and profit statements nervously, doctors and insurance executives proclaimed that Medicare would undermine individual initiative and open the door to socialized medicine, another fateful step in the liberal drive to convert America into a welfare state. The third roadblock was Mills, a fiscal conservative and chair of the powerful House Ways and Means Committee. Medicare was still languishing in Congress when LBJ came to the presidency that fateful day in November 1963.

Johnson had long known and respected Wilbur Cohen. He made it clear that he wanted him to stay on as HEW assistant secretary for legislation. In his first State of the Union message in January 1964, LBJ declared, "We must provide hospital insurance for our older citizens financed by every worker and his family under Social Security." A month later he dispatched to Congress a special message on health, with Medicare at the top of the list. Johnson hoped that the Eighty-Eighth would enact the administration's proposal in time for him to bandy it about during the forthcoming presidential election. Prospects for passage in the Senate looked good. The 1962 elections had seen a net loss of six Senate opponents of Medicare and a net gain of twelve supporters. Public opinion polls were showing a two-to-one margin in favor of some type of national medical insurance for the elderly. Many middle-class families had reached the point where they had to choose between proper medical care for aged parents and a college education for children. A quick head count showed that the King-Anderson bill—Medicare—would pass by a vote of 54 to 46. The real cockpit of battle would be the House. And, because King-Anderson was a revenue bill, it had to originate in the lower chamber. Established procedure called for it to be referred to the Ways and Means Committee, the most powerful of the House's standing committees.

Traditionally charged with overseeing tariff and tax matters, the twenty-five-member Ways and Means Committee was one of Congress's so-called control committees. It was expected to look beyond special interests and the constituent concerns of individual congressmen and congresswomen and see to the integrity of the House and its processes. It considered itself a kind of congressional brain trust and relied heavily on the expertise of economists and tax specialists. Heading this formidable body in 1964 was Congressman Wilbur Mills of Kensett, Arkansas. Mills, a stocky man of average height, was noted, like Robert McNamara, for his slicked-back hair and steel-rimmed glasses. Mills was obsessed with maintaining the fiscal integrity of existing government programs, especially Social Security. "In the Social Security field," Wilbur Cohen observed, "Mr. Mills is probably the only man out of the five hundred and thirty five people in Congress who completely understands the actuarial basis of [the system]."[73]

The Arkansan was not opposed to the notion of health care for the aged, but he believed that King-Anderson would bankrupt Social Security.

Existing benefits under Social Security were cash payments funded by pay-roll deductions and employer contributions. They could be predicted and controlled. Under the pending Medicare proposal, Social Security was to pay for medical services the cost of which could neither be predicted nor controlled. Experts told Mills that the most workers would agree to have withheld from their paychecks without rebelling was 10 percent. Mills could see King-Anderson producing costs that would spin out of control.[74]

"He's certainly in the Medicare ball park," Larry O'Brien reported to LBJ in May 1964, "[but] he's feeling his way along very slowly and carefully and he's manipulating and maneuvering . . . he isn't pinning anything down that can't be unwound."[75] Johnson chose not to run over the Arkansan; in-deed, he saw his support for Medicare as essential. "If you can get something you can possibly live with," he told Mills, "and defend that these people will not kick over the bucket with, it'll mean more than all the bills we've passed put together and it'll mean more to posterity and to you and to me."[76]

Throughout 1964 Wilbur Cohen barely left Mills's side. He read the transcripts of the chairman's speeches, quipped Cohen's biographer, "the way that Sinologists studied statements from Mao."[77] Despite their excel-lent working relationship, Mills and Cohen were not able to put together a satisfactory Medicare compromise before the election. A bill providing for federal subsidies to private insurers (Kerr-Mills) was still on the table, and conservatives were not yet willing to abandon it. "The Wilbur Mills situation has deteriorated totally," O'Brien reported to Johnson in the late summer. "He said he just can't put this thing together. He is suggesting just reporting out a social security bill in the morning with just an increase in benefits."[78] LBJ was tempted to force a vote on King-Anderson—"I'd be prepared to have nothing rather than not have Medicare," he told O'Brien—but then thought better of it.[79] "Now they've [Republicans and the AMA] got us screwed on Medicare," he told Congressman Carl Albert (D-OK). "We're screwed good."[80]

Then came the election of 1964, with LBJ's sweeping mandate and the additions to the already large Democratic majority in the House. More-over, three anti-Medicare Republicans on Ways and Means went down to defeat. The morning following the election, Mills informed reporters that he "would be receptive to a Medicare proposal in the upcoming session."[81] Desperate, the AMA backed an expanded Kerr-Mills bill, which it dubbed

Eldercare, that would allow persons over sixty-five years to purchase Blue Cross/Blue Shield or commercial insurance and pay all or none of the cost, depending on their income. The cost would be borne by the states and the federal government.

Then, on February 4, 1965, Republican John Byrnes introduced "Bettercare," a plan that would cover hospital and doctor bills as well as selected patient services; the government would pay two-thirds of the cost from the general fund, and the remainder would be covered by premium payments scaled to income. To Wilbur Cohen's horror, Mills told Byrnes that he liked the idea behind Bettercare. But unbeknownst to Cohen and the White House, the chair viewed the GOP plan as a supplement to King-Anderson, not an alternative to it.[82] Mills then proposed what he called a "three-layer cake." The bottom layer would be an expanded Kerr-Mills plan to take comprehensive care of those without means. Medicare or King-Anderson would be the middle layer, providing hospital care for those covered by Social Security. Topping the confection would be Bettercare, a voluntary system to cover doctor bills. Cohen was stunned, delighted. No sooner had Mills made his proposal than everyone in the committee room knew "that it was all over," said one committee member. "The rest would be details. In thirty seconds, a $2 billion bill was launched, and the greatest departure in the social security laws in thirty years was brought about."[83] The subsequent "debate" in the House lasted one day. When Mills stepped to the podium to present his plan, he received a standing ovation from both sides of the aisle.[84] The House passed the three-layer cake by a vote of 313 to 115.

The votes for passage in the Senate were clearly there, but the existence of a majority in that chamber had never assured a bill's success. Its procedures were set up to protect the rights of the minority, and during the Johnson presidency the chief protector was Harry Byrd, chair of the Senate Finance Committee. True to his small-government, pro-business philosophy, the Virginian was an archenemy of Medicare.

On the morning of March 26, after Mills's committee had voted out the Social Security Amendments Act of 1965, LBJ summoned the congressional leadership of both houses to the White House for a discussion of the measure. Unknown to his guests, Johnson had arranged for television coverage of the White House–Congressional summit. Before the cameras, LBJ praised Mills and his three-layer cake and then turned to the venerable

Byrd: "Senator Byrd, would you care to make an observation?" Startled, the chair of the finance committee said he had not studied the measure but was prepared to hold hearings on it. "And you have nothing that you know of that would prevent that coming about in reasonable time?" "No," said Byrd quietly. "So when the House acts and it is referred to the Senate Finance Committee, you will arrange for prompt hearings?" "Yes," Byrd replied, even more quietly.[85] As he was leaving, the Virginian observed wryly to reporters that if he had known he was going to be on television, he would have dressed more formally.[86]

Byrd was as good as his word. Hearings proceeded without a hitch, and on July 9 the Senate approved the amendments to the Social Security Act of 1965 creating Medicare by a vote of 68 to 21.[87] "Biggest Change since the New Deal," trumpeted a *Newsweek* headline.[88] Johnson was ecstatic. "[This] gives your boys [in Congress] something to run on if you'll just put out that propaganda," he chortled to Larry O'Brien. " . . . That they've done more than they did in Roosevelt's Hundred Days."[89]

There was one final hurdle to be cleared. Political intelligence had it that the members of the AMA might refuse to participate in Medicare and Medicaid. The Ohio Medical Association, representing ten thousand physicians, had already adopted a resolution to boycott the new programs. When subsequently some twenty-five thousand doctors gathered in New York City on June 20 for the AMA convention, the group's House of Delegates directed its officers to meet with the president to discuss implementation of the legislation. When AFL-CIO president George Meany called to express his concern about the AMA, Johnson said, "George, have you ever fed chickens?" "No," Meany answered. "Well," the president said, "chickens are real dumb. They eat and eat and eat and never stop. Why they start shitting at the same time they're eating, and before you know it, they're knee-deep in their own shit. Well, the AMA's the same. They've been eating and eating nonstop and now they're knee-deep in their own shit and everybody knows it. They won't be able to stop anything."[90]

On June 29, the AMA leadership assembled in the West Wing and was promptly given a large dose of the Johnson treatment. LBJ began by saying what wonderful people doctors were, recalling how the local physician in Johnson City had made numerous house calls to treat his ailing father. He stood and stretched; they stood. He sat. They sat. LBJ then delivered a moving statement about "this great nation and its obligation to those who had helped make it great and who were now old and sick and helpless through no fault of their own." He stood again. They stood. He sat, and they followed suit, now perfectly clear as to the prerogatives of the office that LBJ held.[91]

Suddenly, Johnson brought up Vietnam. Would the AMA help in arranging for physician volunteers to serve for short periods in that country to help the civilian population gain a modicum of health? "Your country needs your help. Your President needs your help." In unison the AMA officials said they would be glad to create a volunteer program for Vietnam. "Get the press in here," Johnson shouted to a lieutenant. To the journalists, the president announced the AMA's commitment to help in Vietnam and praised their patriotism. One of the reporters asked if the AMA was going to boycott Medicare. Johnson piped up with mock indignity: "These men are going to get doctors to go to Vietnam where they might be killed. Medicare is the law of the land. Of course, they'll support the law of the land. Tell him," LBJ said, turning to the head of the delegation. That worthy nodded, "We are, after all, law-abiding citizens, and we have every intention of obeying the new law." A few weeks later the AMA announced its intention to support Medicare.[92]

THE SOCIAL SECURITY AMENDMENTS OF 1965, AS THE THREE-LAYER cake was officially dubbed, introduced health insurance, both hospital and medical, for the aged. Under Part A, present and future recipients of old-age pensions would be automatically covered by hospital insurance at age sixty-five. There would be ninety days of care for each illness, with the patient paying a $40 deductible for sixty days and $10 a day thereafter. Funding would come from payroll deductions and employer contributions beginning at the combined Social Security rate of 7 percent in 1966 and rising to 11 percent in 1973–1975 on the first $6,600 of annual earnings. The new legislation established, in addition, a system of voluntary medical insurance available to anyone sixty-five years or older, with the individual paying $3 a month and the Treasury $3 a month into a Medical Insurance Trust Fund, Part B. Together these two provisions would become known as Medicare.[93] Finally, a provision based on the Kerr-Mills concept would provide medical care to the needy of all ages, including those who were blind or disabled and families with dependent children. States would administer the program with federal matching funds ranging from 55 to 83 percent. This layer of the Mills-Cohen-Johnson confection came to be known as Medicaid.[94]

With much pomp and circumstance, LBJ signed the Social Security Amendments of 1965 into law on July 30, 1965, at the Truman Presidential Library in Independence, Missouri. Some of Johnson's advisers had warned against associating the bill with the former president because Truman had wanted a program that reached everyone, regardless of age or financial condition. During the debate over Medicare, conservatives and the AMA had continually expressed two fears. One was that the program was only a way station on the road to national health insurance; the other was that the passage of Medicare would provide an opening through which the federal government could regulate the practice of medicine. Supporters of the act repeatedly assured naysayers that Medicare, once passed, would not become the basis for a national health insurance program—the dreaded "socialized medicine." "The problem of the aged is a unique problem," declared Robert Ball, the Social Security Commissioner. "The younger members of the population do not have the same problem."[95] None of the principal players in the Johnson administration saw their job as challenging hospitals or the medical profession to do a better job; rather, they wished to encourage these institutions to serve a new target group, the elderly.

The struggle to persuade Congress to enact the legislation creating Medicare and Medicaid was just half the battle. Medicare was so massive and complex that Johnson feared it might never get off the ground. He told his HEW secretary, "If you miscalculate [concerning the bureaucratic effort required to launch Medicare], we're both going to look like the worst kind of damn fools."[96] Some in the medical community were still bitter and unreconciled, and there was the looming problem of segregated southern hospitals.

The White House worried that during the first days of Medicare's operation, in July 1966, the elderly would overwhelm the hospitals with their pent-up demands for medical services. President Johnson asked the Social Security Administration to identify hospitals likely to come under siege, and he instructed the Army and the Veterans Administration to stand at the ready with helicopters in case patients needed to be shifted from overcrowded hospitals to those with empty beds. Medicare's launch came off without a hitch, however, and the airlift proved unnecessary.[97] "The application of Medicare to twenty million people on July 1 was perhaps the biggest single governmental operation since D-Day in Europe during World War II," Wilbur Cohen subsequently observed.[98]

Part B of Medicare was voluntary, but for it to be fiscally viable, the vast majority of citizens who signed up for Part A would have to opt for the Part B coverage as well. Administrators were required to obtain a pledge one way or the other from every Medicare beneficiary. The government conducted a massive outreach program that included even sending Forest Service rangers into remote wilderness areas in search of hermits and getting their Part B declarations.[99]

As was true of many of the Great Society programs, Medicare had a civil rights component. In those hospitals and doctor's offices that participated, "colored" and "white" signs disappeared from waiting rooms, restrooms, and water fountains, but that did not mean an end to discrimination. Presidential adviser Harry McPherson remembered that in the days following passage of the act, the White House was deluged with letters and telegrams from outraged southerners. Noting that federal law required hospitals and clinics not to discriminate and to desegregate in order to receive federal funds, one correspondent told the president, "And they won't Lyndon. You know that. Do you want to be responsible for closing the St. Francis Hospital in Biloxi, Mississippi? That's what will happen if you put this thing into effect. . . . Doctors won't treat the coloreds, and the nurses won't treat them." It was a great gamble, McPherson recalled. "Whatever he decided," he said of the president, "thousands of people, either the elderly or the blacks, might have been deprived of hospitalization. It was an excruciating decision to make, but he made it. Comply. And they did."[100]

The legislation creating Medicare required the government to certify hospitals for participation. Among other things, this meant that they could not segregate their patients and had to admit black doctors. The Social Security Administration issued a stern warning to medical care facilities in the South, and the Public Health Service dispatched a thousand inspectors to Dixie to ensure compliance by conducting onsite inspections of hospitals suspected of discriminating. In one facility in Louisiana, members of the team were dismayed to see that blood was labeled "black" or "white." At the nursery at the same hospital they found black babies alongside white ones but subsequently learned from one of the nurses that integration had been quickly arranged after someone had come into the nursery to warn that "the feds" were coming.[101] About sixty-nine hundred hospitals complied immediately, and another fifty-five hundred did so after visits from the inspectors. By October 1966, the number of segregated medical facilities in the South had dwindled to twelve.[102]

By early May 1966, 16.8 million—88 percent of those eligible—had voluntarily enrolled for medical insurance. Over 90 percent of the nation's accredited hospitals and more than 80 percent of the nonaccredited had applied for participation in the program. In the years that followed, Medicare and Medicaid transformed the lives of millions of American families. The impoverished elderly and dependents no longer had to go without health care; middle-class families no longer had to choose between college for their children and proper medical care for their grandparents. But Wilbur Mills had been right to be worried. There were no effective controls on costs. Hospitals and physicians were entitled to be reimbursed for reasonable costs, which were whatever hospitals and physicians said they were. In 1967 a new theme appeared in President Johnson's messages to Congress on health; costs were rising in a disturbing and, if left unchecked, potentially disastrous manner. Total Medicare expenditures amounted to $3.5 billion in the first year of the program; by 1993 total costs had risen to $144 billion, and Americans were spending approximately 15 percent of the gross national income on health care.[103]

CHAPTER 6

MARCH TO FREEDOM: SELMA AND THE VOTING RIGHTS ACT

THE CAMPAIGNS FOR REFORM IN EDUCATION AND HEALTH CARE unfolded in the midst of the ongoing struggle by black Americans to gain the franchise in the South. The *Brown* decision of 1954 had opened the door to school integration, and the Civil Rights Act of 1964 had outlawed Jim Crow in parks, theaters, hotels, and public transportation, but in seven southern states—Alabama, Georgia, Louisiana, Mississippi, South Carolina, and Virginia—the vast majority of blacks could not vote.[1] During the Freedom Summer of 1964, the Council of Federated Organizations (COFO) and SNCC had established freedom schools in Mississippi to build support for the Mississippi Freedom Democratic Party. More than eighty thousand black Mississippians had voted for the MFDP delegation that traveled to Atlantic City to attend the Democratic National Convention. But that political process had taken place outside the regular voting mechanism, still dominated by the white power structure and still closed to African Americans.[2] In Mississippi and Alabama, only 6 and 19 percent, respectively, of voting-age blacks were on the rolls.[3] In some counties in those two states in which the majority of residents were black, not a single one was registered to vote. White registrars in league with local sheriffs used the poll tax and literacy tests to discourage black voting, but if these did not suffice, those seeking to exercise the franchise could be fired from their jobs, arrested on trumped-up charges, or simply beaten up.

Given his philosophy and experience, LBJ believed that the vote was everything. In a series of remarkable conversations with NAACP head Roy Wilkins, Johnson spelled out his faith in democracy. Their only hope for African Americans, LBJ told the civil rights leader, was to get behind the movement for mass enfranchisement and registration for poor whites as well as blacks. "I know you get disheartened," he told Wilkins:

> and I do, and you think that there is no use trying to get an illiterate [white] truck driver and tell him what is best for him because he has been mistreated—and how he will not cooperate and so forth. I feel that way every day. . . . [But] this old farmer that rides looking at the back end of the mule on the cultivator all day long—he just sits there and thinks. It is his boy that is in Viet Nam, his sister that is out of a job, his brother-in-law that got his car repossessed—and somehow or other, they just add up and they will do what is right. . . . I will resign my office twelve months from now if I am not right, you will see the people [blacks] come into power in every southern state if you will let them vote. . . . Everyone of these states that you consider the worst ones in the Union will wind up being the best.[4]

Enfranchisement was the path to power and self-realization in more senses than one, the president told Wilkins in another conversation. "We cannot register them from Washington," Johnson said. "Now the only ones that can register them [that is, persuade southern blacks to register] are the Negroes themselves. . . . It is your patriotic duty—just like going to fight in Vietnam."[5] In his January 1965 State of the Union address, the president informed lawmakers that he was going to press for the elimination of "every remaining obstacle to the right and the opportunity to vote." Privately, he asked Nicholas Katzenbach, the acting attorney general, to draft legislation that would enforce the constitutionally mandated right of every adult American to cast the ballot.[6]

WORKING CLOSELY WITH LBJ IN THE EFFORT TO SECURE THE FRAN-
chise for black Americans was Martin Luther King. From the beginning,
their alliance was an uneasy one. Throughout his political career, LBJ had
preferred to deal with black leaders such as A. Philip Randolph, Roy Wilkins,
Whitney Young, and even Adam Clayton Powell.[7] They were people from
the world of politics, or they were associated with interest groups that sought
protection and power in the political arena. Johnson had leverage with them;
they were subject to deal making and compromise. They seemed willing to
trust his superb sense of political timing and his prioritizing. Not so King.
The head of the SCLC was both an intellectual and a spiritual leader. His
and Johnson's values were similar, but they relied on dramatically different
means for putting those values into action. Like William Lloyd Garrison, the
famed abolitionist, Martin Luther King lived in the tension between conscience and law. Practitioners of civil disobedience assume that conscience
must obey not statutory or constitutional law but a higher moral law.[8]

In the South, King and his associates realized that the law was the bulwark
of injustice and thus morally invalid in many cases. Consequently, King deliberately flouted the law and went to jail, and he encouraged others, including children, to do the same. Johnson valued the parliamentary process, the
orderly working of democracy, as much as the social justice that the system
was supposed to produce. He believed in this sense that means and ends
were inseparable. Demonstrations, deliberate flouting of the law, the politics
of confrontation—all of which King and the SCLC practiced—made LBJ
extremely uncomfortable. "I don't look for any overwhelming crisis on the
part of the white people," Richard Russell told Johnson a week after the
1964 presidential election. "I don't know how much some of your extreme
colored brethren are going to kick up. If they go to raisin' cane, of course,
it will cause trouble."[9] Confrontation could easily spiral out of control into
violence, black rage, white backlash, and even, ultimately, racial war. At the
same time, LBJ understood the political value of demonstrations and sit-ins;
he realized that they created the energy necessary for reform. Moreover, he
recognized that the laws that the white power structure in the South were
trying to enforce were often in violation of the Constitution.

Then there was the religious dimension. King was first and foremost a
Christian minister, a preacher, a spiritual leader. As a mass movement, the

Second Reconstruction was in no small part an evangelical religious phenomenon. Johnson appreciated the validity of prophets and preachers, but the world in which they lived was alien to him. Out of faith and an experience of the divine came social values, and it was proper at times to invoke religion in behalf of social justice as part of the rhetoric of politics, but Johnson feared a world in which religion transcended law and politics. In this he was not unlike other liberals of his day. The Schlesingers, Galbraiths, and Lippmanns were ambivalent about civil disobedience and social action through faith and testimony. Liberals felt most at home in the orderly world of courts and laws, of science and universities; the nonviolence practiced by King and his followers was rooted in the southern black evangelical church, with all its fervent spirituality and emotion.[10]

For his part, King understood and appreciated Johnson, but unlike Wilkins and Young, insisted on holding him at arm's length. In his recorded conversations with the president, King is cordial but formal and restrained. If the civil rights game had been played solely by Lyndon Johnson's rules, King believed, the Second Reconstruction would have died aborning.

Johnson met with King on December 3, 1963. The civil rights leader briefed reporters afterward, and the president was pleased except for one thing. King had told the media that he had made clear to LBJ that "we will have demonstrations until the injustices that have caused them are eliminated." Johnson thought that King had nodded in agreement to his request for a cessation of marches and sit-ins, which had been curtailed for thirty days during the official mourning period for JFK. Assuring King that the civil rights bill then pending in Congress had the White House's full support, LBJ had urged the SCLC chief to concentrate on registering voters and lobbying Congress. According to Lee White, Johnson's aide for civil rights, who had attended the meeting, the incident raised doubts about King's reliability.[11]

But each man needed the other. Without their tacit alliance, the Second Reconstruction would have wilted on the vine. The two men shared a common goal and tended to attract similar friends and like-minded enemies. Both King and Johnson were caught up in a youth movement that they struggled to control. At the founding of SNCC at Shaw University in Raleigh, North Carolina, in April 1960, Ella Baker, an activist and organizer who had advised King during the Montgomery Bus Boycott, urged the students to maintain their independence. She believed that King and the other SCLC ministers were too authoritarian, that they spent too little time helping poor blacks organize at the grassroots level.[12] The signers of the 1962 Port Huron Statement would later accuse LBJ of being an elitist liberal out of tune with the times and out of touch with the poor, the young, the disinherited of the earth.

The relationship between King and Johnson was further complicated by the machinations of FBI director J. Edgar Hoover. The director was obsessively protective of the reputation of the bureau. The first time Martin Luther King's name came across his desk was on an SCLC memo to the incoming Kennedy administration, pointing out that the FBI was one of those federal agencies with virtually no black employees other than janitors and maids. As such, it was much in need of integrating. Hoover, who thought blacks unworthy of the bureau anyway, was indignant. Then, in 1962, when asked why he thought the FBI had not arrested whites who had openly assaulted nonviolent protesters in Albany, Georgia, King had speculated that the local FBI agents were white southerners who were culturally and emotionally linked to local racists.[13] In August 1963, the FBI labeled King "the most dangerous Negro to the future of this nation," and Hoover persuaded Attorney General Robert Kennedy to authorize wiretaps of King's home and his SCLC offices in Atlanta and New York.[14] As noted earlier, since coming to Washington, Johnson had carefully cultivated Hoover. He was obviously a powerful man and a dangerous enemy. During LBJ's vice presidency, the director was not a problem LBJ had to confront directly. When LBJ became president, that changed.

In December 1963, the FBI began delivering massive amounts of raw data to the White House on a variety of subjects. Hoover thought the information might be "of interest" to the new president. These were the famous "raw files," consisting of uncorroborated secondhand information and excerpts from wiretaps that, though spun by the bureau, still provided valuable political intelligence. These reports went sometimes directly to LBJ and sometimes to Bill Moyers or Walter Jenkins; they were kept in a safe tended by Mildred Stegall, Jenkins's secretary. Among the communications were special memos signed by Hoover himself designed to portray Martin Luther King as dangerously unstable and a tool of communists who had allegedly infiltrated the civil rights movement. Every communication ended with a paragraph listing the "communist credentials" of King's top aides. A March 9, 1964, letter was typical: "As of July, 1963, [Stanley] Levinson [adviser and fund-raiser for King] was a secret member of the Communist party, USA. [Clarence] Jones [another King aide] has been identified as a person in a position of leadership in the Labor Youth League . . . designated as subversive pursuant to Executive Order 10450. . . . [Bayard] Rustin has admitted joining the Young Communist League in 1936."[15]

As he turned to confront the ongoing issue of racial justice during the first weeks of his presidency—the most compelling and potentially divisive issue facing America—Johnson was chilled by the knowledge that Hoover and the FBI were waiting in the wings, ready to provide segregationist senators and congressmen with intelligence, real or manufactured, that the Second Reconstruction was nothing more than a Trojan horse for the Communist International and that Martin Luther King was nothing less than a stooge of the Kremlin. Matters were further complicated by the fact that the Justice Department had to rely almost entirely on the bureau to investigate civil rights crimes and gather the evidence necessary to bring the guilty to justice. In its criticism of the bureau, an increasingly outraged black leadership might push Hoover into open alliance with Senators Russell and Eastland. Conversely, if the federal government did not legislate equality and protection for black Americans and then protect them in the exercise of those rights, it would deliver the movement into the hands of extremists. The line he would have to walk, LBJ perceived, was fine indeed.

Then, in early 1964, the FBI's campaign against King reached a new low. On the night of January 6, agents with the cooperation of the management of the Willard Hotel in Washington installed bugs in King's suite. Following a day of business, the civil rights leader and several of his assistants returned to the hotel room. At least two women were already there. The FBI recording machines picked up the sounds of clinking glasses and cocktail party conversation. As the hours passed the gathering became livelier, eventually resulting in group sex. At one point King's voice could be heard above the others: "I'm not a Negro tonight!"[16] Upon hearing the tapes Hoover was both appalled and ecstatic. "King is a 'tom cat' with obsessive, degenerate sexual urges," the director wrote in a memo. He decided to do everything possible to discredit King and destroy him as America's preeminent civil rights leader. In February, FBI Deputy Director Deke DeLoach delivered the FBI's voluminous file on King and his associates to the White House, proving in the FBI's collective mind that the civil rights leader was a sexual pervert and communist dupe. DeLoach warned that if the contents of the files became public, they could derail the 1964 Civil Rights Act then pending in Congress.

Johnson was shocked that King would commit the indiscretions recorded at the Willard. But LBJ was hardly one to hold nonmonogamous activity against another man. When a friend urged King to be more circumspect, he replied, "I'm away from home twenty-five to twenty seven days a month. Fucking's a form of anxiety reduction."[17] Morality wasn't as much the issue as the potential damage to the movement. When Whitney Young heard a rumor of the existence of the King sex tapes and pictures, he went directly to Johnson to ask whether it was true. The president said, "Yes, it's true." Young asked to see some of the evidence, and LBJ obliged. Appalled, the civil rights leader remarked to Johnson, "This is terrible. You've got to do something. What are you going to do about it?"—meaning, what was the president going to do about reining in the FBI. Johnson replied, "Well, what are you going to do about it? You're the civil rights leader!"—meaning, what was Young going to do to force King to be more discreet.[18]

According to Hoover, on November 27, 1964, Wilkins called at the FBI and spoke with Deke DeLoach. "Wilkins said that personally he would not mind seeing King ruined," the director reported to President Johnson, "but he felt that while King was no good, the ruination of King would spell the downfall of the entire civil rights movement. Wilkins stated that he personally knew King was a liar and had little respect for him."[19] But there was a silver lining. Johnson did not want King ruined and the civil rights movement discredited, but given King's penchant for independence, White House knowledge of his illicit sexual activities might come in handy.

As befitting his role as a minister of God, King asked to smoke the peace pipe with Hoover. After some prodding from the White House, the director accepted, and the two men had a polite if formal encounter at FBI headquarters. King apologized for remarks attributed to him criticizing the bureau, and he told Hoover that as a Christian he could never accept communism.[20] Hoover appeared mollified, but on that very day he sent to the White House a thirteen-page FBI report titled "Communism and the Negro Movement." It provided detailed descriptions of King's "personal debauchery" and repeated accusations that he knowingly associated with Communists. "Your advice is requested," Hoover asked Johnson, "as to whether we should disseminate this document to responsible figures in the executive branch of government."

After consulting with the president, Moyers, who had replaced the disgraced Jenkins as liaison with the FBI, told Deke DeLoach that the director should use his own judgment about sending out the report.[21] If he did not at least seem to go along with the director's vendetta against King, the president reasoned, Hoover could turn on him. Among other things, the director could threaten to make public Johnson's orders to the FBI to spy on the MFDP and Bobby Kennedy at Atlantic City. LBJ had already decided to keep Hoover on beyond the mandatory retirement age, commenting famously to aides that he would rather have him "inside the tent pissing out, than outside pissing in." Then there was the president's ongoing ambivalence about King—his stubborn refusal to bend to the presidential will; in addition, Johnson believed that King and other civil rights leaders were never willing to give him the credit he deserved. Finally, Johnson had lived through the McCarthy era and was as afraid as any other Democrat of being labeled "soft on communism."

In October it was announced that Martin Luther King had been awarded the Nobel Peace Prize. On December 18, 1964, the Johnsons (rather reluctantly on LBJ's part; the president was jealous) had welcomed Martin and Coretta King to the White House following their return from the festivities in Oslo. In his acceptance speech, King had declared, "All that I have said boils down to the point of affirming that mankind's survival is dependent upon man's ability to solve the problems of racial injustice, poverty and war." LBJ could not have put it more succinctly. But in separate remarks, the civil rights leader had also called for a US boycott of South Africa, linked apartheid in South Africa with Jim Crow in Mississippi, and, after charges were dismissed against three white men accused in the Cheney-Schwerner-Goodman murders, called for an economic boycott of Mississippi. In private conversation, LBJ had questioned the wisdom of such statements.[22]

During their post-Nobel tête-à-tête, King informed the president that he would soon be launching a massive voting rights campaign in Alabama; his goal was to demonstrate that blacks could not register to vote in the former Confederacy without federal legislation. "Martin, you are right about that,"

Johnson replied. "I'm going to do it eventually, but I can't get voting rights through in this session of Congress. . . . Now, there's some other bills that I have here that I want to get through in my Great Society program, and I think in the long run they'll help Negroes more, as much as a voting rights bill. And let's get those through and then the other." King reminded the president of his oft-stated belief in the fundamental importance of participation in the political process by all citizens. Johnson responded, "I can't get it [a voting rights bill] through, because I need the votes of the southern bloc to get these other things through. And if I present a voting rights bill, they will block the whole program." The SCLC chief had the last word, however. The campaign for voting rights legislation would begin in Selma on January 2. "We'll just have to do the best we can," he said as he took his leave.[23]

Johnson's reluctance to move at once on a voting rights bill was somewhat puzzling. King was right about the president's belief in the primacy of the franchise. Perhaps he was, as usual, worried about losing control. But there was also the fact that voting qualifications had long been within the purview of states and localities. As a conversation he had with Nicholas Katzenbach at about the same time he was meeting with King indicated, Johnson was conflicted. "I basically believe that we can have a simple, effective method of gettin' 'em registered," Johnson told the attorney general (Katzenbach had succeeded Robert Kennedy). "Now, if the state laws are too high and they disqualify a bunch of them, maybe we can go into the Supreme Court and get them held unconstitutional. . . . If the [local] registrars make them stand in line too long, maybe we can work that out where the [US] postmasters can do it. Let's find some way." When Katzenbach suggested that it would take a constitutional amendment to establish federal government control over voter registration, the president replied, "If you think we ought to have a constitutional amendment on voting, let's have it."[24]

On the appointed day in Selma, King addressed a cheering crowd of several hundred: "Today marks the beginning of a determined, organized, mobilized campaign to get the right to vote everywhere in Alabama," he proclaimed. "If we are refused, we will appeal to Governor George Wallace. If he refuses to listen, we will appeal to the legislature. If they don't listen, we will appeal to the conscience of the Congress. . . . We must be ready to march. We must be ready to go to jail by the thousands. . . . Our cry to the state of Alabama is a simple one. Give us the ballot!"[25] What King wanted was an ironclad national voting rights bill. So did LBJ, but he was not sure it could or should be done in 1965.

LBJ continued to see himself as the hope of the white South, the unenlightened as well as the enlightened. "We've got to have some understanding," he told Ed Clark, an old Austin friend whose son was a white liberal then living in the Deep South. "We've got to have some leadership; we've got to have some sympathy; we've got to have some kindness. I called them in South Carolina . . . yesterday and Georgia and told them that as long as I was in the White House the door would be open to them and they would be treated with respect." But in the end they would come around, he said. Again, LBJ saw himself as redeemer of all of the South, not just the black South. "Lincoln went back to Springfield," he observed after his victory in the 1964 election:

> . . . after he was president and he went down the street of the town wherever he had lived his life. He said there was not one person in it who would speak to him, not one . . . it made him mighty proud that he'd done what he'd done and he was mighty sorry for those folks. . . . We've got to educate 'em [white southerners] and you can't be putting 'em off by themselves. . . . The first thing that happens the sociologists say is that . . . you develop an inferiority complex and the rest of your life you're hitting at people when you think they're going to strike you even when they're not.[26]

Indeed, it may have been that domestically, LBJ's greatest impact was on white southerners. "I ran for governor in 1958," Buford Ellington recalled, "and was elected on an anti–civil rights stand here in Tennessee, because I just couldn't bring it to my mind that anybody had any business telling us what we had to do in our state. Yet in less than two years I was traveling the country for this man, trying to help him in his fight to bring it about."[27]

Martin Luther King, too, was interested in redeeming the white South, but he was determined to do it sooner rather than later and even if the recipients of his beneficence had to be dragged kicking and screaming to grace. Montgomery civil rights leader Reverend James Bevel was named to head a statewide voting rights campaign that would begin in Selma. Large numbers of blacks would appear at the courthouse on registration days, and there would be marches and demonstrations until all were registered. Selma, a city of some twenty-nine thousand, was still entirely segregated as of 1965. The *Brown* decision and the 1964 Civil Rights Act seemed to have made no impression at all. Parks, restaurants, schools, water fountains, public toilets—all were segregated.

In Dallas County, of which Selma was the county seat, there were 14,400 whites and 15,115 blacks of voting age. Exactly 156 of the latter, or 1 percent, were registered. Chief enforcer of Jim Crow in Dallas County was Sheriff Jim Clark, the stereotypical southern lawman with paunch, jowls, campaign hat, pistol, and cattle prod. He had at his command not only his deputies and the Selma police but also white "posse" members to discourage marches and break up demonstrations. The mayor, Joe T. Smitherman, was somewhat more progressive. He felt the sight of police dogs and water hoses being used against black women and children would not be conducive to the continued economic development of the community. But he was a segregationist nonetheless, and his hold over Clark was quite tenuous. In league with Clark was Circuit Judge James Hare, an amateur anthropologist who believed that Alabama blacks were particularly retrograde because they were descended from the Ibo tribesmen of Nigeria and had no Berber (Arab) blood.[28] Presiding over all of this was Governor George Corley Wallace, who having stood in the schoolhouse door in an attempt to block integration, was not going to concede the right to vote to African Americans.

Though Bevel was the chief organizer for the Selma voting rights effort, King was to be its icon. Judge Hare had issued a decree forbidding some fifty named individuals and fifteen organizations from holding meetings of more than three persons. Among other things, King intended to convene gatherings in defiance of the order and get himself arrested. Beginning Monday, January 18, he led waves of local blacks to the courthouse to register, where they were confronted by Clark and ordered to disperse. They did but then returned. They were duly arrested, made bail, and returned again. As the organizers had anticipated, Clark's temper began to fray, and he ordered his officers to employ physical intimidation. During the second week of the demonstrations, Clark shoved Mrs. Annie Lee Cooper. Mrs. Cooper, a dignified, sturdy woman, hit him in the face and, as he staggered backward, delivered two more punches, knocking him to the ground. Enraged Clark got up, threw Cooper to the ground, and jumped on top of her, baton in hand. The next morning that picture appeared on the front page of the *New York Times*. On February 1, the next regular registration day, King was arrested and thrown in jail.[29]

In Washington, meanwhile, LBJ and Nick Katzenbach were monitoring events closely. The Justice Department had dispatched trouble-shooter John Doar to the scene to try to keep a lid on things. The first week in February, he persuaded US District Judge Daniel Thomas to issue an order suspending Alabama's literacy test and demanding that Selma speed up registration of black voters. King was still not satisfied. From jail, using his aide Andrew Young as a messenger, he asked LBJ to send a personal representative to Selma, declare his support for voting rights in Alabama, and use his office and his influence with Congress to see that those rights were realized.[30] Johnson was not willing to do everything King wanted, but the day after his release from jail, the White House announced that it was going to send a voting rights bill to Congress before the end of 1965.[31] On February 9, King traveled to Washington to meet with Katzenbach and Vice President Humphrey. Somewhat reluctantly, LBJ agreed to a fifteen-minute chat.[32] Emerging from the Oval Office, King assured reporters of the president's commitment to voting rights, but he returned to Alabama in a fairly pessimistic mood. The state, the nation, and the president would need additional prodding, he believed.[33]

Arriving back in Selma, King found tempers on the rise. Black Muslim leader Malcolm X came to town, but to the relief of the SCLC, he delivered a restrained speech calling for all Negroes to unify behind King. But then police shot and killed a young demonstrator, Jimmie Lee Jackson, who was planning a march to protest the arrest of a local SCLC leader in the nearby town of Marion. King delivered a moving, fiery eulogy at the interment, and James Bevel announced that there would be a march from Selma to Montgomery, the state capital lying some fifty-four miles to the east on Highway 80. The Reverend King would lead the way and at march's end present petitions to Governor Wallace and the state legislature demanding that all voting-age Alabamians be enfranchised. The march would get under way Sunday, March 7. Throughout, it was Martin Luther King who guided and inspired. J. L. "Ike" Chestnut, a Birmingham lawyer with Selma roots who all but lived in the Dallas County courthouse while representing the jailed marchers, concluded that "no one else [but King] could have unified the collection of ministers, gangsters, self-seekers, students, prima donnas, and devoted, high-minded people we had in Selma that winter."[34]

On the evening before the march to Montgomery, word came that Governor Wallace had declared the event to be an unauthorized assembly and dangerous to the public order. He ordered Albert J. Lingo, head of the Alabama State Police, to assemble his troopers just outside the Edmund Pettus Bridge, which boosted Highway 80 over the Alabama River just east of Selma, and use whatever means necessary to stop the march. Wallace had personally recruited Lingo, who had a reputation for being "hell on niggers." The state police commander was a man with an uncontrollable temper who had Confederate battle flags bolted onto the front bumper of each state patrol car after he took office.[35] King, then in Atlanta, had planned to return to Alabama to lead the procession but was persuaded by Bevel and others to stay put. There had been threats on his life, and they felt the risk of assassination was too great.

As the five hundred or so marchers crossed the Pettus Bridge on March 15, they came face to face with Major John Cloud and his troopers. Lurking behind them were Sheriff Clark and his deputies. Whites lined the south side of the road. Cloud ordered the marchers to disperse. When they did not, his troopers, many on horseback, charged. Several fired tear gas canisters into the crowd. As the knot of demonstrators broke and ran for town, state police rode them to ground where Clark's men beat them with billy clubs, kicked, and stomped them. Amid the flowing blood and screams, the line of white spectators cheered. Some fifty-seven marchers were seriously injured. At the Brown Chapel, where the march had originated, volunteer nurses and doctors from around the country treated bloody heads and broken limbs. The television network ABC interrupted its regularly scheduled programming on Sunday night to present a long televised report on the brutality. The next day a vivid, blow-by-blow account of what came to be known as "Bloody Sunday," appeared on the front page of the *New York Times*.[36] In pictures and prose *Newsweek* depicted the bloodletting and gassing under the headline "An American Tragedy."[37] King immediately flew from Atlanta to Selma and announced that the marchers would try again on Tuesday. King called for sympathetic volunteers from around the country to come and march with them. Stirred by images of violence on television and in the newspapers, hundreds did so.

As he had feared, LBJ was caught between King and the civil rights activists, on the one hand, and Wallace and the segregationist power structure
in Alabama, on the other. On the scene, John Doar; LeRoy Collins, head
of the Federal Mediation Service; and Buford Ellington tried to work out
a compromise. Somewhat ironically, Wallace wanted federal intervention. If
LBJ was forced to nationalize the Alabama National Guard and send in the
troops, the governor could claim to bitter-end segregationists that he had
been overwhelmed by a greater force. "You remember what he did there at
the University of Alabama," Lister Hill, the moderate Democratic senator
from Alabama and a friend of LBJ's, told the president. "He went there and
stood in the doorway and wouldn't let anybody come in until the federal
troops [arrived]. . . . He wanted to show the people of Alabama he fought
to the bitter end. . . . That's what you're up against now. . . . That's a hell
of a decision to have to make, because when you move in there, the people
down home are going to think, My God, he [LBJ] just moved in there and
took over for this King!"[38]

LBJ most certainly did not want to send an occupying force to Alabama.
Neither did his advisers. "I just think it's disastrous when you get troops in,
frankly," Katzenbach told him.[39] Katzenbach later observed in his oral history that both Kennedy and Johnson shared his misgivings. "Both of them,
I think shared the philosophy . . . that you never were going to succeed on
civil rights until you could use the force of voluntary compliance with the
law and not simply sending in troops and marshals and taking responsibility
away from local law enforcement. . . . And the second you substituted for
local law enforcement, they had an out."[40] As a southerner, LBJ had grown
up with the memory of Reconstruction, both real and imagined. "If I just
send in federal troops with their big black boots, it will look like Reconstruction all over again," he remarked during the Selma crisis. He told his
aides, "They know deep in their hearts that things are going to change. They
may not like it, but they will accommodate. But not if it looks like the Civil
War all over again! That will force them right into the arms of extremists
and make a martyr of Wallace. . . . I may have to send in troops, but not until
I have to, not until everyone can see I had no other choice."[41]

Meanwhile, in Selma, the Reverend James Reeb, a Unitarian minister
working for the American Friends Service Committee in Boston who had
flown to Selma to march with King, was assaulted with two other white

ministers by four thugs. One of them shattered Reeb's skull with a three-foot-long bludgeon. He died in a Birmingham hospital on Thursday evening, March 11. King, who confided to Doar and Katzenbach that he was in fear for his own life—more so than usual—led some two thousand marchers across the Pettus Bridge the next day. The procession halted before Lingo, Clark, and their massed forces. The group sang "We Shall Overcome," knelt in silent prayer for several moments, and then got up and walked back into town. King put everyone on notice, however, that those who had gathered to support voting rights for black Alabamians remained determined to make the journey to Montgomery.

In an effort to retake the initiative from King and Johnson, Wallace asked for a summit meeting with the president to take place on February 13. In fact, the president had already decided to invite the governor to the White House when he received Wallace's request.[42] Just before noon on the appointed day, a smiling Johnson welcomed Wallace and his attorney general, Seymore Trammel, to the Oval Office. The president had the diminutive Wallace sit in the large overstuffed sofa and positioned himself in the rocking chair opposite, which he pulled so close that when he leaned forward his nose nearly touched the top of the governor's head.

It seemed to him, Johnson offered in a friendly voice, that all the demonstrators wanted was the right to vote. "You cannot deal with street revolutionaries," Wallace replied sternly. "You can never satisfy them . . . first, it is a front seat on a bus; next, it's a takeover of parks; then it's public schools; then it's voting rights; then it's jobs; then it's distribution of wealth without work."[43] Johnson pulled closer, reached over, and gripped Wallace's knee and launched into an hour-long monologue on his vision of a just and prosperous America. "You can be a part of that," he kept saying. Stop "looking back to 1865 and start planning for 2065." As Wallace seem to shrink, Trammel tried to interrupt, invoking "the growing menace of the Communist demonstrators in Alabama." Johnson turned slowly. "He looked at me like I was some kind of dog mess," remembered Trammel. Johnson thrust a pencil and tablet in his hands and told him to take notes. Why, oh why was Wallace abandoning his liberal roots? "Why are you off on this black thing? You ought to be down there calling for help for Aunt Susie in the nursing home." Then to the crux. "Why don't you let the niggers vote?" Wallace protested that he had no power over county registrars. Johnson suddenly stiffened. "Don't you shit me, George Wallace," he said.[44] Rising he put both hands on the back of the sofa, leaned over Wallace, and said, "George, you're fucking over your president. Why are you fucking over your president?"

After three hours, Wallace emerged looking like a wilted plant. In the subsequent press conference in the Rose Garden, Johnson continued to dominate. "The Governor expressed his concern that the demonstrations which have taken place are a threat to the peace and security of the people of Alabama," he told the more than one hundred reporters who had assembled for the occasion. "I said that those Negro citizens of Alabama who have systematically been denied the right to register and to participate in the choice of those who govern them should be provided the opportunity of directing national attention to their plight. . . . I am firmly convinced, as I said to the Governor a few moments ago, that when all of the eligible Negroes of Alabama have been registered, the economic and the social injustices they have experienced throughout will be righted, and the demonstrations, I believe, will stop."[45]

Lyndon Johnson was not a man to ignore the power of circumstance. His advisers and his instincts told him that the time had come for the administration and the federal government to join hands with Martin Luther King and his followers and lead rather than follow in the struggle for dignity and equality for African Americans. "What the public felt on Monday [the day following Bloody Sunday], in my opinion, was the deepest sense of outrage it has ever felt on the civil rights question," Harry McPherson, whom LBJ would increasingly look to as the administration's conscience on civil rights, told the president. "I had dinner with Abe Fortas Monday night. That reasonable man was for sending troops at once."[46] On the evening of March 14, LBJ met with congressional leaders of both parties. The president told them he was considering a televised address to a joint session to denounce the Selma outrages and introduce his voting rights bill. Mansfield and Dirksen were negative. What if Congress did not rally? The president and the voting rights acts would fall flat on their faces. Speaker McCormack disagreed and made an impassioned plea in behalf of a televised speech. He had of course been carefully primed by Johnson. The tide quickly turned, and by the time the meeting closed, the group was unanimous in supporting an address to a joint session.

The White House had but twenty-four hours to prepare. Johnson summoned McPherson, Goodwin, Busby, Valenti, and company. "I sat with my

staff for several hours," Johnson later recalled. "I described the general outline of what I wanted to say. I wanted to use every ounce of moral persuasion the Presidency held. I wanted no hedging, no equivocation. And I
wanted to talk from my own heart, from my own experience."[47] According
to Goodwin, he drafted the speech, but the substance and, in the end, the
wording were entirely Johnson. "It was by me," he said, "but it was for and
of the Lyndon Johnson I had carefully studied and come to know."[48]

As the time for LBJ's March 15 address approached, the Capitol and the
nation sensed that something extraordinary was about to happen. Word
went out that the president's speech to the joint session was not to be missed.
LBJ entered a packed House chamber a little after nine in the evening. In
addition to the legislators, all of the Supreme Court justices, the entire ambassadorial corps, and the cabinet were present. Even the aisles were filled,
an unprecedented occurrence. Overhead, the galleries were jammed with
whites and blacks, some in street clothes fresh from demonstrations and
others in neat business attire. Lady Bird and Lynda sat among them in the
presence of an odd special guest—J. Edgar Hoover. A few members of Congress had deliberately absented themselves: the entire Mississippi delegation,
for example. Virtually all Americans were aware of the historic moment and
had their TV sets on in anticipation.

Tall, erect, smiling, Johnson made the customary handshakes and proceeded to the podium. He wasted no time. "I speak tonight for the dignity
of man and the destiny of democracy," he began in a slow, melodious tone.
"At times history and fate meet at a single time in a single place to shape
a turning point in man's unending search for freedom," he intoned. "So it
was at Lexington and Concord. So it was a century ago at Appomattox. So
it was last week in Selma, Alabama." Those who were there remembered
almost total silence, a collective holding of breaths. The nation had reached
a moral juncture brought about by "the cries of pain and the hymns and
protests of oppressed people [who] have summoned into convocation all
the majesty of this great government . . . rarely in any time does an issue lay
bare the secret heart of America itself," Johnson declared, his voice rising, his
pace quickening. "The issue of equal rights for American Negroes is such
an issue. And should we defeat every enemy, should we double our wealth
and conquer the stars, and still be unequal to this issue, then we will have
failed as a people and as a nation. . . . For with a country as with a person,
'What is a man profited, if he shall gain the whole world and lose his own

soul.'" He was interrupted by the first burst of applause, hesitant, solid, then thunderous. No president, not even Abraham Lincoln, had identified himself, the Constitution, the values of the country with the cause of equal rights for African Americans. One shrewd heartland politician was finishing what another had started.

The next great step in the march to equality was a national voting rights law, LBJ declared. No law could be effective unless local officials were willing to enforce it. He was, he said, sending to Congress immediately following his speech a special message that would put in place machinery to register black voters in areas where local officials were unwilling to do so and to provide protection to them in their exercise of the franchise. What president who took his oath of office seriously could do less? By now LBJ's voice was inspired, rolling, ringing, a Texas version of the southern Baptist rhythm and tenor that Martin Luther King had mastered. "There is no Constitutional issue here," LBJ declared. "The command of the Constitution is plain. There is no moral issue. It is wrong—deadly wrong—to deny any of your fellow Americans the right to vote in this country. There is no issue of States rights or national rights. There is only the struggle for human rights."

The real heroes of the hour were the civil rights activists who were demonstrating, going to jail, and dying, LBJ continued. "Their cause must be our cause too. Because it is not just Negroes, but really it is all of us, who must overcome the crippling legacy of bigotry and injustice."[49] And then, the president of the United States, remarkably, paused and then proclaimed slowly, deliberately: "we—shall—overcome!" The assembled throng rose almost as one and delivered a roaring, prolonged ovation. In the galleries and on the floor, longtime laborers in the vineyard of civil rights wept openly. At home watching, black Americans sat stunned, daring to hope that at last their dream of full citizenship might actually come true. As Lady Bird and Lynda departed the chamber, a reporter asked the president's eldest how she felt about the speech. "It was just like that old hymn," she said, "'once to every man and nation comes a moment to decide.'"[50]

JOHNSONIAN RHETORIC NOTWITHSTANDING, MARTIN LUTHER KING intended to keep the pressure on. Alabama was a long way from Washington, and he sensed no softening in the attitudes of the George Wallaces, Al

Lingos, and Jim Clarks of the world. On March 17, Federal District Court Judge Frank Johnson, sitting in Montgomery, issued an order declaring the governor's action in outlawing a march from Selma to the capital unconstitutional. The SCLC could hold its march, and participants were entitled to state protection. Wallace was at last trapped. On March 18, he called the president. "These people are pouring in from all over the country," he whined. "Two days ago . . . James Forman suggested in front of all the nuns and priests that if anybody went in a café and they wouldn't serve 'em, they'd 'kick the fuckin' legs of the tables off.' . . . It inflames people. . . . I don't want anybody to get hurt. . . . A Negro priest yesterday asked all the patrolmen what their wives were doing, whether some of their friends could have dates with their wives. You know, trying to provoke them. . . . These fifty thousand people. . . . They're going to bankrupt the state." LBJ listened patiently but remained firm. It would be much better, much less divisive if the National Guard acted as a state rather than a federal force. But Wallace would not give.[51]

That night the governor told the Alabama legislature in a televised speech that the state could not afford to activate the National Guard. He demanded that the president send federal authorities to Alabama. LBJ was furious. "You're dealing with a very treacherous guy," he told Buford Ellington. "He's a no good son of a bitch. . . . Son of a bitch! He's absolutely treacherous."[52] Later, Wallace wired the White House that he did not have the assets available to protect a march from Selma to Montgomery. The effort would require 6,171 men, 489 vehicles, and 15 buses. Absurd, Johnson told reporters. The governor had available to him 10,000 Alabama national guardsmen, but if he could not or would not call them up, he as president would order in more troops to protect King and his fellow demonstrators.[53] True to his word, the president issued orders federalizing the Alabama National Guard and dispatched a sizable contingent of regular Army troops to Maxwell Air Force Base to stand by.[54] "Be sure whatever we do is measured, fitting, and adequate—like in Viet Nam," he told Katzenbach, Ellington, and Justice Department official Burke Marshall.[55]

On March 21, some 392 civil rights activists with King at their head set out on foot from Selma to Montgomery. This time there were no state troopers or Selma police to stop them. Federalized guardsmen did their duty, and there were only minor incidents along the way. The entire march was covered by television cameras and print journalists. The trek, some fifty-four miles, took several days. It was bitterly cold at night, and King slept in a trailer that followed the column. By the time the contingent reached the outskirts of Montgomery, the ranks of the marchers had swelled to twelve hundred, including show business celebrities Peter, Paul, and Mary, Joan Baez, Dick Gregory, Frank Sinatra, and Marlon Brando.[56] The morning after the marchers arrived on March 24, King addressed a throng of some twenty-five thousand gathered on the plaza in front of the state capitol. The redoubtable Wallace peeked at the proceedings from behind venetian blinds in his office.[57]

That night a white civil rights activist from Detroit, Mrs. Viola Liuzzo, was shot in the head and killed as she drove Le Roy Moton, a young black man, back to Selma from Montgomery.[58] In his subsequent report on the incident, Hoover informed LBJ that "we found numerous needle marks indicating she had been taking dope although we can't say that definitely because she is dead." To Katzenbach he reported that Mrs. Liuzzo "was sitting very, very close to the Negro in the car . . . it had the appearance of a necking party."[59] The White House ignored Hoover's innuendoes and ordered the FBI to apprehend the perpetrators at once.[60] "Looks like we ought to give some thought [to how we can] really move in on that Klan more effectively," LBJ observed to Katzenbach. "Is there anything that we can do in the way of legislation on that? . . . Pretty well outlawing them."[61] In response to questions from reporters concerning the Liuzzo murder, the president described the Klan as a "hooded society of bigots."[62] The thing to do, Johnson subsequently told Katzenbach, was to turn the House Un-American Activities Committee loose on them.[63] That would spike Hoover and the segregationists' red-baiting guns.

FOCUS NOW SHIFTED TO CONGRESS AND THE VOTING RIGHTS BILL. "We needed something where you didn't have to litigate for fifteen years before you finally get . . . some relief," Deputy Attorney General Ramsey Clark later said.[64] There was some real doubt, however, that the federal government had the constitutional power to establish and regulate voter qualifications beyond those explicitly based on race. The Constitution, as it was ratified, gave each state complete discretion to determine voter qualifications for its residents. Following the Civil War, Congress had passed and the states had ratified three amendments that affected voting rights. The Thirteenth prohibited slavery; the Fourteenth granted citizenship to anyone "born or naturalized in the United States" and guaranteed every person due process and equal protection under the law; and the Fifteenth stipulated that "the right of citizens of the United States to vote shall not be denied or abridged by the United States or by any State on account of race, color, or previous condition of servitude." In 1957 in the wake of the *Brown* decision, the Montgomery Bus Boycott, and the Little Rock Crisis, Congress had enacted a civil rights bill that authorized the attorney general to sue for injunctive relief on behalf of persons whose Fifteenth Amendment rights were being violated. It also created a Civil Rights division within Justice to pursue any necessary litigation. In the years that followed, however, the Justice Department was largely stymied by recalcitrant southern registrars and judges.

Even as the Johnson administration prepared to move ahead with a comprehensive voting rights measure, there were dissenting voices from within. As was the case in the argument against sending federal troops into the South to protect civil rights protestors, the establishment of a federal voter registration system would remove the onus from the indigenous white population, Horace Busby argued. Local communities must be brought to the realization that discrimination was immoral and unconstitutional and act on their own. The imposition of federal registrars would merely provide Dixie with another chance to decry federal intervention and to avoid responsibility.[65] Citing the obstacles placed in the way of the Justice Department in the wake of the 1957 law, Attorney General Katzenbach told the White House, "While I agree with Mr. Busby that the political consequences of the proposed message are serious, I see no real alternative."[66]

In short, by the spring of 1965 Johnson, King, and, it seemed, the nation as a whole were not willing to wait for the South to come around on its own. In the days following Bloody Sunday and the president's speech to Congress in support of the Voting Rights Act, a surge of support for the civil rights movement crested across America, quickening the tempo of the social revolution Lyndon Johnson had dreamed about from the first night of his presidency. "The might of past empires is little compared to our own," LBJ had declared in his "We Shall Overcome" speech. "But I do not want to be the President who built empires, or sought grandeur, or extended dominion. I want to be the President who educated young children to the wonders of their world. I want to be the President who helped to feed the hungry . . . who helped the poor to find their own way, who protected the right of every citizen to vote."[67] There was the horror of Selma but also the buoyant optimism generated by the promise of expanded educational opportunity, adequate health care for the elderly, and hope for the poverty-stricken. A Gallup poll showed that four out of five Americans favored a voting rights law. Even in the South, a majority of white Americans supported legislation to ensure the right of black Americans to cast the ballot.[68]

The legislation that the White House presented to the Hill on March 17 began by echoing the Fifteenth Amendment. It prohibited the denial of the right to vote on the basis of race or color. The measure invalidated "any test or device" that was used to discriminate in any federal, state, or local election in areas in which, as of November 1, 1964, more than 50 percent of the persons of voting age were not registered and had not voted in the last presidential election. Twenty or more residents of a jurisdiction were empowered to petition the attorney general to ask for relief from voter discrimination. If the complaint was authenticated, the Civil Service Commission, which oversaw the hiring and firing of government employees, would appoint examiners to check the qualifications of voter applicants and certify them to vote if they were twenty-one years of age or older and legal residents. Finally, no person could be denied the right to vote for failure to pay a poll tax.[69]

The bill was referred to the Senate Judiciary Committee, whose chair, Senator James Eastland (D-MS), was perhaps Congress's most outspoken segregationist. To prevent him from keeping the measure bottled up indefinitely, Majority Leader Mansfield offered a motion on the Senate floor requiring the committee to report the bill out by April 9; his proposal passed by an overwhelming margin. Led by Robert Kennedy, who had been elected to the Senate from New York following his resignation as attorney general, liberals in the Senate made a brief but unsuccessful attempt to toughen the administration's measure by outlawing the poll tax entirely.[70] Although the Twenty-Fourth Amendment to the Constitution banning the use of poll taxes in federal elections had been ratified a year earlier, the administration and the amendment's sponsors did not include a provision in the Voting Rights Act explicitly prohibiting the use of poll taxes (as distinct from turning an individual away for failure to pay) in state elections because they feared the courts would declare the entire measure unconstitutional. Furthermore, by excluding poll taxes from the definition of "tests and devices," the coverage formula would not apply to Texas, mitigating opposition from that state's powerful congressional delegation.

Johnson, of course, believed that the move to outlaw the poll tax in all elections was just one more attempt by the Kennedys to upstage and embarrass him. He observed to Senator Birch Bayh (D-IN), who wanted to vote for the amendment, that he could not understand the Kennedys. Attorney General Katzenbach was their man, and he had taken the position that the poll tax amendment the liberals had put forward was unconstitutional. "They brought him from Yale, they pulled them together and he loves them and he is loyal to them, he is devoted to them. . . . I took their lawyer because I foresaw this very problem. I foresaw that I would be charged with not being quite strong enough on Civil Rights."[71]

On April 22, the full Senate began debate on the bill. Dirksen was unequivocal in his support. The black vote was coming to the South, and the GOP did not want to be left out. Bitter-enders like Strom Thurmond (R-SC) proclaimed that the bill would lead to "despotism and tyranny," while Senator Sam Ervin (D-NC) argued that the measure was unconstitutional because it deprived states of their right under Article I, Section 2 of the Constitution to establish voter qualifications. Russell Long let the White House know that he was going to vote for the measure, and he predicted that he would be able to carry eleven other southern senators with him. On May 25, the Senate voted for cloture 70 to 30, thus overcoming the threat of filibuster. The Voting Rights Act of 1965 passed the Senate by a vote of 77 to 19 the following day. The majority included 5 southern and border state Democrats.

The scene of action then shifted to the House, where the Judiciary Committee's ranking Republican, William McCulloch (R-OH)—he who had played such a key role in passage of the 1964 civil rights bill—generally supported expanding voting rights, but he opposed both the poll tax ban and the coverage formula. He proved unable, however, to prevent the committee from reporting the voting rights measure out with a "do pass" recommendation. On the floor, McCulloch introduced an alternative bill that would allow the attorney general to appoint federal registrars after receiving twenty-five bona fide complaints of discrimination and to impose a nationwide ban on literacy tests for persons who could prove that they had a sixth-grade education. The White House feared the worst, but after Representative William M. Tuck (D-VA), a McCulloch ally, stated publicly that he opposed the Senate version because it would ensure that blacks could vote—implying that that was the Ohioan's true goal—support for the McCulloch alternative dwindled. The House followed the Senate's lead on July 9 by a vote of 333 to 85. Among the majority were 33 Democrats and 3 Republicans from the South. On August 6, 1965, LBJ proudly presided over a televised signing ceremony in the rotunda of the Capitol.[72]

Throughout the fall and indeed for the remainder of his administration, LBJ badgered Justice, local officials, and civil rights leaders to launch one voter registration drive after another. "I don't care if you are Mexican, American, Negro, Baptist, Catholic, Jew—just vote," he remarked to Roy Wilkins. Questions of race and religion would then disappear; with every person voting his or her best interests, social justice would inevitably follow and it would be based on democracy, on "home rule" rather than "federal edict."[73] But the federal government could not make long-disenfranchised blacks vote. It could not overcome the apathy instilled by years of abuse and neglect. African American leaders were going to have to spur their community to political action. One of Johnson's converts was Thurgood Marshall, the pioneering civil rights lawyer Kennedy had appointed to the US Court of Appeals. "I told them [other civil rights leaders] the last time I met with them," he told the president, "that there was nothing in the Voting Bill or Constitution or any place else that required the Attorney General to go down into the bayous and pick up the Negro in his Cadillac and take him to vote."[74]

By July 14, 1965, federal agencies had identified eight counties each in Alabama, Mississippi, and Louisiana, along with four in Georgia, that did not meet the 50 percent rule. Operating from Civil Service offices in Atlanta and Dallas, supervisors opened local offices in the affected areas. By the end of January 1966, the campaign had registered 93,778 new voters, 91,212 black and 2,566 white. Progress was slow but steady. In March 1966, the Supreme Court held the basic components of the Voting Rights Act to be constitutional.[75] By the 1968 presidential election, Mississippi had reached 59 percent, and black registration in the eleven former Confederate states averaged 62 percent. In 1980 only 7 percent fewer blacks, proportionately, than whites were on the nation's voting rolls.[76]

LBJ's faith in the ballot as a means to empower African Americans was not misplaced, but the benefits of enfranchisement had their limits. Blacks in the North had long had the legal right to vote, but that had not brought ghetto-dwellers economic opportunity and social justice.

CHAPTER 7

CULTURES OF POVERTY

IF THE ARCHITECTS OF THE GREAT SOCIETY HAD LEARNED NOTHING else during the debate over the poverty bill, they had learned that the story of the disadvantaged in America was a complicated one and that, even if white attitudes changed quickly, the culture of poverty among African Americans would still persist. And the White House began to get an inkling by the summer of 1965 that the number one racial battleground in the future would be the large urban areas of the Northeast and Midwest, where millions of southern blacks had settled between 1940 and 1970. In August 1965, *Newsweek* ran a piece entitled "New Crisis: The Negro Family." The article, citing a Department of Labor report, painted a dismal picture of overpopulated urban ghettoes teeming with unemployed youths, fatherless children, drug addicts, gang members, rats, and predatory white shopkeepers. "The evidence—not final, but powerfully persuasive—is that the Negro family in the urban ghettoes is crumbling. . . . This is the time bomb ticking at the very heart of America's 'most dangerous social problem.'"[1]

In his conversations with black leaders and the architects of the Great Society, LBJ had made it clear that he considered the Office of Economic Opportunity and other facets of the War on Poverty to be civil rights programs. Equality under the law, equal access to public facilities and institutions, and voting rights were not enough. The history of the American Negro was quite different from that of other ethnic, immigrant groups. Slavery had deliberately fractured families, prohibited literacy, and denigrated notions of self-worth. The sharecrop, crop-lien system and Jim Crow were steps up from slavery but miles short of equality. Even with *Brown,* the Civil Rights Act of 1964, and the Voting Rights Act of 1965 in place, blacks were not simply working-class whites ready to move up to the next rung on the socioeconomic ladder. By virtue of education, income, IQ, and other accepted measures of achievement and potential, African Americans had not been given the opportunity to measure up.

The War on Poverty had spawned a number of government studies that sought to uncover the historical and social roots of the culture of poverty. One of those, a report on the black family by Assistant Secretary of Labor Daniel Patrick Moynihan, had been circulating in the West Wing and throughout the federal bureaucracy for four months. The Moynihan report ticked off the statistics and then focused on that most widely accepted criterion of social stability and progress—the family. Nearly one-quarter of city-dwelling black women who had ever been married were now divorced, separated, or deserted—22.9 percent compared to 7.9 percent for whites. As a result, one black family in four was fatherless. More than half of all Negro children would have lived in broken homes by their eighteenth birthday. One-fourth of all black babies born in America were illegitimate compared to 3.07 percent for whites. As a result, recipients of Aid to Families with Dependent Children (AFDC), a Social Security program to provide aid to families with children that had low or no income, had become primarily unmarried black females and their dependent children. More than half of all Negroes subsisted on AFDC checks at some time during their childhood. At the same time, the birth rate for ghetto-dwelling blacks was 40 percent higher than for whites.[2]

The intention of the report, Moynihan later recalled, was not to indict the black family but to use it as "the best point . . . at which to measure the net, cumulative plus or minus impact of outside forces on the Negro community. All the abstractions of employment, housing, income, discrimination, education, et al. come together here."[3]

With its focus on the black family, the Moynihan report was a bombshell. Harry McPherson recalled that when Moynihan, a close friend and intellectual soulmate, finished his study, he, McPherson, was laid up in the hospital recovering from a hernia operation. Moynihan showed up with the document and a full bottle of Johnny Walker Black scotch. As McPherson read, he grew drunker and increasingly alarmed. The report would be fodder for every racist who was trying to discredit the values and morality of African Americans.[4] Black activists, especially the more radical in SNCC and CORE, were sure to insist that the government was trying to blame the victim for the crime. It seemed to be saying that if only blacks would take control of their lives, embrace monogamy, and nurture their children, all would be well. But where would the jobs come from, where the schools, where the rat-control programs, where the health care? How could inner-city blacks reach the suburbs, where the jobs were, without transportation?

During his vice presidency, which included chairing the Equal Employment Opportunity Commission (EEOC), LBJ had come to know and trust Whitney Young, the Atlanta University Law School dean who was named to head the Urban League in 1961. Informally in conversations with Johnson, and formally at the 1963 national convention of the national Urban League, Young had advanced the notion of a Marshall Plan for the American Negro. Historic abuse rooted in racial prejudice and economic exploitation had left the average African American poorly equipped to take advantage of the opportunities that were being opened to him or her. Young called for a "special effort" by government and the private sector to provide poor blacks in the rural South and urban ghettoes with job training and educational opportunity. In his book *To Be Equal,* he suggested that the best schools and the best teachers be placed in Negro communities and that jobs be provided preferentially to Negros "where two equally qualified people apply," especially if a company had never before hired blacks.[5]

By the summer of 1965, LBJ had come to embrace what would become known as affirmative action. The first week in June of that year, the president delivered the commencement address at Howard University, in which he justified and defined affirmative action. "You do not take a person who, for years, has been hobbled by chains and liberate him, bring him up to the starting line of a race and then say, 'you are free to compete with all the others,' and still justly believe that you have been completely fair." It was not sufficient simply to open the gates of opportunity; all must be able to enter those gates. Equipping black Americans to take advantage of the opportunities available to them would be "the next and more profound stage for the battle for civil rights. We seek not just freedom but opportunity. We seek not just legal equity but human ability, not just equality as a right and a theory but equality as a fact and equality as a result." Summarizing the Moynihan report, LBJ emphasized the historical role that racial prejudice and exploitation had played in blighting black youth and their families.[6] "Ability is stretched or stunted by the family that you live with," Johnson told his all-black audience, "and the neighborhood you live in—by the school you go to and the poverty or the richness of your surroundings." It was the responsibility of all Americans to see that this blight imposed by the culture of poverty was lifted from those who suffered from it. Typically, LBJ quoted scripture:"I shall light a candle of understanding in thine heart, which shall not be put out."[7]

"The strategy of the speech," Moynihan later observed," . . . was that by couching the issue in terms of family . . . white America could be brought to see the tired old issues of employment, housing, discrimination and such in terms of much greater urgency than they ever evoke on their own." Moreover, family as an issue raised the possibility of enlisting the support of conservative groups for quite radical social programs. The architects of the Howard speech recognized that "the intense moralisms of conservative Catholic and Protestant religion" were "simply a clumsy effort to maintain standards of family stability that most of us regard as eminently sane."[8]

In fact, the administration got the worst of both worlds. Conservatives for the most part chose to view the disintegration of the black family as proof of the innate depravity of inner-city blacks, and many blacks chose to view the Moynihan report and references to the family in the Howard speech as attempts by the white power structure to blame the victim. And then there was the reaction to affirmative action, especially to Johnson's new, more radical definition of it. LBJ had not developed the notion of affirmative action with any specificity, but his allusion to equality of condition as well as equality of opportunity pointed to the righting of historic wrongs with the implication of hiring quotas and preferences. Traditional civil rights leaders such as King, Young, Randolph, and Wilkins hailed the Howard address as historic. Some white liberals who had participated in the struggle for equality under the law and nondiscrimination were not so sure, however. Quotas and preferences violated the "American philosophical creed," libertarian Daniel Bell wrote. Special subsidies for the poor were acceptable, but a plan that would end up discriminating "against others" was not. The managing editor of *Christian Century,* Kyle Haselden, agreed. "Compensation for Negros is a subtle but pernicious form of racism," he editorialized. "It requires that men be dealt with by society on the basis of race and color rather than on the basis of their humanity."[9]

At this point, George Reedy recalled, Johnson and his staff were not willing to accept preferences for blacks with the notion of hiring quotas that it implied. He would claim that affirmative action originated with the EEOC and "did not contemplate hiring quotas or pressure to force employees to 'favor' minorities." Rather, Reedy asserted, "it meant efforts to let blacks know that the jobs were available and to make certain that qualifications were truly being reviewed without bias."[10] Johnson's call upon the white power structure to guaranty equality in condition aside, Title VII of the 1964 Civil Rights Act and the guidelines put forward by the EEOC bore out Reedy's contention.

IN PART, THE HOWARD SPEECH WAS AN ATTEMPT TO DISSIPATE THE storm that was gathering in the nation's ghettoes before it burst upon the nation and created a white backlash that might threaten all that LBJ and his colleagues had been trying to accomplish. But, despite its promise, the administration's embrace of affirmative action was too little, too late.

In August, just days after LBJ signed the Voting Rights Act, rioting erupted in Watts, Los Angeles's teeming black ghetto.[11] The violence began when a white policeman attempted to arrest a black youth for driving under the influence. As the officer tried to push the young man into the patrol car, the young man began to struggle. By this time the youth's mother had arrived and summoned a crowd from nearby street corners. Suddenly, she and the onlookers began pelting the police with rocks and bottles. Police reinforcements arrived, and the confrontation ballooned. Within two hours, an angry mob was attacking white drivers and setting cars aflame. Dawn brought a momentary lull, and community leaders called for calm. With the coming of nightfall, however, black rage, fueled by chronic unemployment, poor schools or none at all, rat-infested tenements, police brutality, and the general hopelessness and frustration of ghetto living, boiled over. A mob estimated at five thousand roamed the streets, looting stores, attacking whites, and fire-bombing white- or Korean-owned businesses.

When police and firefighters responded, isolated sniper fire from surrounding rooftops greeted them. Mobs rampaged up and down Avalon Avenue, setting fires and looting retail stores. A Molotov cocktail thrown at a passing auto caused a four-car pileup. From two of the vehicles several whites were dragged and then beaten. The first death occurred when a twenty-seven-year-old deputy sheriff was shot dead by looters he surprised in a store.[12] At this point, the governor of California called in the National Guard. Still, the looting and violence continued. Crowds of angry young blacks chanted "Burn, baby, burn" and prevented fire fighters from dousing flames. After imposing a curfew, soldiers and police officers began shooting indiscriminately. For nearly a week Watts was turned into a combat zone. When the rioting was finally quelled six days after it had begun, thirty-four lay dead, a thousand were injured, four thousand had been arrested, and large sections of the ghetto had been reduced to smoldering ruins.[13]

"If a single event can be picked to mark the dividing line" of the sixties, *LIFE* editorialized, "it was Watts." The outburst of violence "ripped the fabric of democratic society and set the tone of confrontation and open revolt."[14] Martin Luther King had flown to the scene of the rioting to appeal for calm only to be heckled by young militants. A feud had long been brewing between the older generation of civil rights leaders such as King, Young, and Randolph and younger, more radical elements in CORE and SNCC who had grown disillusioned with the American political process and even with the tactic of nonviolent civil disobedience.

Revolutionary activists such as Stokely Carmichael, H. Rap Brown, and Bobby Seale took over existing organizations or formed new ones that called for whatever means necessary, including violence, to achieve equality and opportunity for African Americans. They were aided and abetted by black writers and intellectuals such as Eldridge Cleaver (*Soul on Ice,* 1967) and James Baldwin (*The Fire Next Time,* 1963) who moved beyond authors Richard Wright and Ralph Ellison in their anger and their vision of an apocalyptic end to the struggle of African Americans against oppression and exploitation. The new militants even questioned the value of integration. "Integration," Stokely Carmichael wrote, "speaks to the problem of blackness in a despicable way. As a goal, it has been based on complete acceptance of the fact that in order to have a decent house or education, blacks must move into a white neighborhood or send their children to a white school. This reinforces, among both black and white, the idea that 'white' is automatically better and 'black' is by definition inferior. This is why integration is a subterfuge for the maintenance of white supremacy."[15]

The ultimate prophet of the new militancy that the press dubbed "the black power movement" was Malcolm X, who had risen to the leadership of the Black Muslims, or Nation of Islam. The organization was a puritanical association of African Americans that practiced a variation of the Islamic creed and that drew its converts primarily from the pimps, drug pushers, and generally down-and-outs of the big-city ghettoes. Malcolm argued that blacks had been abused and reviled for so long that the only way they could liberate themselves spiritually as well as politically and economically was through violent struggle. "If someone puts a hand on you," he told his followers, "send him to the cemetery." *Newsweek* called him a "spiritual desperado . . . a demagogue who titillated slum Negroes and frightened whites."

For Johnson, the rioting in Watts was the ultimate nightmare. Up to this point he had been relatively successful in denying conservatives use of the "law and order" issue. During the 1964 campaign, Goldwater and the ultra-conservatives had tried to raise the specter of lawlessness, subtly attempting to link civil rights demonstrations with communist subversion and inner-city crime.[16] Their appeal, echoed by George Wallace, had struck a chord with some, but not enough to reverse the political tide. Johnson had turned the law-and-order table on conservatives by comparing the Klan to the Communist Party and pointing to the lawlessness of anti–civil rights forces in the South. Indeed, his final, unanswerable appeal to southern whites faced with the Second Reconstruction was the demand and the expectation that they "obey the law." Now the nation was faced with the reality of black violence and worse—black leaders who were hailing the therapeutic value of violence and denouncing white society and its political processes as impotent and irrelevant. Johnson's first reaction to Watts was incredulity and then denial. "How is it possible," he asked, "after all we've accomplished? How could it be?" When he first received word that mass violence had erupted in South Los Angeles, LBJ was at the ranch, celebrating the signing of the Voting Rights Act. Stunned, he drove over pastures and through woods alone for hours, refusing to return calls from White House aide Joseph Califano, who was then being besieged by California governor Pat Brown, Los Angeles mayor Sam Yorty, and other state officials pleading for federal aid.[17]

On the second day of the rioting, LBJ began to emerge from his shell and grapple with the situation. He was loath to send in regular Army units because he did not want to admit "that city government, state government,

county government is impotent in this country and that I am a dictator."
If it proved, however, that state and local authorities were insufficient and
that they really wanted federal help, he would be willing to authorize it.[18]
LBJ and his advisers at once realized how symbolically important would be
the manner in which the federal government reacted to Watts. There was
obviously an overriding need to get at the roots of the rioting, lest other
American cities go up in flames.

Since the emergence of juvenile delinquency as a national issue in the
1950s, members of the Kennedy-Johnson administration had been aware
of the unique problems facing inner-city blacks, but Watts took them by
surprise. For one thing, the Justice Department seemed largely unaware of
the history of police brutality against minorities in the nation's major urban
areas, an issue that future studies would show to be paramount. "We always
thought of . . . these big fine police departments up there," recalled Assistant
Attorney General Ramsey Clark. "One of our problems in the South was
always your skepticism about the police themselves. . . . In the North, we
didn't think of that as a problem."[19] A second issue was lack of reliable intelligence. "The Student Non-Violent Coordinating Committee doesn't really
have direct communications . . . strong ties, or much influence with the
deep ghetto," Clark observed. "And the major leadership units, the Urban
League and the NAACP and others are very, very remote from the hardest places."[20] This was true in part because there was very little organized,
identifiable leadership in the nation's ghettoes. The uprising in Watts, as in
other urban areas, was spontaneous and free-form, with violence ebbing and
flowing, driven by its own momentum.

The White House had hoped that the leaders of the principal civil rights
organizations would stay away from the rioting in Los Angeles. "In the first
place," George Reedy observed to Johnson, "there is very little they can do
as people who smash liquor store windows and loot groceries are not likely
to respond to cultivated minds like Roy Wilkins and Whitney Young. In the
second place, unless they are extraordinarily careful, the Civil Rights leaders
run the risk of identifying their movements with ordinary hooliganism and
savagery."[21]

At one point, Johnson believed that the entire Watts uprising, if not a
conspiracy to embarrass moderate civil rights leaders, was going to be used
by radicals to discredit them. "'See that Hoover is in there up to his ears in

everything that happens . . . in Los Angeles," he instructed Attorney General Katzenbach. "I sure do not think that [the riot] is an accident. I think that it is pre-meditated. I would think that they are going to want to jump on Martin Luther King or someone of that type."[22]

But some, namely, Dick Gregory, the comedian and civil rights activist, and Martin Luther King felt that they would be derelict if they did not try to intervene. For his trouble Gregory was shot in the leg by rioters, and King was abused by both black militants and white authorities. The SCLC leader met with Yorty and Police Chief William Parker at City Hall. Yorty did his best to avoid being photographed with King, and Parker blew his top when he suggested a civilian review board to hear complaints of police brutality. "They are insensitive to the problem and the need for a cure," King subsequently reported to LBJ. He then met with three hundred angry blacks in the heart of the ghetto. When they were finally persuaded to stop heckling him, King began, "We must join hands. . . . " "And burn!" came a shrill voice from the crowd. He tried to begin again: "You are all God's children. There will be a better tomorrow. . . . " "When, damn it, when?" a voice broke in.[23] From Watts, King flew to Washington to meet with the president. "What should we do?" LBJ asked. "Get the Poverty Program going in L.A.," King replied.[24]

Like Johnson, King was a southerner who had viewed racial injustice in the South primarily through the lens of Jim Crow. Watts brought home to both men just how much more needed to be done. It was during Watts that King came to a fuller awareness that the two great civil rights laws of 1964 and 1965 had addressed the evils of southern segregation but had barely touched the ghetto's problems of poverty, joblessness, isolation, family dis-integration, and hopelessness. With Watts, King began moving toward a far more radical critique of American society, one that focused on institutions and cultures. "I worked to get these people the right to eat hamburgers," he told Bayard Rustin the night he was in Watts, "and now I've got to do something . . . to help them get the money to buy them."[25]

In the aftermath of his meeting with King, Johnson ordered Katzenbach to put together an emergency task force to develop summer job programs and funnel government funds into the rehabilitation of recreation centers and playgrounds. The government had initiated such programs in Washing-ton, DC, where violence had been predicted during the summers of 1963 and 1964. At the very least, Katzenbach subsequently observed, such initiatives would "show the children and juveniles that their government cared about their problems."[26] But such aid would have to be discreet lest the federal government appear to frightened whites to be rewarding violence and lawlessness. "The riot had, you know, just stunned and polarized the community there particularly, but also the nation," Ramsey Clark noted. Gun sales to white suburbanites skyrocketed, and so did the popularity of law-and-order candidates like actor-turned-politician Ronald Reagan. "And there was great concern that what we would do might appear to reward rioters," Clark observed. "Both the immediate and long range repercussions of such an impression would be very great. This lent a certain ambiguity to our mission."[27] Joe Califano, who had moved over from the Defense Department to the White House to handle domestic affairs after Moyers became press secretary, recalled how worried the president was that out of frustration, hopelessness, and ignorance, poor blacks would lash out and undermine the very programs he was creating to help them.[28]

Despite his frustration, disappointment, and occasional anger, however, Johnson had no intention of abandoning inner-city blacks to their fate. "We are on a powder keg in a dozen places," he told John McCone, former CIA director and a Republican, whom he was trying to persuade to head up an inquiry into urban unrest. "You just have no idea of the depth of the feeling of these people. I see some of the boys that have worked for me, have 2,000 years of persecution, now they suffer from it. They [ghetto dwellers] have absolutely nothing to live for, 40 percent of them are unemployed, these youngsters live with rats and have no place to sleep, and they all start from broken homes and illegitimate families and all that narcotics circulating around. . . . We have just got to find some way to wipe out these ghettos and find some housing and put them to work."[29] At the same time that he appealed to the compassion of liberals, he tweaked the fears of conservatives. "I got 38 percent of these young Negro boys out on the streets," he told Arkansas senator John McClellan. "They've got no school to go to and no job. And by God, I'm just scared to death what's going to happen . . . you take an old hard-peckered boy that sits around and got no school and got no job and got no work and got no discipline. His daddy's probably on relief, and his mama's probably taking morphine. Why, he ain't got nothing hurt if he gets shot. I mean, he's better off dead than he is where he is."[30] By the end of August, the administration had allocated more than $29 million to help rehabilitate Watts alone.[31]

In the months ahead, LBJ would turn his attention once again to the War on Poverty, now perceived as both an exercise in idealism and as an emergency fire station to keep the American house from burning down. At the same time, the president increasingly appropriated the language of law and order. A few days before announcing the new federal programs for Watts, he addressed a White House Conference on Equal Employment Opportunities. "A rioter with a Molotov cocktail in his hands is not fighting for civil rights any more than a Klansman with a sheet on his back and a mask on his face," he declared. "They are both more and less what the law declares them: lawbreakers, destroyers of constitutional rights and liberties, and ultimately destroyers of a free America. They must be exposed and they must be dealt with."[32] But more and more Americans would come to believe that the Great Society, in general, and the War on Poverty, in particular, were not antidotes to urban unrest, but the abettors of it.

IN SOME WAYS THE GREAT SOCIETY AND THE WAR IN SOUTHEAST ASIA stemmed from the same root; the moral awakening among middle-class whites that provided much of the impetus for the Second Reconstruction and programs such as Medicare also provided much of the energy that fueled the Vietnam consensus. By the spring of 1964, the Vietcong, the military wing of the communist-dominated National Liberation Front, controlled more than 40 percent of the territory and 50 percent of the population of South Vietnam. The military junta headed by General Nguyen Khanh that ruled the country from Saigon was autocratic and increasingly out of touch with the citizenry. The Army of the Republic of Vietnam (ARVN) was undermanned and suffering from poor morale. Buddhists and Catholics continued to distrust each other, and the intelligentsia bridled at government censorship. In the summer of 1964, North Vietnam mobilized its own forces to support the insurrection in the south and accelerated work on the Ho Chi Minh Trail, which would transform it into a modern logistical network. In April of that year, the first North Vietnamese Army (NVA) regulars had been spotted moving down the trail and into the Central Highlands and the Delta.

In response to the deteriorating security situation in South Vietnam, some of Johnson's advisers devised a plan that called for the president, after first obtaining permission from Congress, to authorize a gradually escalating bombing campaign against North Vietnam. The White House would need a trigger to make its air assault credible, however. It was not long in coming. On the nights of August 1 and 4, 1964, American naval vessels on patrol in the Gulf of Tonkin reported being attacked by North Vietnamese gunboats. Citing this, the Gulf of Tonkin incident, as justification, LBJ went to Congress and obtained a resolution authorizing him to take "all necessary measures to repel any armed attacks against the force of the United States and to prevent further aggression."[33]

In February 1965, with coup and countercoup plots hatching all around him, General Khanh resigned. The US mission in Saigon and the more hawkish of his advisers urged Johnson to authorize the "carefully orchestrated bombing attack," to use the Pentagon's phrase, that had been in the works since spring. Fearing a repetition of the Korean War quagmire, LBJ balked. But then, on February 6, 1965, Vietcong units attacked a US Army barracks in Pleiku and a nearby helicopter base. A month later, communist guerrillas destroyed an enlisted men's barracks at Quinhon. In the wake of these provocations, the president bought in to the argument that the communist insurgency could not survive without aid from Hanoi, and he ordered a bombing campaign against North Vietnam codenamed Rolling Thunder.

Anticipating retaliatory attacks by the NVA and Vietcong, General William Westmoreland, the US commander in Vietnam, requested combat troops to protect the giant American air base at Danang. On March 8, 1965, the day after Bloody Sunday in Selma, two Marine battalions splashed ashore, the first regular combat units to be sent to Vietnam. But Westmoreland and the Joint Chiefs of Staff wanted to do no less than change basic American strategy. By mid-March they had concluded that if the war in Vietnam were to be won, the United States would have to assume a direct role in the fighting. Consequently, Westmoreland asked for two Army divisions, one to be stationed in the Central Highlands and the other in and around Saigon. At a high-level conference in Honolulu in April, the US military leadership decided to put forty thousand troops in Vietnam and continue the bombing campaign against North Vietnam for six months. The Rubicon had been crossed. The aerial assault on North Vietnam would continue throughout the remainder of the Johnson administration, and by the time the Texan left office, there would be half a million American troops in South Vietnam.

Lyndon Johnson was in basic agreement with the foreign policies of the Kennedy administration: military preparedness and realistic diplomacy, he believed, would contain communism within its existing bounds. To keep up morale among America's allies and satisfy hard-line anticommunists at home, the United States must continue to hold fast in Berlin, oppose the admission of Communist China to the United Nations, and continue to confront and blockade Cuba. Washington would stick with its "flexible response" of military aid, economic assistance, and technical/political advice in response to the threat of communism in the developing world. There was nothing wrong, however, with negotiating with the Soviet Union, which Washington perceived to be an increasingly conventional member of the international community, in an effort to reduce tensions.

Nevertheless, Johnson was no more ready than his predecessor to unilaterally withdraw from South Vietnam or seek a negotiated settlement that would lead to neutralization of the area south of the 17th parallel. A member of the Greatest Generation, Johnson was particularly sensitive to the Munich analogy, the notion that appeasement of an aggressor nation always led to further aggression. In addition, as he would later observe, he felt duty bound to continue the policies of his predecessor. Kennedy's top foreign policy advisers, whom LBJ retained in toto, were united in their belief that the United States must draw a line in Southeast Asia and that South Vietnam was the best place to do so. Too, Johnson feared that right-wing adversaries would tear him to pieces should South Vietnam fall to communism, just as Harry Truman had been hounded and his policies circumscribed by Senator Joseph McCarthy after the fall of China. Finally, in 1964 and 1965 when LBJ was faced with crucial decisions regarding Vietnam, he was trying to push through Congress the 1964 and 1965 civil rights bills, Medicare, and federal aid to education. He needed if not the outright support of the anti–big government, states-rights South, then its acquiescence. But the former Confederacy was traditionally the most hawkish section of the country. Johnson perceived that he could not ask the region to swallow civil rights accompanied by a dramatic increase in federal power, on the one hand, and the loss of Southeast Asia to the communists, on the other.[34]

In the context of the Cold War and America's embrace of liberal internationalism, how could the United States abandon a nonwhite people struggling for freedom in Southeast Asia while helping American blacks to full citizenship and equal opportunity in the United States? By the mid-1960s, this refrain had become particularly popular with members of the Americans for Democratic Action—Hubert Humphrey, Arthur Schlesinger, John Roche—and liberal internationalists in general. JFK's inaugural address, a call to arms, had inspired an entire generation. For Kennedy, excellence at home was necessary primarily to defeat communism abroad. Johnson tapped into that idealism to generate support for the Great Society. He was much more reluctant to embrace nation building in the developing world than had been Kennedy. Yet when faced with the exigencies of the Cold War, Johnson was as quick to prick the country's conscience to support the war in Vietnam as he had been for the War on Poverty. "We will carry on the fight against poverty and misery, and disease and ignorance in other lands and in our own," he had declared in his speech to a joint session of Congress on November 27, 1963. There was in his philosophy the assumption that human beings everywhere, especially at the individual and family levels, were the same. "For what do the people of North Viet-nam want?" he asked rhetorically in his 1965 Johns Hopkins speech. "They want what their neighbors also desire: food for their hunger; health for their bodies; a chance to learn; progress for their country; and an end to the bondage of material misery."[35]

Members of the audience at Howard University listen to LBJ deliver their 1965 commencement address, in which he broached the notion of affirmative action. (LBJ Library photo by Yoichi Okamoto)

Signing ceremony for the 1965 Immigration Act. (LBJ Library photo by Yoichi Okamoto)

LBJ on the Appalachian poverty tour, 1964. (LBJ Library photo by Cecil Stoughton)

The Johnsons try to exploit southern chivalry to open hearts and minds. (LBJ Library photo by unknown)

Vietnam War protestors at The March on the Pentagon. (LBJ Library photo by Frank Wolfe)

LBJ and Martin Luther King at the signing of the Civil Rights Act of 1964: Uneasy partners in a common cause. (LBJ Library photo by Yoichi Okamoto)

LBJ as student principal at Welhausen, the all-Hispanic school in Cotulla, Texas, 1928: A firsthand experience with institutionalized racism. (LBJ Library photo by unknown)

Robert F. Kennedy: LBJ's nemesis throughout his presidency. (LBJ Library photo by Yoichi Okamoto)

President Johnson tries to justify the war in Vietnam to Senator J. W. Fulbright, the powerful chair of the Senate Foreign Relations Committee and a leading opponent of the war. (LBJ Library photo by Yoichi Okamoto)

Whitney Young, executive director of the National Urban League: a man in the middle, caught between Black Power advocates and traditional civil rights leaders. (LBJ Library)

President Johnson and his elementary school teacher, Katie Deadrich Looney, at the signing of the Elementary and Secondary Education Act at Stonewall, Texas, 1965. (LBJ Library photo by Yoichi Okamoto)

J. Edgar Hoover: Longest-serving FBI director and sworn enemy of Martin Luther King. (LBJ Library photo by Yoichi Okamoto)

George Corley Wallace: The personification of white resistance to racial justice in the South. (LBJ Library photo by Yoichi Okamoto)

CHAPTER 8

PROGRESSIVISM REDUX: THE CHALLENGES OF SOCIAL ENGINEERING

THE WAR ON POVERTY REMAINED AT THE VERY CORE OF THE GREAT Society. It was perceived to be the key to social justice, putting an end to class animosities, providing substance to the civil rights movement, quelling urban unrest, and demonstrating to the world that capitalism was superior to communism. In February 1965, LBJ proudly reviewed the status of the War on Poverty for Congress. Through the Community Action Program, Neighborhood Youth Corps, Volunteers in Service to America, Aid to Families with Dependent Children, Job Corps, and various extracurricular education programs, Sargent Shriver and the Office of Economic Opportunity were getting help to millions of poor Americans. Specifically, local antipoverty programs were already under way in forty-four states, and fifty-three Job Corps centers, many of them at converted military bases, were processing six thousand applications a day. Some twenty-five thousand welfare families were receiving employment training, and ninety thousand adults were enrolled in adult education programs. Neighborhood Youth Corps were operating in forty-nine cities and eleven rural communities, and some four million Americans were receiving benefits under AFDC.[1] In March, LBJ submitted a $1.5 billion request to Congress to continue and expand these programs. One of the most significant increases was for Operation Head Start, a preschool program primarily for inner-city children designed to compensate for cultural disadvantages and to get them up to speed for the first grade.

But as the House and Senate took up the administration's 1965 poverty bill, the war was receiving mixed reviews. Complaints came pouring in from the poor that bureaucratic red tape was preventing mass access to OEO and other programs. "The pipeline is getting clogged up," Senator Abraham Ribicoff (D-CT), a supporter of the poverty program, told LBJ. "And we are going to have indigestion in the country . . . you have oversold the program. Everybody says President Johnson says it is great and everybody thinks it is great—and it is, but the trouble is this is going to start kicking back in everybody's teeth within the next year. . . . And that is dealing with a damned clean State [Connecticut]."[2]

The most controversial component of the War on Poverty was the Community Action Program (CAP). Title II of the Economic Opportunity Act established Community Acton Programs that were to provide "services, assistance, and other activities of sufficient scope and size to give promise of progress toward elimination of poverty or a cause or causes of poverty through developing employment opportunities, improving human performance, motivation, and productivity, or bettering the conditions under which people live, learn, and work." Under the act, $315 million was available to enable state and local agencies to work with private nonprofits to carry out a coordinated attack on local poverty problems.[3] The fundamental notion driving the CAP was that the poor and powerless, by participating in decisions affecting their local communities, would benefit not only materially but psychologically.

"Maximum feasible participation," which became something of a catchphrase in the OEO after it was established, had its roots initially in the New England townships that served as stable political bases through the War for Independence and the early days of the Republic. Later, in the late nineteenth century, the aggrieved farmers of the South and Midwest who established the Populist Party came to see in the cooperative movement a vehicle to achieve social and economic justice. During the Progressive Era and the New Deal, collective bargaining was inextricably linked to the republican ideal of "industrial democracy." There could be no more "political democracy" in contemporary America, Progressive attorney Louis Brandeis declared in 1915, without an "industrial democracy" that gave workers actual participation in the governance of the firms for which they worked.[4]

During the Kennedy administration, New Frontiersmen came to see local action as an antidote to juvenile delinquency, a mechanism that would eradicate the conditions that were producing delinquency. "The people of the other America do not, by far and large, belong to unions, to fraternal organizations, or to political parties," Michael Harrington wrote in 1962. "They are without lobbies of their own; they put forward no legislative program." Because they had no voice, the government would have to step forward itself and empower them.[5] The idea of participatory democracy also found clear expression in the Port Huron Statement issued in 1962 by the SDS. Authentic democracy required more than economic security and social equality; it required a politics of maximum citizen participation. In part, it was this call for participatory democracy that separated the New Left from the Old Left.[6]

LBJ and the architects of the Great Society have been, with some justification, portrayed as advocates of big government, seeing the federal bureaucracy as the ultimate backstop for social and economic justice in America. There is no doubt that the 1964 and 1965 civil rights acts, Medicare, the Elementary and Secondary Education Act, and other measures and programs greatly enhanced the power of the federal government. But there is also much evidence that LBJ had doubts that the Great Society could be built and sustained solely from the top down. Johnson had been an enthusiastic and effective state director of the Texas National Youth Administration (NYA). The NYA, headed by the militant southern liberal Aubrey Williams, was both more idealistic and less bureaucratic than most other New Deal agencies. Its programs were administered from state offices and under state relief administrations that were encouraged to develop innovative grassroots reforms.[7] Johnson, Busby, and other 1960s reformers believed that in the South the assertion of federal power was necessary to eliminate discrimination, but once African Americans, specifically, and the poor, in general, were empowered, then states and localities could become the "laboratories of democracy" that Progressives had envisioned.

In truth, however, LBJ accepted community action almost by default. He had given the poverty task force a mere six weeks to come up with a

workable plan. He made it clear that he did not want either increased welfare payments, income subsidies, or an expensive new jobs program. Many
of the personnel Shriver staffed OEO with had worked for the Kennedy
administration's President's Commission on Juvenile Delinquency (PCJD).
They had already embraced community action and maximum feasible participation, and they naturally put it forward as a principal component of the
War on Poverty. But as time would quickly tell, maximum feasible participation meant different things to different people. Johnson saw the CAPs as
mechanisms enabling the poor to work cooperatively with state and local
bureaucracies and political machines. Others saw community action as a
means to challenge those bureaucracies and party organizations. Sargent
Shriver would later acknowledge a deeper purpose—"to change institutions
as well as people," to challenge "hostile or uncaring or exploitive institutions" in an attempt to make them responsive to the peculiar needs of the
"whole community."[8]

For many black activists, the call for maximum feasible participation was
the most compelling aspect of the Economic Opportunity Act. The notion
of Community Action Programs resonated with a black community that had
a long history of self-help organizations—from participant-owned insurance
companies to literary societies, from black churches to civil rights organizations. All of these had emphasized the importance of self-improvement
in service to community betterment. Not only radicals but established civil
rights organizations such as the NAACP and the Urban League were swept
up in the growing enthusiasm for community action by the poor. In the
first year of the War on Poverty, over one thousand CAPs across the country
received federal funding; by 1968, four-fifths of them were being run by
private, nonprofit organizations directly funded by OEO.[9]

Samples of undertakings by OEO-funded CAPs were summer day camps
for poor children in Detroit, fencing classes for underprivileged kids in
Harlem, and a university-run health center in Boston. Hardly revolutionary.
But in August 1965, Philadelphia's poor used OEO funds to travel to Har-
risburg to demonstrate against Governor William Scranton's planned veto of
several welfare measures. And members of the East New York–Brownsville
antipoverty council had hardly been elected before they were talking about
demanding improved public services from the city—better garbage collection and rigorous housing inspection.[10]

Mayors and governors complained with increasing shrillness about Shriver's willingness to give control of poverty funds to private organizations that circumvented local political machines. Welfare had long constituted the base of political power for big-city organizations, and they were loath to give it up. Leading the charge was the powerful mayor of Chicago, Richard Daley, and Adam Clayton Powell, who's HARY-YOU project in Harlem was one of the major relief projects in New York City. "What in the hell are you people doing?" Daley asked Bill Moyers. "Does the president know he's putting money in the hands of subversives? To poor people that aren't a part of the organization?"[11] Southern governors joined northern mayors in clamoring for control. Their motives, Shriver and his staff suspected, were not the purest. Initially, OEO stuck to its guns, insisting that the poor could constitute a majority on local CAP boards and that segregationists be removed from positions of power in the poverty program in Louisiana and other southern states. The ever-tanned and energetic Shriver came under increasing attack as a result. In an effort to appease critics, he agreed to give up the Peace Corps to concentrate on poverty, but the assault continued.

Abe Ribicoff, an increasingly influential voice in matters of poverty and urban unrest, argued to LBJ that for the War on Poverty to work,

> you have to have the political establishment, you have to have labor, you have to have industry, and you have to have civil rights and the poor. Now setting up what they [OEO] are doing now, setting up a new power base with the poor is absolutely dynamite because it has to lead to anarchy when the vicious men who have never been able to achieve power, seek power through the poor. Now you have to start with smart mayors and work all of them in together.[12]

LBJ agreed. "I am against subsidizing any private organization," the president told Bill Moyers in August 1964. "I would prefer Dick Daley do it than the Urban League. . . . I just think it makes us wide open and I don't want anybody to get any grants."[13] The problem was that "the poor" and many urban civil rights leaders sided with Shriver and the OEO radicals. Labor was split, with George Meany of the AFL-CIO backing the establishment, and Walter Reuther and the United Auto Workers (UAW) working to set up local nonprofits outside the existing political order. Meanwhile, representatives of the National Governors Conference lobbied to have amendments attached to the Economic Opportunity Act of 1965 providing for a gubernatorial veto of all poverty program decisions in their respective states.[14]

If LBJ was ambivalent about community action, he was totally committed to the Job Corps, a reincarnation in his mind of the New Deal's Civilian Conservation Corps. But by 1965 it, too, was being attacked by both liberals and conservatives. Many Great Society officials saw the Job Corps as the answer to the culture of poverty. It would, recalled Christopher Weeks, special assistant to Shriver, remove the poorest youth, aged sixteen to twenty-one, from their home environments—"ghetto tenements and rural shacks"—and send them to "a clean, healthful center where massive injections of remedial education and job training would turn them into law-abiding, tax-paying good neighbors."[15] Though envisioned as a program for men, Congress added women, stipulating that one-third of the openings would be reserved for them. At its height the Job Corps included six large (1,000 to 3,000) urban centers for men, at least eighty rural centers for men (100 to 250 per unit), and seventeen for women (300 to 1,000 per unit). All offered health care and counseling as well as education and training. From the outset, OEO officially denied that the corps was intended primarily for African Americans, but they were simply trying to avoid the ire of segregationist legislators during congressional consideration of OEO. Of those remaining in the corps six months, nearly two-thirds were African American, while just a quarter were white. Very quickly both civil rights supporters and civil rights opponents came to see the corps as a program to help inner-city blacks. In the wake of Watts and other urban uprisings, conservatives denounced the Job Corps as a federal program to reward black criminals. When a riot erupted at the Job Corps Center at Camp Breckenridge in Kentucky over discriminatory hiring practices at the facility, conservatives denounced the camps as no more than breeding grounds for urban revolutionaries.[16]

The Job Corps, indeed, the entire War on Poverty, was designed to reinforce the traditional family model with an employed father and a homemaking mother. Women received "intensive training in home and family life and the development of values, attitudes, and skills that would contribute to stable family relationships and a good child-rearing environment," the Job Corps announced. There was no vocational training that would allow women to compete for jobs in the larger workforce, thus stigmatizing and penalizing single mothers. Female trainees who became pregnant were summarily dismissed.[17]

Inevitably, the War on Poverty had to address the thorny issue of birth control. Economists and demographers estimated that over a generation, one million poor women practicing contraception meant 500,000 less poor children. Under existing Department of Health, Education, and Welfare guidelines, the agency could provide federal funds for family planning but only if states requested and administered such aid. HEW chief Anthony Celebrezze, a Catholic, insisted that federal activity in the area of birth control ought to go no further. Shriver, also a Catholic, violently disagreed. He, along with Harry McPherson and Bill Moyers, believed that the federal government through the OEO ought to undertake an aggressive campaign of sex education and provide free contraceptives not only to married poor women but also to the unmarried as well. Indeed, it was unmarried women and women not living with the fathers of their children who were responsible, biologically, for the population explosion. "If the purpose of our policy is to slow down the making of babies in conditions of squalor and intellectual degradation," McPherson observed to Moyers, "the choice seems clear."[18]

Johnson was leery. The subject was a minefield. As McPherson pointed out, the great mass of Catholics would prove acquiescent, but if the Vatican chose to make an issue of the matter, there would be trouble, particularly if it allied with white religious fundamentalists who would see federal birth control programs as attempts to subsidize immorality. Finally, there would be those within the black power movement who would cry genocide. Nevertheless, the OEO proceeded to make grants to private nonprofits to distribute information and contraceptives among both inner-city and rural poor regardless of color or marital status.[19]

In late July, the president took time off from lobbying for the poverty bill to secure longtime friend and confidant Abe Fortas's appointment to the Supreme Court. LBJ had never forgotten the political disaster that had followed on the heels of FDR's infamous court-packing plan. He knew how ground-breaking and controversial were the Great Society programs that had been created and were being contemplated, and he wanted to ensure that the liberal majority on the Warren Court remained intact. Moreover, he could depend upon Fortas to keep him abreast of the changing mood of the court as it responded to personalities and changing circumstances.

Fortas had always insisted that he did not want to leave his lucrative law practice for a seat on the court, but LBJ and Lady Bird suspected otherwise. Ever since LBJ had become president, Fortas, egged on by his wife and fellow attorney Carol Agger, had deflected talk of an appointment to the court. She wanted him to wait five or six years until the couple had ensured their financial security and Abe could enjoy the ermine of the bench in his declining years. But as Fortas biographer Laura Kalman observes, he "was a pragmatist who knew that history could be managed only up to a point. The opportunity had arisen now, and it might not occur again."[20] There-upon LBJ and Fortas entered into an elaborate charade in which it was made to appear that the former dragged the latter onto the court almost against his will. On July 19, Fortas wrote the president a letter declining his offer of a seat on the highest court in the land. On July 28, LBJ summoned his friend to the White House and told him that in minutes he was going to address a press conference announcing that he was sending an additional fifty thou-sand troops to Vietnam and that he was nominating Fortas for the vacant position on the Supreme Court.[21] Faced with a fait accompli, he dutifully and gratefully accepted.

During Fortas's confirmation hearings in August, some senators expressed worry that his close relationship with the president might compromise his judicial independence. "There are two things that have been vastly exagger-ated with respect to me," the nominee declared with some disingenuousness. "One is the extent to which I am a Presidential adviser and the other is the extent to which I am a proficient violinist. I am a very poor violinist but very enthusiastic, and my relationship with the President has been exaggerated out of all connection with reality." Despite the fact that members of the John Birch Society and other right-wing groups flooded Washington with tele-grams urging rejection of the nomination on the grounds that Fortas was a Jew, a liberal, and even, possibly, a Communist, he was approved unanimously.[22]

As the debate in Congress over the 1965 poverty bill raged during the summer and early fall, LBJ stepped up the pressure, calling congressmen and -women and senators, urging labor leaders and civil rights organizations to enter the fray, and subtly threatening conservatives with the specter of urban revolution if new appropriations for OEO were not forthcoming.[23] The latter threat was not hollow. The uprising in Watts and an earlier less destructive riot in Harlem, with its potential to create a massive white back-lash, frightened and depressed Johnson and Shriver. They saw the legislation increasing funding for the poverty program for 1966 as a crucial safety valve. The president demanded that Congressman Charles Halleck support his effort to force the poverty bill out of the hands of Howard Smith, the Rules Committee chairman.

But many Republicans were less than enthusiastic because they believed that in aiding the poor the War on Poverty was just enabling people who were bound to vote Democratic.[24] "That's a good bill," the president told Halleck, "and there's no reason you ought to keep a majority from voting on it. If you can beat it, go on and beat it, but you ought to give me a fair shake."[25] The president then turned to southern conservatives, many of whom saw the Job Corps as just another liberal scheme to promote racial integration. "I'm going to take tax-eaters and make tax-payers out of them . . . and I'm going to stop those damn riots," he told Congressman George Mahon (D-TX). "I got them [civil rights leaders] to agree today . . . no more demonstrations and they're asking please, put these people to work . . . and I'm going to put 150,000 of them [to work] in 90 days."[26]

Finally, after five weeks, the bill reached the floor. Johnson proceeded to enlist the help of labor leaders, including Meany of the AFL-CIO and Reuther of the UAW. In conversation with the latter, Johnson argued that not only the poverty bill but the remainder of the Great Society agenda was on the line. "They're going to beat our poverty bill, and we can stand that, we can survive it," he told Reuther. "But one thing we can't survive is just getting beat this time of the year, because it's like Roosevelt's Supreme Court. They're going to say 'the king's dead.' If Johnson can't pass a little $900 million poverty bill, he damn sure can't pass anything else. And that's what's bad. . . . It's going to de-nut him [the president]."[27]

On October 9, Congress passed the Economic Opportunity Act Amendments of 1965—without a gubernatorial veto of Community Action Programs. It was a very close thing. The vote in the Senate was 44 to 43.[28] By the end of 1965, the OEO was alive and well, and it was only 20 percent of what had become nearly a $20 billion War on Poverty that included Social Security, direct relief, Food Stamps, HEW aid to slum schools, federal expenditures for public housing, and area redevelopment.[29]

NOT ONLY HAD THE WHITE HOUSE LOBBIED INTENSELY FOR PASSAGE of the 1965 EOA amendments bill, it had also focused poverty programs on south Los Angeles in an effort to convince future potential rioters that there was hope. On August 26, LBJ announced that the federal government was going to immediately spend between $200 million and $300 million in Watts on, among other things, a special employment program, pilot child care centers, a small-business center to foster black-owned enterprises in the ghetto, a vigorous back-to-school program, construction of low-income housing, and an expanded surplus food distribution program.[30] But Abe Ribicoff, Walter Reuther, and others advised the president that special programs beyond OEO and AFDC were needed to address the complex problems facing the nation's cities—problems such as mass transit that would bring the poor to available jobs, slum clearance programs that would do more than simply replace tenements with middle-class housing that the poor could not afford.

"There is no imagination to pull together as I see it what you do with schools, what you do with parks, what you do with roads, what you do with housing, what you do with urban renewal," Ribicoff observed to LBJ; "all it has been up until now is a method to eliminate the poor and to substitute it with a middle-class and a lot of men to make a lot of money on big office buildings and big markets and big real estate developments. Now this has been a tragedy because . . . we have not helped the poor or the Negro but we have hurt him by forcing him to go into more and more crowded areas as we have destroyed the hovels in which he has lived."[31]

Independently, Walter Reuther attempted to sell the White House on a "pilot cities" program in which business, labor, and the federal government would cooperate "to carve out significant portions of decayed areas of center cities and rebuild them with rehabilitation, new housing, new commercial buildings, new workers, professional people, Negroes, Whites, etc."[32] LBJ was sympathetic despite his dislike of Reuther.[33] It was no accident, he commented to journalist Al Friendly, that Watts simultaneously demonstrated the highest population density, the highest disease rate, the highest unemployment rate, and the highest rate of narcotic use in the country. "If we don't face up to the problems [that we have now] ultimately [we will] not only have to face up to the ones we got now, but we face up to a bunch we have created that flow from failure to face up to the ones we got."[34] Standing in the LBJ Ranch swimming pool at the beginning of August, Johnson declared to his new domestic adviser, Joseph Califano, "I want to rebuild

American cities. . . . I want a bill that makes it possible for anybody to buy a house anywhere they can afford to."[35] The upshot was a proposal for a new cabinet-level department—Housing and Urban Development (HUD).

Johnson's vision of a new Department of Housing and Urban Development went far beyond what the Kennedy administration had in mind when it proposed and Congress rejected a housing and urban affairs bill. HUD would be an institution of both the Old Politics and the New. It would simultaneously solve the malaise created by mass society—anonymity, powerlessness, and isolation—and ease racial tensions in inner-city ghettoes by promoting employment and raising living standards. At the signing ceremony for HUD on September 9, 1965, LBJ exclaimed, "It is not enough for us to erect towers of stone and glass, or to lay out vast suburbs of order and conformity. We must seek and we must find the ways to preserve and to perpetuate in the city the individuality, the human dignity . . . the devotion to individual responsibility that has been part of the American character and the strength of the American system."[36] HUD would be an instrument in service to the New Individualism, a new America produced by a society committed to both negative and positive rights.

Although the president was required to name a cabinet secretary for HUD no later than November 1, he agonized for more than three months before announcing his choice. Since his accession to the presidency, LBJ had made noises about naming the first black Supreme Court Justice [he did—Thurgood Marshall in 1967] and the first black cabinet member. Nearly everyone anticipated that Johnson would choose Robert Weaver, the administrator of the Housing and Home Finance Agency and a Negro, to head HUD.

But as LBJ confided to Roy Wilkins, he had serious misgivings. He was aware of the tremendous symbolic importance of appointing a black cabinet officer. He knew "how many little Negro boys in Podunk, Mississippi" would be uplifted by it. "Now I am very anxious, in the limited time the Good Lord is going to give me, to just not talk but to do and to do by example and to put the coon skins on the wall and not just talk and promise and then make big speeches," he told Wilkins. Moreover, he liked Weaver, he said; he was a fair, intelligent if unimaginative man. But would racism in Congress and within the urban power structures prevent Weaver from getting the job done? "I rather think that a white man can do a hell of a lot more for the Negro than the Negroes can for themselves in these cities," he observed to Wilkins.[37] "In my judgment you are liable to get yourself in the same shape you did after the reconstruction and it will take you another hundred years to get back," the president confided to Katzenbach. "I doubt that this fella can make the grade and he will be a flop and he will be exhibit number one."[38]

LBJ had other reasons for delaying. He wanted to use Weaver's potential appointment to compel civil rights leaders to follow the path he had chosen, and he wanted to impress upon Weaver the importance of his appointment and the debt he would owe to the president for it. In his conversation with Wilkins, he indirectly chided the leadership of the traditional civil rights organizations for not anticipating urban unrest and doing more to prevent it, for fostering demonstrations that contributed to the white backlash, and for not getting out and registering black voters.[39] Significantly, Wilkins told LBJ that he and the blacks that he knew would abide by whatever decision regarding the HUD secretaryship he made. "I can criticize you and will," he told LBJ, "but I still believe in your heart."[40] All the while LBJ kept Weaver and the black community in suspense, however, he had been running interference for his appointment with Richard Russell, Russell Long, and other southern senators. When LBJ finally sent Weaver's name up in January, the Senate took a mere four days to give its unanimous consent.[41]

THE FIRST WEEK IN OCTOBER 1965, THE NATION WAS ONCE AGAIN reminded that racism was alive and well in the South. In August, in Lowndes County, Alabama, Thomas A. Coleman, a highway engineer and unpaid deputy sheriff, had emptied his shotgun into two civil rights workers, Jonathan M. Daniels, a twenty-six-year-old white Episcopal seminarian, and Richard Morrisroe, a Catholic priest of the same age, killing the former and gravely wounding the latter. Coleman's trial took place in the slave-built, white-washed courthouse in Haynesville. Circuit Judge T. Werth Thagard refused to allow Alabama Attorney General Richmond Flowers to direct the prosecution, and he refused to delay the trial until Morrisroe was well enough to testify. The clerk of the court was Coleman's cousin; the local football field had been named for his father. The local prosecutor, Arthur E. "Bubba" Gamble, dominated the proceedings. Joyce Bailey, a thin, nineteen-year-old Negro, took the stand and described the scene at the Cash Store, which a mixed group was trying to integrate. She recounted Coleman's order to Daniels—"Get off this property, or I'll blow your god-damn heads off, you sons of bitches." Gamble joined the jury and spectators in prolonged laughter. She described the blast as it hit Daniels—"He caught his stomach and then he fell back." With Father Morrisroe, she started run-ning. After he was shot down, she testified, "I was still running." More laughter from the gallery, and then somebody yelled, "Run, you niggers." More laughter. Coleman was duly acquitted.[42]

The White House was as repelled as most of the rest of the nation. Reedy and his cohorts mulled over various options, including reviving the Force Acts (Reconstruction-era measures empowering the president to use fed-eral troops to protect citizens in the exercise of their constitutional rights), federal legislation to reform the jury system, and a sub-rosa campaign to convince southern officials that if they did not put a halt to these courtroom farces, the civil rights movement would be driven underground "where it is likely to act like the Viet Cong." But in the end there was nothing in the short run that the administration could do.[43] In November, however, the Justice Department did intervene on the side of Charles Morgan Jr., a Bir-mingham lawyer who had been run out of Alabama for his liberal heresies; he had filed suit in federal court charging discriminatory jury selection in Haynesville.[44]

In his Howard speech the previous June, LBJ had called for the conven-ing of a White House Conference, "To Ensure These Rights," to be held in the spring of 1966. In November, some two hundred civil rights leaders gathered at the Washington Hilton to plan for the meeting. By this point, the black backlash against the Moynihan report was in full swing. If Negroes had a family problem, declared Bayard Rustin, "it is not because they are Negro but because they are so disproportionately a part of the unemployed, the underemployed and the ill-paid." Honorary chairman A. Philip Ran-dolph, seventy-six, the courtly president of the Brotherhood of Sleeping Car Porters, called for a $100 billion "freedom budget" to be spent on eradicat-ing ghettoes.[45] Moynihan, among others, agreed. "Pat's answer was rather simple," Harry McPherson recalled, "a family allowance plan. He took the position that all the remedial programs in the world were for naught unless there was an income base in the family. You could build on that; they would stay home and you'd have an interacting family. . . . This was a Catholic middle-class view."[46] Given LBJ's commitment to consensus, his determination to sell antipoverty and civil rights to conservatives as well as liberals, and the mounting costs of the war in Southeast Asia, such an approach, which could cost $11 billion to $12 billion a year, was an impossibility.

TO SIMULTANEOUSLY FINANCE THE WAR IN SOUTHEAST ASIA AND THE Great Society, it was imperative, LBJ believed, to hold down prices and wages in order to prevent runaway inflation. Beginning in August 1964, the Johnson administration had worked to persuade labor and management to adhere to an unofficial guideline of 3.2 percent in wage and price increases annually. The first great challenge to this standard, which corresponded to the estimated annual growth rate in productivity, came from the steel industry.[47]

The United Steel Workers, headed by newly elected I. W. Abel, and the steel industry, represented by R. Conrad Cooper, had negotiated throughout the summer, but to no avail. The union demanded wage increases of approximately 5 percent, with steel offering half that amount. If it was forced to go above that offer, industry spokesmen said, prices would increase well above 3.2 percent. Abel had been elected on a promise to achieve the same wage increase recently won by the can and aluminum workers, and he would not budge. Cooper, banking on White House intervention, also remained adamant.

On August 17, LBJ summoned Abel to the White House to try a little persuasion. "I made commitments to the members who elected me," Abel told the president defensively. "You're starting to sound just like Dick Russell," Johnson retorted, cunningly. "He sat on that very couch talking to me about my civil rights bill in 1964. I asked him not to filibuster. 'We've got to make a stand somewhere,' he said. He sounded just like you.'" Smiling, LBJ softened and told Able an anecdote. "I told Dick Russell the story about the Negro boy in bed with the white gal, whose husband arrived home unexpectedly. 'Hide! Hide,' she whispered. 'He'll kill you and then he'll kill me.'" The president described how the black youth hid in the closet. "At this point," Joe Califano, who was at the meeting, recalled, "Johnson bolted from his rocker, stood upright, arms stiff at his side, legs straight, tight together, back and shoulders ramrod straight. He described the enraged husband charging through the bedroom shouting that he knew someone was there, banging doors open. Finally he came to the closet where the culprit was hiding. 'What the hell are you doing here?' this little white gal's husband shouts, fire in his eyes. 'Everybody's gotta stand somewhere, boss,' this Negro boy answers." Everybody laughed. Johnson leaned into Abel and said softly, slowly, "Everybody's gotta stand somewhere," he repeated. Just "like that Negro boy he wanted to keep down, Russell stuck himself in a closet with nowhere to go on civil rights. Mr. Abel, I know you gotta stand somewhere. But you gotta stand where you can move around a little, not just pinned in the linen closet."[48]

Initially, Johnson tried to leave it to Willard Wirtz and John Conner, his secretaries of labor and commerce, respectively, to work out a deal, but he found them too closely tied to the positions of their constituents. When the two closeted themselves with Abel, Cooper, and their lawyers in a suite in the Executive Office Building next to the White House, the best they could come up with was an eight-day postponement of the strike deadline. LBJ then brought former governor LeRoy Collins of Florida, successful negotiator of civil rights disputes; Senator Wayne Morse (D-OR), whose domestic expertise centered on labor-management conflict resolution; and former labor lawyer Arthur Goldberg into the picture. Following an extended breakfast meeting on August 30, all three expressed pessimism that the 3.2 percent guideline could be adhered to.[49] Johnson then decided to jump into the fray himself. The stakes were too high. He appealed typically to both parties' patriotism. A strike would end the nation's fifty-five-month economic expansion. Price rises on steel would percolate throughout the economy, providing justification for price increases on thousands of consumer items. A recently conducted Harris poll indicated that 87 percent of America's housewives were worried about inflation.[50] Negotiators pushed LBJ to permit selective price increases that would allow a better wage offer to the union. "No price increase," he told Califano. "None. Zero," making a circle with his thumb and forefinger.[51]

Observers remarked on the enthusiasm, confidence, almost joy with which LBJ intervened in the steel dispute. He continued to pop in on union and industry negotiators while at the same time sending Clark Clifford, counsel to Republic Steel, to tell company executives that there would be no guideline-busting settlement and Goldberg to union leaders to tell them the same thing.[52] On September 3, a gleeful Johnson flanked by Abel and Cooper, both of whom were obviously less than gleeful, appeared at a press conference to announce that a settlement had been reached and that it was well within the administration's 3.2 percent guideline. Commentary in the press and the public were generally laudatory. "'Masterful' is the word for the way you brought the steel crisis to a successful solution," economist Walter Heller wrote him. "You struck a key blow for continued cost-price stability and the country's economic health."[53]

In reality, LBJ's ostentatious intrusion into the steel dispute ended his honeymoon with the business community. "Business people are generally scared stiff by the tactics that have been followed in the aluminum, copper, and now the steel situation where individual companies have been singled out and expressions used that indicate that the administration leaders might look upon them as profiteers or unpatriotic," Secretary of Commerce Connor reported to LBJ. His boss was not impressed: "Allright for them to call their President a son of a bitch but if he replies, he ought to go to jail. Is that the meat of it?"[54]

In the midst of the steel brouhaha, conservative economist Milton Friedman wrote an article for the *National Review* entitled "Social Responsibility: A Subversive Doctrine." A businessperson's first and overriding obligation must be to his or her stockholders, Friedman proclaimed. To introduce other factors into the decision-making process would be to subvert the free-market system. It was his experience, Friedman wrote, that "the appeal to 'social' responsibility or 'voluntary' restraint has always occurred when the governmental agency which is responsible for the area of policy in question has been unable or unwilling to discharge its own responsibility." Here was an attack on the whole notion of Johnsonian corporatism, the concept of business-labor-government cooperation to bring stability and predictability to the marketplace.[55]

Executives and business academics chastised LBJ for undermining the very system he was trying to save. George Shultz, dean of the Graduate School of Business at the University of Chicago and a prominent labor arbitrator, warned that "it undermines private collective bargaining to have the President and government come in so strongly." Lawrence Harvey, president of California's Harvey Aluminum, agreed: "Soon there will be no more unions, in effect, and no more collective bargaining. The government will control the terms of every contract."[56] A Washington cynic looked up Johnson's favorite biblical quotation, "Come now, and let us reason together" (Isaiah 1:18), and found that the passage continued: "If ye be willing and obedient, ye shall eat of the good of the land; but if ye refuse and rebel, ye shall be devoured with the sword."[57]

In the end, LBJ's attempts to limit price-wage increases without mandatory controls proved futile. In January 1966, John V. Lindsay, the newly elected liberal Republican mayor of New York, agreed to give transit workers a 6.3 percent pay raise. In the summer, steel defied LBJ by increasing prices. A subsequent settlement between the International Machinists and Aerospace Workers (IMA) and the country's airlines gave the union a 4.9 percent raise and in the words of the IMA president "destroy[ed] all existing wage and price guidelines now in existence."[58]

Nevertheless, the Great Society marked a watershed in the history of labor-management relations in the United States. Some of the change had to do with intent, some with long-term trends, and some with unintended consequences of collateral legislation. In the years following World War II, even as union membership grew, organized labor came under attack from both the Right and the Left. There was the Taft-Hartley Bill of 1947 whose section 14b permitted right-to-work laws, measures outlawing agreements between unions and employers making union membership a condition of employment. States where unions were weakest, principally in the South and West, proved most likely to pass such laws. But even in the industrial states of the Northeast and Midwest, unions faced a business community that had begun to mobilize against union bargaining clout. At the same time, critics on the left denounced unions for selling out to big business. In 1952 sociologist Daniel Bell labeled modern trade unionism "the capitalism of the proletariat," arguing that unions as a market-shaping interest group were inevitably winning out over organized labor as an ideological force. By the early 1960s, Bell's was no longer a voice crying in the wilderness. A generation of intellectuals, jurists, journalists, academics, and politicians had come to see the unions as little more than a self-aggrandizing interest group, no longer a force for progressive change.[59]

Union critics on the left were overstating the case. During the Johnson administration, both the AFL-CIO's more conservative wing under George

Meany and the CIO, which included the powerful Auto Workers Union headed by left-leaning Walter Reuther, proved to be consistent supporters of Great Society legislation, although southern unions continued to discriminate and northern unions would man their seniority systems as bastions against affirmative action. While he readily appealed to the social consciences of labor union members, LBJ had no problem with modern unionism. He was a thoroughgoing corporatist, and in his view consensus within organized labor was a positive thing. But in the view of most businessmen and some unionists, LBJ's ostentatious and ongoing intervention into labor-management disputes—indeed, corporatism itself—was undermining the whole concept of collective bargaining. What Johnson did was nothing new for Democratic administrations, which beginning with that of Franklin Roosevelt had politicized collective bargaining, putting unionists, capitalists, and government labor relations experts in the Oval Office, the halls of Congress, and the chambers of the Supreme Court. Employers decried this development and worked to reprivatize industrial relations, thus taking the "labor question" out of the realm of politics and returning it to the far more favorable terrain of the firm-centered welfare state.[60] But what really delivered the coup de grace to collective bargaining was the "rights revolution."

Title VII of the 1964 Civil Rights Act, which prohibited discrimination in hiring or firing because of race, sex, or national origin, would come to equal the Wagner Act, which created the National Labor Relations Board (NLRB) to enforce fairness in collective bargaining in importance in the world of work. Within just a few years of its creation, the Equal Employment Opportunity Commission would become an even more high-profile agency than the NLRB, and the judicial interpretation of Title VII became every bit as significant and controversial as any Supreme Court labor law ruling. Title VII opened the floodgates to a host of new laws that were classified as civil rights initiatives but were actually central to the expansion of work rights in the factory, office, mine, and salesroom. In 1968 came the Age Discrimination in Employment Act, in 1969 the Mine Safety Act, in 1970 the Occupational Safety and Health Act, in 1973 the Rehabilitation Act, and in 1974 the Employee Retirement Income Security Act.[61] Labor's reliance on collective bargaining came to seem far less potent and universal than the rights discourse generated by the state's conception of substantive justice and equal protection under the law.[62] In brief, more and more workers sought redress of their grievances in court rather than in the union hall.

But as the glorious Eighty-Ninth Congress neared its end and one Great Society coonskin after another was nailed to the wall, the growing alienation of business and labor was not yet apparent. Increasingly, LBJ permitted himself the luxury of comparing achievements of the Great Society with those of the New Deal and himself with FDR. As was the case with the New Deal, there was to be something for everyone, even the venomous and ungrateful intellectuals and artists who were then criticizing Johnson for everything from his Vietnam policy to his haircut. Unlike the New Deal's efforts in this area—the Federal Writers' Project, the Federal Theater project, and others—the Great Society's programs were designed to be permanent.

During his brief appearance at the White House Festival of Arts in June 1965, LBJ had observed that it was the role of the federal government "as representative of all the people" to stimulate and nurture the creative arts.[63] Indeed, the previous March the president had submitted to Congress legislation creating a National Foundation on the Arts and a National Foundation on the Humanities. The proposals had sped through the Senate and bogged down briefly in the House. A little presidential prodding, however, freed the bills from the conservative coalition's embrace. On September 29, LBJ signed the new measures and promised that a National Theater, a National Opera, and a National Ballet would follow. The legislation created two 24-member bodies, a National Council on the Arts/Humanities to select projects worthy of funding, and a National Endowment on the Arts/Humanities to administer the grants awarded. Thus was launched the first comprehensive and sustained effort by the federal government to materially support artists, historians, musicians, writers, critics, philosophers, sculptors, painters, and dancers.[64] As chairman of the Arts Council, the White House selected Roger Stevens, playwright, art impresario, and, not coincidentally, an intimate of the Kennedys.[65]

CHAPTER 9

NATIVISM AT BAY: IMMIGRATION AND THE LATINO MOVEMENT

ON THE AFTERNOON OF OCTOBER 3, AT THE BASE OF THE STATUE OF Liberty, LBJ signed the Immigration Act of 1965, thus putting in place one of the least-noticed but most important components of the Great Society. Citizenship in the United States was not to be based on blood, national origin, kinship, heredity, or color but on a commitment to certain governing political principles.[1] This, allegedly, was what made America unique among all other polities. However, as particular ethnic, religious, or racial groups within the United States struggled to gain or maintain political and cultural dominance, state and federal laws sought to identify American nationality as peculiarly white or Protestant or Anglo Saxon. In turn, Congress passed citizenship laws that institutionalized those myths. Throughout most of the history of the United States, laws were on the books that declared the vast majority of the peoples of the world legally ineligible to become full citizens solely because of their race, origin, nationality, or gender.[2] Even indigenous peoples were not immune from discrimination.

The Founding Fathers embraced immigration as a necessity to populate the vast hinterlands of the new nation. Indeed, high on the list of Thomas Jefferson's grievances against King George III was the charge that he had endeavored to prevent the peopling of the American colonies by obstructing naturalization laws and making immigration from countries other than Great Britain or its colonies difficult. The framers of the Constitution clearly intended to encourage immigration when in Article I Section 8 they authorized Congress to "establish a uniform rule of naturalization" and made immigrants eligible for all federal offices save president and vice president.[3] At the same time, many Americans evidenced hostile feelings toward immigrants in general and those from certain countries in particular. Benjamin Franklin did not like Germans. Reacting to an influx of Germans into Pennsylvania, he wrote in 1751:

> Why should the Palatine boors be suffered to swarm into our Settlements, and by herding together establish their Language and manners to the Exclusion of ours? Why should Pennsylvania, founded by the English, become a colony of Aliens, who will shortly be so numerous as to Germanize us instead of us Anglifying them, and will never adopt our Language or Customs, any more than they can acquire our Complexion?[4]

In the 1830s and 1840s, violent anti-Catholic riots swept the cities of New England and Pennsylvania. The 1850s gave rise to a new political party, the Know-Nothings, as their critics labeled them, which focused primarily on limiting further immigration and restricting the rights of the foreign-born already in the country. The Civil War, which saw members of various ethnic groups fighting side by side under both flags, ended, for a time, the anti-immigrant furor. The adoption of the Fourteenth Amendment—which begins "All persons born or naturalized in the United States, and subject to the jurisdiction thereof, are citizens of the United States and of the State wherein they reside"—established for the first time a national citizenship and bestowed citizenship on former slaves who had been born in the United States.[5]

During its first one hundred years, the American Republic was overwhelmingly peopled by immigrants from northern and western Europe—the British Isles, Scandinavia, Germany, and France. But beginning in the late nineteenth century, a flood of some twenty million immigrants entered the country from eastern and southern Europe, most of them of darker skin, many of them Catholics and Jews. In 1907 alone, 1,285,349 persons from nations stretching from Greece to Russia came through Ellis Island. In addition, there was in the late nineteenth century a flurry of immigration from China and Japan, mostly manual laborers who were willing to work on the railroads, in the mines, and in the white households of the booming West. It was this influx that produced the infamous Chinese Exclusion Act of 1882. US naturalization laws had always discriminated, limiting access to citizenship to "whites," but the 1882 measure was the first to single out a nonwhite nationality by name.

By the turn of the century, the pseudoscience of "eugenics" (from the Greek, meaning "noble in heredity") began to take root in the United States. Appealing alike to white southerners who were busily erecting Jim Crow statues and to nativists who wanted to keep the impure from America's shores, eugenicists such as Dr. Harry H. Laughlin were writing popular articles positing a chain of being, setting up racial classifications in descending order, with the whitest and hence most civilized and most intelligent at the top and the darkest and hence least intelligent and least civilized at the bottom. Others equated race with nationality. Thus, Poles, Italians, Russians, and Jews were biologically different from the English, Scots, Germans, and Norwegians. The former, it came to be believed, were "inferior" and the latter "superior." By the eve of the Great War, a vast nativist movement had emerged, insisting that immigration to the United States had to be regulated on the basis of national origin.[6] The Immigration Act of 1917, passed over Woodrow Wilson's veto, assuming that western Europeans were literate and southeastern Europeans were not, imposed a literacy test on would-be immigrants. It also established an Asiatic Barred Zone, but citizens of the increasingly powerful and nationalistic Japan were exempted.

Then came the Red Scare of 1919–1920, which featured mass deportations of suspected subversives and which helped to create the preconditions for the broader restrictionist movement to come. The Red Scare was fueled by wartime superpatriotism, by apprehension about job stealing among the working class, and by fears of many old-stock Protestant Americans who saw the ongoing influx of non-Protestants as a threat to their status and values. The Immigration Act of 1924, which included the Asian Barred Zone, limited the annual number of immigrants who could be admitted from any country to 2 percent of the number of people from that country who were already living in the United States in 1890.[7]

By the late 1950s, primarily because of the post-*Sputnik* crisis of confidence and the perceived need to compete with the communist bloc for the allegiance of the peoples of the developing world, attitudes toward immigration had changed dramatically. In 1960, for the first time, the Democratic Party platform approved at the presidential nominating convention denounced the national origins system as "a policy of deliberate discrimination" that "contradicts the founding principles of this nation." The Republicans, expressing a point of view not seen since William Howard Taft's administration, declared that immigration had been a major contributing factor to the growth of the nation and observed that its ongoing decline was not serving the nation's interests.[8]

The leading congressional proponent of immigration reform in the 1960s was Representative Emmanuel Celler (D-NY). The entire concept of quotas based on national origin was racist, he argued. To have on the books laws that validated the notion of "prepolitical" civil identity based on clan, tribe, race, or soil was un-American. Jack Kennedy had been receptive to Celler's entreaties, and despite the fact that Lyndon Johnson had voted for the restrictive McCarran-Walter Act, so had he. Shortly after he became president, LBJ met with Celler; Myer Feldman, the White House aide who had handled immigration issues for Kennedy; and Abba Schwarz, a Jewish activist and expert on displaced persons. LBJ, who had helped smuggle European Jewish refugees into the United States before and during World War II, needed no persuading to support a new immigration bill. On January 13, 1964, he met with sixty representatives of church, nationality, and labor groups that supported immigration reform as well as with congressional leaders. LBJ left no doubt that he wanted prompt and positive action on the bill the Kennedy administration had devised and introduced in the House. Nevertheless, nativists kept the measure bottled up in committee until after the 1964 election. The large Democratic majorities elected to both houses opened a window of opportunity for the newly mandated Johnson, who included immigration reform on his "must" list.

In the House, the key to victory was Congressman Michael Feighan (D-OH), who had been in Congress since 1942 and who headed the key subcommittee. Johnson gave him the full treatment: midnight calls, invitations to White House soirees, trips on Air Force One. Feighan embraced the Immigration Act of 1965, and it passed the House by a vote of 320 to

70. In the Senate, James Eastland, one of a minority of two on the Judiciary Committee's Subcommittee on Immigration opposed to the House version of the bill, signaled his surrender by appointing Senator Edward Kennedy (D-MA) to manage the bill. Senator Sam Ervin (D-NC) took up the nativist flag and denounced the administration's measure. He insisted that the McCarran-Walter Act was not discriminatory but was rather "like a mirror reflecting the United States . . . recognizing the obvious and natural fact that those immigrants can best be assimilated into our society who have relatives, friends, or others of similar background already here."[9] But the tide had turned, and the Senate approved the Immigration Act of 1965 on September 3 by a vote of 76 to 18.

Under the provisions of the law, the national origins system, the central feature of US immigration policy for forty years, was to be phased out by July 1, 1968. Thereafter, immigrants would be admitted by preference categories—family relationships to American citizens and resident aliens, and occupational qualification—on a first come, first served basis without reference to country of birth. The bill imposed overall hemispheric limits on visas issued each year: 170,000 for persons from the Eastern Hemisphere, 120,000 for those from the Western Hemisphere. (A 1976 update of the bill did away with hemispheric quotas and established an annual limit of 290,000 immigrants.) The 1965 measure exempted certain close relatives from both preference requirements and numerical limits. Another provision admitted refugees of all kinds, who, as it turned out, came in unprecedented numbers. On the very day he signed the 1965 Immigration Act, LBJ issued an open invitation to Cubans hoping to flee the communist regime of Fidel Castro.

Standing at the foot of the Statue of Liberty after signing the measure, LBJ proclaimed that the new law repaired "a very deep and painful flaw in the fabric of American justice." The national origins system, he said, "violated the basic principle of American democracy—the principle that values and rewards each man on the basis of his merit as a man . . . it has been untrue to the faith that brought thousands to these shores even before we were a country."[10] Johnson made it clear that in his mind the intent of the bill was to right past wrongs, not wreak a major demographic change on American society. "This bill that we sign today is not a revolutionary bill," he declared. "It does not affect the lives of millions. It will not reshape the structure of our daily lives or really add importantly to our wealth or power."[11] For once, LBJ's vision failed to match his actions.

As intended, the Immigration Act of 1965 did ensure that America remained a land of diversity whose identity rested upon a set of political principles rather than blood-and-soil nationalism. As not intended, the measure led to an increase in immigration so that America in 2000 was as diverse as it had been in 1900. Illegal immigration had something to do with this, but the 1965 measure exempted from preference and numerical requirements relatives of US citizens and permanent resident aliens, skilled workers, and refugees from communist countries.[12] By 1965, western Europe was prosperous, thus eliminating a primary motive to emigrate to the United States, and the peoples of eastern Europe were prohibited from emigrating by their communist governments. By the 1980s, more than four-fifths of all legal immigrants came from either Asia or Latin America.[13]

THE SECOND RECONSTRUCTION WAS PART OF A BROADER MOVEMENT of ethnic minorities, including those who traced their heritage to Latin America, for equal treatment under the law and greater cultural autonomy. By far, the largest Hispanic group was Mexican Americans, many of whose ancestors had been living in the American West and Southwest before the arrival of the first "Anglo" settlers. Like Native Americans, they found themselves victims of exploitation and discrimination, relegated in most cases to second-class citizenship. Galvanized by the rhetoric of the 1941 Atlantic Charter, the Anglo-American promise of a new world of equal opportunity and justice, and by their contributions to the war effort, Mexican Americans began organizing after World War II in an effort to penetrate the white-dominated power structure.

Similar to the civil rights movement for black Americans, the Hispanic empowerment movement stressed both pride in native culture and assimilation into the mainstream white society. The League of United Latin American Citizens (LULAC), founded in Texas in 1928, increased its membership after the war to fifteen thousand. LULAC and the Mexican American GI Forum, established in 1948, also in Texas, stressed English literacy, education, and exercise of the franchise. LULAC successfully guided two cases through the federal court system that anticipated *Brown*. In 1947, the Supreme Court in *Mendez v. Westminster* upheld a lower court ruling that prohibited the segregation of Mexican Americans in public facilities. In 1954, LULAC lawyers obtained an order from the high court forbidding the exclusion of Mexican Americans from Texas jury lists. These breakthroughs did not end segregation and discrimination, but they did establish a firm legal basis from which Mexican American activists could attack racial barriers.

The number of Mexican nationals coming to the United States had increased dramatically during World War II, when the American and Mexican governments cooperated in establishing the bracero program. Under this arrangement, approximately three hundred thousand Mexicans entered the United States as temporary laborers, working primarily on farms and railroads. The labor shortage, and along with it the bracero program, continued into the postwar period. Agribusiness in the West and Southwest gradually became dependent on this cheap source of farm labor, and despite harsh working conditions, low pay, and lack of social services, immigration mounted annually. Thousands of braceros and their children took up residence in urban ghettoes, called barrios, in Los Angeles, Denver, San Antonio, and El Paso in search of better jobs and conditions.

Despite the harshness of life in the barrios and on American farms, economic opportunity in the United States was far greater than in Mexico. As a result, during the 1950s tens of thousands of *mojados,* or "wetbacks"—so named because many swam the Rio Grande to gain entry—entered the United States illegally. Beginning in 1954, the Eisenhower administration launched "Operation Wetback," and over the next few years some 3.7 million allegedly illegal immigrants were rounded up and deported. Immigration officials often ignored due process, and consequently, legal aliens and even some American citizens were caught up in the deportation process. Operation Wetback broke up families and left an enduring legacy of anger and mistrust of Anglo culture and politics among many Hispanics.

Despite the Eisenhower administration's mass deportation scheme, by 1960 Mexican Americans constituted the second-largest ethnic group in the United States. Although numbering only 3.5 million and representing 2.3 percent of the national population, Hispanics made up 12 percent of the combined populations of California, Texas, Colorado, and New Mexico.[14]

A Texan, Lyndon Johnson came from a culture that was heavily influenced by its large Hispanic minority. The Lone Star State was a primary breeding ground for Mexican American political activists, the birthing ground of both LULAC and the GI Forum. There is no doubt that LBJ's experience as principal at the Welhausen School in Cotulla played a key role in his developing social consciousness. His exhortations to the students to have the same aspirations as any other American left no doubt about his attitude toward equal rights and equal opportunity for the browns of the nation. Shortly after his election to the Senate, Johnson garnered favor among Mexican Americans when he intervened in the case of Felix Longoria, a World War II veteran from Three Rivers, Texas. When a white-owned funeral home refused to accept Longoria's body, Johnson condemned it and arranged for the young soldier to be buried in Arlington National Cemetery in Virginia. But as senator, representing a state with vast agricultural interests that depended on cheap Mexican labor, LBJ felt he could not oppose the bracero program, and he refused to raise his voice against the existence of separate and vastly inferior schools for Mexican children.[15]

After ascending to the presidency, Johnson moved to appoint prominent Mexican Americans to federal positions, one of the primary goals of LULAC and the GI Forum. In the spring of 1964, Johnson called Assistant Secretary of State Thomas Mann to urge appointment of a Mexican American as ambassador to Mexico and suggested Daniel Luevano, finance commissioner for the state of California. When Mann observed that "the Mexicans don't like what they call '*pochan*,'" a derisive term for those born in the United States but who called themselves Mexican Americans, the president replied, "I don't godamned think I understand that. . . . Go get me a good one. I want to help 'em. We've been miserable to the Mexicans." He had better luck with Secretary of Defense McNamara, whom he urged to appoint Luevano to a prominent post in the Pentagon. "He's a Mexican boy and we got 'em dying all over the world as privates but we never do put any of them in any of these top jobs," Johnson complained. "The Mexicans just are all raising hell that you've got Negros all over the government but you haven't got any Mexicans, and California's got 23 percent of all the Mexicans in the United States." Luevano was sworn in as assistant secretary of defense on July 1, 1964.[16]

Mexican Americans benefited from both the intended and unintended consequences of the Great Society. To a degree, the Mexican American community in the United States was for Johnson a model of what African

Americans could become politically. Early in his career, LBJ had established a strong working relationship with Doctor Hector P. Garcia of the GI Forum. Johnson looked to Garcia to deliver the Mexican American vote, and in return Garcia expected and received for his constituents the benefits of state and federal New Deal/Fair Deal, New Frontier, and Great Society programs. The Forum and LULAC were Johnson's kind of civil rights organizations. Garcia and others supported English-language-only schools and looked to the political and legal arena for the redress of grievances. There was some disillusionment when in the wake of the failed White House Conference on Civil Rights in 1966, Johnson refused the Forum and LULAC's request for a White House gathering to discuss the state of the Hispanic community. Nevertheless, relations between the old-line organizations and the Johnson administration were generally positive. Though LULAC and the GI Forum lacked the professional staff that enabled the NAACP and the Urban League to develop specific legislative proposals and file an unending series of court cases, Mexican Americans benefited from initiatives emanating from the black community. By the end of the decade, Hispanic activists had largely dismantled segregation as it had operated in the Southwest.[17]

The Great Society's emphasis on community action and maximum feasible participation may have, next to the Equal Employment Opportunity Commission, had the longest-lasting effect on the Mexican American community. The Great Society provided people of color, including Mexican Americans, at the local level the opportunity to become politicized and consequently demand more of their government. Indeed, Johnson's War on Poverty produced the same unintended consequences within the brown community as it did in the black. Many Office of Economic Opportunity–funded projects in Texas served as training centers for activists who subsequently went on to promote meaningful change in their communities. For example, following a fire in an El Paso barrio that killed three children, members of a community action group called MACHOS, which stood for Mexican-American Committee for Honor, Opportunity, and Service, led a successful campaign for safer housing. In Wisconsin, migrant farm workers from Texas, embracing the notion of maximum feasible participation, took control of an OEO-funded agency called United Migrant Opportunity Service. Founded by white liberals, the organization was originally intended to dispense temporary aid to temporary residents. Under the control of the farm workers, UMOS became a hotbed of labor activism that enabled its members to earn a living wage and secure permanent residency in Wisconsin.[18]

The Mexican American rights movement experienced the same generational conflict that the African American civil rights campaign did. Traditional activists in LULAC and the GI Forum stressed racial advancement through political action and assimilation. By the late 1960s, however, a new generation of activists emerged to advocate direct action as a means to improve wages and living conditions for Mexican Americans. Like black power leaders, they preached cultural autonomy rather than assimilation as a means to race empowerment. A pioneer in this new wave, known as the Chicano movement, was Cesar Chavez, a Mexican American farm worker who organized the United Farm Workers Association in 1963 and who between 1965 and 1969 led a series of dramatic strikes and boycotts that forced growers to recognize the union and bargain with it. Meanwhile, in Texas, Jose Angel Gutierrez established a new political party called La Raza Unida. La Raza celebrated the Hispanic heritage and lobbied for bilingualism in schools. Young activists declared that "brown is beautiful," and movement newspapers such as *El Papel* and *La Raza* appeared in Albuquerque and Los Angeles.[19]

In the wake of World War II, Mexican Americans had developed a civil rights tradition that pointed to ethnic group patriotism and particularly military service as justification for granting first-class citizenship. During the Vietnam War, these traditionalists, particularly leaders of the GI Forum, clung to that approach, strongly supporting LBJ and the war effort in Southeast Asia. By the mid-1960s, Chicano activists were challenging that tradition. Not only did they object to Vietnam for draining funds from the War on Poverty, they also protested the disproportionately high casualty rates among Mexican American soldiers. Increasingly, Chicano activists expressed empathy with the people of Vietnam as common victims of US imperialism.[20]

CHAPTER 10

THE NEW CONSERVATION

THE GREAT SOCIETY OFFERED PROTECTIONS FOR THE ENVIRONMENT, consumers, and workers as well as ethnic minorities and the poor.

During the Progressive Era, the conservation movement had had two goals: John Muir's drive to preserve the beauty of nature, its forests, mountains, lakes, and rivers, by withholding them permanently from the grasp of developers, and the promotion of sustainable economic development through state and federal regulation of grazing, timber cutting, and mining. Theodore Roosevelt, the first great conservation president, was, like the movement of which he was a part, willing to limit individual freedom for the good of the nation. Political insurgents from the western states, most of them members of Roosevelt's own party, resented the meddling of easterners and experts—what Republican Representative Herschel Hogg of Telluride, Colorado, called the "goggle-eyed, bandy-legged dudes from the East and sad-eyed, absent-minded professors and bugologists."[1] The westerners declared that conservation would doom economic development and threaten civilization.

On March 4, 1907, Roosevelt staged his famous end run around anti-conservationists who were trying to block him. His chief forester, Gifford Pinchot, had been steadily enlarging the federal forest preserves to the annoyance of timber companies and land speculators. Western congressmen tacked onto an appropriations bill an amendment forbidding Pinchot from carrying on his work in certain states. Roosevelt felt he couldn't veto the bill, but he held it for the full ten days allowable under the Constitution while proclaiming twenty-one new areas, totaling nearly sixteen million acres, as preserves. In the end, however, Pinchot; President Woodrow Wilson, who shared some of his arch-opponents' concern for natural preservation; and others were unable to build a sense of shared public urgency about conservation that would overwhelm opponents; the fate of grazing lands did not alarm most Americans in the way that the fear of eating poisoned beef did (thus the Pure Food and Drug Act and Meat Inspection Act of 1906). Instead of conjuring up a broad national-interest-based political coalition, the conservation movement became largely a battle with different producer interests vying for favor. Roosevelt's heavy-handed use of federal authority had only activated latent fears about centralized power and threats to property rights.[2]

Like other aspects of the Great Society, environmental protection had its roots in the Kennedy administration. In 1961 JFK had named Arizona congressman Stewart Udall as secretary of the interior. He was the first Arizonan to be selected for the cabinet. Before completing his college studies, Udall had worked for two years as a Mormon missionary. After serving in World War II, he practiced law in Tucson with his brother, Morris. Beginning in 1954, Udall served his first of three terms as a United States congressman. He was a member of the "conservation bloc" on the Committee on Interior and Insular Affairs. Udall and Kennedy had become friends in the 1950s, and the Arizonan played a key role in delivering his state to the Democrats in the 1960 presidential election. Instead of running Interior as a loose-knit group of bureaus and agencies that promoted resource development and protected western interests, he envisioned its mission as serving national environmental needs. He readily admitted that as a congressman he was "pro-dam." As he later observed, "I voted for the upper Colorado project that flooded Glen Canyon. I instinctively identified my values more with the Sierra Club than with dam building, except that I was from Arizona, and so you had to be for water. You couldn't go to Congress and be against dams."[3]

Udall and the environmentalists of the 1960s went beyond the narrowly gauged conservation movement that had characterized environmentalism since the Progressive Era. In line with the liberal philosophy being espoused by Arthur Schlesinger Jr. and John Kenneth Galbraith, Kennedy and Udall insisted that the goal was not simply to conserve pockets of beauty, wildlife, and natural resources but also to preserve and enhance the "quality of life" in cities and towns as well as mountains, forests, lakes, and deserts. In his book *The Quiet Crisis,* Udall articulated his philosophy: "America today stands poised on a pinnacle of wealth and power, yet we live in a shrinking open space, and in an overall environment that is diminished daily by pollution and noise and blight. This, in brief, is the quiet conservation crisis of the 1960s."[4]

The Kennedy administration had sponsored a White House conference on the environment in 1962 and pushed through Congress legislation creating the Cape Cod National Seashore, but it was not until publication of Rachel Carson's *Silent Spring* (1962) that nationwide support began to build in behalf of the new environmentalism. A marine biologist with the US Fish and Wildlife Service, Carson had written a celebrated series of nature essays collected and published in 1951 as *The Sea Around Us.* As the economy exploded in the years after World War II, Carson had become increasingly disturbed by the pollution of the nation's rivers, lakes, and underground aquifers by DDT and other pesticides. Because it was used to eliminate malaria-carrying mosquitoes and insects that destroyed food and fiber crops, DDT had been hailed as a wonder chemical and used indiscriminately. In *Silent Spring* Carson demonstrated through massive research that indiscriminate use of toxic chemicals was poisoning the nation's water supply and food sources, thus threatening the health of human beings and animals alike. A number of magazines, pressured by their food advertisers, refused to serialize *Silent Spring.* Finally, *The New Yorker* agreed to publish her findings. Though pesticide manufacturers mounted a massive campaign to discredit Carson as an hysteric, *Silent Spring* became the text of the burgeoning environmental movement.

Nature, Carson argued, did not exist to be exploited by humans; rather, humankind was part of nature and had an obligation to live in harmony with it, enhancing the quality of the natural habitat as human beings were enhanced by it. She and her disciples did not call for the elimination of pesticides, merely their regulation. She claimed that private companies and public agencies did not have the right to contaminate the environment with toxic substances without the knowledge of the public. Like Upton Sinclair's *The Jungle,* a turn-of-the-century exposé of the brutal exploitation of labor and grossly unsanitary conditions in the meatpacking industry, Carson's *Silent Spring* sparked a public demand for regulatory legislation.

Environmentalists were initially pessimistic about LBJ and the environment. They remembered him as the oil senator from Texas. But once again, reformers were pleasantly surprised. In truth, Johnson's background revealed a man who since the early days of his political career had devoted himself to soil conservation, water preservation and control, and publicly owned power. Many New Dealers—and Johnson was one to the core—believed that the Great Depression had been triggered by an imbalance between the income of rural areas and the earning power of city dwellers. The solution, then, lay in a determined effort to improve the lot of agricultural areas with soil and range conservation, multipurpose river development, rural electrification, and recreational opportunities. Policymakers, of which LBJ was one, believed that if a region's natural resources were both owned by the people closest to them and fairly distributed, the economic balance between city and farm could be restored.[5]

The Hill Country of Central Texas, the rural heart of Johnson's district, was beautiful but daunting, with rocky outcrops, thin soil, persistent drought, and intermittent flooding. As the congressman from 1937 through 1948 representing the Tenth Congressional District, Johnson entrenched himself politically by serving the interests of his rural constituents, by making political allies of the land and water. "All our rich topsoil was wasting away," he later recalled in an interview: "And so we started to do something about it. We had to dig some wells, we had to terrace our land. We had to remove some of the small cedars and trees. . . . We built six dams on our river. We brought the floods under control. We provided our people with cheap power. . . . That all resulted from the power of the government to bring the greatest good to the greatest number."[6]

Congressman Johnson was at the forefront of a movement to have the state of Texas create an independent agency, the Lower Colorado River Authority (LCRA), to develop a comprehensive plan to dam the Colorado River, which bisected the Hill Country from northwest to southeast, creating lakes and reservoirs that would provide a reliable source of water to local farmers. Following their construction, the dams not only did that but also made available a source of cheap power to the population of Central Texas through their hydroelectric generators. With the support of the Roosevelt administration, Johnson worked to ensure that his constituents could buy power from the publicly controlled LCRA rather than the privately owned Texas Power and Light.[7]

Udall admired JFK, whom he considered a "modern president," and worried whether LBJ would extend his legacy. The secretary of the interior regarded Johnson as a superb politician, but "ruthless," and he had opposed him in the 1960 primaries. But Johnson could boast strong ties with Arizona politicians such as Carl Hayden and former Senate Majority Leader Earnest McFarland; he had supported the Central Arizona Project and the Bridge Canyon Dam when he was senator. The two men never became close personally, but Udall came to view Johnson as an environmentalist in the fullest sense of the word.[8]

Between 1963 and 1968, President Johnson signed into law approximately three hundred conservation, beautification, and environmental measures—more than during the preceding 187 years combined. He convened nine task forces focusing directly on the environment. The breadth of the legislation and scope of the task forces were impressive—everything from land policy to pollution control to consumer and worker protection. Congress was an active participant, sometimes leading, more often following. JFK had favored federal funding for sewage treatment plants, air pollution control, national park expansion, wilderness preservation, and expanded recreational facilities. But he was unable to garner much congressional support.[9]

In environmentalism, consumer and worker protection, and beautification, LBJ saw an opportunity to get behind those quality-of-life issues that Richard Goodwin and Bill Moyers, Schlesinger and Galbraith, the New Left, and the American intelligentsia in general seemed to think were so important. Here, truly, was a bridge from the interest-based Old Politics to the cause-based New Politics, from the Old Left, which focused on issues of economic justice, to the New Left, which homed in on quality-of-life issues. In his speech at the University of Michigan, LBJ had claimed that the Great Society was "a place where the city of man serves not only the needs of the body and the demands of commerce but the desire for beauty and the hunger for community. . . . It is a place where men are more concerned with the quality of their goals than the quantity of their goods."[10]

FIRST ON THE ADMINISTRATION'S ENVIRONMENTAL LIST WAS POLLU-tion control. "You'll recall this Rachel Carson book, *Silent Spring*," Secretary of Agriculture Orville Freeman prompted his boss in mid-1964. "I think it's very important politically that we be doing something about this

because we've got to use pesticides in agriculture and in our forests . . .
we've just got to go ahead and do the right thing." (That is, regulate their
content and use.)[11] Throughout his first year and a half in office, LBJ invoked
the memory of Theodore Roosevelt and promised to take up where the
Rough Rider had left off. "There is no excuse for a river flowing red with
blood from slaughterhouses. There is no excuse for paper mills pouring tons
of sulphuric acid into the lakes and the streams of the people of this country. There is no excuse—and we should call a spade a spade—for chemical
companies and oil refineries using our major rivers as pipelines for toxic
wastes."[12]

Under the Water Quality Act of 1965, all states were required to enforce
water-quality standards for interstate lakes and rivers within their borders.
The following year, Senator Edmund Muskie (D-ME) pushed through
Congress the Clean Waters Restoration Act. The measure authorized more
than $3.5 billion to finance a cleanup of the nation's rivers, streams, and
lakes and to block further pollution through the dumping of sewage or toxic
industrial waste. From that point on, LBJ tended to take violation of his
environmental standards personally. White House staffer Lee White recalled
that when the president received a series of complaints that waste was being
allowed to contaminate drinking water in a particular locale, he called up
Udall. "I don't know what the hell you guys are doing but that dirty-water
program just ain't working. I've got all kinds of complaints." Udall replied,
"Mr. President, that may be the case, but the truth of the matter is that that
program is in the Health Service, in the Department of Health, Education
and Welfare." Incredulous, the president exclaimed, "What's it doing there?"
"That's where it's always been," Udall answered. Johnson said, "Well, I think
that's outrageous. When I think of dirty water, I think of you." He then
turned to White and Califano, who had also been present during the conversation, and ordered them to use the president's reorganization authority
and get the clean water program transferred from HEW to Interior.[13]

It was a natural step for environmentalists to move from concern about
water purity to a focus on clean air. President Johnson's Task Force on Environmental Pollution, established in 1964, documented the damage being
done to the environment by toxic emissions from coal-burning factories and
auto exhaust systems. The nation was shocked to learn that air pollutants
created "acid rain" that fell back to earth, tainting food crops and further
corrupting the water supply. On Thanksgiving Day, 1965, New York City

experienced an ecological catastrophe: an air inversion that concentrated almost two pounds of soot per person in the atmosphere. Eighty died and hundreds were hospitalized. In the wake of the Third National Conference on Air Pollution in 1966, Congress passed the Air Quality Act of 1967, which set progressively stricter standards for industrial and automobile emissions. The polluting industries had invested billions of dollars in lobbying for crippling amendments. As a result, standards were to be set jointly by industry and government. In 1969 Congress passed the National Environmental Policy Act requiring, among other things, that federal agencies file environmental impact statements for all federally funded projects. The following year the House and Senate established the Environmental Protection Agency (EPA). These were but the first shots in the ongoing battle to protect the public and nature from air and waterborne pollutants.

On another environmental front, Udall joined with Lady Bird Johnson to launch a preservation and beautification movement that would protect wilderness areas and make inhabited areas as visually attractive as possible. In 1889 John Muir had formed the Sierra Club in an effort to save the giant redwoods of California's Yosemite Valley. During the years that followed, that organization and other wilderness preservation groups made some headway, but they were no match for the lumber companies and mining interests, which insisted on the unrestricted right of private enterprise to exploit the public domain. From the time LBJ had been director of the National Youth Administration in Texas, Lady Bird Johnson had taken an intense interest in preserving portions of the environment in their natural state and cleaning up the American landscape. During the 1930s, she had cofounded a movement to establish a system of roadside parks. She, along with her husband and Stewart Udall, helped persuade Congress to pass the Wilderness Act of 1964, a legislative initiative the Sierra Club and the Wilderness Society had been touting for ten years. The measure set aside nine million acres of national forest as wilderness areas, protecting them from timber cutting and strictly regulating public access. The following year, the Wild and Scenic Rivers Act extended federal protection over portions of eight of America's most spectacular waterways. Mrs. Johnson was gratified by these successes, but she was determined to do something about inhabited areas as well.

At the first lady's behest, the president convened in 1964 the Task Force on the Preservation of Natural Beauty. The national beautification movement focused first on Washington, DC. Determined to convert the nation's capital into a model community, Mrs. Johnson worked through the National Park Service and private donors to beautify Pennsylvania Avenue and create a system of parks throughout the city. She and LBJ subsequently championed the Highway Beautification Act of 1965 in the face of stiff opposition from the Outdoor Advertising Association. Beautification was good business, LBJ declared. Tourism in Europe was booming, but it was declining in the United States. "Yet a few men are coming in and insisting that we keep these dirty little old signs up in these dirty little old towns," he proclaimed to an environmentalist group, "and that this is going to affect free enterprise."[14] The highway bill cleared the Senate but stalled in the House. LBJ sent word to the Hill that he considered a vote against highway beautification "a matter of personal honor" for him and his wife. The day that the measure came up for a vote, October 7, Lady Bird was to host a previously scheduled White House dinner. LBJ sent word that no member of Congress would be welcome at the executive mansion unless and until the highway bill was voted through.[15] As finally passed, the compromise law banned or restricted outdoor billboards outside commercial and industrial sectors and required the fencing of unsightly junkyards adjacent to highways.[16]

Critics of the administration dismissed leaders of the beautification movement as dilettante elitists, "the daffodil and dogwood" set. Rats, open sewage, and unsafe buildings were more of a problem than green space, advocates for inner-city dwellers argued. Mrs. Johnson responded by persuading University of Chicago historian and Democratic activist Walter Johnson to head the Neighborhoods and Special Projects Committee, a body whose goal was to clean up and beautify the mostly black, poorer neighborhoods of Washington, DC. Compared to racism, war, poverty, and social injustice, the beautification movement paled, but it was an authentic aspect of the larger environmental movement and important in part because it involved members of the American aristocracy.

That portion of the environmental crusade that sought to protect human beings and the natural habitat from polluting industries reinforced and was reinforced by the consumer protection movement. Congress's enactment of a bill imposing the first federal standards on automobile emissions marked a victory for both groups. In 1965 Ralph Nader, a muckraking young lawyer who would become the guru of consumer advocacy, published *Unsafe at Any Speed,* an attack on giant automobile companies such as General

Motors, which allegedly placed design and cost considerations above safety. He played a key role in securing passage in 1966 of the Fair Packaging and Labeling Act and the Automobile Safety Act. Near the close of Johnson's term, Congress enacted the landmark Occupational Health and Safety Act (OSHA), which imposed new federal safety standards on the American workplace.

The speed with which the modern environmental movement took hold in America was breathtaking. On April 22, 1970, environmentalists gathered to celebrate Earth Day. The staff of Environmental Action issued a manifesto declaring that on that day "a generation dedicated itself to reclaiming the planet. . . . A new kind of movement was born—a bizarre alliance that spans the ideological spectrum from campus militants to Middle Americans." Across the country as many as twenty million Americans gathered to celebrate Earth Day, purportedly "the largest, cleanest, most peaceful demonstration in America's history."[17]

In a way, the Great Society as a whole was an environmental movement in the sense of scientific engineering of the social and natural milieus. Medicare, federal aid to education, the War on Poverty and its various programs, public broadcasting, the national endowments for the arts and humanities, as well as the wilderness acts and the clean air and water measures were designed to improve America's social, economic, political, and cultural environments. Speaking for the Kennedy and Johnson administrations, Stewart Udall had declared: "No longer is peripheral action—the 'saving' of a forest, a park, and a refuge for wildlife—isolated from the mainstream. The total environment is now the concern, and the new conservation makes man, himself, its subject. The quality of life is now the perspective and repose of the new conservation."[18]

IN THE LATE FALL OF 1965, THE "FABULOUS EIGHTY-NINTH," AS THE press labeled the sitting session of Congress, adjourned. Its record of achievement was unparalleled: Medicare; Medicaid; voting rights; federal aid to education; the National Endowment for the Humanities (NEH) and National Endowment for the Arts (NEA); a massive battery of antipoverty programs; highway beautification; a heart, cancer, and stroke bill that pumped new funds into the National Institutes of Health for research; area redevelopment;

and a new department of Housing and Urban Development. LBJ was intensely proud of what he and Congress had done; he desperately wanted to be compared to his hero, FDR.

It was not to be. "The President has been lucky," Senate Majority Leader Mike Mansfield told reporters. "Don't overlook that. If Clarence Cannon were still alive, he'd have plenty of headaches with his appropriation bills. But the House Appropriations Committee is headed by George Mahon of Texas who is a close friend of the President's."[19] Others pointed out that every measure that Congress had passed had had the support of a majority of Americans. The one item that did not—repeal of section 14b of the Taft-Hartley Act, the so-called right-to-work proviso—was voted down in both houses. The Republican National Committee estimated that the cumulative cost of the top fifty Great Society bills would be $112 billion. "Think of it!—$112 billion!" exclaimed National Committee chair Ray C. Bliss. "This spending program dwarfs into utter insignificance all past spending programs, by all nations, all over the world."[20] Columnists who were willing to give LBJ the credit he felt he deserved for the legislative achievements of 1965 were careful to couple their praise with a critique of the Johnson foreign policies that portrayed them as aimless and reactive.[21]

Unfortunately, LBJ did not take these blows gracefully. He could not believe that he was not getting credit for resolving some of the great issues of the twentieth century, resolving them in favor of the poor, oppressed, and disadvantaged without polarizing the nation and stoking the flames of class warfare. In the fall of 1965, he agreed to give an interview to political historian William Leuchtenburg, an admirer of Schlesinger. LBJ picked up on Leuchtenburg's condescension immediately. "Mr. President, this has been a remarkable Congress," Leuchtenburg said. "It is even arguable whether this isn't the most significant Congress ever."[22] LBJ responded, "No, it isn't. It's not arguable." He then launched into a two-hour tirade against the press, liberals, and the inflated reputations of both FDR and JFK. Roosevelt, he declared, "was like the fellow who cut cordwood and sold it all at Christmas and then spent it all on firecrackers. . . . Social Security and the Wagner Act were all that really amounted to much, and none of it compares to my education act." Johnson was aware that his guest was the author of an admiring account of the New Deal. "No man knew less about Congress than John Kennedy," LBJ followed up. Every press story he read was full of lies. "We treat those columnists as whores," he shouted to Leuchtenburg. "Anytime an editor wants to screw 'em, they'll get down on the floor and do it for three dollars."[23]

Johnson subsequently ordered his staff to put together a series of White House dinners that turned into tributes to LBJ and the Great Society. "A moment ago I left the White House at the conclusion of another of the President's great circuses," Orville Freeman recorded in his diary, "where the business community is beguiled, seduced, enraptured and then coaxed into thunderous applause about the great God LBJ. . . . At my table a Mexican-American who started as a shoeshine boy made his statement of dedication to America and of course LBJ. Then two Negros also spoke. . . . There wasn't a single critical note in the crowd. What does it mean? I really don't know. On the one hand I feel a sense of purpose and direction, consensus, mobilization, and it's good. . . . The troublesome thing is, it is kind of enshrined in a kind of hero worship, exhibitionism."[24]

And, as usual, there was the impulse in LBJ to try harder. On the phone with Congressmen Gerald Ford and Hale Boggs, the House minority and majority leaders, respectively, on the verge of adjournment in late October 1965, LBJ burst out, "Oh hell, do you want me to tell you all what you didn't do? Twenty three major items that you all just ignored me." He ticked off Home Rule for Washington, DC, 14b (Taft-Hartley's right-to-work amendment), firearms control, truth in packaging and lending, amending the Fair Labor Standards Act, reforming the Electoral College, and amending the Water Resources Act.[25] There would be no rest for either Congress or the man in the White House.

CHAPTER 11

GUNS AND BUTTER

IN OCTOBER 1965, WHILE LBJ WAS IN THE HOSPITAL RECUPERATING from gallbladder surgery, John Kenneth Galbraith wrote, urging him to take an extended vacation. "While no one who lives in the eye of the hurricane will ever think so," he observed to the president, "historians will describe these as rather tranquil times. There is no depression; no fighting except for a minor jungle conflict with a fourth-rate power; no major legislative battle impending here at home."[1] If only you knew, LBJ must have thought. His advisers were telling him that the war in Vietnam was going to require another hundred thousand troops at least, and even that might not do the job. He was going to have to go to Congress and the American people and ask for another $15 billion to $20 billion to fight the war, which would knock the notion of a balanced budget into a cocked hat, raise the hackles of conservatives, and threaten present and future Great Society programs. Meanwhile, moderate civil rights leaders such as Martin Luther King, increasingly driven to take more radical positions on public issues by the burgeoning black power movement, were speaking out against the war. The antiwar impulse among blacks coupled with ongoing urban rioting would alienate working-class whites, thus shattering any hope LBJ had of fashioning a rainbow coalition that would ensure ongoing peaceful change in the United States. Something had to be done.

PERHAPS MOST WORRISOME TO JOHNSON AND HIS ADVISERS WAS THE impending budget crisis, apparent to them if not to anyone else by the fall of 1965. On July 8, LBJ had Moyers summon the heads of the various task forces he had put together to design components of the Great Society. In the White House mess, LBJ thanked Robert Wood, John Gardner, and the other action intellectuals who had devised everything from Head Start to Medicare. "In an extraordinary evening lasting until after one the next morning," Wood writes, "Johnson conveyed his appreciation, his determination to continue his domestic initiatives, and his conviction that guns for Vietnam and butter for the cities were possible simultaneously. Toward the end of the evening, several academics politely questioned that assumption."[2]

But LBJ would have none of it. At that point, his economists were telling him that the American economy was more than robust enough to turn back the communists in Southeast Asia and feed the hungry, educate the ignorant, and train the unemployed in America. When he talked with the task force heads, he still had before him the Council of Economic Advisers' estimate that the GNP would continue to grow at a rate of 4.1 percent through the 1960s, leading to a 51 percent growth in productivity during the decade. Liberal economist Leon Keyserling criticized this figure as much too low. There was a current gap between actual production and full potential of $80 billion a year, he argued in an article in the New Republic. In September 1964, the CEA had advised Johnson that the current rate of growth and inflation could be maintained if the fiscal year 1966 budget was kept between $101 billion and $104 billion.[3]

Then, on December 1, 1965, McNamara stunned his boss by telling him that in order to continue to fight the war in Vietnam at present levels, the Department of Defense (DOD) would have to ask Congress for an $11 billion supplemental to the FY 1966 budget. And that was not the worst of it. If phase two of the war was implemented—that is, more troops and more extensive bombing—the DOD request for FY 1967 would be $61 billion, putting the total budget over $115 billion.[4] Told of the news, Gardner Ackley, chair of the CEA, advised the president that such a budget would require a huge tax increase. The GNP for 1966 would otherwise have to be 7.5 percent to pay the bill, and that was not going to happen. Such a tax increase could touch off a recession; at the same time, to prevent inflation there would probably have to be mandatory wage-price controls.[5]

LBJ's first reaction to this unwelcome news was to attempt to split money for Vietnam out of the regular budget.[6] Told that such a tactic would not alter the impact total federal spending would have on the economy, the president turned to economies in existing programs. He summoned the cabinet heads to the Ranch and ordered them to scour existing programs for cuts. There would have to be priorities in the administration of existing Great Society programs and in the creation of new ones. LBJ had no intention of abandoning his dream of a just and prosperous republic, but the emphasis would in the future have to be on quality-of-life programs that cost little or no money, with special attention to the problems of the inner cities.[7] And the president ordered all-out cost cutting in Defense Department programs that were not directly related to the war in Southeast Asia, even to the point of drastically reducing America's military presence in Europe. Thus did the administration come into direct and ironic conflict with portions of the military-industrial complex in the fall of 1965 even as it planned for a major escalation of the war in Southeast Asia.

The target of budget cutters in the Pentagon continued to be domestic military bases. McNamara was still willing to be the front man for guns and butter. "It's a myth," he had declared in May, "that education, or welfare, or health or other civilian needs have to be cut back to meet our defense requirements. This is a rich and powerful country, and we can do whatever needs to be done to educate our people and fight poverty and at the same time we can spend what needs to be spent to assure an adequate national defense."[8]

The chief advocate of the military-industrial complex in Congress was Congressman L. Mendel Rivers (D-SC), head of the House Military Affairs Committee and "Admiral of the Charleston Navy Yard," as the press derisively dubbed him. On Vietnam, Rivers was the most outspoken of hawks. In late August, he had announced to a *New York Times* reporter, "I will accept nothing but total and complete victory in Viet Nam." LBJ was understandably incensed. "Who in the hell is 'I,'" he asked Speaker McCormack, incredulously. "What meat does this Caesar feed on, John? The damned fool is out here advocating bombing Peking and he has no business being chairman of the committee. He should be removed."[9]

And then, as the number of base closings in the United States mounted, Rivers introduced into Congress a military construction bill providing that the president could not propose a reduction of mission or the closing of any military facility without giving Congress 120 days' notice. He also began to impound funds allocated to but not spent by the OEO and other Great Society agencies. "You tell Rivers that if he wants a veto and full scale political war, he can have it," Johnson exploded to McCormack. "He has been playing with McNamara. McNamara does not know how to fight but I have a good sharp knife and I am going to cut off his peter and tuck it in my pocket, as Mr. Rayburn used to say."[10] Either he was commander in chief or he was not, LBJ ranted to Assistant Attorney General Ramsey Clark. To so restrict his power to close military bases would be unconstitutional.[11] Finally, Johnson called Rivers directly and browbeat him into a compromise. He would settle for a bill that imposed a thirty-day notification period, and he gave verbal assurances that he would effect no closings while Congress was out of session. "I follow the Constitution and I follow my President more than anybody else," Rivers whined. LBJ just snorted.[12]

The encounter with Rivers was an indication of just how complex the attempt to have guns and butter would be. Many hawks on the war were opposed to the OEO and AFDC but supported all of the corporate welfare that Congress would fund. The country could not afford the largesse of superfluous bases, but by dismantling them, LBJ was risking alienating hardline supporters of the war in Southeast Asia.

Finally, partially as an effort to have guns and butter simultaneously, LBJ converted the DOD itself into an antipoverty agency. In late 1965, planning began that would produce Project 100,000, a scheme to use "advanced educational and medical techniques," in the words of its architects, to qualify a hundred thousand of the approximately six hundred thousand young men who failed the Armed Forces Qualification Test (AFQT) each year.[13] The experiment, which had its roots in the Kennedy administration, was designed simultaneously to increase the pool of individuals available for service in the military; to ensure that the number of nonwhites in the military matched the number in the general population; to reinforce the poverty program by providing education, job training, discipline, and employment to impoverished young men; and to undercut discontent in inner-city ghettoes—40 percent of those who failed the AFQT were African Americans—by removing their most volatile populations.[14]

In 1962, a report from the director of Selective Service indicating that, as usual, 50 percent of the individuals called up had failed the AFQT had come to the attention of the Labor Department, specifically the assistant secretary for planning, Daniel Patrick Moynihan. As part of a Task Force on Manpower Conservation, Moynihan conducted an in-depth study of the problem, an endeavor that would lead to his controversial report on the Negro family two years later. He and his colleagues found that the rejectees were already young men in trouble. Four out of five were dropouts. One in ten had a court record. Three-quarters worked in unskilled, semiskilled, or service jobs. Their unemployment rate (28 percent) was four times that of their age group as a whole. A large percentage came from broken families that were on AFDC.[15] In its report, entitled "One-Third of a Nation," the Moynihan task force recommended that the military accept a certain number of those who failed the AFQT, train and educate them to pass the exam and serve in the military, and in the process equip them with the skills and discipline to live a full and productive life once they returned to the civilian sector. The Kennedy administration had attempted a small-scale program, the "Special Training and Enlistment Program," but it was scuttled in Congress, the victim, so Moynihan argued, of southerners who controlled key committees and who were aware of the advantages that would accrue to Negroes through military service. There was also, of course, the resistance of career military officers to acceptance of low-aptitude recruits.[16]

The task force report was duly submitted to LBJ in January 1964. He was fascinated and excited by its recommendations. "I've seen these kids all my life," he remarked in a cabinet meeting. "I've been with these poor children everywhere. I know that you can do better by them than the NYA or the Job Corps can. The Defense Department can do the job best." Go to it, he told McNamara.[17] The DOD chief needed no convincing. Here was a program, if ever there was one, that could demonstrate his and the Pentagon's commitment to the social justice goals of the Great Society, to the notion, "that Defense Department operations can be shaped to support both military and social objectives without significant penalties to military readiness."[18]

LBJ believed that the African American community would welcome a program to train disadvantaged young men through military service. Throughout the nation's history, black leaders, aware that military service constituted the ultimate badge of citizenship, had fought for the right to wear the uniform of the United States military branches, and especially to serve in combat units. On the basis of information that Moynihan supplied in 1965, however, Johnson and his advisers came to include the military among those American corporations that were doing a particularly poor job ending job discrimination. "The single most important and dramatic instance of the exclusion of Negro Americans from employment opportunities in the United States is that of the Armed Forces," Moynihan reported to the White House. "If there was a proportionate racial balance in the Armed Forces, the unemployment rate for young Negro men would be lower than that for whites!"[19] Then came the skyrocketing budget projections of December. "I just hung up with Bill Moyers," LBJ reported to McNamara. "I'm trying to get him to sit with Shriver and tell him if you'll let Bob McNamara take 300,000 of your boys and take care of them in the service for their education and health . . . if you will just get along with what you had last year, we'll give you the first supplemental when the war ends."[20] When the OEO chief and black activists protested, Johnson had Moyers threaten Shriver: "I'm ready to kill it [the poverty program] quietly through George Mahon [chair of the House Appropriations Committee] and then get the damn thing out of the way if the niggers are just going to be that mean to me and Shriver's group is going to be disloyal."[21]

In August 1966, appearing before the Veterans of Foreign Wars, the most hostile possible audience, McNamara announced Project 100,000. He was, he said, going to uplift the "subterranean poor" by taking into the military each year a hundred thousand young men who would normally be rejected.[22] Unlike Kennedy's Special Training and Enlistment Program, which called for an initial appropriation of $32.1 million, Project 100,000 would be accommodated within the existing DOD budget. McNamara anticipated blowback from Richard Russell, telling LBJ, "He's just reluctant to see anything done that takes more Negros into military service." Johnson offered some advice: "[Tell him] we'll take these Negro boys in from Johnson City, Texas and from Winder, Georgia. We get rid of the tape worms and get the ticks off of him and teach him to get up at daylight and work to dark and to shave and to bathe. . . . When we turn him out we'll have him prepared to at least drive a truck."[23] The Georgian grumbled but did not attempt to block appropriations for Project 100,000. Immediately, various branches of the service began accepting "New Standards" men, as they were called. Unfortunately for LBJ, Project 100,000 and other attempts to realize the goals of the Great Society on the cheap yielded only very anemic dividends.

AS THE THIRD YEAR OF THE JOHNSON PRESIDENCY BEGAN, THE WHITE House staff experienced some important changes, and they were important because in the world of LBJ, individuals were far more significant than organizations. When television executive Robert E. Kintner, whom the president had brought on board to provide advice on how the president could improve his public image and how to make the West Wing more efficient, attempted to put together a chart of the White House organization, Bill Moyers set him straight. Such an effort would be "a gross misuse of a good man's time," he said; "nothing useful can come from it, since the White House staff reflects the personal needs of the President rather than a structural design. If there is a design, it is radial—like the spokes of a wheel radiating out from the hub. Each person has a special relationship to the President and does what the President needs done. . . . Work, furthermore, flows not from one layer to another, but directly from the President's needs."[24]

Unfortunately, Johnson was never able to find a replacement for Walter Jenkins, who had had to resign over a sex scandal in the fall of 1964. Several months after the 1964 election, LBJ had named W. Marvin Watson to be his appointments secretary with the title of Special Assistant to the President. It was an unfortunate choice. In the first place, Watson was a genuine Texas conservative. He had grown up in Huntsville in the shadow of the Texas State Penitentiary, worked his way through Baylor, served as a combat Marine in the Pacific, and then returned to Texas, where he rose to become the right-hand man of E. B. Germany, the reactionary president of Lone Star Steel Company. He was loyal, hard-working, and unimaginative. He was also literal-minded and tactless. When LBJ told Watson to do something, he, unlike Valenti, Moyers, and McPherson, did it, no matter how outrageous or counterproductive. Where Jenkins had been solicitous and attentive to all with the slightest bit of influence with or importance to his boss, Watson was frequently brusque and dismissive.[25] More ominously, Watson served as a tacit ally of J. Edgar Hoover in his effort to instill in LBJ an anticommunist paranoia. "He [Watson] was the keeper and processor of personnel reports from the FBI and they are a disaster," Harry McPherson said. The "raw" reports typically featured a mountain of positives on the individual coupled with a bit of unsubstantiated material linking a candidate for office with a suspicious organization through a distant relative. "Marvin was fascinated with the 'con' evidence," McPherson recalled, "and his inability to bring an historical sense to the material caused real problems. He did not understand that the situation in the 1930s is not the same as it is now."[26]

Shortly after Watson came on board, Jack Valenti departed to head the Motion Pictures Association of America. Horace Busby, upset at Bill Moyers's burgeoning influence and LBJ's mercurial temper, returned to Texas to create his own consulting firm. Following his foot surgery, George Reedy had returned to the White House as "a sort of resident, long-range idea-man" on civil rights and labor especially. He, too, departed in May 1965 to take a lucrative job as vice president of a New York public relations firm.[27]

The vacuum that was left by Valenti's, Busby's, and Reedy's departures was partially filled by Joseph A. Califano Jr., who had come to the White House in the fall of 1965 to replace Moyers, who had moved on to become publisher of *Newsday,* as chief domestic adviser. The thirty-three-year-old Califano was a native Brooklynite, the son of an Irish American mother and an Italian American father. He had graduated from Holy Cross and Harvard Law School. His distinguished record at the latter institution landed him a job with the New York law firm headed by Thomas E. Dewey, the former GOP presidential candidate. Califano, who like Pat Moynihan was a member of the Catholic social work movement and a liberal Democrat, and Dewey proved to be uneasy bedfellows. Thus, Califano jumped at the chance when the opportunity arose to become one of McNamara's Department of Defense whiz kids.[28] After LBJ lured him to the White House, Califano took over the task forces from Moyers and began building relationships with those departments and agencies most concerned with domestic affairs. He proved to be devoted to the Great Society and to his boss, ruthless in defending both. Moynihan once asked Califano how one acquired power in the White House. "You take it," he replied. "There are vacuums everywhere, and if you do it, if you take it and seize it and run with it, it's yours, and you develop a certain right of adverse possession."[29]

Second only to Califano on the domestic front on the White House staff was S. Douglass Cater Jr. Cater had joined the staff of *The Reporter* magazine as its Washington correspondent. Born in Alabama and Harvard-educated, Cater was LBJ's kind of man. His father had been a state legislator, and Cater had written speeches for Senator John Sparkman (D-AL) when he had run for the vice presidency in 1952. In covering LBJ as majority leader, Cater had been critically approving. Johnson believed that Cater could be honest with him and at the same time absolutely loyal.[30]

Almost unnoticed by the press—which gratified LBJ—was the growing influence of Harry McPherson, the literate, open-minded Texas liberal who became counsel and then special counsel to the president. From the summer of 1966 on, McPherson was the chief architect of all of Johnson's speeches. McPherson's humanity, his Christian realism, his political experience and sensitivity, his independence of mind, and his loyalty would serve LBJ as he descended into the paradoxes of American history in the 1960s.

Conspicuously absent from Johnson's inner circle was Hubert Humphrey. When the president learned that Joe Califano had asked Humphrey to participate in the planning for phase two of the Great Society, he exploded. "You are never, never to let the Vice President attend any meeting on the legislative program," he roared at Califano. "He has Minnesota running-water disease. I've never known anyone from Minnesota that could keep their mouth shut. It's just something in the water out there." It turned out that Humphrey had alluded in public to Walter Reuther's suggestions for the creation of demonstration cities—a scheme to eradicate inner-city slums in selected metropoles through a government-business-labor partnership—and Whitney Young's ideas for a Marshall Plan for urban areas in several speeches. Johnson told Califano to tell the vice president to shut up. "The President will talk about what he wants to do in the State of the Union message and he doesn't need the Vice President to try to commit him to some crazy, goddamned expensive idea that Congress will never approve anyway."[31]

JOHNSON APPROACHED THE 1966 STATE OF THE UNION ADDRESS with a troubled mind. He would have to rally the country to stay the course in Vietnam. At this point, LBJ and his advisers still held out hope that, if things went fairly well on the battlefield, at the negotiating table, and in the political arena in South Vietnam, the United States could begin withdrawing troops in 1967. A number of his advisers were warning him that given the billions needed for the war, the economy would not be able to produce enough largesse in 1966 for guns and butter. Both Mike Mansfield and Harry McPherson recommended a slowdown on the domestic front in 1966, with the focus on implementing existing programs rather than funding new ones.[32] Budget Director Charles Schultze pointed out that appropriations were not matching amounts authorized when various Great

Society bills were passed. "States, cities, depressed areas and individuals have been led to expect immediate delivery of benefits from Great Society programs to a degree that is not realistic. This leads to frustration, loss of credibility, and even deterioration of state and local services as they hang back on making normal commitments in order to apply for Federal aid which does not materialize." He informed his boss that $2.5 billion more would be required during the coming year just to meet existing expectations.[33]

There was no question about funding existing programs, but LBJ was for a variety of reasons also opposed to a moratorium on new ones. He would still have liberal majorities in both houses of Congress in 1966, something he could not count on after the midterm elections in November. Many Great Society programs were also civil rights programs. To back away at that point would have been to undercut moderate leaders such as Whitney Young and Martin Luther King and open the way for a takeover of the movement by Stokely Carmichael, Floyd McKissick, who had succeeded James Farmer as director of CORE in 1966, and other black fire-breathers. That would in turn exacerbate the white backlash, fueling racial tensions in the nation's cities and giving encouragement to segregationists everywhere.

During a nose-to-nose conversation with Joe Califano in the pool at the Ranch in August 1965, LBJ had been emphatic about the thing he wanted in addition to a Department of Housing and Urban Development. "I want a fair housing bill," he had told the frantically dog-paddling Califano. "We've got to end this Goddamn discrimination against Negroes. Until people whether they're purple, brown, black, yellow, red, green [he jabbed his besieged aide hard on the shoulder as he enumerated each color] or whatever—live together, they'll never know they have the same hopes for their children, the same fears, troubles, woes, ambitions."[34]

Most important, LBJ continued to believe that it was his moral and religious duty to bring a better life within reach of as many people as possible. During the early months of 1966, LBJ carried around two quotations from scripture in his pocket. The first was from Acts: "Then Philip went down to the city of Samaria, and proclaimed unto them the Christ. And the multitude gave heed . . . when they heard and saw the signs which he did. For some of those that had unclean spirits that came out crying with a loud voice and many that were palsied and were lame were healed. And there was much joy in that city." The second was from Second Peter: "And besides this, giving all diligence, add to your faith, virtue; and to virtue, knowledge; and to knowledge, temperance, and to temperance, patience; and to patience, godliness; and to godliness, brotherly kindness; and to brotherly kindness, love. For if these things are yours and abound, they make you to be not idle nor unfruitful to the knowledge of our Lord Jesus Christ. For he that lacketh these things is blind, seeing only what is near having forgotten the cleansing from his own sins."[35] In April, he would deliver the keynote speech on the Bicentennial of American Methodism, in which he proclaimed "The Social Creed of the Methodist Church," written in 1940, to be the "perfect description of the American ideal [and] the American commitments in the 1960s."[36]

Over the summer and fall of 1965, Joe Califano had set up a series of new task forces to plan the second phase of the Great Society. Government officials and distinguished citizens (from Kingman Brewster, president of Yale, to Walter Reuther to John Kenneth Galbraith and historian Barbara Ward) focused on pollution control, transportation, urban renewal, population control, education, housing, foreign aid, and civil rights. On December 29, at the Ranch, Califano had taken LBJ through the proposed program. Johnson was enthusiastic about 90 percent of it. He was particularly taken with a vast international health initiative that, among other things, aimed at eradicating smallpox from the face of the earth by 1975. LBJ insisted on expanding a proposal to enrich kindergarten and summer programs for poor children by making free lunches available to all disadvantaged children. The idea for free lunches had come to the White House through aide Larry Levinson, whose friend Father Charles Woodrich, a Denver priest, had experimented successfully with the concept as part of the local poverty program. There, lower-priced meals were served in one secondary and three elementary schools; immediately, attendance improved, attention spans widened, and dropout rates and disciplinary problems declined significantly.[37]

Thus, as the date for the 1966 State of the Union address approached, LBJ knew what he wanted to ask Congress to support, but he was unusually tentative. Aides remembered that the process by which the 1966 speech was prepared was the wildest, most hair-raising to date. Valenti suggested bringing Richard Goodwin back on board to draft the domestic portions. LBJ, now seeing the speechwriter as a confirmed Kennedyite, at first flatly refused, but then when Valenti and Califano presented him with several unsatisfactory drafts, he gave in. To Goodwin's intense irritation, however,

LBJ insisted on editing every line, and he refused to meet in person with him. At four o'clock in the morning on January 12, the day of the speech, Goodwin, Califano, and Valenti sent what they anticipated would be the final draft to the president's bedroom for approval. Instead, LBJ summoned six aides, excluding Goodwin, and told them to rewrite the whole thing, reducing it by a third. Work on the address continued until just an hour and a half before delivery.[38]

More than half the speech dealt with Vietnam. That which did not focused on the Great Society phase two and consisted of an uninspiring laundry list. The president began well enough with an uncompromising call to arms. "We will not permit those who fire upon us in Vietnam to win a victory over the desires and the intentions of all the American people," LBJ declared. "This Nation is mighty enough, its society is healthy enough, and its people are strong enough, to pursue our goals in the rest of the world while still building a Great Society here at home." But then he simply ticked off, without embellishment or inspiring rhetoric, the goals of his domestic policy: continuation of "the great health and education programs," including the antipoverty program, enacted the previous year; more money for foreign aid "to make a maximum attack on hunger and disease and ignorance in those countries that are determined to help themselves"; "a program to rebuild completely, on a scale never before attempted, entire central and slum areas of several of our cities"; a clean water act; a measure prohibiting discrimination in jury selection; a new Department of Transportation; a fair housing measure; consumer protection laws; repeal of section 14b of Taft-Hartley; and a constitutional amendment extending the terms of members of Congress to four years to match that of the president.[39] Johnson admitted that the war in Vietnam would create budget constraints, but by economizing in government, holding down inflation through keeping a lid on prices and wages, and maintaining the pace of growth, the nation could have both guns and butter.[40]

In truth, the recommendations for LBJ's second hundred days differed from those of the first almost as much as FDR's did for the so-called first and second New Deals. The emphasis of phase two of the Johnson program would be on regulation and reform rather than relief. Demonstration cities and to a lesser extent transportation were big-ticket items, but the rest were not. Consumer and environmental protection, fair housing, and nondiscriminatory jury selection were largely regulatory proposals designed to improve the quality of life for Americans by preventing encroachment on their rights traditionally defined.

LBJ and his lieutenants spent an inordinate amount of time during 1966 in an effort to preserve the economic space that would make guns and butter possible. LBJ lashed the National Aeronautics and Space Administration (NASA), Agriculture, Interior, and Defense (in non-combat-related areas) to cut their budgets. He made sure that many of these reductions were in areas of vital concern to congressmen and -women and senators, knowing that they would be restored, and he went out of his way to point out to the press and public that when all was said and done, Congress had appropriated $4.5 billion for projects for which he had requested cuts. When conservatives began to threaten funding for Great Society programs, he let them know that he might veto their favorite pork-barrel schemes and notified the public that it was Congress, and not him nor the war in Vietnam, that was unbalancing the budget.[41] "It came through," Orville Freeman recorded in his diary, "that he was rather enjoying the position he had Congress in where he could contend that he was being so frugal and careful and that Congress was not going along with these cuts . . . but insisting on increasing all of them . . . at the same time this protects some of the other programs such as rent subsidy, poverty program, [and] teachers corps that he is bound and determined to hold regardless."[42]

AS SPRING TURNED INTO SUMMER, THE ECONOMY CONTINUED TO grow at a healthy pace, with unemployment remaining low, but the rate of inflation crept steadily upward. A fight broke out between the White House and organized labor over the minimum wage. David Dubinsky of the International Ladies Garment Workers Union (ILGWU) and Jacob Potofsky of the Amalgamated Clothing Workers were struggling with industries that were taking their union shops from the high-wage North to the low-wage South. Speaking for them, Meany insisted that the administration propose legislation that would establish a $1.60 minimum wage beginning immediately and moving to $1.75 or $1.80 by 1968.[43] Califano and Gardner Ackley, chairman of the Council of Economic Advisers, informed the president that either move would be grossly inflationary. Johnson agreed. "I don't see how I can break [my own] guidelines," he remarked to Califano.[44]

LBJ let it be known that he found $1.60 acceptable, but it would have to be phased in over a four-year period. Dubinsky, Potofsky, and other labor leaders denounced the administration in the press, and a confrontation with AFL-CIO chief George Meany ensued. "I don't mind telling you that I've got a very unhappy bunch of boys here," the labor leader said. "Well, I am unhappy too," LBJ replied. "I have worked and fought and bled and died for them, and am still ready to do it, but I don't want my motives questioned and I don't want my sincerity questioned."[45] The 1966 amendments to the Fair Labor Standards Act passed on September 23 raised the minimum wage to $1.60 an hour by 1971 and expanded coverage to include seven hundred thousand federal employees.

If conservatives were mollified by Johnson's restraint on the minimum wage issue, there was no sign of it. By June, William McChesney Martin and his compatriots on the Federal Reserve Board were talking about raising the prime interest rate by at least a percentage point, while Gardner Ackley, Budget Director Schultze, and Treasury Secretary Henry Fowler pressed for an immediate tax increase.[46] The president was opposed to both. A lifelong low-interest man, Johnson believed that high rates penalized farmers, blue-collar workers, and small businesspeople first and foremost. He was most reluctant to suggest a tax increase until he absolutely had to. It would, he believed, open the door to the "hawks," who were for the most part conservative on socioeconomic matters. They would prey on the public's antipathy to new taxes and attempt to use the war in Vietnam to obstruct and then dismantle the Great Society.[47] To make this clear to Fowler, Ackley, and his other pro-tax advisers, LBJ sent them up to the Hill to see Wilbur Mills. For an across-the-board tax increase to have any chance, "the right environment would have to be created," Mills told the president's men. In brief, LBJ would have to balance the budget and reduce nondefense expenditures, not only from future budgets but from the present one.[48]

The storm refused to pass, however. Public unrest over the steadily rising rate of inflation, which increased from 1.5 percent in early 1965 to 3.5 percent in January 1966, grew apace during 1966. "Rising Prices: How Long, How High?" a Newsweek headline asked.[49] In August, pollster Lou Harris called the White House to report "a crisis of major proportions" for the president. An informal survey of corporation heads and investment bankers had revealed a total lack of confidence in LBJ on the issue of inflation. The

latest nationwide poll gave LBJ a 90 percent unfavorable rating on his handling of the economy.[50] LBJ understood that inflation had destroyed more
governments in modern history than any other issue. Nevertheless, he per-
severed: no let up on the domestic front or in Vietnam and no tax increase.
"I think it is as important to take care of our poor that are on social security
or on relief as it is to meet our commitments under some treaty," he told
congressional leaders in September. "Because I don't think we can do those
things [enforce collective security agreements] if we neglect the health and
the education and the economic well-being of our people. I think that in
an economy that is running 750 billion dollars a year, gross national product,
I think that we can do what we are doing in Vietnam and do these other
things without taking it out of the hides of the poor, or the head start kids,
or the education bill."[51] Johnson began carrying a new Bible verse in his
pocket, one from the 72nd Psalm: "He shall deliver the needy when he cri-
eth; the poor also, and him that hath no helper."[52]

With Vietnam, inflation, and the need for a surtax converging, and conservatives waiting in the wings, LBJ perceived that he had a narrow window
of time in which it might be possible to realize phase two of the Great
Society. As his commitment to beautification indicated, Johnson wanted
to improve the quality of life for all Americans, not just the poor, disadvantaged, sick, and elderly. Like McNamara's, Califano's, Moynihan's, and
McPherson's, LBJ's vision of Utopia was solidly middle class. To the degree
that the peoples of the earth were able to experience enough social and
economic security to be able to raise their families, live independently, and
look forward to a better future, to that extent would there be social stability
and international peace. Moreover, there was the political angle. During the
fifteen years following the end of World War II, the vast majority of Americans had joined the middle class. Without their support, Johnson realized,
there could be no civil rights campaign, War on Poverty, or commitment to
hold back the communist tide in Southeast Asia. This awareness had had as
much to do as anything else with measures such as Medicare and various
education bills.

BY 1966, THE NATION'S TRANSPORTATION SYSTEM WAS IN DANGER OF
being overwhelmed by a tangle of conflicting authority and bureaucratic

red tape. For a century and a half, Congress had provided funds or land to construct a system of roads and canals linking the East with the Trans-Appalachian West, for subsidizing the construction of a national rail system, and finally for establishing a national network of highways. As of 1966, more than thirty agencies and bureaus were attempting to regulate the trucking, airline, and railroad industries, to oversee the merchant marine, and to build and regulate airports, harbors, and inland waterways. Transportation, so vital to the domestic economy and to any foreign conflict in which the United States might find itself, cried out for a central authority.

In March, LBJ sent a dramatic "Special Message on Transportation" to Congress. The president asked the House and Senate to bring together the almost hundred thousand employees and almost $6 billion currently allocated to transportation in the federal government under one cabinet-level Department of Transportation. Pointing out that nearly fifty thousand Americans had died in traffic accidents the previous year, he proposed creation of a National Transportation Safety Board under the new secretary of transportation and passage of the Traffic Safety Act of 1966 that would, among other things, set safety standards for motor vehicles operating in the United States.[53] LBJ and Joe Califano had spent endless hours with the constituencies involved—railroad executives and unions, truckers, auto manufacturers, shipbuilders, airline industry executives—getting them on board. It was a gargantuan task that perhaps only a person of Johnson's energy and drive could have accomplished.

After the White House reluctantly agreed to exclude the Maritime Administration from the new department—shipbuilders, their workers, and the Merchant Marine had joined forces to lobby for its exclusion, fearing that LBJ would find it easier to reduce federal subsidies for shipping than would Congress—the transportation bill passed the House. In the Senate the principal obstacle would be the hard-drinking conservative senior senator from Arkansas, John McClellan, who headed the Commerce Subcommittee that would conduct hearings on the bill. McClellan's pet scheme was the McClellan-Kerr Navigation Project, which was intended to transform the Arkansas River into a major inland waterway. He objected to the administration's bill because it gave to the federal government the power to set standards for the construction and operation of such navigation systems.

During the early stages of the hearings on the transportation bill, McClellan refused to even meet with Califano. Upon hearing this, LBJ proposed that his aide leak a story to the press to the effect that the Arkansan was holding up the bill because he wanted the Corps of Engineers to build a dam on property he owned, enabling him to realize a huge profit when the government condemned and bought the land. Califano asked if this was true, and LBJ responded by telling him a story from his earliest days in politics:

> The first time Mr. Kleberg ran for Congress, he was back home making a tub-thumper campaign speech against this opponent. I was sitting on the steps at the side of the platform, listening. Mr. Kleberg said: "It isn't easy, but I guess I can understand why the good citizens of the hill country might let themselves be represented in Washington by a man who drinks too much. It isn't easy, but I guess I can even understand why the good citizens of the hill country might let themselves be represented by a man in Washington who carouses with city women while his wife and children are back here working the land. But, as God is my witness, I will never understand why the good people of the hill country would let themselves be represented by a man who takes female sheep up into the hills alone at night!" Well, I jumped up and shouted, "Mr. Kleberg, Mr. Kleberg, that's not true." He just looked down at me and said, "Then let the son of a bitch deny it!"

LBJ laughed and said, "Let the son-of-a-bitch deny it." According to Califano, they did not have to resort to the leak; the president instead talked directly to McClellan. Suddenly, the president's man was welcome.[54]

Over the next two weeks, Califano and McClellan negotiated standards for the Corps of Engineers water projects. Upon reaching an agreement, Califano returned to the West Wing and proudly presented it to his boss. After quickly reading the compromise, LBJ told his aide to stand up and unzip his pants. Califano smiled nervously, not because he took Johnson literally but because he suspected he had erred. "Unzip your fly," LBJ said again, standing up, "because there's nothing there. John McClellan just cut it off with a razor so sharp you didn't even notice it." LBJ had the White

House operator get McClellan on the phone. "John," he said, "I'm calling about Joe Califano. You cut his pecker off and put it in your desk drawer. Now I'm sending him back up there to get it from you. I can't agree to anything like that."[55] Eventually, the transportation bill cleared a House-Senate conference committee almost as it had originally been received. LBJ was so mad at the leaders of the maritime corporations and unions that he did not even invite them to the signing ceremony.[56]

JOHNSON HAD ESTABLISHED THE DEPARTMENT OF HOUSING AND Urban Development to solve the problem of urban blight, to give ghetto dwellers from Los Angeles to Newark hope, and to build a backfire against the urban rioting that loomed in 1966 and 1967. But he and Califano believed that HUD would have to do more than expand the programs and practices of the past. Despite his dislike and distrust of Walter Reuther, Johnson was enthusiastic about his "demonstration cities" plan. Up to this point urban renewal had consisted almost exclusively of demolishing existing slums and replacing them with low-cost public housing that inevitably turned into slums themselves. Demonstration cities proposed to create local action committees consisting of business, labor, government, and local residents—both blacks and whites—to improve not only housing but also local education, health care, transportation, and recreation. "Instead of urban renewal programs that moved poor people out of their neighborhoods, and homes," Joe Califano remembered, "he [Johnson] envisioned a program that would allow them to stay there, in remodeled or new dwellings, with jobs, police protection, recreation, and community health centers."[57]

In the wake of the Watts riot, LBJ had instructed Califano to put together a task force specifically for the purpose of fleshing out Reuther's ideas. Leading lights on that body were HUD undersecretary for metropolitan development Charles Haar, Senator Abraham Ribicoff of Connecticut, and Ben Heineman of the Chicago and Northwestern Railroad. Haar wanted to focus on one city. Reuther had proposed six. LBJ settled on sixty-six—6 with populations over 500,000, 10 between 250,000 and 500,000 people, and 50 with fewer than 250,000 people. LBJ pointed out that to get demonstration cities through Congress, urban areas of all sizes and regions would have to be included. Estimated costs were $2.3 billion over five years with the federal government providing 80 percent and local entities 20 percent. Federal funds would be concentrated in housing and in block grants to neighborhoods for specific projects.[58]

Members of Congress reacted to the demonstration cities bill as if a dead fish had been thrown among them. Conservatives insisted that the nation could not afford such a costly experiment in time of war. Liberals complained that the funding envisioned was woefully inadequate. Mayors, convinced that their cities would not be picked, weighed in. Those caught up in the white backlash seized on the project's title, proclaiming that the measure was nothing more than a scheme to reward demonstrators and looters. In May, the *New York Times* declared the measure dead.[59]

LBJ ordered Califano and Humphrey to begin to line up those interests that would benefit from the bill and get them to mobilize their lobbyists on the Hill: persuade the House subcommittee to bring its hearings to a close and report the measure out, but then have the House as a whole to hold it up. In an election year, the House would not act unless the Senate was first committed. The Senate would be a problem, congressional liaison O'Brien pointed out. The chair of the Banking and Currency Subcommittee on Housing was John Sparkman of Alabama, a moderate segregationist who was up for reelection. Second in seniority was Paul Douglas of Illinois, who was an enthusiastic supporter of the bill but who was facing a tough reelection campaign against the popular Charles Percy; Douglas would not have the time to give. That left Edmund Muskie of Maine, a senator representing a rural state whose concern with urban decay was minimal. When Califano pointed out that Muskie did not have a single city in the state of Maine that would be eligible for the program, LBJ chuckled and replied, "Well, he has one now."[60]

Muskie labored mightily, but a head count by O'Brien indicated that demonstration cities would fail in subcommittee. The administration needed one more vote and settled on Senator Thomas McIntyre, a Democrat from New Hampshire who was up for reelection. Unfortunately, the Portsmouth Naval Base, which employed a large number of McIntyre's constituents, was scheduled for closure. Moreover, New Hampshirites were renowned for their frugality. Nevertheless, after the White House promised to delay the base closing until after the election and allowed McIntyre to amend the bill to reduce the amounts requested from $2.3 billion to $12 million for planning grants and $900 million for the first two years, he switched his vote; demonstration cities cleared committee on August 19.[61]

Having run the conservative gauntlet, the bill now faced the wrath of liberals. A subcommittee of the Government Operations Committee headed by Abe Ribicoff was then holding hearings on urban unrest. For the rest of August, Ribicoff, Bobby Kennedy, and GOP senator Jacob Javits of New York took turns blasting the administration for not doing enough for the cities and especially the black ghetto dwellers who lived in their decaying cores. LBJ saw the "City Hearings," as they were called, as a vehicle to promote Bobby's presidential candidacy. As for Ribicoff, "Abe wants to be America's first Jewish Vice President." To divert public attention from the hearings, LBJ embarked on a three-day swing through the Northeast to gin up support for his urban renewal bill. Upon his return, he called Ribicoff. "Abe, if you want to eat from the cake, don't piss on it," he said.[62] The Senate passed the bill on August 16. The House followed suit on September 1. At the signing ceremony held in the East Room on November 3, LBJ referred to the measure as the Model Cities Act and instructed administration officials to refer to it as such from thence forward. Leaving the ceremonies with Califano, Johnson turned to his aide and said with mock hostility, "Don't ever give such a stupid Goddamn name to a bill again."[63]

Johnson and the framers of the Model Cities Act were determined that it not turn out to be just another pork-barrel measure, but they were equally committed to seeing that it did not fall into the hands of irresponsible radicals. Guidelines for plans were stringent: they had to be integrated in terms of housing, education, health, jobs, and recreation; and integrated in terms of race; integrated politically by involving local political establishments and politically marginalized neighborhood dwellers; integrated in terms of business and labor participation. For the first two years of Model Cities, all HUD did was process applications—by May 1967, the department had received 193 of them. Over the next year and a half, Secretary Weaver and his lieutenants approved 108.

Model cities was a noble dream. "Along with new buildings to replace the crumbling hovels where slum dwellers wore out their deprived existences," Johnson wrote in his memoirs, "we needed to offer those slum dwellers a genuine opportunity to change their lives—programs to train them to jobs, the means of giving their children a better chance to finish school, a method for putting medical clinics and legal services within their reach. The proposal was an approach to the rebuilding of city neighborhoods in a total way, bringing to bear on a blighted community all the programs that could help in that task."[64] But there was no flood of new jobs, no new health and transportation infrastructures, few new housing projects and parks, little or no immediate relief. There was only the beginning of local political/administrative structures that would over the years hone their skills as grant writers and win support and trust from local residents and city halls alike.[65]

That a model cities bill passed Congress at all in 1966 was a remarkable achievement, however. In the summer of that year, pollsters had asked Americans whether they had a "favorable" or "unfavorable" opinion of the Great Society. Of all respondents, 32 percent answered favorable, 44 percent unfavorable, with 24 percent giving no opinion.[66]

CHAPTER 12

THE SEARCH FOR A NEW KIND OF FREEDOM

THE ONE CONSTANT IN THE GREAT SOCIETY WAS CIVIL RIGHTS. IT was a complex, transitioning phenomenon that was never far from LBJ's mind. "I will sleep tonight in the house where Lincoln slept," Johnson told the White House Conference on Civil Rights in June 1966. "It was 100 years ago that a civil war was fought in this country to free the Negro from slavery. The Negro won that war, but he lost the battle still to come. Emancipation was a proclamation," Johnson told the twenty-five hundred delegates assembled at the rambling Washington Sheraton Hotel, "but it was not a fact. I came here tonight to tell you that in the time allotted me, with whatever energy and ability I have, I do not intend for history to repeat itself."[1]

But since the Watts riot and the white backlash that surged in its wake, LBJ had felt the power to affect the course of civil rights in America slipping from his hands. Watts was but a prelude. That outburst was followed by upheavals in the summer of 1966 in thirty-eight cities, including Minneapolis, Atlanta, Philadelphia, Chicago, and Cleveland. Images of black youth yelling "Burn, baby, burn!" as they torched stores and stoned the firefighter who came to douse the flames sent waves of fear and anger through respectable middle-class America, scabbing over the very consciences that the civil rights movement had depended upon to succeed. Surveys taken at the end of the summer indicated that 86 percent of whites believed that blacks were getting a better break in finding jobs than they had five years previously. Of those polled, 54 percent were convinced that Negro children were receiving as good an education as whites. But 70 percent were of the opinion that blacks "are trying to move too fast." Virtually all who so responded blamed the federal government, in general, and Lyndon Johnson, in particular, for opening Pandora's box.

The most dramatic shift in opinion was in the North and West. For both North and South, the issue seemed to be physical proximity. White enthusiasm for the civil rights movement spread across a spectrum, with the right to vote and enjoy equal protection under the law garnering the most support, and fair housing laws compelling residential integration the least. Socioeconomic status continued to matter; the poorer the white and the less educated, the greater the hostility to blacks in general and the civil rights movement in particular. Articles in *Newsweek* and *US News & World Report* on "Negro Progress in America" outlining significant gains in education, income, and jobs for black Americans reinforced the notion among whites that the time had come to "cool it." A July 1966 congressional survey of twelve thousand constituents showed that a large majority favored cutting poverty programs, welfare, and urban renewal to finance the war in Vietnam. There was support for consumer protection and environmental measures, but an astounding 90 percent opposed additional civil rights measures.[2] "For the first time," Abe Fortas wrote Jack Valenti, "I am becoming concerned about the signs of resentment and reaction which I see, even in persons who have been sturdy advocates of the Civil Rights program."[3]

The problem was not that African Americans were not making prog-ress—they were, and the vast majority acknowledged the fact. Of those surveyed in an August 1966 poll, between 50 percent and 60 percent tes-tified that they felt more satisfaction with their jobs, found it easier to eat in restaurants, believed that their children were getting a better education, and found it easier to vote in 1966 than they had in 1960. The problem was that, as Pat Moynihan put it, "things were going to hell at the bottom." From 1960 to 1965, family income in the nation went up 14 percent, and nonwhite family income rose 24 percent. But a government survey follow-ing Watts found that in south Los Angeles, with a quarter of a million black residents, family income went down 8 percent during the same period.

The number of female-headed households went up, the proportion of adult males in the population went down, and the proportion of persons living with both parents dropped from 56 percent to 44 percent. The median age of males in Watts dropped to 13.5 years. As much as anything else, it was the self-comparison of ghetto dwellers with the rest of the country that bred such frustration and anger.[4]

With the focus of the civil rights movement shifting from South to North and the outbreak of race riots in northern and western cities, the movement as a whole underwent a transformation. The rhetoric and philosophies of its leaders were more secular and less religious; its stratagems departed from Gandhian nonviolence and integration and became more militant and separatist; and its focus shifted from the immorality of segregation to a harsh critique of the social and economic order.[5]

In truth, the riots that had such a profound impact on white attitudes were the work of a very small minority of urban-dwelling blacks. The black activism that manifested itself in the Northeast and Midwest beginning in the mid-1960s was a complex and significant phenomenon that transcended the sporadic looting and burning. There would be profound differences between the civil rights movements in the South and the North. The struggle in Dixie with which LBJ and Martin Luther King were so familiar was akin to a morality play that pitted the forces of good against the forces of evil.[6] Nonviolent protesters with their roots in the southern black church were the heroes of this tale, while southern segregationists spearheaded by racist politicians and law enforcement officials were the villains. From Montgomery to Selma, America was treated to a tale of suffering and redemption complete with true-life martyrs and prophets, with segregationist Pharaohs and Pharisees dedicated to the maintenance of an unjust status quo.

African Americans in northern cities, largely transplants from the rural South, were caught between two cultures—unable to reproduce the milieu that they had left, and unable to gain entrance to the white middle-class existence they had encountered. Black urban dwellers could not, like those who had been left behind, live off the land when matters were at their worst.[7] Participants in the Great Migration, the mass exodus of millions of blacks from the South to the North during the Great Depression and World War II, were exposed to the materialism and the insensitivity of the industrial workplace, an insensitivity heightened by racism. "The church decays; the family reverts to the matricentric pattern," social critic Christopher Lasch observed. In school black children were expected to live up to middle-class norms, and when they failed they were written off as "unteachable." Meanwhile, the mass media flooded the ghetto with images of affluence, which black residents absorbed while "rejecting the ethic of disciplined self-denial and postponement of gratification which had traditionally been a central component of the materialistic ethic; for them such habits had brought little or no result."[8]

The movement in the North as it unfolded in the mid-1960s was fundamentally different. The publicity given to atrocities committed against blacks in the South and the ongoing struggle to overthrow the Jim Crow regime had created a false sense of virtue and moral superiority among northern whites. In fact, racial prejudice was endemic in the North. During the years of the Great Migration, more southern whites had migrated to the cities of the Northeast and Midwest than southern blacks. Cleveland, Detroit, and Newark did not put up signs to designate separate black and white facilities; blacks were not systematically disfranchised; and schools and public facilities were not segregated by law. Nonetheless, public policies, market practices, and private behavior created and reinforced segregation and discrimination. Public policy and the market confined blacks to decaying neighborhoods; informal Jim Crow excluded them from restaurants, hotels, amusement parks, and swimming pools and relegated them to separate sections of theaters. All but a small number of northern blacks attended racially segregated and inferior schools. African American adults were excluded from whole sectors of the labor market.[9]

The Civil Rights Acts of 1964 and 1965 had not been without their effect in the North, but they were largely tangential to the needs of northern blacks. Title VII of the 1964 measure, which prohibited discrimination in hiring and firing, was phased in slowly, meaning that large businesses with more than a hundred employees were affected in 1965, but employers with twenty-five workers or fewer did not have to stop discriminating until 1968. Less than 10 percent of companies in the nation hired more than twenty-five workers; large corporations employed only about 40 percent of the workforce. The newly created Equal Employment Opportunity Commission did not have the power to file suits or issue "cease and desist" orders.[10] Moreover, blacks frequently could not pass the skills tests required for employment because of poor vocational education opportunities or none at all.[11] Unions, out of ingrained racism or a desire to protect the seniority system, were among the worst discriminators.

To make matters worse, it was frequently impossible for ghetto dwellers to obtain loans either from public or private sources. As a group of civil rights activists told a White House staffer, if inner-city residents could obtain loans to buy the houses they inhabited, they would be spending less than the rent they paid to slumlords. The Watts rioters burned down the houses in which they lived because they did not own them and because they were symbols of exploitation. This same group pointed to the fact that big-city machines were exploiting welfare and poverty programs for their own gain. The bosses and precinct captains used the War on Poverty to control black votes and provide employment for their supporters. "So long as this condition persists," the activists declared, "the city political bosses will continue to oppose any action to organize the masses, since, if they are organized, they can only be organized to fight the status quo."[12]

In the North few activists at the time saw the battle to strike down segregation—de jure or de facto—as an end in itself. Rather, it was one part of a larger, multifaceted battle that included a struggle against discrimination in the workplace, the opening of housing markets, the availability of quality education, the economic development of impoverished communities, and unrestricted access to the consumer marketplaces. Unequal education was a particular sticking point. In Watts's schools, black children had different curricula and even different diplomas from those provided to students who attended predominantly white schools. School buildings for African American children had not been earthquake-proofed; those for whites had.[13]

PROFOUND DIFFERENCES EXISTED WITHIN THE BLACK COMMUNITY as to the best approaches to achieve nondiscrimination and equal opportunity in the North and to bring blacks who had been oppressed and exploited for generations up to a level where they could compete. Every northern and midwestern metropolis had its own Harlem. In Philadelphia, Cleveland, and Detroit, the ghettoes could boast a rich cultural life—a vibrant music scene, literary societies, powerful black churches and mosques, and a social and political elite. They also featured rundown tenements, high crime rates, neighborhoods virtually without public services, and troubled community-police relations. Activists were confronted with an angst-filled dilemma: should the ghettoes be eliminated entirely in the name of racial equality, or should they be preserved and nourished as wellsprings of self-determination and community empowerment?

In New York, two black civil rights leaders confronted this dilemma and came up with radically different solutions. Jesse Gray and his followers argued that the solution to the problems of the inner city lay in tapping the power of the poor and directing it into community-based movements to improve everyday living conditions. Gray and many of his followers, disproportionately women, accepted the concentration of poor blacks in the nation's inner cities as a given. He was, among other things, a pioneer in the tenants' rights movement. Clarence Funnye, on the other hand, joined forces with the open housing movement, pushing for the "deghettoiza-tion" of America's Harlems as the first step toward full economic and racial equality.[14]

Civil rights leaders who focused on the North in the 1960s were conflicted over an even deeper issue, namely, whether racial justice could be achieved through altering white attitudes, or whether racism was so deeply embedded in the American political and economic institutions that systemic change was required. Actually, this debate was not new. From the 1930s on, northern activists such as A. Philip Randolph had argued that changing white attitudes would not be sufficient to the end. To achieve racial equality, blacks must contest power—reforming or fundamentally transforming key American institutions, including the real estate industry, city governments, the welfare system, and, in the view of the most radical, such as Bayard Rustin, American capitalism itself. Randolph believed that matters of class and economics were more important than considerations of race. He, Rustin, and other leftists, echoing W. E. B. Dubois (the turn-of-the-century black intellectual who had authored the uncompromising *Souls of Black Folk*) and some early Populists, argued for working-class solidarity in which the proletariat would use the democratic process to either modify capitalism or establish a socialist state. Others, particularly those activists who were associated with black churches, insisted that racism was primarily an individual moral and psychological problem—a flaw in the white moral and ethical order. Their efforts focused on changing the boundaries of discourse and modifying representations of race. A subset of this approach was the ongoing efforts of Thurgood Marshall and the NAACP to compel white America to respect the constitution, which lay at the very heart of the nation's civil identity.

The tension between the behavorialists and the institutionalists played out in the mind and actions of the era's most conspicuous civil rights leader—Martin Luther King. King was simultaneously a Baptist minister, an intellectual steeped in the history of Western political thought, and a Gandhian practitioner of nonviolent civil disobedience. The thrust of King's early activities as leader of the Southern Christian Leadership Conference had been to prick the consciences of white America, especially Christian white America, through peaceful demonstrations and nonviolent civil disobedience. Confronted with the immorality of personal and institutional racism, white Christians would come to embrace the cause of racial justice. But King shared Rustin's worries that racial resentments would fester unless the government relieved job competition at the bottom by expanding the pie for everyone.

King's receipt of the Nobel Peace Prize and his trip to Oslo to accept it in December 1964 broadened his horizons considerably. The SCLC chief came to oppose not only racism, poverty, and disfranchisement but also imperialism. Increasingly, he would refer to the US civil rights movement as simply one expression of an international human rights revolution against oppression, exploitation, and colonialism. Whiffs of Franz Fanon, the radical black psychiatrist who wrote *Wretched of the Earth,* began to appear in his speeches. According to David Garrow, a King biographer, by 1966 the SCLC chief had transformed himself from a "reassuring reformer" into "a radical threat" to America's class system and dominant institutions. In November King confided to an associate that it was his belief that the movement's greatest obstacles "were economic rather than legal, and tied much more closely to questions of class than to issues of race."[15]

Like other civil rights leaders and liberals in general, King by 1966 was being torn over the question: Should African Americans regard themselves as individuals entitled to equal opportunity, and plug into the emerging rights revolution, or as members of a group entitled to "special treatment" as compensation for historic and ongoing racism? A 1959 trip to India had familiarized him with that government's array of special programs designed to assist the untouchables. By the time he had testified before the platform

committee at the Democratic National Convention in 1964, he was publicly advocating federal spending on public works and preferential treatment
for African Americans.[16] Critics within the black community declared that
King was destroying any hope for a black-white working-class alliance. On
May 19, 1964, George Wallace had won a white majority and a 43 percent
plurality in the Maryland Democratic primary. Alabama state historian L. D.
Redick wrote to King urgently from Maryland on June 10. Stop demanding "preferences or compensatory treatment," Redick pleaded, and instead
advance proposals centered on the principles of "opportunity" and "to each
according to his need." African Americans would still benefit disproportionately simply because their needs were greater.

Reddick offered a seminal view of the Rainbow Coalition—the broad-
based, multiethnic political coalition that emerged in the 1970s to push for
change in America—in place of the narrow politics of affirmative action.
The Negro must join "all the disadvantaged"—white Appalachians, Native
Americans, Asian Americans, and Latinos. In response King began to substitute "opportunity" for preferential treatment in his speeches.[17] King was
not directly involved in the controversy over the Moynihan report on the
Negro family or the White House Conferences of 1965 and 1966. He did
go on record disagreeing with the "paternalistic" assumptions that underlay
the report and the War on Poverty in general. He acknowledged that "pa-
thology" and self-destructive behavior afflicted poor blacks, but he insisted
that ongoing racial exclusion and class exploitation accounted for these
problems. He explicitly rejected metaphors describing poverty as a cycle or
culture in which parents transferred deviant norms to their children across
generations.[18]

Randolph, King, and others who advocated working-class solidarity faced
a number of obstacles: not only with racism and fears of job competition
but also with the fact that some black workers had long believed capital a
better friend than labor, swallowing business propaganda and willingly serving as strikebreakers. Eventually, for King and his cohorts the answer to the
dilemma of special treatment versus opportunity—and the threat the former
posed to class politics—was to advocate a federally guaranteed minimum
income for those outside of the labor market regardless of color. A society
built on abundance could no longer distribute its rewards only on the basis

of traditional forms of work. Service, self-fulfillment, and citizenship were public goods worthy of remuneration.[19]

IN JUNE 1966, JAMES MEREDITH, WHO HAD DESEGREGATED THE UNIversity of Mississippi in 1960, decided to return to his native state after three years of study in Nigeria and at the Columbia University School of Law. He had been haunted by continuing stories of repression and persecution of blacks in his native South. Meredith decided that if he could walk unarmed across Mississippi during the approaching primary season, the pilgrimage would encourage other blacks residing in the rural South to come out and register to vote. Clad in a pith helmet and yellow sports shirt, and carrying an ebony walking stick presented to him by a Sudanese village chief, Meredith set out from the Sheraton-Peabody Hotel in Memphis followed by a small group of supporters. On the second day, the little band walked past the big "Welcome to Mississippi—the Magnolia State" sign and crossed the state line. A mile south of Hernando, a white unemployed hardware clerk from Memphis rose up out of the underbrush and shot Meredith twice with birdshot from a 16-gauge shotgun. Meredith fell to the ground wounded, but not mortally. Within minutes he was on his way to a Memphis hospital.

As news of the shooting flashed across the nation over television and radio, civil rights leaders—King of SCLC, Floyd McKissick of CORE, and Stokely Carmichael of SNCC—rushed to Meredith's bedside. The shooting was "bigger than Selma," King confided to Assistant Attorney General Ramsey Clark, who would shortly take over the Justice Department from Nick Katzenbach.[20] It was decided immediately to continue the march with all groups participating. "It was raggedy and impromptu," *Newsweek* reported; "there were no tents to sleep in or places to pitch them; no mobile canteens or portable toilets."[21] That evening, the big three shuttled back to Memphis to confer with the NAACP's Roy Wilkins and the Urban League's Whitney Young, who had flown down from New York. At a mass meeting, the civil rights leaders discussed the meaning of the march.

In the end, the radicals prevailed. The statement that the march organizers issued denounced the white-dominated power structure in America and criticized the Johnson administration specifically. It demanded that the federal government saturate six hundred southern counties with marshals and voting examiners, and it called for a multi-billion-dollar "freedom budget" to rescue America's impoverished blacks. Late in the march at Greenwood, Carmichael was arrested when the marchers violated a city ordinance by pitching tents on the grounds of a black school. Freed on bond, he told an agitated crowd of six hundred, "Every courthouse in Mississippi ought to be burned tomorrow to get rid of the dirt. . . . Now, from now on when they ask you what you want, you know what to tell 'em?" Then he answered his own question: "Black power!" As he repeated the slogan, the crowd thundered back time and again, "Black power, black power!"[22]

In a poll taken in August 1966, Carmichael's approval rating with African Americans stood at only 19 percent compared to 88 percent for King.[23] But Carmichael, McKissick, and to a degree Malcolm X spoke for those at the bottom for whom things were "going to hell." Over the next two years, it was black power that would capture the nation's headlines and that would come to symbolize the civil rights movement as a whole for many white Americans.

Johnson initially had little understanding of the changing dynamic of the civil rights movement as it shifted its focus from South to North. LBJ was close to Louis Martin, a black publisher and journalist. A devoted Democrat, Martin was the Texan's connection to black journalists, politicians, and church leaders. Every year, Harry McPherson recalled, "the Rose Garden would be filled with three or four hundred black faces," all of them elected officials and Johnson acolytes. "It was a love fest every time," McPherson recalled. The Martin connection served LBJ well, but it also blinded him to a degree to the festering problems of the ghetto.[24] As early as 1962, Whitney Young had warned of an impending urban crisis that only vigorous government action could forestall.[25] Young, LBJ's most trusted black adviser, conveyed some of his concerns to the president, but Johnson believed that the War on Poverty in its various manifestations was the answer to the problem. He had opposed a massive jobs program advocated by Secretary of Labor Willard Wirtz and a Marshall Plan for African Americans as too expensive and politically unachievable.

Johnson's response to the black power movement and urban rioting alternated between outrage and empathy. In conversation with congressional friends and advisers, he would rail against the handful of "hoodlums" and "commie agitators" who were stirring up America's ghetto dwellers. But when he paused and reflected, the occupant of the White House knew that this simply was not true. "God knows how little we've really moved on this issue," he said. "As I see it, I've moved the Negro from D+ to C–. He's still nowhere. He knows it. And that's why he's out in the streets. Hell, I'd be there too. It was bad enough in the South—especially from the standpoint of education—but at least there the Negro knew he was really loved and cared for, which he never was in the North, where children live with rats and have no place to sleep and come from broken homes and get rejected from the Army. And then they look on TV and see all the promises of a rich country." But he also understood and to a degree empathized with working-class whites who were repelled and angered by urban rioting and black power doctrine. "There are thousands of people . . . who've worked hard every day to save up for a week's vacation or a new stove," he said, "and they look around and think they see their tax dollars going to finance a bunch of ungrateful rioters. Why, that's bound to make even a non-prejudiced person angry."[26]

LBJ realized that, tragically, the black power movement and urban rioting were costing black Americans the moral high ground in their struggle to achieve economic and social justice. The post–World War II civil rights movement had been through the early 1960s as much an evangelical religious movement as a political or economic one. Like Martin Luther King, LBJ recognized that religious and moral sensibilities were African Americans' greatest allies. Even more so than during the crusade to abolish slavery, advocates of racial justice during the 1950s and early 1960s had been able to seize the moral high ground, a crucial achievement given the evangelical Christian leanings of so many southern segregationists. Moreover, LBJ and his allies had been able to exploit white America's affinity for law and order. George Wallace, Al Lingo, and Paul Johnson were violating the Constitution and, worst of all, employing violence to maintain a status quo that was not only unjust but illegal. The black power movement's rejection of "the system," and the violence and lawlessness associated with the urban riots, threatened to forfeit the legal high ground as well as the moral.

In September 1966, LBJ addressed the Bishops' Council of the African Methodist Episcopal Church. He noted the fundamental importance of the black church in the modern civil rights movement: "Headquarters for the battle in almost every community have always been a church and often an AME church. . . . The battle cry was not a shout, it was a song. The victory was not conquest, but was reason and reconciliation." But the movement was on the verge of taking an ominous turn. "What if the cry for freedom becomes a sound of a brick cracking through a store window, turning over an automobile in the street, or throwing of rocks, or the sound of the mob. . . . If that sound should drown out the voices of reason, frustration will replace progress and all of our best work will be undone." Do not abdicate, he pled with the bishops, but there was a tone of hopelessness, of resignation in his voice.[27]

The only thing Johnson knew to do was to press ahead with existing and future programs, to appoint more blacks to the federal bench and to see that as many were hired by the federal bureaucracy as possible, to use the Armed Forces as a tool to integrate American society and to provide job training for blacks, to ask for new legislative initiatives, and to expand and refine the poverty program. He could not and would not admit that the existing social and political order could not accommodate the stresses and strains of the Second Reconstruction.

Throughout the fall of 1965 and spring of 1966, LBJ had pressed the case of school integration, mandating daily reports on the progress southern school districts were making. By 1966, 88 percent of school systems had filed compliance plans, and the number of black children attending integrated facilities tripled. But this was a drop in the bucket. The administration had available to it two instruments for compelling integration: the federal courts and Title VI of the Elementary and Secondary Education Act (ESEA). Title VI had authorized more than $1.3 billion in aid to schools in economically depressed areas. To receive these funds, a school district had to certify that it was in compliance with the 1954 *Brown* decision. Commissioner of Education Francis Keppel warned the seventeen southern and border states that they risked losing a total of $867 million in federal funds if they did not take specific steps to desegregate their schools, integrating four out of twelve grades by the start of the new school year.[28] Still, integration of the southern education system moved at a snail's pace, with the vast majority of the school districts dragging their feet, seeking to comply with court orders and Department of Health, Education, and Welfare (HEW) guidelines under Title VI with token integration.

Until 1966, HEW and the courts had used freedom of choice as the principal criterion for judging compliance: districts could not block black students from attending white schools but did not have to do anything to actually encourage it. In practice, most schools remained segregated, with only a small minority of black students choosing to attend white schools, and virtually no white students opting for black schools. That year, everything changed. Under new guidelines, the criterion for compliance was to be the number of black students actually attending formerly all-white schools. Conservatives screamed that the federal government had embraced quotas and reverse discrimination, but the courts upheld the 1966 guidelines, and integration in the South began to move at a much brisker pace.[29] Progress there was, but much of it was painful. In September, when 150 black students showed up for the first day of class at formerly white schools in Granada, Mississippi, many of them had to run a gauntlet of spitting, cursing whites. A group of white men in their twenties beat a twelve-year-old black boy bloody. A seventy-year-old apostle of Jim Crow told fourteen-year-old Emerald Cunningham, "You are a fool to try to go to a white school. We'll kill all of you, black ass nigger." He then attacked her with an iron pipe.[30]

Compelling southern school districts to integrate was one thing, but forcing compliance on northern counties and districts was another. As the Johnson administration was soon to learn, it had built a political coalition to force equality of opportunity and access on the South with northern constituencies that were not themselves committed to those principles. In October, Keppel announced that HEW was withholding $30 million from the Chicago school system because of widespread complaints of discrimination. Both Senator Everett Dirksen (R-IL) and Congressman Roman C. Pucinski (D-IL) announced that their respective bodies were going to open investigations into HEW's administration of Title VI. Chicago Mayor Richard Daley rushed off to New York to confront LBJ, who was there to sign the immigration bill and meet with the Pope, who was visiting.

After LBJ became president, both he and Daley had put the 1960 convention—during which the Chicagoan had supported JFK and lobbied against LBJ being chosen for second place on the ticket—behind them and had become cordial political allies. Daley had helped deliver the Illinois congressional delegation on a number of important Great Society votes. "I am a Daley man," LBJ had proclaimed to the mayor shortly after the 1964 election.

Nevertheless, the two men came from different worlds. Daley was an apostle of the patronage system. "A patronage job," writes his biographers, was for him "a reward for hard work, and for loyalty to the political hierarchy—a secular equivalent to Catholic concepts of getting into heaven through a life of religious duty."[31] Conversely, LBJ had little patience with the notion of patronage. He believed in campaigning for and supporting Democratic candidates, but he wanted expertise, honesty, and a commitment to diversity in those he appointed to office. Political affiliation and effort expended on partisan matters appeared far down on his list.[32]

When Daley reached Johnson in New York, the mayor was incoherent with anger. Keppel was an idiot, he declared. If this was how the administration was going to treat its friends, then he wanted no part of it, the mayor said. The president was not unsympathetic. Politics aside, withholding funds would hurt the poor as well as the rich, black children as well as white. "Its punitive power—the cutting off of funds—hurts most those whom the programs were designed to help, i.e. the poor disadvantaged Negro children in the community," Doug Cater advised the president.[33]

Upon his return to Washington, LBJ called on the carpet Keppel and HEW secretary John Gardner and gave them unstinted hell. HEW under secretary Wilbur Cohen was immediately dispatched to Chicago to confer with Daley and school system superintendent Benjamin C. Willis. Willis insisted that no discrimination had taken place, and Cohen emerged from the meeting to announce that Chicago's Title VI money was being restored. Keppel was transferred from his post as commissioner and resigned from the administration later in the year.[34]

As LBJ contemplated his next move in the area of civil rights, the political intelligence he was receiving was not encouraging. Congress was in no mood to expand the Second Reconstruction, especially in the field of housing, which polls continued to show as a flashpoint in white attitudes toward the civil rights movement.[35] The Republicans were not anxious to hand the president another series of victories, especially in an election year. Everett Dirksen had already gone on record as opposing a fair housing measure.[36] Uncharacteristically, he spoke out early and often against such a bill. He told colleagues that he could not accept the "ugly compulsion and illegality" of federally enforced open housing.[37] Besides, whites were hearing from the new generation of black leaders that African Americans did not want to integrate. But LBJ was not to be deterred. He continued to assume that "racial isolation" was perpetuating racism and inequality, and he perceived that the problem went beyond segregation imposed by law to include "housing patterns, school districting, and economic stratification and population movements."[38]

Many of the president's friends and advisers were telling him to pull back, warning that the housing issue in particular was one on which he could only lose. "I remember discussions in December of '65," Assistant Attorney General Ramsey Clark recalled, "in which most of the administration leaders in the civil rights field and even many of the civil rights leaders in the movement felt open housing legislation would be unwise because it could not be passed; it would raise expectations; and it would manifest an unwillingness of the American people to really come all the way toward equal justice."[39] Plus, warned the Justice Department, such a law would be difficult to enforce. But, as Harry McPherson, increasingly the voice LBJ listened to on civil rights, told him:

> You are the principal civil rights leader in the country—in a time of turmoil, as in a time of unity and progress. . . . In my judgment, you cannot shake off that leadership. You are stuck with it, in sickness as in health. . . . If you do nothing to exercise your leadership, you will be damned by the Negroes, who will turn increasingly toward extremist leaders, and by the whites, who will still identify you as the Negroes' protector. . . . The pressure will grow for you to silence the protests. . . . But the Negro is not about to return to subservience now. . . . He will not listen to—and will bitterly resent—those who tell him to stop where he is now and consolidate his gains.[40]

In April 1966, LBJ sent a new message on civil rights to Congress. In it he asked the House and Senate to pass legislation expanding the powers of the Justice Department and the size of the FBI to protect citizens from violence as they set about exercising their constitutional rights; prohibiting discrimination in jury selection; allowing the attorney general to file suit to compel school desegregation on his own initiative without having to wait for a specific complaint; and forbidding racial discrimination in the sale and rental of housing. "The ghettoes of our major cities—North and South, from coast to coast—represent fully as severe a denial of freedom and the fruits of

American citizenship as more obvious injustices," he declared. "As long as the color of a man's skin determines his choice of housing, no investment in the physical rebuilding of our cities will free the men and women living there."[41] LBJ called civil rights leaders from Young to King to McKissick to the White House and assured them of his commitment to open housing, but he warned them that "the situation in Congress is a good deal different with respect to civil rights than it was in 1964 or 1965." It would not just be a matter of lining up labor, the big-city machines, and northern liberals to beat up on the segregationist South. Housing represented a new frontier. As Nick Katzenbach put it, "The difficulty with housing legislation is that this is the first civil rights proposal which has a major impact outside a few states in the South." They were going to have to lobby as they never lobbied before, Johnson told his visitors.[42]

LBJ decided to seize on the posthumous bestowal of the Medal of Honor on Private First Class Milton Olive II, the first Negro Medal of Honor winner from Vietnam, in an effort to prick the consciences of whites clinging to residential segregation. "If Negroes can give their lives for their country," he declared at the award ceremony, "surely a grateful nation will accord them opportunity to live in any neighborhood they can afford, and to send their children to any school of their choice to be educated and developed to their fullest capacity."[43] LBJ's drift was clear: Milton Olive had died for your sins. But when it came to housing, the northern white psyche proved impervious to Johnson's guilt trips.

By early 1966, Martin Luther King was searching for an opportunity to "bring the movement" to what he called the "un-led Negro communities" of the North. During the summer, he decided to focus on Chicago, a hotbed of housing activism. Sharp frontiers divided the city into racial boroughs. Blacks lived on the vast South Side, extending from the Loop for more than sixty blocks down the lakefront, and in the old, run-down working-class neighborhoods of the West Side. Whites inhabited large areas of the North Side and Far South and Southwest Sides. Mayor Daley's own Bridgeport neighborhood, which bordered mostly black sections of the city, was protected from the "Negro invasion" by gangs of vigilante white youths. "Our primary objective," King announced to a press conference, "will be to bring about the unconditional surrender of forces dedicated to the creation and maintenance of slums."[44]

In August, Martin Luther King's lieutenants in Chicago sent racially mixed teams into two all-white residential sections, Gage Park–Chicago Lawn, a mostly Lithuanian, Polish, and German area on the Southwest Side, and Belmont Cragin, a Northwest-Side colony of Poles and Italians. In both "tests," real estate agents offered to sell to whites, but not to blacks. Thereupon, King personally led protest marches into the two neighborhoods. In Belmont Cragin, a howling mob that eventually reached fifty-four thousand, waved rebel flags, sported Nazi insignia, and pelted the marchers with rocks and beer bottles. In Gage Park, a white mob taunted and assaulted marchers to the tune of a ditty entitled "Alabama Trooper":

> *I wish I were an Alabama trooper,*
> *That is what I would truly like to be;*
> *I wish I were an Alabama trooper*
> *'Cause then I could kill the niggers legally.*

Bruised and battered, King commented, "I think on the whole, I've never seen as much hate and hostility before, and I've been on a lot of marches."[45]

By October, Congress had made it clear that it would not pass a civil rights bill with a fair housing section in it. LBJ and his advisers decided that it was better to have no bill at all than one without housing. The White House let it be known that it was giving up—but only for the moment. It would be back again after the midterm elections, however they might turn out. Meanwhile, Congress busied itself with the white backlash. The House Un-American Activities Committee announced plans to investigate "subversive elements" that were no doubt responsible for the riots. The Judiciary Committee began hearings on a stack of eighty separate antiriot bills.[46]

In the wake of its failure to get a civil rights measure through the Ninetieth Congress, the White House stepped back to take stock. Everyone agreed that it was pointless to try to deal with the likes of Carmichael and other black power advocates. But Young, Wilkins, and Randolph were too old and too identified with the white establishment. McPherson wanted the president to build bridges to a new generation of moderate black leaders. The problem was that no such group could be found.[47] In Pat Moynihan's opinion, King and white liberals such as Schlesinger, Bobby Kennedy, and Joe Rauh, counsel to the United Auto Workers and the Mississippi Freedom

Democratic Party, had abandoned the administration, kowtowing to Carmichael and the militants and frightening off moderates. "The President was badly let down by the white liberal community which panicked at the thought that it might have to pursue for a moment a line of thought unpopular with the Negro militants, leaving the administration in a hopelessly exposed position from which it had to withdraw."[48] Typical of the new, radicalized liberal was Andrew Kopkind, who, in the *New York Review of Books,* had attacked King, and implicitly LBJ, for being out of date and irrelevant. Racism and capitalism had joined hands in a "practically invulnerable" alliance, he declared. The efficacy of nonviolent civil disobedience was always an illusion. "Morality, like politics, starts at the barrel of a gun."[49]

Through violent or nonviolent means, a radical restructuring of the socioeconomic system in the United States in the 1960s was a political and practical impossibility. Some in the black community recognized that fact and sympathized with Johnson, among them the distinguished black intellectual Ralph Ellison. "He [LBJ] is far ahead of most of the intellectuals—especially those Northern liberals who have become, in the name of the highest motives, the new apologists for segregation," he declared in a magazine interview in early 1967. "President Johnson's speech at Howard University spelled out the meaning of full integration for Negroes in a way that no one, no President, not Lincoln nor Roosevelt, no matter how much we love and respected them, had ever done before."[50] But Ellison's voice was obscured by the fires of burning ghettoes and drowned out by the cacophony of black power advocates on the left and law-and-order enthusiasts on the right.

More disturbingly, those around the president concerned with civil rights began to suspect that in confronting the problem of the urban ghetto they were moving into uncharted seas. Evidence began to mount that none of the programs that the administration was implementing was having any impact at all on the denizens of America's inner cities. If the solution was the black family, as Moynihan had argued, the problem was the black family, and no amount of integration, job training, park construction, or improved sewage could change attitudes ingrained by decades of oppression, economic deprivation, and social disorganization. The massive Coleman report (*Equality of Educational Opportunity,* 1966, a study headed by University of Chicago sociologist James Coleman that fleshed out the justification for the *Brown* decision) on black education was submitted to Congress toward the close of the year. It found that spending money on special classrooms and equipment did not help black students much. Neither did a low pupil-teacher ratio, superior teachers, or integration. What did make a difference was family and peer attitudes, a sense to the student that education mattered and that it was truly possible for a black, ghetto-dwelling youth to "control his own destiny."[51]

WITH THE RACIAL SITUATION IN THE NATION'S URBAN AREAS SEEM-ingly intractable, the reformers in the White House diverted themselves to less divisive reforms. Labor historian Irving Bernstein has penned the standard view of Lyndon Johnson and high culture:

> The notion of Lyndon Johnson as a latter-day Lorenzo de Medici, patron of the arts, is ludicrous on its face. He was a Texas hill country philistine. There is no evidence that he ever read a poem or a novel of his own choice. His interest in painting seems to have been confined to the noted western artist Peter Hurd who painted the first official portrait of Johnson, which the President hated. Music, the theater, opera, ballet held no attraction. At the Kennedy White House parties for artists, writers, and musicians he stood about with his hands in his pockets and a sour expression on his face.[52]

And yet, as Bernstein readily admits, no chief executive in American history did more for high culture. As of 1960, public support for the arts in America was practically nonexistent. Among the elite of the Republican Party were some of the most generous and enthusiastic patrons of music, painting, sculpture, and dance, but the official position of the GOP was that this support should remain private and philanthropic. The Democratic Party in the first half of the twentieth century, dominated for the most part by representatives of farmers, laborers, and the petit bourgeoisie, did not give the fine arts a high priority. With the advent of Jack and Jackie Kennedy that changed. The first couple turned the White House into a stage for violinists, sopranos, ballerinas, and novelists and threw their support behind the establishment of a National Cultural Center. LBJ preferred Tony

Orlando to Robert Merrill, but he recognized that the fine arts should be nurtured by any society that considered itself great. Under his leadership the federal government matched the $15.5 million that had been raised by private subscription for the center. The legislation appropriating the funds, passed in January 1964, renamed the facility, completed in 1971 at a final cost of $71 million, the John F. Kennedy Center for the Performing Arts. As noted earlier, the president, taking further advantage of the Kennedy legacy, had encouraged Congress to put public funding for cultural matters on a permanent footing by creating the National Endowments for the Arts and Humanities.

In 1966, Lyndon and Lady Bird approached the multimillionaire art collector Joseph Hirshhorn about donating his magnificent collection of paintings and sculpture to the Smithsonian Institution. Hirshhorn agreed, but only on the condition that the federal government erect a separate building to house his treasures. Harry McPherson, who was acting as liaison, urged the president to comply. "Hirshhorn's collection is among the very best in private hands anywhere," he advised LBJ. "Washington has long lacked a significant connection with the world of 20th century art, and this will provide it. It is the sort of thing the art, magazine, and education worlds will remember about your Administration." Johnson needed little urging. "I agree with all this," he replied, "and get the message ready for me—the strongest one ever written—I want to see that our people go to see every member of that Committee [responsible for arts funding] and explain it to them."[53] Following a year of intense lobbying by the White House and various cultural entities, Congress appropriated the necessary funds. The Hirshhorn Museum—with its nearly six thousand Rodins, Degases, Renoirs, Picassos, Calders, and Matisses—was one of the Johnsons' greatest gifts to the nation.[54]

Another landmark contribution to the nation's cultural life came in 1967, when LBJ induced Congress to create the Corporation for Public Broadcasting with a one-year appropriation of $10.5 million for construction and $9 million for operations. From this initiative grew National Public Radio and its television companion, the Public Broadcasting System.[55]

If high culture did not resonate personally with Lyndon Johnson, wilderness preservation did. "Everybody needs beauty as well as bread, places to play in and pray in," wrote John Muir, the pioneering environmentalist who had played the central role in preserving California's redwood forests, "where Nature may heal and cheer and give strength to body and soul alike."[56] LBJ could not have agreed more. He had benefited immensely and continuously from his almost transcendental relationship with the Texas Hill Country; he believed that all Americans—"the mechanic that gets Saturday off, who wants to pack his six children, his wife, and mother-in-law into a station wagon to relax a little bit, to free himself from some of the 20th century frustrations"—ought to have that experience open to them.

LBJ identified three stages in the conservation-environmental movement. The first comprised federal and state legislation fencing off areas of natural beauty, protecting them from the ravages of modern civilization, especially development. The second involved soil conservation and water power development projects such as the TVA. The third put government in the business of building and maintaining a system of national parks and recreation areas.[57] The Johnson presidency distinguished itself in both the first and third categories. In September 1964, LBJ had signed legislation creating the National Wilderness Preservation System. Starting with 9.1 million acres of Forest Service lands, classified as wilderness, the system grew to eventually include more than 100 million acres, or some 5 percent of the nation's land mass.[58] Then in 1966 alone, LBJ signed six separate bills designating new National Park and Recreation Areas, including the Fire Island Seashore in New York, Pictured Rocks National Lake Shore in Michigan, and the Big Horn Canyon National Recreation Area in Montana.[59]

CHAPTER 13

THE IMP OF THE PERVERSE: COMMUNITY ACTION AND WELFARE RIGHTS

"MAKE NO LITTLE PLANS," WROTE SIXTEENTH-CENTURY DANISH astronomer Tycho Brahe. "They have no magic to stir men's blood."[1] Lyndon Johnson was no maker of little plans; his schemes more often than not stirred men's and women's blood—but often in unforeseen ways.

One of the overriding goals of the Great Society was to achieve a basic redistribution of power in America. It was not that the Johnson administration was unconcerned with redistributing the nation's wealth—it was, albeit in a modest fashion. LBJ and his fellow liberals, including Hubert Humphrey, Bayard Rustin, and A. Phillip Randolph, had long dreamed the liberal dream of a farmer-worker-Negro-Hispanic alliance that would, by voting their bread-and-butter interests, achieve a degree of economic and social justice never before seen in America. As Joe Califano observed in his commencement address to the students of Mercy College in 1968, the Johnson administration was concerned with economic redistribution, to finish what FDR had started: "We are now asking the many to give to the relatively few—the 15 percent of our society who comprise the remaining 'have nots' in the wealthiest nation in the world."

And in that quest, the White House had achieved a remarkable degree of success in a very short period of time. By the end of 1967, federal expenditures on education would have tripled from $4 billion to $12 billion. There was more than a tripling of spending on health, from $5 billion to $16 billion. By then the federal government was spending $4,000 a year on each poor family of four—four times the amount expended in 1961.[2] In 1959, America defined 38 million of its citizens as poor; in 1967, 25.9 million. The 14 percent of whites and 47 percent of nonwhites in poverty had declined to 10 percent and 35 percent, respectively.[3] But as the Moynihan and Coleman reports observed, jobs, education, and health care alone would not break the cycle of poverty. "This mood of our people is captured in large measure in Paul Goodman's phrase, 'the psychology of being powerless,'" Califano said. If the disinherited could become convinced that the good things in life were coming to them through the exercise of their own political muscle rather than the charity of philanthropists or government, they would be rid of the enervating feelings of dependency and powerlessness.[4]

This, of course, was the rationale for the Community Action Program. Poverty warriors, and especially LBJ, saw maximum feasible participation by the poor as a counter to the dole, as a gateway to opportunity. As such, CAP and the War on Poverty would be able to appeal to traditional American values of hard work and self-reliance. If ever there was a believer in the virtues of access to political power, it was Lyndon Johnson, and he initially thought of the CAPs as effective vehicles to achieve that end.[5] The National Youth Administration, in which LBJ had played such a prominent part, had been cited by the 1943 National Resources Planning Board for avoiding bureaucratic torpor and for effectively linking itself to the grassroots aspirations of the people it served.[6] The problem was that by 1966, the more than one thousand CAPs that had sprung into existence were being invaded by community activists, black power advocates, and representatives of the New Left, who saw maximum feasible participation as an antidote and not a complement to the existing political system.

Community action was a particularly useful concept to SNCC, CORE, and black power groups attempting to organize and empower the nation's ghetto dwellers. "The poor in our cities," Bill Moyers observed, "they have been the wards of the political machines. The machines needed them to exist, and they needed the machines to survive, and the benevolence of the politicians toward the poor kept the arrangement going. . . . Suddenly we discovered that these people wanted more than merely the illusion of being in, they wanted political power, a sense of control. They were no longer contented with the meager paternalism by which the system had been held together."[7] Under the flag of maximum feasible participation, CAPs challenged local political leaders and established institutions such as schools, welfare agencies, and housing authorities that vied with the existing power structure for control of poverty funds.

Inevitably, there were abuses, or at least abuses from the standpoint of the established political order. No less a liberal than Jim Rowe directed LBJ's attention to a story in the *New York Times* featuring a Syracuse, New York, CAP whose $300,000 OEO grant was being used to finance protests by the poor against the city's Housing Authority. In Washington, DC, furthermore, "high minded . . . innocents," in the words of the *Times* article, at the OEO's national headquarters were "giving instructions and grants to local private groups for the purpose of training the Negro poor on how to conduct sit-ins and protest meetings against government agencies, federal, state, and local."[8] Tired of being sued, demonstrated against, and having their offices occupied by sit-in protestors, the US Conference of Mayors, led by Richard Daley and Sam Yorty of Los Angeles, passed a resolution condemning the CAPs for promoting "class struggle and insisting that local programs remain under the control of local officials."[9]

For conservatives, community action was nothing more than a mechanism to create and perpetuate dependency. They cited the efforts of welfare activists to extend government benefits and loosen the rules determining who could receive those benefits to prove their point. And, in truth, expanded welfare rights was a major, if unintended, consequence of the Great Society initiative. From the days when the Puritans were torn between their sympathy for the poor and downtrodden and their Calvinist belief that outward prosperity was a badge of inner sanctification, Americans had struggled with the issue of "welfare." The social security programs of the New Deal and Great Society have their roots in the Civil War pension system and in the "mothers' pensions"—laws authorizing public expenditures for widowed mothers that were enacted across forty US states during the 1910s. Benefits for mothers caused little controversy, but that was not true of soldiers' pensions. The years following the Civil War witnessed massive abuse of the pensions provided to veterans of the Grand Army of the Republic. By 1889 when politicians—generally Republicans—had finished liberalizing eligibility for payments to Civil War veterans, over a third of all the elderly men living in the North, along with quite a few elderly men in other parts of the country as well as many widows and dependents across the nation, were receiving quarterly payments from the US Pension Bureau.[10]

During this same period, millions of immigrants flooded into the United States, driving down wages and creating pockets of urban poverty. On the nation's farms, overproduction, high freight rates, and monopolistic practices by middlemen impoverished vast regions of the rural Midwest and South. The Gilded Age saw a growing cultural divide between America's middle class and its working class. The Victorians of the late nineteenth century believed the individual could be free only if he was self-disciplined. Determined to accumulate wealth and avoid dissipation, the nineteenth-century middle class had glorified hard work, limited leisure, and cast a wary eye toward consumption.[11] Of necessity, working men, women, and children lived by a different set of cultural rules. In 1900, more than half the population—men, women, and children—toiled with their hands on docks, roads, and farms and in factories, mines, and other people's households. Given the dangers and indignities of wage labor, there was little chance that laboring men would mimic the Victorians and glorify self-denial.[12]

Many Progressive reformers viewed Civil War pensions as a prime example of government profligacy and a major contributor to laziness and dissolution among the working class. Between 1900 and 1916, a number of measures were enacted into law regulating big business and protecting consumers and workers, but not those calling for new public spending on old-age pensions or other kinds of workingmen's social insurance. The United States thus did not follow other Western nations on their journey toward a paternalist welfare state during the first quarter of the twentieth century.

Depression and war did not change matters. Despite passage of the Social Security Act in 1935, no comprehensive American welfare state emerged from the New Deal and World War II. By midcentury, the United States could boast of only one national program, contributory retirement insurance. Unemployment insurance was a federally mandated program, with the states left in charge of taxes, coverage, and benefits. Public assistance

programs were eligible for federal subsidies, but the states were left responsible for devising and administering policies.[13]

Perhaps the most conspicuous feature of US welfare policy, such as it
was, was the division between public assistance and social insurance. Public
assistance was means-tested relief, what is usually thought of as welfare. Its
major programs were Aid to Families with Dependent Children (AFDC)
and General Assistance. Social insurance—unemployment and old age—was
not means tested. It was an entitlement for everyone eligible by virtue of
fixed, objective criteria, such as age, disability, or unemployment, and its
benefits crossed class lines. With a strong middle-class constituency, social insurance had carried no stigma. Public assistance, which became synonymous
with welfare, was, of course, restricted to the very poor, with its recipients
bearing the cross of the unworthy indigent. As a consequence, they were
sometimes ill-treated.[14] Amendments to Social Security in 1939 made a
distinction between the widowed, who were judged to be deserving because
their deceased husband could have qualified for social insurance, and the
divorced or never-married, who were frequently considered undeserving.
The former received survivor's insurance, whereas the latter were left to the
more arbitrary state-run welfare programs. The 1956 amendments to Social
Security began the transformation of welfare from assistance to workfare, a
movement away from a right of a mother to choose caring for her children
as an occupation to a requirement to earn; social welfare advocates began
arguing for "rehabilitation," the notion that training, education, and other
social services would enable families on welfare headed by women to become self-supporting by placing mothers in the workforce.[15]

Aid to Families with Dependent Children emerged as the program least
able to extend rights of social citizenship on a fair and equitable basis to its
beneficiaries. It was the most decentralized program in the Social Security
Act. In determining client eligibility, "suitable home" rules were used to
scrutinize the lives of potential beneficiaries, evaluate their child-rearing
and housekeeping abilities, and examine the school and church attendance
of their children. Some states and localities used "man-in-the-house" rules
to withdraw aid from women suspected of or found to have "male call-
ers."[16] Case workers in state and local welfare bureaucracies were sometimes
told by their supervisors that the withholding of assistance might be more

beneficial to the client than the furnishing of assistance. Supervisors scrutinized only decisions to grant benefits, ignoring decisions to deny, and thus systematically discouraging case workers from erring on the side of liberality. In some instances, welfare authorities would issue bus tickets back to the South instead of accepting applications for assistance.[17]

LBJ had sold the War on Poverty as a means to convert poor Americans from "tax eaters" to tax payers. One of the primary stated objectives of the Great Society was to shrink the nation's welfare rolls. Johnson and his colleagues advocated policies that privileged those employed in the marketplace; their programs reinforced the notion that employment was the norm for full citizenship for women as well as men, for mothers of small children as well as for other women. Like the New Deal, the Great Society aimed to shore up the traditional male-centered family. In his 1965 Howard University Speech, LBJ declared, "The family [understood as the heterosexual nuclear family] is the cornerstone of our society. More than any other force it shapes the attitude, the hopes, the ambitions and the values of the child."[18] The implicit conclusion of Moynihan's report on the black family was that the government should do everything it could to nurture the traditional family model in the nation's ghettoes; presumably this was to be accomplished by additional acculturation of blacks into white, middle-class, Protestant norms, including the work ethic, male breadwinning, and sexual restraint.[19]

For those nuclear families headed by women, the goals should be to turn the head of household into a breadwinner, which in turn would qualify her for full citizenship and all of the positive rights that accrued to it. Title VI of the Economic Opportunity Act of 1964 targeted "parents who are eligible for aid because of their unemployment." Most significant, work programs reached out to "women caring for children who are old enough that, with proper safeguards for their care, they can safely be left while their mother learns and works so that she may eventually become employable." Increasing the skill levels of such mothers, Secretary of HEW Anthony J. Celebrezze argued in 1964, would not only make them better workers but also "strengthen family life."[20]

There was also the political aspect. By the mid-1960s, welfare had become increasingly stigmatized in the public mind because of increased number of participants, a shift in recipient population from white widows to African Americans and those who had never married, and reports of fraud. "Bob

Byrd [Senator Robert Byrd (D-WV)] is just raising hell about us putting in this money for these illegitimacy women," Johnson exclaimed to an aide in 1964. "He is talking about aid to families of dependent children. . . . Ones that just stay up there and breed and won't work. . . . We don't want to take care of all of these illegitimate kids; we want to make 'em [the parents] get out there and go to work."[21]

Resistance on the part of poor single mothers to the campaign to force them into the workplace proved significant. Despite the fact that its payments were minimal, AFDC was an enormously important program for African Americans, especially in the North. In 1961, in the six northern states with the largest black populations (New York, Pennsylvania, New Jersey, Illinois, Michigan, and Ohio), the percentage of welfare recipients who were black ranged from 40 percent to 73 percent. Poor women had a love-hate relationship with welfare: it often allowed them to escape abusive relationships, and monthly checks also saved many families from hunger and homelessness.[22] It enabled mothers to raise their own children rather than putting them up for adoption, placing them with relatives, or sending them to orphanages. Their rights talk began to challenge the growing expectation that even mothers of young children should join the labor force. Claiming to be working already for their own families, welfare recipients and aspirants began organizing and, as they did, presenting an alternative understanding of citizenship that broke the link between market labor and social benefits. Public assistance was a "right" that should not be tied to marketplace employment.

In Manhattan's Lower East Side in the winter of 1965–1966, the OEO, ironically given LBJ's welfare philosophy, began funding the establishment of the Committee of Welfare Families. The object of the organization was to get as many mothers and children on the welfare rolls as possible. Struck by the fact that only about half of those eligible for public assistance under the existing terms of the Social Security Act received relief, Richard Cloward and George Wiley, who had just been defeated by Floyd McKissick in the contest to become national director of CORE, formed the National Welfare Rights Organization (NWRO).

The goal of the new group was a massive drive to recruit the poor onto the welfare rolls, just the opposite of what LBJ had been promising middle-class America that the War on Poverty would achieve.[23] The NWRO hired lawyers to sue state and local welfare agencies for applying criteria that were of dubious constitutionality; the legal assault on overly restrictive welfare practices was supported and sometimes funded by the OEO. Federal courts struck down state resident laws, man-in-the-house rules, "substitute father" rules, and employable mother rules. In *Goldberg v. Kelly*, the Supreme Court even required that recipients be allowed to challenge welfare decisions through quasi-judicial administrative proceedings called "fair hearings."[24] From 3.1 million people on AFDC in 1960, the number rose to 4.3 million in 1965, and to 6.7 million in 1969. At the same time, the percentage of nonwhites on welfare grew steadily from 32 percent in 1950 to 46 percent in 1967. OEO activists worked to bring legal services to the residents of America's inner cities, but they soon found that welfare recipients wanted to use those services in contravention of the rehabilitation goals that the poverty warriors brought with them. Planners wanted strong families; ghetto residents used legal services to obtain divorces. The actions and attitudes of legal aid lawyers tended to make the system more permissive rather than more rehabilitative.[25]

By late 1966, many liberal activists and civil rights leaders were becoming disenchanted with the Great Society's emphasis on opportunity and rehabilitation. What the poor needed were jobs and money, the second through the first if possible, but without it if necessary. "With its titanic rhetoric and piddling appropriations," wrote activist Penn Kemble, an associate of Randolph, Rustin, and Michael Harrington, "it [the War on Poverty] has raised the hopes of many of the poor people whom it has reached without significantly affecting their living standards."[26] In Oakland, California, a local poverty warrior complained that "in the form of services these people are getting less than $1 per person."[27] One of the objectives of the NWRO, secretly supported by Richard Cloward of the New York University School of Social Work as well as by others working for the OEO, was to fill the welfare rolls to the breaking point to destabilize the system, forcing a reassessment of antipoverty strategies. The only option available to the White House, they believed, would then be to support a guaranteed annual income.[28]

WHAT BOTHERED LBJ MORE THAN THE PERVERSION OF THE WAR ON Poverty from opportunity to entitlement and the challenge the CAPs were posing to local political machines was the perception that the OEO had become a Trojan horse within his administration to advance the fortunes of one Robert F. Kennedy. The internecine warfare between the Kennedy and Johnson camps had if anything intensified since 1964. LBJ naturally gravitated toward those who had a low opinion of the Kennedys. John Roche, the political scientist who had replaced Eric Goldman as White House intellectual, was typical. "While I had immense admiration and respect for John Kennedy, I thought Bob Kennedy was a little shit," he later told an interviewer. "Ted Kennedy seemed to me to be a genial idiot. There's nothing wrong with Ted that, say, a hundred points in I.Q. wouldn't help, you know."[29]

For his part, Bobby continued to view LBJ as something of a monster. "Our president [JFK]," he told his Hickory Hill friends, "was a gentleman and a human being, and . . . this man is not. He's mean, bitter, vicious— an animal in many ways."[30] There was the sniping on Vietnam, but RFK's principal strategy seemed to have been to use a liberal-Negro alliance to challenge LBJ for the presidency in 1968. "He is trying to put himself into a position of leadership among liberal Senators, newspapermen, foundation executives, and the like," Harry McPherson advised his boss. "Most of these people mistrusted him in the past, believing him (rightly) to be a man of narrow sensibilities and totalitarian instincts. A number of brave votes for pure liberalism, and a number of internationalist . . . speeches such as the one on nuclear proliferation, and he will seem to them like St. George slaying the conservative dragons . . . as we know, the intellectuals are as easy a lay as can be found."[31] In October 1966, *Newsweek* ran an article on RFK under the banner headline "The Bobby Phenomenon."[32] Straw polls indicated that Democrats favored RFK over LBJ for the 1968 nomination.[33]

The temptation for the president to turn his back on the poverty program, and especially community action, was great. It would throw a bone to conservatives and to big-city mayors who continued to swamp the White House with complaints. "It's [community action] the most dangerous problem we've got facing us today," Richard Daley complained to LBJ. "You've got a lot of people on poverty that are subversive . . . they're [members of inner-city gangs] going in and telling the people, you'll either pay us off or we will knock your windows out or give you a Molotov Cocktail. . . . We've gotten our city reports on RAM [Revolutionary Action Movement] which is a pro-Castro outfit operating out of New York. I think it's going to happen in every major city."[34] In distancing himself from the poverty program, Johnson could outflank Bobby on the right. The junior senator from New York had joined with Jacob Javits and Abraham Ribicoff to conduct hearings on America's urban problems, hearings that generally laid the blame on the doorstep of the Johnson White House. If Kennedy wanted to take charge of the urban problem, why not let him?

By late 1965, Sargent Shriver, a Kennedy in-law, had begun arousing presidential suspicions by pressing continually for more funds for OEO and by refusing to rein in the radicals in his organization who were giving grants to local CAPs to stage demonstrations and sit-in strikes. LBJ subsequently complained to HEW under secretary Wilbur Cohen that everybody at OEO was "disloyal to him . . . always trying to undermine him."[35] On a couple of occasions, the White House did intervene to try to circumscribe OEO projects that its political allies in Congress or city hall found particularly objectionable, most notably a literacy program conceived by black activist James Farmer that Mayors Daley and Yorty objected to and to the Child Development Group of Mississippi, which had set up eight Head Start centers in forty communities staffed by poor blacks, objected to by Senate Appropriations Committee chair John Stennis.

Generally, however, LBJ was content to let matters take their course. He rejected suggestions that he break up OEO and transfer its entities to other government agencies, and he refused to fire Shriver. Johnson, despite all the angst he experienced over the Kennedys, chose to follow Harry McPherson's advice. "It is possible, in my opinion, for people to work hard for you, maintain confidences, and still find the Kennedys attractive and adventurous," he had told his boss. "The test of our people should be whether they are smart, imaginative, and working to carry out your policies."[36] Nor did the White House declare war on the CAPs. In 1967, Congress modified the original OEO legislation to allow mayors and governors to take over community action entities if they so desired. The White House opposed the legislation; although it passed, ironically, of the 940 mayors with CAPs in their jurisdiction, only 40 chose to take them over.[37]

CHAPTER 14

REFORM UNDER SIEGE

ON JANUARY 31, 1966, LBJ ORDERED AN END TO THE CHRISTMAS bombing halt of North Vietnam. The president had authorized the halt as part of a dual effort to bring Hanoi to the negotiating table and to sidetrack the antiwar movement in the United States that was beginning to gather steam. That same evening, Senator J. William Fulbright appeared on "CBS Evening News" to declare the war morally wrong and counterproductive to the interests of the country. The administration, the chairman of the Senate Foreign Relations Committee (SFRC) declared, was still a prisoner of the Munich analogy, a comparison that was totally inapplicable to Southeast Asia. To him, Vietnam did not represent Sino-Soviet aggression, but a genuinely indigenous revolt against colonialism. He subsequently announced that the SFRC would hold public hearings on the war in Southeast Asia in the immediate future.

Fulbright's hearings stretched across more than two weeks in February. Administration officials refused to testify, so the SFRC chair turned to prominent establishment figures who were having doubts about the war. General James Gavin presented the case for the enclave strategy—limiting American combat troops to action within a certain number of miles of their base—that Fulbright and columnist Walter Lippmann had earlier advocated and that the Johnson administration had already discarded. On February 11, Fulbright pulled out his big gun: George Kennan. The former head of the State Department's Policy Planning Staff and the author of the containment

policy toward the Soviet Union agreed with Gavin that it was essential to
avoid further escalation, and he urged that the war be ended "as soon as this
could be done without inordinate damage to our prestige or stability in the
area."[1] Like the Kefauver crime hearings of 1951 and the Army-McCarthy
hearings of 1954, the Fulbright hearings were watched and discussed by
millions.

Congressional doubters were echoed by a variety of groups in the general population. Traditional pacifists such as A. J. Muste and the organizations they headed, the Fellowship of Reconciliation and the War Resisters
League, spoke out against the ongoing carnage in South Vietnam because
they were against all wars. The taking of human life, no matter what the
reason, was immoral. Antinuclear activists who had organized the Committee for a Sane Nuclear Policy (SANE) in the mid-1950s opposed the war
in Vietnam because they feared it would lead to a nuclear confrontation
between the United States and the communist superpowers. Student activists who, energized by the civil rights movement, formed the Students for
a Democratic Society in 1960 enlisted in the antiwar movement as part of
a larger campaign to fundamentally alter American society. Indeed, by late
1966, opposition to the conflict in Southeast Asia had become an article of
faith for members of the New Left. Building on the economic determinism
of Charles Beard and Fred Harvey Harrington, New Leftists insisted that
because it was a capitalist society, America was dominated by financiers and
manufacturers who, having subdued the American proletariat and exploited
the nation's resources in the nineteenth century, had set out to establish their
economic hegemony throughout the rest of the world in the twentieth.
Because politics always follows economics, the government and military
were permanently and primarily committed to Wall Street's agenda. Liberals
of a more moderate stripe, concentrated in one wing of the Americans for
Democratic Action, had become convinced by the end of 1965 that the
war in Southeast Asia was a perversion of the liberal internationalism that
they had espoused since the end of World War II. In its quest to protect democracy and liberty from communist totalitarianism, the United States was
allying itself with brutal military dictatorships and facilitating the murder of
thousands of innocent people.

Joining the growing antiwar chorus were religious leaders. In October
1965, the Reverend Richard Neuhaus, Rabbi Abraham Heschel, and Father

Daniel Berrigan formed Clergy Concerned about Vietnam, a particularly ominous development for LBJ and the architects of the Great Society, who had tapped into deep currents of Judeo-Christian beliefs to generate support for domestic reform. "A year ago . . . it seemed that the United States might be about to undergo something of a social revolution," Senator Fulbright observed. "But for the present at least, the inspiration and commitment of a year ago have disappeared. They have disappeared in the face of deepening involvement in an Asian war, and although it may be contended that the United States has the material resources to rebuild its society at home while waging war abroad, it is already being demonstrated that we do not have the mental and spiritual resources for such a double effort."[2]

"Washington is a city obsessed by Vietnam," journalist and historian Ronald Steel wrote in the *New York Review of Books* later in the year. "It eats, sleeps, and particularly drinks the war. There is virtually no other subject of conversation worthy of the name, and no social gathering or private discussion that does not inevitably gravitate toward the war. . . . The administration . . . has not had the time, or the aptitude, or perhaps the understanding to explain this war in terms that could reconcile it with traditional American values. As a result, it has lost the support of much of the nation's intellectual community."[3] Steel was right.

In a spate of essays and books, LBJ was portrayed as a power-mad Machiavellian figure who was establishing in America an "imperial presidency," to use Arthur Schlesinger's famous phrase. Typical was a series of articles written by University of Chicago political scientist Hans Morgenthau. Johnson was about power, he declared in one piece; intellectuals (read: dissenters) were about truth. The two could never meet.[4] In an essay entitled "The Colossus of Johnson City," Morgenthau wrote, "What is so ominous in our present situation is not that the President has reasserted his powers, but that in the process he has reduced all countervailing powers, political and social, to virtual and seemingly permanent impotence. What the Founding Fathers had feared has indeed come to pass: the President of the United States has become an uncrowned king. Lyndon B. Johnson has become the Julius Caesar of the American Republic."[5] "Who could have foreseen it?" opined the *New Republic*. "The Great Society exponent, the practitioner of common sense compromise and consensus, has become The War President—sworn to prevent at any cost one set of Vietnamese (unfriendly, we have guaranteed that) from overcoming other Vietnamese (who could not hold power without us.)"[6]

The burgeoning antiwar movement, not surprisingly, left LBJ distraught. He was particularly disturbed by those who were arguing that the administration was deceiving and manipulating the public and those who questioned the efficacy of the political and economic system. "There's a great infiltration in the government and in the press particularly and in the networks of folks that have little faith in our system and who want to destroy it every way in the world they can," he complained to a Texas friend.

> They are making an all-out pitch against everything—getting out of Vietnam. . . . I think we're going to have to start a drive to run 'em underground because they're getting to a point now where they're dangerous. . . . No mother and no daughter and no married woman wants her husband or her son to go to Vietnam. The only thing that would . . . compel 'em to go would be love of country and their honor and their duty. But they no longer think it's an honor or duty; they think it's a terrible thing to do. . . . It's just too cruel, too brutal. It's all right if they have an alternative and debate the alternative, but to say that you're maneuvering 'em and lacking candor and you're lying . . . it just goes a little bit further than it oughta go.[7]

AS THEY PREPARED FOR THE 1966 MIDTERM ELECTIONS, LBJ AND THE Democratic Party had much to boast about. During Johnson's thirty-six months in office, the unemployment rate had dropped from 5.7 percent to 3.7 percent. Industrial production had risen by 25 percent. GNP had increased by 17 percent, and the average American's real income had risen by 14 percent. While four million Americans moved above the poverty line, both profits and wages had increased. Medicare had helped three million elderly Americans to obtain access to health care, eight million new workers were covered by the minimum wage law, and Jim Crow was on the run in the South.[8]

Yet for all this, Democratic leaders approached the elections with apprehension. "The American people are concerned about Vietnam," Secretary of Agriculture Orville Freeman wrote in his diary. "There is a dark void there, and they don't know exactly where we're going as a Nation. . . . The same thing seems to be true about the economy. The President's obsession with it, with inflation, with what should be done about it, and the failure to act . . . and certainly these civil rights disturbances and riots everywhere and the whole white backlash problem is another [area] where there is such doubt and indecision."[9]

Although LBJ had won in a landslide in 1964, and Democrats had coat-tailed to large majorities in both houses, the major elements of the Great Society had carried only by an average 235 to 200 vote in the House. A shift of a mere 18 votes would have meant the failure of much of the president's program.[10] In general, except for the Civil Rights Act of 1964, a suprapartisan, centrist consensus favoring liberal programs for poor, powerless, neglected segments of the American population did not seem to exist. Less than a month before LBJ signed the Civil Rights Act of 1964, a Gallup poll showed that 57 percent of its respondents expected race relations to worsen during the next six months. In a May 12, 1965, poll, a plurality of nonsouthern whites claimed that LBJ was "pushing integration too fast," while only 8 percent said that his backing was not strong enough. Only 35 percent of poll respondents supported the enactment of a fair housing law.

By contrast, two of the Big Four domestic policy goals of the Great Society, the income tax cut and Medicare, enjoyed consistent, widespread public support in the opinion surveys. Opposition to tax increases remained strong even if for the purposes of reducing inflation and avoiding a budget deficit.[11] If the tax cut, Medicare, public television and radio, federal support for the arts and higher education, clean air and water legislation, and consumer safety were all initiatives to buy white middle class support for programs focused on poverty and racial injustice, they had failed in their objective. Indeed, what white middle class support there was for the War on Poverty may have stemmed more from fears that the situation in the nation's cities would get worse if the government did not act than from an aroused social conscience.

Matters were not helped by the fact that the president had grossly neglected the party and its machinery. Indeed, Johnson was proving to be one of America's least partisan presidents. "I hear rumors you were a politician," presidential adviser John Roche memoed the president, "but have no evidence of it."[12] The Johnson administration featured a running feud between John Macy, LBJ's chief talent scout who was also head of the Civil Service Commission, and Democratic Party operative Jim Rowe. Without success, Rowe hounded Macy to recommend some good party loyalists for appointment to government office. In filling federal jobs, LBJ was motivated by his search for excellence and expertise as well as by his determination to be beyond reproach. "You know," he told Rowe, an old friend from New Deal days, "I can only feel safe if I pick civil servants or military men, because their whole life has been under such complete scrutiny, they won't surprise me. . . . You lawyers, you are not trustworthy, you have always got a client some way or other that's embarrassing."[13] Johnson's neglect of the Democratic National Committee was common knowledge.

AS THE CAMPAIGN SEASON GOT UNDER WAY, THE JOHNSON ADMINIS-tration discovered that the two-party system was alive and well. By 1966, the GOP was on its way back to the center of political life in America. Heading this resurgence was a new, sleeker, more relaxed Richard Nixon. Since his 1960 presidential defeat and his loss in the 1962 California gubernatorial contest, Nixon seemed to have shed the insecurity and humorlessness that had plagued him. "Remember when the Democrats tried to run with LBJ?" Nixon told a whooping throng of Republican loyalists. "Now they're trying to run away from him."[14]

The Kennedys were of two minds about the election. They wanted the Democrats to retain their majorities in both houses, but they wanted to see the Johnson administration discredited. Above all, the warriors of Camelot had their sights set on 1968. RFK worked to stake out an alternative position: on the war in Vietnam (the administration was too inflexible), on the Great Society (the administration was quitting too early), and on the plight of the cities (the administration was not doing enough). Polls by both Gallup and Quayle taken in the first week in September indicated that Democrats favored Bobby 40 percent to 38 percent for the 1968 presidential nomination and that independents would vote for him by a margin of 38 percent to 24 percent. The "exquisitely modulated battle," as *Newsweek* termed it, between RFK and LBJ was having an immediate and detrimental impact on the Democrats' prospects in the midterm elections.

Martin Luther King did his best to help with the upcoming elections. On September 29, he extracted a promise from Stokely Carmichael, chair of SNCC, that he would, until after the midterm elections were over, stop using the term "black power" or advocate the use of nonviolence and refrain from organizing street demonstrations. The moving force, ironically, behind King's efforts to rein in the tempestuous Carmichael was J. Edgar Hoover's number one red bait, Stanley Levison. SNCC had organized demonstrations in Atlanta that had turned violent. Levison and others blamed the gubernatorial nomination of arch-segregationist Lester Maddox on those disturbances. "Stokely must be politically isolated," Levison declared.[15] But it was all to no avail.

Election Day proved to be humbling, if not disastrous, for the Democrats. The GOP gained forty-seven seats in the House, three in the Senate, eight governorships (including California's Ronald Reagan), and perhaps most significant, over five hundred seats in state legislatures. Critics of the administration were elated.[16] Liberals predicted a revival of the Dixiecrat–conservative Republican coalition. Some Democrats saw a silver lining, however. "It is, I think, a brand-new ballgame," political activist Frank Mankiewicz wrote Bobby Kennedy after the elections. "In every contested election the young, attractive, more non-political candidate won. And the oldest, least attractive, most political candidate is LBJ."[17] Vietnam was not as important in explaining GOP gains, Schlesinger told reporters, as "the picture—true or false—which people have about President Johnson's character."[18] LBJ tried to put the best face on the outcome. Democratic margins had been reduced from 249 to 187 in the House and 64 to 36 in the Senate—still working majorities. And though he did not say it, LBJ believed that some of the newly elected Republicans might be easier to get along with than some of his liberal fellow Democrats.[19]

IN DECEMBER 1966, BILL MOYERS LEFT THE WHITE HOUSE TO BE-come publisher of *Newsday*. A break had been in the offing since he first took the job as press secretary. At the time, Moyers had remarked to his wife, "This is the beginning of the end, because no man can serve two masters," meaning LBJ and the press.[20] Particularly when those two masters were so continually and vexatiously at odds. Johnson was dissatisfied with his relationship with the media, and increasingly he tended to blame his press secretary. For its part, the White House press corps began to view Moyers less as a witty, informed, sincere individual who was doing his best to defend them than as the defender of the paranoid, arbitrary, dishonest man in the

White House. In the summer of 1966, Moyers had gone to the hospital with a bleeding ulcer.

Despite Vietnam, his trouble with the press, and GOP gains, LBJ's appetite for reform had not abated. As he prepared for his fourth State of the Union address, he was as determined as ever to forge ahead on the domestic front. Shortly after Christmas, Joe Califano arrived at the Ranch to go over the next year's program. For months, Johnson had been thinking about upgrading nursing homes. At the president's direction, Califano had put together a task force to make recommendations. LBJ's charge to the members had been memorable. As he described some of the conditions he had witnessed, his voice rose and he became more agitated: "Fire traps, rat traps, a disgrace . . . no one of you would let your mother near one." He invoked the Bible and the commandment to honor thy father and mother. "I want nursing homes that will be livable, happy places for people to serve out their old age, places where there will be a little joy for the elderly, but most of all places that take care of their special needs." There needed to be "flat floors, and grades, so that the wheelchairs can easily be used. . . . And when you design toilets . . . "—at this point he leaned sideways on his left buttock, put his elbow on the arm of his chair, took his right arm and hand, and strained to twist them as far behind himself as he could, and, grunting and jabbing his hand behind his back, he continued—"make sure that you don't put the toilet paper rack way behind them so they have to wrench their back out of place or dislocate a shoulder or get a stiff neck in order to get their hands on the toilet paper."[21]

Califano suggested legislation requiring tobacco companies to reveal the tar and nicotine content of cigarettes on their packaging. LBJ was sympathetic but did not want to do anything to further alienate the tobacco states. His civil rights initiatives were doing enough of that. LBJ was enthusiastic about lowering the voting age to eighteen but wanted to wait a year (he proposed a constitutional amendment to that effect in June 1968). He wanted a truth-in-lending bill, the president told his advisers. And more consumer protection. Earlier that year, Califano's young son, Joe, had swallowed the contents of an aspirin bottle and had had to have his stomach pumped out. "There ought to be a law that makes druggists use safe containers," LBJ declared on hearing of the accident. "There ought to be safety caps on those bottles so kids like little Joe can't open them." Thus was born the Child Safety Act, which Congress eventually passed in 1970.[22]

LBJ and his advisers picked the evening of January 10, 1967, for the State of the Union address. Johnson did not want to conflict with Everett Dirksen's birthday party scheduled for the 11th, and he did not want to shoulder aside popular television programs. "I don't want millions of people looking at me for an hour and thinking, 'This is the big-eared son of a bitch that knocked my favorite program off the air,'" he told Califano.[23] Still, the 10th turned out to be an unfortunate choice. "On the Hill today there had been a death [the aged Congressman John E. Fogerty of Rhode Island] and an expulsion," Lady Bird recorded in her diary. "Adam Clayton Powell had been expelled from the House [for misuse of public funds and other offenses] in an atmosphere tense with violence and hatred."[24]

Observers noted a different LBJ who strode into the House chamber that January evening. There was a diffident, almost apologetic smile on his face. His tone was subdued, his rhetoric measured. He admitted that sundry "mistakes" and "errors" had marred his leadership. He alluded to the need sometime in the future for a tax increase. He promised safer streets, maintenance rather than expansion of most Great Society programs, and, as in 1966, emphasis on quality-of-life issues. Johnson mentioned civil rights only briefly. The theme of the speech was not what the federal government was going to do for America, but what could be achieved in partnership with state and local government.[25] James Reston of the *New York Times* hailed the speech as the beginning of a new and creative federalism. In a laudatory column entitled "Johnson and the Age of Reform," Reston wrote:

> This is not a conservative but a radical program. He is not trying to follow but to transform the New Deal. He is not proposing to console the poor in their poverty but to give them the means of lifting themselves out of poverty. He is not using Federal funds to keep them where they are or to impose Federal control over the states and cities, but to finance the passage of the poor into useful, effective jobs, and create new partnerships between Washington and the state capitals and the cities and other political centers in the world.[26]

Johnson seemed to be saying to the South Vietnamese, to African Americans, to the white middle class, to labor, to management that he had carried forward and modernized the Rooseveltian vision; he had put in place the tools with which to achieve the goal of a just, peaceful, diverse, and democratic society. Now it was up to the people to determine whether they had the will and the wisdom to sustain that vision. On the war itself, the president offered little solace. "I wish I could report to you that the conflict is almost over," he said. "This I cannot do. We face more cost, more loss, and more agony. For the end is not yet. I cannot promise you that it will come this year—or come next year."[27] America and its allies would stay the course, Johnson declared.

Given the facts that civil rights leaders and representatives of the poor in general were complaining that the money spent on the War on Poverty was insignificant and that the Great Society's obsession with the cult of opportunity was insufficient to the day, that conservatives were demanding law and order to include a government crackdown on both ghetto rioting and nonviolent civil disobedience, that hawks on the Vietnam war believed that the administration was not doing enough, and that doves were insisting that Washington was doing too much, it was not a message many people wanted to hear, Reston notwithstanding.

Two weeks later, the United States endured its first manned space tragedy. Air Force Lieutenant Colonel Virgil I. Grissom, Navy Lieutenant Commander Roger B. Chaffee, and Air Force Colonel Edward H. White II were burned to death when a ball of flame engulfed their *Apollo I* spacecraft at Cape Kennedy as they rehearsed one of the steps designed to take man to the moon. Grissom, Chaffee, and White were buried on a clear, wintry day in Arlington Cemetery. Both Lyndon and Lady Bird attended the service. The Greatest Generation had suffered yet another blow to its collective ego. Increasingly, it seemed, all things were not possible.

BEGINNING IN 1966, ALLARD LOWENSTEIN, A FORMER STUDENT AC-tivist at the University of North Carolina at Chapel Hill, a past head of the National Student Association, and a leader of the reform wing of the Americans for Democratic Action, launched a campaign to persuade the ADA to support someone other than Lyndon Johnson for president in 1968. Though Lowenstein did not succeed, the national board at its annual meeting in Washington in the spring of 1967 did denounce the war in Vietnam. At the same time, a group of antiwar enthusiasts in New York opened the "Citizens for Kennedy-Fulbright" headquarters in preparation for the 1968 presidential election.[28] In July the group organized some fifty former delegates to the Democratic National Convention, who sent a public letter to the president urging him not to run in 1968. Because of deep divisions over foreign affairs, they declared, "millions of Democrats will be unable to support Democratic candidates in local, state or national elections."[29] From that time on, Lyndon Johnson viewed the ADA as nothing less than a "Kennedy-in-exile" government.

There had always been a complicated but crucial connection between the civil rights movement in the United States and the war in Vietnam. The moral imperative that Lyndon Johnson, Martin Luther King, and others had invoked to persuade white, middle-class America to support the drive for racial equality had reinforced and been reinforced by the liberal internationalist notion that the United States had an obligation to help the peoples of the Third World—most of whom were nonwhite—resist communist domination. Johnson's talk of internationalizing the Great Society and of transforming the Mekong Delta (the river system that dominated Southeast Asia) into another TVA had woven the connecting fabric tighter and tighter. But as the black power advocates co-opted the civil rights movement and intimidated white liberals, and as a new wave of urban rioting swept the nation's cities, a white backlash had erupted that threatened not only the Great Society—especially the Second Reconstruction—but the war in Vietnam as well. Liberals who surrendered to the New Left and who joined with Tom Hayden and Stokely Carmichael in indicting American institutions and political processes played their part in eroding the Vietnam consensus, but it was the growing doubts among the average American that the Judeo-Christian ethic could or should be applied to social problems at home and abroad that did the real damage.

Harry McPherson persuaded LBJ to take advantage of Lincoln's birthday anniversary on February 12, 1967, to speak out on race, to affirm the administration's continuing commitment to equal opportunity and equality under the law both at home and abroad.[30] Standing before the majestic Lincoln Memorial, LBJ gestured to the statue designed by Daniel Chester French and called the crowd's attention to the aura "of brooding compassion, of love for humanity; a love which was, if anything, strengthened and deepened by the agony that drove lesser men to the protective shelter of callous indifference." Speaking for himself as well as the Great Emancipator, LBJ declared, "Lincoln did not come to the Presidency with any set of full-blown theories, but rather with a mystical dedication to the Union—and an

unyielding determination to always preserve the integrity of the Republic."
Then he forged the link between civil rights and internationalism: "Today,
racial suspicions, racial hatred and racial violence plague men in almost every
part of the earth. . . . The true liberators of mankind have always been those
who showed men another way to live—than by hating their brothers."[31]

What Johnson and McPherson were trying to do was to persuade
black Americans to acknowledge a positive connection between the Second Reconstruction and the war in Vietnam: both were struggles for self-
determination, campaigns to spread the blessings of freedom and democracy
to nonwhite peoples. "I have come to speak . . . about the morality of
nations," LBJ had declared in a commencement address at Catholic University back in June 1965. "For while I believe devotedly in the separation of
church and state, I do not believe it is pleasing in the sight of God for men to
separate morality from their might. . . . What America has done—and what
America is doing around the world—draws from deep and flowing springs
of moral duty . . . we of the United States cherish the right of others to
choose for themselves what they shall believe and what their own societies
and institutions shall be."[32]

Instead, the black power movement, the SDS, the SNCC, and the leadership of the SCLC, including Martin Luther King, were joining hands
to portray the war in Southeast Asia as just another attempt by the white
power structure in the United States to exploit and oppress colored people
everywhere. There was a link between the struggle for black civil rights
in America and for social and economic justice in South Vietnam, they
acknowledged, but black soldiers ought to be fighting with the Vietcong
against American imperialism rather than with the Armed Forces of the
United States. Only the most radical went that far, of course, but, increasingly, black revolutionaries such as Floyd McKissick and New Left leaders
such as Tom Hayden were joining with evangelical civil rights activists like
King in calling for an immediate withdrawal from Vietnam in order to free
up funds for the antipoverty program and other aspects of the Great Society.

The SDS and SNCC were thorns in the administration's side, but nothing
compared to King, whose decision to publicly question US policy in Vietnam had grown out of his December 1964 trip to Oslo to receive the Nobel
Peace Prize. At the annual convention of the SCLC in Birmingham on August 12, 1965, he announced that he planned to write to the Vietnam combatants, calling on them to reach a negotiated settlement. He subsequently

abandoned the project but then, after meeting with UN ambassador Arthur Goldberg, issued a public statement calling on the United States to include the Vietcong in peace negotiations, to stop bombing North Vietnam, and to support Communist China's bid for a seat in the United Nations.[33]

Following the Watts riot, Johnson and King had met at the White House. The president noted that members of Congress had "the impression that you are against me in Vietnam. . . . You better not leave that impression," he said. "I want peace as much as you do, and more so, because I am the fellow that wakes up in the morning with a report that fifty of our boys died last night. These folks just will not come to the conference table."[34] In this conversation and ones to follow, the president and the head of the SCLC shadowboxed over Vietnam. King knew full well that if he followed his moral inclination to speak out against the president's foreign policy, it would seriously risk his ability to influence Johnson on poverty and civil rights. In September 1965, the civil rights leader assured the White House that he was not strong enough to carry on two struggles at the same time—the civil rights battle and the Vietnam peace struggle. He intended to get back to civil rights.[35] But as the war continued to escalate and King's conviction that racism and imperialism stemmed from a common root hardened, he decided he had to speak out.

In the spring of 1966, King and Dr. Benjamin Spock, a prominent pediatrician and antiwar leader, led a Holy Saturday procession of eighty-five hundred people down State Street to the Chicago Coliseum. Then, on April 4, 1967, came King's memorable speech at New York's Riverside Church. The war in Vietnam was a "symptom of a far deeper malady" that throughout history had prompted the United States to oppose revolutions in behalf of social justice and self-determination by the nonwhite peoples of the Third World.[36] He declared that there was an inseparable connection between the battle for civil rights and antipoverty programs at home and the war in Vietnam. "A few years ago," he said, "there was a shining moment in [our] struggle. It seemed as if there was a real promise of hope for the poor—both black and white—through the poverty program there were experiments, hopes, and new beginnings. Then came the buildup in Vietnam and I watched the program broke and eviscerated as if it were some idle political plaything of a society gone mad on war." He had finally realized, he said, that "I could never again raise my voice against the violence of the oppressed in the ghettos without having first spoken clearly to the greatest

purveyor of violence in the world today—my own government." His comments provoked a firestorm. A *Washington Post* editorial called his remarks
"bitter and damaging allegations that he did not and could not document."[37]

Actually, King's position on the war was fairly moderate: bombing halt,
cease-fire, negotiations, and implementation of the 1954 Geneva Accords.
But the White House, recognizing his significance as the moral arbiter of the
civil rights movement, came to see him as "the crown prince of the Viet-
niks," as Harry McPherson put it.[38] Johnson's dismay turned to "cold anger,"
the president's new press secretary, George Christian, recalled.[39] LBJ and his
advisers believed that by blaming the war in Vietnam for society's ills, King
was undercutting their efforts to bring the Second Reconstruction to fruition. Conservatives were aching for a justification to starve the Great Society
of funds. While the administration argued for guns and butter, leaders of the
conservative coalition could cite the "dubious loyalty" of figures like King
to block further appropriations.[40] From this point on, LBJ refused to view
King as a troublesome partner but saw him instead as an avowed enemy.

King's apostasy on the war played directly into the hands of J. Edgar
Hoover and others who were determined to establish a link between the
forces of international communism and the civil rights movement. If the
ghetto uprisings and the violent rhetoric of the black power movement
were not enough, King, whose principal advisers were former communists
or communist sympathizers, would do the trick. Hoover continued to benefit from an ally within the inner sanctum of the Oval Office, Chief of Staff
Marvin Watson. He was an avid reader of the raw reports on King's activities
that arrived at the White House on an almost daily basis. His summaries
for the president unerringly ended with the Hoover-like coda: "One of
King's advisers is still Stanley Levison who is a long-time Communist" and
"[Harry] Wachtel is a former member of the National Lawyers Guild, which
has been cited as a communist front."[41] Following the Riverside speech,
Johnson asked George Christian to quietly start contacting "reliable" reporters and columnists and supplying them with information about King's
ties with the "secret Communist" Stanley Levison.[42]

Not surprisingly, the administration did everything in its power to mobilize and publicize black supporters of the war. And there were supporters,
although most were unenthusiastic. A. Philip Randolph, Whitney Young,
Roy Wilkins, and even James Farmer had varying reservations about the

conflict in Southeast Asia. They, like King, worried that it would divert attention and funding away from antipoverty and other programs vital to African Americans, but they kept these sentiments to themselves. "I felt that the civil rights movement should not get involved in this," Farmer later recalled. "I felt it would simply confuse the issue."[43] Wilkins and Young recognized the idealism, misguided though it may have been, that was responsible for America's decision to go to war. The White House encouraged Young to make a trip to Vietnam and applauded when he subsequently reported to the Saigon press corps that black soldiers seemed to be faring no better or worse than their white counterparts, that they generally supported the war, and that, for the most part, they saw service in the military as a way to get ahead in the world.[44]

The board of directors of the NAACP voted on April 10, 1967, that any attempt to merge the civil rights and peace movements would be "a serious tactical mistake."[45] At the prompting of the White House, General Louis B. Hershey and the Selective Service Board made a concerted effort to get blacks on local draft and appeal boards in the South. As a result, between December 1966 and June 1967, the number of blacks on local boards increased from 267 to 413, including Florida with 5 and Louisiana with 8. The White House ordered a study to determine whether African Americans were fighting and dying in Vietnam in a higher proportion than their percentage of the draft-age population. The study found that blacks were serving in disproportionately high numbers in combat, but those in combat were dying at the same rate as whites.[46]

Ironically, LBJ's staying the course in Vietnam won him scant credit with the ultranationalist white South. Although most whites approved of the war, they continued to disapprove of him. A September 1966 poll in Louisiana showed the president's job rating at 31 percent favorable and 69 percent unfavorable. When divided by race, the numbers stood at 16 percent to 84 percent among whites and 94 percent to 6 percent among blacks. As hawkish South Carolina congressman Mendel Rivers told White House aide Henry Wilson, his constituents loved the bombing but hated the federal registrars.[47]

Soon, however, Americans were to be confronted with two insurgencies: one in South Vietnam and one in the black ghettoes of their own cities.

CHAPTER 15

WHIPLASH: URBAN RIOTING AND THE WAR ON CRIME

JOHNSON, McPHERSON, CALIFANO, AND RAMSEY CLARK, WHO HAD been serving as acting attorney general, were anticipating another summer of unrest in the nation's inner cities. During late 1966 and early 1967, they had continued to struggle with causes and remedies. Moynihan's focus on the dysfunctional black family seemed logical, but what to do about it, especially in the short run? To make matters worse, the Moynihan report continued to be denounced almost daily by black power spokesmen as just another racial slur.[1] More parks, more summer camps, more job training, more subsidized housing, and better education opportunities seemed the only answer.[2]

On February 15, 1967, LBJ delivered a special message to Congress on equal justice. He called on lawmakers to enact a fair housing law, provide specific punishments for those interfering with the exercise of existing federal rights, approve a measure that outlawed discrimination in jury selection (previously rejected by Congress), and extend the lives of both the Equal Employment Opportunity Commission and the US Civil Rights Commission.[3] LBJ was most specific about fair housing. Under his plan, a flat ban on discrimination would go into effect for large apartment houses and real estate developments in 1968, and for all housing in 1969. "I am proposing fair-housing legislation again this year," he said, "because it is decent and right." And there was also an effort to mobilize sentiment, if not for the war in Vietnam, for the soldiers fighting there in behalf of civil rights. "The bullets of our enemies do not discriminate between Negro marines and white marines." And he recalled the promise of the Howard University speech. "Freedom," he declared, "is not enough. You do not wipe way the scars of centuries by saying: Now you are free to go where you want, do as you desire."[4]

Thurgood Marshall's confirmation to be associate justice of the Supreme Court in 1966 and Johnson's message to Congress may have swelled the hearts of the vast majority of African Americans, but it did not do a thing for urban ghetto dwellers confronted with a landscape of unremitting hopelessness. Moreover, unlike their rural brethren, they were in a position to vent their anger. The second week in July, violence erupted in Newark, New Jersey, when police arrested a black cab driver on traffic charges and scuffled with him outside a station house. A glowering crowd from an adjacent housing project gathered, shouted insults, and then rocks and bricks from the knot of angry blacks and finally a Molotov cocktail were hurled at police. Ghetto dwellers by the hundreds poured onto the streets, setting fires and looting. Police and firefighters who responded to calls were stoned and eventually fired on by snipers. Rioters dragged passing whites out of their cars, mauled a Good Humor ice cream vendor, and overturned and set fire to his truck. "We're getting bombed out here," one cop radioed his station. "What should we do?" "Leave," responded his dispatcher. Six days of rioting took twenty-six lives, injured fifteen hundred, and left much of the inner city a burned-out shell. After regaining the initiative from the rioters, state and local police had responded with a vengeance.[5]

LBJ wanted to avoid a federal presence in Newark. Whatever the administration did, conservatives who would say it wasn't doing enough, and liberals who were saying it was too much, would whipsaw US marshals and troops. As with Selma and Watts, the president wanted to avoid the appearance of federal occupation, a charge that conservatives would level at the same time they accused the administration of being soft on crime. As luck would have it, New Jersey Democratic governor Richard Hughes was one of Johnson's strongest supporters. The president quietly offered aid, but to his great relief, Hughes replied that state and local authorities could handle matters. On Saturday afternoon, July 15, United Press International reported that Vice President Humphrey had called the governor and offered "federal aid." Johnson was furious. He ordered Califano to rein in the vice president: "He has no authority, spell it out N-O-N-E, to provide any federal aid to Newark or any other city, town or county in America."[6] Humphrey subsequently denied to Califano that he had made any such promise, but LBJ remained unconvinced. In truth, Johnson was taking his anger at white liberals out on Humphrey. All the while Congress was whittling away at his Great Society programs, and Bobby Kennedy, Abe Ribicoff, and Joe Clark, the liberal Democratic senator from Pennsylvania, were blasting the administration for abandoning the nation's cities.

Congress found itself in the grip of a Newark backlash almost immediately. In a special message to the House and Senate on urban and rural poverty earlier in the year, LBJ had proposed the Rat Extermination Act to provide federal funding to control and exterminate the millions of rats that bred in collapsed buildings and bit terrified children. The measure had breezed through the Senate, and the administration expected quick passage in the House. But three days after Newark, a coalition of southern Democrats and Republicans by a vote of 207 to 176 blocked the measure. They derided it as a "civil rats" bill and suggested that the president allocate funds to hire an army of cats.[7] Johnson was appropriately appalled. He issued a scathing statement the afternoon of the defeat, calling the House action a "cruel blow to the poor children of America. . . . We are spending Federal funds to protect our livestock from rodents and predatory animals. The least we can do is give our children the same protection we give our livestock."[8] Following a massive lobbying effort by the White House, the House reversed itself and added a rat extermination provision to the Partnership for Health Act, which the president signed on December 4, 1967.[9]

By 1967, black power and the riots were fueling each other, even if most black power organizations were too small and too ineffectual to play any role in fomenting urban unrest, and most urban rioters were not members of radical organizations. The riots were not part of a conspiracy. But it was impossible for many to make sense of the ghetto uprisings—the form that they took, the meanings that they assumed for both black and white Americans, and, especially, the language and self-perception of their participants—without placing them in the context of black radicalism.

As historian Thomas Sugrue has noted, "Rebellion depends on frustration with the status quo but a belief in the possibility of change. Above all it requires the summoning of collective energies and resources and the development of shared consciousness and identity."[10] In northern cities in the early 1960s, all these ingredients were present. Various organizations emerged under the rubric of black power that called on African American communities to reject white, middle-class society as a model, to demand equal opportunity and equal protection under the law, and to develop a separate black identity. In addition to the Black Muslims, there was the Revolutionary Action Movement (RAM), established in Cleveland in 1962. Led by Robert F. Williams Jr., the young RAM activists envisioned black activism in the United States as the driving force in a worldwide struggle against Western imperialism and racism. Williams was a fierce advocate of blacks' right to self-defense, to carry arms openly.[11] Of the post-1966 black power groups, the most influential was the Black Panther Party for Self-Defense, founded in Oakland in October 1966. What distinguished the Panthers from other black radicals was their focus on the criminal justice system. They depicted the police as agents of racial oppression, demanded the immediate release of black men in prison, and hammered away at the notion of trial by jury of peers, the definition of peers to include race.[12]

Black power advocates rejected integration as a means to black empowerment. African Americans should concentrate on building their own communities. Rather than trying to become white and middle class, blacks should cultivate their own history and identity; indeed, racial pride and self-esteem were two keys to black liberation. They rejected moderation and liberalism and claimed that they—not traditional, establishment civil rights leaders—were the true voice of the people. The movement should stop trying to change white attitudes; they were immutable. The Great Society was a token effort by the white power structure to derail the drive for racial justice in its fullest meaning. And, finally, radicals such as Stokely Carmichael, Floyd McKissick, and the Black Muslims presented their arguments in an international context, linking the black freedom struggle in America with anticolonial movements around the globe.[13]

AT FOUR O'CLOCK IN THE MORNING ON SUNDAY, JULY 26, DETROIT police staged a raid on a "blind pig," an after-hours drinking club on the city's west side in the heart of the ghetto. As the officers herded some eighty patrons down the stairs of the club, knots of angry blacks gathered in the muggy streets. Soon a crowd had surrounded the police and began hurling rocks and then bricks at them and their cruisers. The besieged officers defended themselves but did nothing to disperse the crowds. Mayor Jerome Cavanaugh had been elected with black votes and had ordered the city's police force to take a "walk softly" approach when dealing with minorities. Encouraged by the cops' passivity, the crowd emptied garbage into the streets and set it afire. Then the looting began. Bricks crashed through shop windows, and roaming gangs set fire to what they did not take. There would be more than fifteen hundred blazes in the days to come. Cavanaugh and Michigan governor George Romney huddled on Sunday the 24th and decided to call in seventy-three hundred national guardsmen to reinforce the city's four thousand police. The guardsmen turned out to be, in *Newsweek's* words, "a ragged, jittery, hair-triggered lot, ill-trained in riot control." Said one young citizen-soldier, "I'm gonna shoot anything that moves and is black." By midmorning, Detroit was paralyzed. A pall of smoke hung over the entire city as intermittent sniper fire crackled in the air.[14]

Just before three o'clock on Monday morning, Romney made the first of a series of calls to Attorney General Ramsey Clark. Romney, a self-styled "Republican with a conscience," was positioning himself for a run at the 1968 GOP presidential nomination. Attractive, articulate, moderate, he would be to LBJ's mind a more formidable adversary than Richard Nixon. Under the 1795 law that governed the federal government's response to civil unrest, the president was authorized to send in troops at the "request" of a governor to put down an "insurrection." In his conversations with Clark, Romney stated that he would probably have to "recommend" that troops be sent in. Each of these conversations was reported to LBJ.

Abe Fortas, still providing political advice despite his position on the Supreme Court, warned that Romney was going to try to draw the administration into the peacekeeping effort in Detroit and then scream federal intervention. From then on, Johnson's political antennae were up. Throughout the morning, Clark and Romney sparred.[15] The governor would have to formally request the troops before they could be sent, Clark said. After Romney agreed, the attorney general insisted that his message to LBJ also include the word "insurrection." The governor angrily pointed out that insurance companies did not pay for damages caused by insurrections and slammed the phone down. He then told the press that he had requested troops, the president had agreed to send them, but that he had then with-drawn his request out of the conviction that federal forces would be needed to put down disturbances in other US cities. The implication was that the government was losing control of the country. In fact, Republican con-gressman Gerald Ford, also of Michigan, had been touting this line, and that very day the Republican Coordinating Committee had issued a statement charging that "widespread rioting and violent civil righters have grown to a national crisis since the present Administration took office."[16]

Meanwhile, Deputy Secretary of Defense Cyrus Vance, whom LBJ had dispatched to the riot scene to represent him, reported that the situation was worsening; more fires, more sniper fire, more shootings by guardsmen. At 10:46 p.m. on July 24, Romney cabled a formal request for federal troops. Johnson ordered McNamara to assemble a contingent of troops at Selfridge Air Force Base, some thirty miles from Detroit. To no one in particular, LBJ remarked despondently, "Well, I guess it is just a matter of minutes before federal troops start shooting women and children."[17] He then told Vance to get on the radio, or loudspeakers, or whatever was available and issue a call for peace and quiet before the soldiers were sent in. There wasn't any time, de-clared J. Edgar Hoover, who had been at the president's elbow since the crisis began. "They have lost all control in Detroit," he said. "Harlem will break loose within thirty minutes. They plan to tear it to pieces."[18] Finally, at 11:22, an exhausted Johnson signed the executive order dispatching federal troops to Detroit. Fortas helped draft a statement for him to read over television. The address was a disaster. The seven-minute statement mentioned Romney fourteen times, spelled out to the minute when the president received the governor's wire and when he responded, and emphasized the "undisputed evidence that Governor Romney of Michigan and the local officials in De-troit have been unable to bring the situation under control."[19] CBS president Frank Stanton, a friend of LBJ's, later observed to Joe Califano that the state-ment was transparently political and beneath the president at such a time.[20]

The violence in Detroit continued for three more days. When peace was finally restored, 43 people lay dead, 33 of whom were black, and another 2,250 were injured. Police had arrested more than four thousand citizens, and property damage was estimated in the hundreds of millions of dollars. *Newsweek* described the scene and summed up the national mood:

Whole streets lay ravaged by looters, while blocks were immolated in flames. Federal troops—the first sent into racial battle outside the South in a quarter century—occupied American streets at bayonet point. Patton tanks and Huey helicopters patrolled a cityscape of blackened brick chimneys poking out of gutted basements. And suddenly Harlem 1964 and Watts 1965 and Newark only three weeks ago fell back into the shadows of memory. Detroit was the new benchmark, its rubble a monument to the most devastating race riot in U.S. history—and a symbol of a domestic crisis grown graver than any since the Civil War.[21]

Even before the ashes of Detroit had cooled, the conservative coalition had moved to blame the rioting on LBJ and the permissive policies of the Great Society. Figures on the right from Gerald Ford to George Wallace, Ronald Reagan to Richard Russell declared that the War on Poverty was fueling urban unrest, not fighting it. They deliberately refused to make a distinction between civil disobedience and urban violence; when challenged, they declared that at best the first led to the second. The Great Society was undermining individual responsibility and personal accountability, conservatives charged. Head Start and the antipoverty program were indirectly subsidizing anarchism and riots and playing into the hands of Hanoi, Moscow, and Beijing.

By the fall of 1967, restoring law and order meant putting down urban riots. Polls showed that the racial crisis was now the nation's chief domestic concern. Even among those without an ideological axe to grind, there was a growing perception that the nation was in the grip of a crime wave and that the vast majority of criminals were black. According to the Uniform Crime Reports, compiled and published by the FBI, the rate of property crime rose 73 percent between 1960 and 1967; the rate of violent crime had doubled by 1969. (Much of this was due to demographics; the baby boomers were increasing the proportion of young men in the overall population, which always led to an increase in the crime rate.) In August 1964, *U.S. News and World Report* had asked, "Is Crime Running Wild?" One year later it had an answer—and a new question: "Crime Runs Wild—Will It Be Halted?" By 1971, African Americans constituted less than 10 percent of the total population but accounted for more than two-thirds of all robbery arrests and almost two-thirds of all homicide arrests.[22]

Many black leftists interpreted the urban riots as protorevolutionary or revolutionary struggles. For their part, many whites, particularly law enforcement officers and elected officials, took black radicals at their word. They viewed the riots as products of a conspiracy hatched by cells of black militants who hoped for nothing short of the overthrow of the white power structure. Left and Right exhibited a common antipathy toward the Great Society. While the Right attributed great influence to the antipoverty program—if only as a negative force—the Left gave it little credit and attacked it as a political sham, a token gesture motivated by white guilt and intended to deflect black demands for structural change.[23] Liberals and moderate Republicans despaired. An editorial in *The Nation* predicted, "Sooner or later, sporadic local uprisings are pretty sure to escalate into action organized on a national scale with some degree of liaison and discipline instead of extemporaneous looting. And then what?"[24]

In the wake of the civil unrest that plagued the summer of 1967, the administration prepared a confidential report entitled "Thinking the Unthinkable," which outlined four potential policy outcomes. In the first scenario, "The Armed Fortress," whites flee to suburban enclaves when "unprecedented violence" erupts in the nation's central cities. Congress guts the War on Poverty. Police forces soon resemble "occupation armies." The UN flees New York for Paris. In scenario number 2, "The Pacified Ghetto," black radicals conclude that initiatives such as Model Cities will work and forgo violence. With more funds available because of the end of the Vietnam War, urban conditions improve. Over time, conditions begin to deteriorate as a result of segregation but remain bearable because suburban whites are willing to send some tax dollars into the central cities as the price of Negro exclusion from their communities. In the third scenario, "The Mini Ghetto," strong open-housing legislation breaks down segregation, granting middle-class blacks access to suburban life and fostering urban renewal that lures young whites back to the city. In the fourth scenario, "The Vanishing Ghetto," society achieves virtually complete residential and political integration. The authors of "Thinking the Unthinkable" declared only the first two projections to be realistic.[25]

The Detroit riot revived the maroon scare, the notion that there was an inextricable link between urban rioting and the international communist conspiracy—red and black blending to maroon—with a vengeance. King's increasingly vocal opposition to the war in Vietnam had provided an opening for segregationist red-baiters; Detroit opened the floodgates. By the fall of 1967, conservatives were able to break the moral link connecting the war in Vietnam with the domestic civil rights movement. While American soldiers were fighting in Southeast Asia to protect the peoples of South Vietnam, Cambodia, and Laos from the scourge of international communism, black radicals in America were openly opposing that effort and actively trying to destroy the very "system" that was fighting for freedom and justice in the Third World.

Critics of the administration on both the right and left drew parallels between the struggle to maintain law and order at home and combat revolutionary nationalism abroad. At the rhetorical level, there was repeated recourse to the language of deterrence and credibility, with the White House eventually charged with creating a "gap" in both the domestic and foreign spheres. An important theme, particularly for many on the right, was that the United States could not contain communism abroad if it could not contain ghetto uprisings, violent student protests against the war in Vietnam, and crime in the streets at home. This argument reinforced the Hooverian notion that urban unrest was the result of a communist conspiracy, representing just as much of a potential victory for the forces of international communism as a North Vietnamese Army–Vietcong victory in Vietnam. On the left, radicals in the civil rights and antiwar movements agreed that the Johnson administration was pursuing a policy of containment both at home and abroad, proving that the black liberation struggle in the United States was part of the worldwide campaign by nonwhite peoples to defeat colonialism.[26]

To the delight of conservatives, in the aftermath of Newark and Detroit, black radical Stokely Carmichael flew to Cuba to address the Organization for Latin American Solidarity. The gathering of Marxists-Leninists from throughout the Western Hemisphere was held in the hotel Havana Libra, whose three-story lobby featured an enormous derrick replete with machine guns, automatic rifles, Molotov cocktails, and banners proclaiming the OLAS motto: "The duty of every revolutionary is to make revolution!"

Carmichael was appropriately radical. "Yankee imperialism has existed too long," he declared. "We are ready to destroy it from the inside. We hope you are ready to destroy it from the outside."[27] His remarks made front-page news in papers across the United States. At the same time, the new national chairman of the SNCC, H. Rap Brown, proclaimed that the organization would thereafter celebrate August 18, the anniversary of the 1965 Watts riot, as Independence Day instead of July 4. One GOP congressman declared that by preaching resistance to the draft and the use of violence to achieve the goals of the civil rights movement, Carmichael had violated the treason laws of the United States. He must be arrested and severely punished. If the president did not take action, the nation could and probably would descend into chaos.[28]

LBJ was tempted to buy in to the notion that the riots were communist inspired. King's apostasy and the black power movement, with its apocalyptic antiliberal rhetoric and advocacy of violence in the nation's inner cities, continued to distress him. How could blacks, for whom he had done so much, be so ungrateful? But if the conservative coalition's plans to derail domestic reform were to be thwarted, the riots and the black power movement must be portrayed as an indigenous aberration, the creations of a misguided, but tiny, minority. Besides, the CIA, which was in a much better position than the FBI to judge what role if any was being played by Russian, Chinese, and Cuban agent provocateurs, found that there was no connection between the riots and the forces of international communism.[29]

As if Johnson and the Great Society did not face enough adversity, Bobby Kennedy continued to attack from the left, using the ongoing cities hearings in Congress to indict the administration for not foreseeing the urban uprisings before they materialized and for responding with "token" programs when they did. Kennedy's hatred of Johnson had never flagged. Egged on by Arthur Schlesinger and others, he began to positon himself for a run at the Democratic nomination in 1968. But he had to have a constituency. There was nothing on the right for him, so he looked to the left on both the domestic and international fronts. In the wake of the Watts uprising, he had expressed sympathy for the rioters. Law and order was not the answer. The legal system, proclaimed Kennedy, had not protected poor blacks "from paying too much money for inferior goods, from having their furniture repossessed," or "from having to keep lights turned on the feet of children at night, to keep them from being gnawed by rats."[30] In an address delivered in late January 1966, RFK had declared that breaking up the ghetto was his ultimate goal but that it would take many years, and in the meantime federal, state, and local authorities should undertake a "total effort" aimed at the regeneration of inner-city communities.

In August 1967 the highly publicized Senate "cities" hearings examining the causes of the urban crisis reconvened. RFK was brutal in his cross-examination of administration officials. He asked Robert C. Weaver, head of HUD, why only four thousand new low-income housing units were under construction nationwide. He blasted the administration for requesting $4 billion for the development of a supersonic plane when a similar figure would have increased by hundreds of thousands the number of children covered by Head Start.[31] RFK then proceeded to take on the welfare system. In a speech before the Day Care Council of New York, he branded it "a second-rate set of social services which damages its recipients" and "destroys any semblance of human dignity."[32]

A *Newsweek* article depicted Bobby as a publicity-seeker more concerned with the television coverage of the Ribicoff hearings and his own exposure in the run-up to the 1968 election than with the poverty budget. But he continued to have enormous public appeal. Testifying before the Senate hearings on urban unrest in November 1967, Katie Ridley, a District of Columbia resident, declared that the only hope for the War on Poverty was RFK. "I feel that Mr. Kennedy is one of the poor man's friends. I do not think this is true of our president." Room 318 of the Old Senate Office Building, crowded with the residents of the nation's capital, erupted in applause.[33]

While Kennedy, Ribicoff, and King assailed the administration from the left, the GOP issued a statement, endorsed by former President Eisenhower, lambasting LBJ for having "totally failed to recognize the problem" of the American city; on that same day its authors appealed to the president to cut back federal spending for the antipoverty program and Model Cities. Republicans denounced Johnson's $10 billion request for urban areas, a 250 percent increase over seven years, as another act of fiscal irresponsibility and part of a continuing scheme to reward rioters.[34]

At Harry McPherson's suggestion, LBJ met with his informal black cabinet—Randolph, Young, Wilkins, et al.—on July 31, 1967; he and his staff found the group discouraged, even despondent, with nothing to offer but the same old remedies. Do not punish the 97 percent of the law-abiding citizens because of the 3 percent who riot. Fund more housing, reconsider Young's Marshall plan for the ghettoes.[35] They seemed to LBJ to be out of touch with the currents that were then running in both the ghettoes and Congress. Columnist Emmet Hughes, a former Eisenhower speechwriter, observed that the "movement" had recently come "to suffer the baleful prominence of two men supremely skilled in the art of alienating—the smirking Adam Clayton Powell and the snarling Stokely Carmichael."[36]

On July 27, with the ashes of the Detroit riot still smoldering, LBJ went on national television to appeal for peace and calm. He designated the following Sunday a national day of prayer and announced that he was establishing the National Advisory Commission on Civil Disorders. LBJ wanted a blue ribbon committee whose report would sensitize white America to the plight of ghetto dwellers, and he wanted to undercut congressional investigations of the riots that were assailing him from both the Right and the Left. To this end, he planned to stack it with white liberals and black conservatives. For chair he chose Illinois governor Otto Kerner, a Democrat, and for vice chair John Lindsay, the Republican mayor of New York City. Both Roy Wilkins and Senator Edward Brooke (D-MA), an African American, were included. In his speech, LBJ condemned the rioters and promised that they would be punished, but he warned, "It would compound the tragedy . . . if we should settle for order that is imposed by the muzzle of a gun. . . . The only genuine, long-range solution for what has happened lies in an attack—mounted at every level—upon the conditions that breed despair and violence."[37]

In the late summer of 1967, the president dispatched his aides to St. Louis, New York, Boston, Washington, DC, and other perceived breeding grounds for urban rioting. Instead of relying on local party leaders and officials for information, he resorted to this unusual method to learn about the state of black America. Indeed, in many cases local and state officials, including Mayor Daley, were not even informed that Johnson's lieutenants were coming.[38] Cliff Alexander, Louis Martin, and Harry McPherson went to Harlem and Bedford-Stuyvesant. McPherson's report was chilling: "It is awful in most parts of Harlem. In one block we saw four separate empty lots . . . that were piled high with rubbish and filth, and that were no doubt breeding rats by the thousands. Harlem looks like Calcutta; filthy streets, broken doorways (affording no security for those who live there), trash in the halls, condemned buildings where junkies sleep overnight and sometimes start fires that threaten the whole neighborhood." And Harlem was Shangri-La compared with Bed-Sty. In their effort to quell discontent before it erupted into violence, Mayor Lindsay and local black leaders sometimes found themselves with strange bedfellows. "We heard of a conversation between Rap Brown and a man named Mumpy Johnson—allegedly the top Negro in the Mafia rackets," McPherson told the president. "After Brown spoke, Johnson told him, 'I agree with a lot of what you said. Except I don't want any riots. I got to raise $60,000 to buy off some people downtown on a narcotics rap. I can't do that if there's a riot. You start a riot and I'll kill you.' Brown is said to have left town the next day."[39]

Predictably, the Detroit and Newark riots hardened racial stereotyping among many whites. Blacks were lazy, immoral, less intelligent—people who wanted something for nothing. White America had extended its hand, and look what happened. Public opinion polls taken in the wake of the rioting showed that whites believed by 71 percent that the uprisings were organized, and by 45 percent that the organizing was done by outside agitators.[40] White backlash, red-baiters, demagogues, and political opportunists aside, there was a growing feeling among well-intentioned Americans that nothing really could be done about the residents of the Third World, whether they lived in inner-city Philadelphia or the rice paddies of South Vietnam. "This kind of world outbreak, the failure to follow law and order and accepted procedures," Orville Freeman confided to his diary, "might very well lead us to what is the big problem in most of the less developed countries around the world that they simply can't get together, work together, and cooperate to get anything done."[41] In the wake of the rioting, LBJ's approval rating fell to an all-time low of 39 percent.[42]

Urban unrest, the men and women the president dispatched to the ghettoes reported, was rooted in the economic but particularly the social landscape of the ghettoes. Surveys taken during and after the riots offered many surprising findings. The majority of those who took to the streets were males aged fifteen to twenty-four. Investigators demolished the widely held theory that rioters were an "underclass" or members of a criminal element. The black revolutionaries' belief that the rebellions were led by the urban "lumpenproletarait" were mistaken. Those arrested for looting, arson, and other riot-related crimes were not the poorest of urban residents. They were better educated than most northern blacks but were disproportionately confined to low-end jobs. One-third were unemployed.[43]

In his summary report on the visits to the ghettoes, White House aide Sherwin Markman noted a pervasive sense of alienation. Housing, education, and employment varied from city to city, but the "disconnection" blacks felt from the rest of America was "not limited to one city or region but [was] nation-wide in its pattern and growing." Going into the nation's inner cities "was almost like visiting a foreign country—and the ghetto Negro tends to look on us and our government as foreign." Markman attempted to defend black power as a cultural and social force. At its core, he said, it meant "an increase in race consciousness and pride" and could in the end produce "positive results."[44] By all accounts, Johnson was deeply moved by these reports. He carried Markman's briefing on the Chicago ghetto around with him and read it to members of the cabinet, Congress, and the press.[45]

BY 1967 LBJ HAD BECOME CONVINCED, VERY RELUCTANTLY, THAT HE could not continue to afford guns and butter without a tax increase. He knew how Americans hated taxes; he knew that "higher taxes and federal spending" were the issues out of which conservatives could always make political hay, but the budget had risen to $126.7 billion for fiscal year 1967 and was projected to reach $135 billion for FY 1968. The administration had estimated that around $12 billion would be needed for Vietnam. Wishful thinking. The figure turned out instead to be $21.9 billion. The Johnson budget called for only $1.9 billion more for Great Society programs—including just $280 million over FY 1967 for the War on Poverty—but the president refused to abandon other programs he regarded as essential.

The Council of Economic Advisers predicted a budget deficit of $10 billion to $12 billion. By contemporary standards, such government red ink figures were absurdly low. But the banking community and the conservative coalition went berserk. "We are in the midst of the worst financial crisis we have had since 1931," William McChesney Martin, chairman of the Federal Reserve Board, charged. The problem, he declared, was one of "perpetually rising budgets," and if the administration failed to get its financial house in order, there would be a worldwide devaluation of currencies and a general depression.[46] Secretary of the Treasury Henry Fowler echoed Martin: "My job is to get the money to pay the bills. . . . To collect the revenue and borrow to maintain a healthy and balanced economy." Borrowing $10 billion to $12 billion would drive interest rates up and create a credit shortage and eventually trigger a financial panic.[47] The Keynesians on the Council of Economic Advisers proceeded to lose their collective nerve. The consensus among Johnson's advisers was that the country could afford—financially, politically, socially—no more than a $2 billion deficit. To pay for guns and butter, LBJ asked Congress to consider enacting a 6 percent surcharge (a tax on a tax) on corporate and individual incomes.[48]

The argument that a balanced federal budget was crucial to the nation's economic health was, as the Keynesians had advised Kennedy and Johnson in 1963 and 1964, rooted more in politics and ideology than in reality. America's World War II economy had demonstrated that the government could engage in planning, production, and consumption and that government debt could be used to finance economic expansion without bringing about the collapse of capitalism or creating runaway inflation. In 1930 the national debt was $131 per capita. In 1940 it was still only $325, despite the New Deal's use of deficit spending as a remedial tool. The war changed that: in 1945 the per capita national public debt was $1,848. The deficit remained fairly stable after the war, and the country simply outgrew it.[49] During the first two years of the Vietnam War, the consumer price index had risen 5.7 percent. For the first two years of World War II and the Korean War, it had risen 19.8 percent and 11.3 percent, respectively.[50]

Some in the business community wanted to balance the budget through cuts in nondefense spending alone, while others publicly supported the president's call for a tax surcharge. The motives of the latter were less than pure. As one of Harry McPherson's confidants told him, "I'm afraid the reason so many businessmen and bankers are supporting you on the surtax is so that they will feel free to increase prices and interest rates after you lose the surtax fight. You won't be in any position to put the screws to them as you did on the steel, copper and aluminum people."[51]

GOP leaders in Congress echoed the wolf-criers in the financial and business communities and continued to blame the crisis gripping the nation's cities on the administration while moving to drastically cut appropriations for Model Cities and the War on Poverty.[52] "They're going to hurt and hurt a lot," Orville Freeman said of the cuts:

but the experts like Joe [Secretary of the Treasury Henry] Fowler say
we need to show our ability to tighten our belt at a time of boom in
our economy . . . in order to reassure those who are watching our
economic performance closely, those who control a lot of dollars and
could call up a lot of gold. I said to Joe at a luncheon in Dean Rusk's
office last week that this bothers me. It appears to me that this great,
rich, strong country with a very stable dollar and an inflation rate
last year of less than 3 percent, smaller than any place in the world, is
reacting awful scared when the international bankers crack the whip.
His only real response was, "Well, that's the way it is."[53]

For six months, the administration's surtax proposal lay dead in the water.
Members of the conservative coalition did not want to give the administration additional funds because they opposed most aspects of the Great
Society program; antiwar liberals did not want to give the administration
more money because they opposed the war in Vietnam and wanted to make
LBJ choose between domestic programs and the conflict in Southeast Asia.
The first week in June, LBJ met with his economic advisers; they presented
him with devastating news. The projected cost of the war was continuing
to increase, as was the cost of Medicare, Social Security, and other domestic
programs. The administration was now looking at a projected deficit for
FY 1968 of between $23 billion and $28 billion.[54] Several days later, the
president presided over a gloomy cabinet meeting. "The country could
not tolerate a deficit of from $25 to $30 billion," Johnson said. Either there
would be new taxes or programs would be cut or eliminated. Each cabinet
officer, each agency head must cultivate every representative and senator
they could gain access to. While they were applying a thick coat of butter to
the solons, he would be "tailing 'em up." He explained that in Texas, when
there was a drought or flood and the cows became very weak and could not
eat and refused to get up, the cowboys would go out and grasp the cow's tail,
twisting it around and around until the animal became so uncomfortable
that it got up on its feet and began to eat.[55]

On July 26, LBJ had Wilbur Mills to the White House. Word had reached
the president that the chairman of the Ways and Means Committee was
in high dudgeon because he had not yet been "consulted" about the proposed tax increase.[56] Why did the economy need a tax cut in 1964 but now

needed a tax increase? Mills inquired. Times and conditions were different, Johnson replied. Mills helped draft a new tax request message to Congress but made it clear he would not come onboard until there were dramatic cuts in domestic programs.[57] On August 3, the president sent his message to Congress, asking this time not for a 6 percent but for a 10 percent surcharge on personal and corporate income taxes. Congress's response was to threaten virtually every component of the Great Society program, from education to Medicare to Social Security to rent supplements to public broadcasting. All right, if they want cuts, LBJ responded, we'll give them cuts. He contemplated telling Congress that if it did not enact a tax increase, he would request the House and Senate to cut all appropriations by 10 percent, including the pork barrel bills so favored by individual House and Senate members. "Including defense," McNamara recommended. "I'd stick it to Mills," he said. It would then appear that the Arkansan was leading a congressional charge that would not only undermine existing domestic programs but threaten the war in Vietnam as well. All the while, Johnson continued to lash his cabinet officers and agency heads, telling them that if they did not lobby the hell out of Congress, he would sacrifice their budgets first. In a spate of interviews with journalists, LBJ laid out the situation and placed the blame at Congress's door. Wilbur Mills, he told columnist Joseph Kraft, was the "chief blackmailer."[58]

In mid-November LBJ held a spirited press conference on the economic situation. He abandoned his podium and teleprompter, instead walking among reporters with a lavaliere microphone pinned to his lapel, speaking extemporaneously: "One of the great mistakes that the Congress will make is that Mr. Ford and Mr. Mills have taken the position that they cannot have any tax bill now. They will live to rue the day when they made that decision. . . . I know it doesn't add to your . . . popularity to say we have to have additional taxes to fight this war abroad and fight the problems in our cities at home. But we can do it with the gross national product we have. Who should do it [if we don't]?"[59]

The day following, the British devalued the pound for the first time since 1949 and raised interest rates. To protect the dollar, the Fed, followed by commercial banks, raised the prime lending rate. Johnson attempted to seize the crisis to push his tax bill and to eliminate congressional add-ons to his budget. But Mills remained unmoved. To Johnson's consternation, the chairman added a freeze on welfare payments for dependent children to the administration's Social Security bill, an amendment that, if enacted, would keep another 1.3 million Americans from rising above the poverty line. In a last-ditch effort to get the Arkansan to back down, LBJ met with him in the Oval Office. The freeze was unfair, LBJ protested. "Mr. President," Mills said, "across town from my mother in Arkansas a Negro woman has a baby every year. Every time I go home, my mother complains. That Negro woman's now got eleven children. My proposal will stop this." Moreover, he reiterated, there would be no tax bill until there were more and deeper cuts in domestic programs.[60]

CHAPTER 16

A "RICE-ROOTS REVOLUTION": THE GREAT SOCIETY IN VIETNAM

IN 1964, JOHNSON, MOYERS, AND GOODWIN HAD HOPED TO HARNESS the youth rebellion and turn it into a powerful engine for reform. In some areas, particularly civil rights, they were successful, but the Students for a Democratic Society's ongoing critique of liberalism and traditional politics proved more of a minus than a plus.

When the authors of the Port Huron Statement assumed leadership of the anti–Vietnam War movement, one of the principal spark plugs was removed from the Great Society engine. From 1966 on, the conflict in Southeast Asia consumed the New Left and the student movement generally. Employing the civil rights movement's Mississippi Freedom Summer as a model, the SDS together with pacifists and disillusioned liberals persuaded twenty thousand people to participate in Vietnam Summer, a series of antiwar protests and demonstrations staged at various points across the country. Then, in the fall of 1967, fifty thousand antiwar protesters gathered in Washington for Stop the Draft Week.[1] They prayed, picketed, protested, eventually packed the bridge connecting Washington and Arlington, and surrounded the Pentagon in an effort to bring the alleged center of the military-industrial complex to a halt. Republican California gubernatorial candidate Ronald

Reagan observed to reporters: "If you ask me, the activities of those Vietnam Day teach-in people can be summed up in three words: Sex, Drugs, and Treason." House Democratic leader Carl Albert declared that the march on the Pentagon was "basically organized by International Communism."[2]

Lyndon Johnson had had grave doubts about the war in Vietnam, but following the crucial decisions of 1965 to escalate, he demanded that the Congress, the media, and the American people get behind the war. Massive public dissent upset and confused him. He believed that he and his colleagues, as elected officials, deserved the respect and trust of the people until the next election. He could understand if not sympathize with the black power movement, but he could not understand and was deeply offended by the participation of King and other civil rights leaders in the antiwar movement. He proved much more willing to view protests and demonstrations against the conflict in Vietnam as communist inspired than he did the ghetto revolts of 1964–1968. In 1964 LBJ had heeded Goodwin and Moyers and included in his Great Society vision elements of the Port Huron Statement. Now the SDS was leading the attack not only against the war in Vietnam but also against liberalism in general. Most frustrating of all, his critics seemed unable or unwilling to recognize that he was attempting to change the very nature of the war in Vietnam, moving from a strategy of search and destroy to counterinsurgency, pacification, and nation building.

The ferocity of the war and the subsequent disillusionment clouded the fact that America's Vietnam experiment was part of a vast reform movement that extended beyond the United States. The impulse toward modernization and international development was implicit in the notions of American exceptionalism and mission. Between the Spanish-American War, which marked the Unites States' coming out as a world power, and World War I, during which the country momentarily embraced Wilsonian internationalism, American statesmen, business leaders, religious figures, and public intellectuals stepped forward to argue that promotion of economic betterment and institutional modernization was both a moral and strategic imperative. Progressives did not limit their vision of a better world through environmental engineering to the United States. Some believed that the United States could only be safe in a world of other liberal democracies, while others believed that modernity would suffice. Power plants, dams, roads, bridges, and other experiments in applied science would change how people lived. New technologies would not only provide material benefits but also fundamentally alter the human condition. Dams and power plants would democratize electricity, raise living standards, and, more important, change the way individuals viewed the world and their place in it.[3]

As JFK and LBJ began their campaign to wrest control of the federal government from the Republicans in 1960, modernization was at the height of its influence globally. Several publications went so far as to declare the 1960s the "Decade of Development."[4] Kennedy rebuked the Republicans for allowing an "economic gap" to develop in the Third World, a phenomenon as dangerous as the heralded "missile gap." The United States must master the global "revolution of rising expectations," he declared. "It is we, the American people, who should be marching at the head of this world-wide revolution, counseling it, helping it come to a healthy fruition."[5] When he created the Peace Corps, President Kennedy asked David Lilienthal, one of the principal architects of the Tennessee Valley Authority, to serve on its National Advisory Council.[6] Chartered by Congress in 1933, the TVA was a federally owned corporation empowered to build and operate a series of dams, electric power facilities, and fertilizer plants throughout the Tennessee River Valley, one of the most economically backward regions of the United States. For the Kennedy administration the TVA remained "an answer to socialism," demonstrating, it believed, the productive potential of coordinated private industry, popular participation, and government aid.[7] Even more than Kennedy, LBJ believed that large-scale programs primed by government intervention could produce remarkable economic change. The Lower Colorado River Authority (LCRA), of which he was a prime architect, was nothing more or less than an iteration of the TVA.

In early 1961, David Lilienthal contacted Undersecretary of State Chester Bowles, urging the administration to consider participating in a TVA experiment focused on the vast Mekong River system in Southeast Asia. Bowles in turn presented the idea to Kennedy. By taking the lead in creating an "International Lower Mekong Valley Authority," the United States could win hearts and minds not only in the region but in the entire developing world. Bowles emphasized both the potential for economic growth and "the political concept surrounding it."[8] JFK's assassination and the decisions to escalate the war in Vietnam momentarily deflated the Mekong development project, but it revived when, in his 1965 John Hopkins address, President

Johnson declared that projects centered on the huge river complex might "provide food and water and power on a scale to dwarf even our own TVA."[9] In 1966 LBJ dispatched none other than David Lilienthal—"Mr. TVA"—to South Vietnam to represent the United States in discussions on postwar reconstruction. From then on, a Mekong River development project remained at the center of reconstruction planning. A TVA for Southeast Asia never materialized, primarily as a result of the exigencies of war: the Vietcong remained a particularly strong presence in the delta, and Cambodian ruler Prince Norodom Sihanouk was determined to hold both the United States and South Vietnam at arm's length. The vision of a TVA for the lower Mekong was pure Great Society, however.

Much more concrete were the development and modernization initiatives associated with counterinsurgency-pacification. There were those in the State Department, Pentagon, and other agencies who believed that if the United States and its allies did not meet the enemy on its own terms in Vietnam and fight a people's war, it would surely lose. Physical security was important, but so were political accountability, a reliable justice system, educational opportunity, and a modicum of economic and social security. US and South Vietnamese forces could kill communist soldiers until the coming of the next ice age, and it would make no difference if South Vietnam did not evolve into a viable polity.

American advocates of counterinsurgency-pacification had been present on the ground in Vietnam and in Washington since the mid-1950s when Ngo Dinh Diem came to power. Edward Lansdale, hero of the victory over the Huk rebellion in the Philippines, argued that the task of winning hearts and minds in South Vietnam was simple: find out what the people wanted and give it to them. But Diem and his brother Ngo Dinh Nhu regarded the emergence of pockets of well-armed, politically motivated South Vietnamese, whether communist or not, as threats to their hold on power.

Following the fall of the House of Ngo in 1963, US officials became aware of just how alienated the countryside was from its national and provincial governments. In an effort to provide security to the villages and hamlets of South Vietnam and generate popular support for the struggle against the Vietcong (VC) and North Vietnamese Army (NVA), the CIA by early 1966 had officers on duty in each of South Vietnam's 44 provinces and 242 districts. Agency operatives gathered intelligence, advised the South

Vietnamese government and its provincial and district security forces, and supervised a variety of paramilitary operations. The emphasis was generally on physical security, on counterterrorism, but there was a civil affairs initiative as well. Medics attached to the Advanced Pacification Program treated more than two hundred thousand patients. US Navy Construction Battalion engineers built and repaired roads, dug wells, and maintained bridges.

Frank Scotton, a United States Information Service (USIS) officer who had begun forming armed propaganda teams in Long An Province in 1964, moved to Saigon where he organized combined Political Action–Counter Terror teams in the six districts around the capital.[10] CIA operatives worked in close cooperation with South Vietnamese pacification officials. Among the most effective was Major Tran Ngoc Chau, a former Viet Minh who had rallied to Diem, but who had grown increasingly disillusioned with Saigon's repressive policies. In Kien Hoa Province, a VC hotbed southeast of Saigon, Chau had developed and implemented the "Census-Grievance program." Members of his counterinsurgency force would move through the province conducting a thorough census, and in the process they would encourage villagers to list their complaints against both the Vietcong and the South Vietnamese government. Chau and his men made it clear to the locals that they understood that before the people could be expected to support their government and its soldiers, its leaders would have to show themselves to be nurturers rather than exploiters.[11] Throughout 1965, however, US-sponsored counterinsurgency-pacification efforts remained localized and compartmentalized.

In an effort to go national with its campaign to win hearts and minds, the CIA in 1966, in cooperation with the Ministry of Rural Development, established the National Training Center for Revolutionary Development Cadre at Vung Tau, the former seaside resort of Cape Saint-Jacques. The center was to train cadre who would work in Scotton's armed propaganda teams or in Tran Ngoc Chau's Census-Grievance program. The curriculum at Vung Tau was the joint creation of Chau and agency personnel. In the pacification manual that he authored, Chau wrote that the rural population in postcolonial Vietnam was divided into three groups by the South Vietnamese government: those who supported the government—the police, civil servants, and military personnel; those who were Vietcong or their active sympathizers; and the great silent mass in between. During the 1940s and 1950s, the vast majority of peasants had rallied to the Viet Minh and fought against the French and their Vietnamese puppets. The Saigon regime and its representatives viewed anyone who had been affiliated with the Viet Minh as communists or communist sympathizers. Nothing could have been further from the truth, Chau wrote. Ninety percent of the villagers in Kien Hoa were nationalists, not communists. It was this group to whom the South Vietnamese government and its American allies must appeal.[12]

By early 1966 there had emerged in South Vietnam a group of counterinsurgency-pacification experts, including CIA officers, USIS personnel, US Army Special Forces, and Foreign Service officers. The clique included John Paul Vann; Frank Scotton; Everett Bumgardner, Scotton's boss and mentor; and Daniel Ellsberg, who had come to Vietnam the previous year as part of Edward Lansdale's second mission. The group boasted powerful friends in the Johnson administration and press corps, the latter including *New York Times* reporters David Halberstam and Neil Sheehan. At a series of working dinners in Saigon, the group put together a position paper on the war entitled "Harnessing the Revolution." The National Liberation Front and the Vietcong were winning the war because their program promised a better life for the average Vietnamese, they wrote. Until and unless Washington and Saigon seized control of the revolution and used it for their own purposes, there could be no progress. The paper called for a different kind of government in South Vietnam, "a national government . . . responsive to the dynamics of the social revolution," a regime that the masses would fight and die for and that would survive the inevitable American withdrawal.[13] Combat had to take a backseat to conversion. The US military and the Army of the Republic of Vietnam must be made servants of an all-out counterinsurgency-pacification program, the report concluded.

In Saigon, Henry Cabot Lodge read "Harnessing the Revolution" and endorsed it. In Washington, William E. Colby, head of the CIA's Far East Division, and Army Chief of Staff Harold K. Johnson lobbied for its adoption. In articles in the *New York Times,* Halberstam and Sheehan applauded the strategy. Perhaps most significantly Westmoreland's deputy in Vietnam, General Creighton Abrams, embraced the group's blueprint for victory through nation building. The counterinsurgency clique's most important recruit, however, was the president of the United States.

By early 1966, the Johnson administration was ready to turn its attention to "the other war," as the president termed it. LBJ never believed that it would be possible to prevail in Southeast Asia by conventional military means alone. Rather, the task at hand was to temporarily interpose American military power between the communists and noncommunists in Vietnam until the latter were strong enough to triumph on their own. Indeed, in terms of building a viable society capable of governing and defending itself, a clear-cut American "victory" would have been counterproductive. Vietnamization, a term Richard Nixon would claim as his own, was always America's policy: the line separating intervention from imperialism was extremely fine, but the White House believed initially that it could be walked. In truth, the concept of nation building lay at the very core of the Johnsonian vision: at home, the president's Great Society itself, especially the Second Reconstruction, was nothing if not an experiment in social engineering. The speech LBJ had delivered to the joint session of Congress that convened on November 27, 1963, immediately following the Kennedy assassination, was meant to evoke memories of JFK, but it was pure LBJ. "We will carry on the fight against poverty and misery, and disease and ignorance, in other lands and in our own," he had declared.[14]

At the outset of his administration, Johnson disavowed any intention to replicate America overseas. But once the exigencies of the Cold War seemed to demand intervention in Vietnam, his mind turned naturally to internationalizing the Great Society. There was, in his philosophy, the assumption that human beings everywhere, especially at the individual and family levels, were the same. "For what do the people of North Vietnam want," he asked rhetorically in his speech at Johns Hopkins University in 1965. "They want what their neighbors also desire: food for their hunger; health for their bodies; a chance to learn; progress for their country; and an end to the bondage of material misery."[15]

In February 1966, President Johnson called an impromptu summit meeting in Honolulu with South Vietnamese president Nguyen Van Thieu and Prime Minister Nguyen Cao Ky. Following the formal opening session, LBJ retired to the King Kalakuau Suite in the Royal Hawaiian Hotel for private talks with Ky and Thieu. He pointed out that 85 percent of their countrymen were peasants who had suffered terribly from the ravages of war during the previous ten years. Their suffering must stop, and the regime must earn the support of the people through programs designed to achieve social and economic security and promote democracy. At the conference's close, the two sides issued the Declaration of Honolulu, in which the United

States and South Vietnam pledged to keep fighting until an honorable peace could be negotiated and to launch immediately an accelerated program of social, economic, and political reform. Before they departed Honolulu, LBJ informed Ky that there would be another meeting somewhere in the Pacific in three to six months "to evaluate the progress toward social justice and democracy that had been made in South Vietnam."[16]

On March 28, LBJ named Robert Komer, a National Security Council staffer and former CIA officer, to the post of special assistant to the president for pacification and rural reconstruction. A short, bespectacled, intense man, the new pacification czar was a Harvard graduate and fervent liberal. "We can spur a socio-economic revolution in a non-country [South Vietnam] even in wartime," he told the president, "but it won't be easy."[17] Some had reservations that "Blowtorch Bob," as the American Mission in Saigon referred to him, was all sail and no anchor, but Colby approved. "He understood what the CIA Station was trying to do in its various experimental programs in the countryside," he wrote in his memoir. "Insisting only that more be done, he provided the policy approval we needed to do it."[18]

The chief engine of rural reform and security in South Vietnam continued to be the Vung Tau Training Center for Rural Development Cadre. The trainees were a microcosm of the society, a reflection of its many ambiguities and contradictions—Catholics, Buddhists, Cao Dai (a religious sect active in central South Vietnam), northerners who had fled south, indigenous peoples, and the sons and daughters of Cambodian and Lao immigrants. Some of the trainees, indeed many, were former Vietcong. "Every effort was made to convert VC sympathizers (and even those who had engaged in guerrilla activities)" Tran Ngoc Chau wrote, "by helping to solve their personal and family problems, usually created by local authorities and troops. . . . If these efforts did not succeed, we tried compromising the individuals in various ways so that they would either have to work with us, or at a minimum be less effective for the other side."[19] The CIA estimated that during all of 1966, 400 villages were brought under South Vietnamese control, for a total of 4,400 out of 11,250. Much remained to be done.[20]

In March 1967, the National Security Council combined all pacification operations, civilian and military, in a new entity, the Civil Operations and Revolutionary Development Support group, or CORDS. Komer was named to head the organization, but within a year he had worn out his welcome within the vast and complex US Mission. In February 1968, in the midst of the Tet Offensive, Bill Colby was named to replace him. The former head of the CIA's Far East Division had long bemoaned the fact that there was only a handful of Vietnamese-speaking Americans in country. The previous year CORDS had moved to remedy that problem, establishing the United States Vietnam Training Center in Arlington, Virginia. The Foreign Service imported a number of Vietnamese English speakers from Southeast Asia to serve as instructors. Some of the students were State Department officers, some were from the US Agency for International Development, and some were from the United States Information Service. A few came from the CIA and the Defense Intelligence Agency. Most were extremely bright and highly motivated individuals, graduates of some of the best universities in the country. A few had previous experience in the Peace Corps. They tended to be independent thinkers, committed but critical. More than a few marched in antiwar parades on their days off.[21] The focus of the program was a year-long, six-days-a-week intensive language course, but there was some instruction in Vietnamese culture, and at the end two weeks at the CIA's paramilitary training facility at Camp Peary, Virginia.[22]

The task facing CORDS was immense. The Tet Offensive, the massive communist assault on South Vietnam's cities and towns that began on January 31, 1968, had added one million new refugees to South Vietnam's already huge displaced population. CORDS officials—military and civilian—moved out into the countryside and set up shop in virtually every hamlet and village. By day, working with US Navy engineers, medical corps personnel, and the US Agency for International Development, they supervised the construction of dispensaries and schools, the rebuilding of bridges and telephone lines, the establishment of first-time electrical grids and education programs to teach modern agricultural techniques. Farmers who had previously brought in one crop a year now brought in three. Rural Development Cadre propagandized in behalf of liberty and democracy and against Marxism-Leninism. By night, CORDS military personnel oversaw patrols conducted by members of Provincial Reconnaissance Units (PRUs) in search of VC. In pacification's most controversial program, codenamed "Phoenix," the CIA and South Vietnamese intelligence identified suspected VC cadre, and the PRUs either captured or killed them.[23]

To some extent the war in Vietnam was an attempt by American liberals to demonstrate that not only were they as staunchly anticommunist as conservatives but also liberalism was the best, indeed, the only antidote to

Marxism-Leninism in the struggle for hearts and minds in the developing world. The conflict, especially its counterinsurgency-reconstruction phase, was not only a programmatic extension of the Great Society, it was an ideological extension. Colby, like LBJ, was a prototypical New Deal Democrat. Any regime not committed to social and economic justice for its citizenry was bound sooner or later to be overthrown. That was certainly the message LBJ had been sending to Richard Russell and other defenders of the American caste system as he demanded their acquiescence in the dismantling of Jim Crow. If the white power structure did not make some structural adjustments, the disinherited might very well burn its collective house down. In Vietnam as elsewhere in the developing world, America's other warriors declared, the United States had to stop aligning itself with the forces of reaction. "If . . . the American position supports the reactionary trends which a new sense of nationalism is attempting to shake off," Colby wrote the State Department's Michael Forrestal, "can we hope to maintain a position in these new emerging nations[?] Even with the use of considerable force as in Vietnam, can we hope to have other than a discouraging stalemate with an aggressive communist movement which aligns itself with the aspirations of the young and arising leadership and repudiated us along with the old and colonialist leadership?"[24] At home and abroad, as long as individuals were denied the rights and opportunities that made life worth living, there was going to be revolution.

The concept that more than any other linked the nation-building effort in Vietnam to the Great Society was community action. Johnson wanted to mold environments to produce the best possible life for the individual. But at some point that meant giving up control. If community action meant anything, it meant empowerment. Through participation in the decisions affecting the fundamental conditions of their lives, members of a community would shed feelings of hopelessness and impotence and become active, responsible defenders and molders of not only their local community but also the larger polity of which they were a part.

This is certainly what William Colby had in mind when he dispatched his armed propaganda teams and Rural Development Cadre, and Sargent Shriver, as he presided over the issuance of Office of Economic Opportunity (OEO) grants to coalitions of local citizens' groups, nongovernmental organization (NGOs), and municipal agencies. No less a figure than Walt

Rostow, MIT economist, development theory pioneer, and an architect of the war in Vietnam, made the connection. "The critical moment [in the modernization process] is not when men begin to share the material benefits of modernization," he wrote the president. "The critical moment is when men feel that they have become active agents in fashioning their own destiny." That was the assumption behind what CORDS was doing in Vietnam and what OEO was trying to achieve in the United States.[25] Problems occurred in Chicago and Bien Hoa province when the empowered groups began to operate outside the established system. Big-city machines were willing to accommodate minorities as long as they did not directly challenge the existing order. In Vietnam, the Diem regime and the military governments that succeeded it tended to see any organized, independent political entity, whether communist or noncommunist, as subversive.

The problem that the United States faced in Vietnam was that there was no constitutional tradition. In the United States all but the most radical looked to the basic law of the land as the final arbiter of the great issues of the day. Johnson insisted that the government of South Vietnam produce a constitution, and it did—but it remained an empty shell. The hidden heart of South Vietnamese politics continued to be the corps commander system. Between 1966 and 1968, these warlords acquired the power to appoint all the key civil and military officials in their zones, including division and regimental commanders and province and district chiefs. Positions generally went to the highest bidders. Utilizing intermediaries—that is, wives, aides, and staff assistants—the corps commander and the aspiring candidate would work out a lump-sum down payment and the monthly tribute that was to follow. These payoffs were made possible by the corruption that came with the post. The key money-collecting official in the system was the province chief, who earned huge sums by raking off funds from various public works projects and payoffs from businessmen for favors and protection. According to Ed Lansdale, who reappeared on the Vietnam scene in the mid-1960s as an adviser to the US ambassador, the corps commander system was much more the control mechanism for the South Vietnamese government and Army of the Republic of Viet Nam (ARVN) than the ministries and channels of authority listed in the official organization charts.[26]

In the United States, liberalism's campaign for equal justice, equal opportunity, and full citizenship for all was a political and moral issue. In Vietnam, it was that but also a strategic and institutional problem. Perhaps, as Mc-George Bundy had remarked to Colby, there was no institutional means by which the United States could nurture a rice-roots revolution that would bring to Vietnam the same blessings that Americans enjoyed. The United States could apply diplomatic and economic leverage to a friendly government—even support coups that pitted one elite against another—but it did not possess the means or the will to foment revolutions that would change the social and political equation in other countries, particularly its allies in the struggle against the forces of international communism.

There were, the architects of the Great Society discovered to their dismay, limits to liberalism in the international as well as the domestic sphere.

CHAPTER 17

ABDICATION

BY THE CLOSE OF 1967, LYNDON JOHNSON'S OFFICIAL LIFE WAS BEING consumed by insurgencies at home and abroad. There was the revolt of the nation's ghetto dwellers against a political and economic system that seemed to have no place for them. There was the rebellion of the New Left against liberalism itself. The antiwar movement had spread beyond the student protest movement to include civil rights leaders and establishment figures such as J. William Fulbright. Black power activists had declared war on traditionalists within the civil rights movement. Then, of course, there was the ongoing communist-led insurgency in South Vietnam.

For Johnson, there was no answer to those in the New Left and antiwar movements who blamed the nation's and the world's ills on liberalism. There was to his mind no alternative to liberal capitalism and constitutional democracy. The administration's strategy at home and abroad had to be counterinsurgency and pacification. It could be argued that, like the Civil Operations and Revolutionary Development Support (CORDS) programs in Vietnam designed to win hearts and minds, the various components of the War on Poverty, Model Cites, and HUD were initiatives to pacify America's have-nots.

By the late 1960s, even some workers in the Great Society vineyard were coming to that conclusion. In *Regulating the Poor* (1971), Richard Cloward and Frances Fox Piven, two of the architects of the War on Poverty, contended that, historically, "relief-giving" was deployed as a means for regulating the supply of cheap labor and, most important, given gathering momentum of the black freedom struggle in the 1960s, social control. The northern urban focus of community action was thus less about a unique extension of participatory democracy than about "absorbing and directing many of the agitational elements of the black population." Social science planners provided "an aura of scientific authority" that minimized white opposition to what really was a program designed to appease African Americans.[1] That was certainly the refrain emanating from the civil rights leadership by 1967 as they insisted that Congress and the administration adopt A. Phillip Randolph's "freedom budget" of at least $30 billion as a means to rehabilitate the nation's ghettos.

In Vietnam, the communist insurgency relied not only on promises of economic and social justice but also on organized and widespread terror campaigns to gain control of the countryside. Counterinsurgency involved military action to secure South Vietnam's villages and hamlets and, in the Phoenix program, tit-for-tat terrorist operations. There were in the United States calls for a coercive response to the ghetto riots and violent antiwar demonstrations. Law-and-order advocates from George Wallace to Ronald Reagan demanded that federal, state, and local authorities respond to civil disruptions with the strongest possible show of force. Not only were there parallels between the insurgencies in the United States and in South Vietnam, they argued, there was an organic connection. Wallace, Reagan, and J. Edgar Hoover depicted the civil rights movement, black power, urban unrest, and the antiwar movement as communist inspired if not communist dominated.

By the fall of 1967, Lyndon Johnson was coming to the conclusion that he and the Great Society had done about all they could do to enhance social and economic justice in the United States and in Vietnam. Mechanisms were in place, people empowered; the rest was up to them. If Americans were fed up with liberalism, and the South Vietnamese preferred Marxism-Leninism, so be it. In truth, by 1967 LBJ was willing to accept the communization of Indochina by peaceful means. "He is prepared for a cease fire and phased withdrawal of all combatants in Vietnam," New York Times columnist James Reston reported. "He is willing to dismantle American bases in that peninsula; he is in favor of neutralization of all Southeast Asia, and he is prepared to let the peoples of South and North Vietnam decide their own political future even if this means a coalition with the Communists."[2] What Johnson could not permit, under any circumstances, was the overthrow of the Saigon regime by force of arms. To do so would threaten the entire containment regime built so painstakingly since World War II.

While the antiwar movement itself was becoming more mainstream, its leading edge—the Students for a Democratic Society (SDS), New Left, and black revolutionaries—seemed to be descending into nihilism. On Labor Day weekend some three thousand delegates from 372 organizations gathered at the Palmer House in Chicago to attend the first convention of the National Conference for a New Politics. No one knew what the "new politics" was, exactly, and the proceedings quickly degenerated into a scene, as one observer put it, "worthy of Genet or Pirandello, with whites masquerading as either poor or black, blacks posing as revolutionaries or as arrogant whites, conservatives pretending to be communists, women feigning to be the oppressed, and liberals pretending not to be there at all."[3] A 150-member black delegation demanded that the gathering pass a resolution denouncing Zionism and calling for immediate reparations payments to all African Americans. Shortly thereafter, forty antiwar radicals met with North Vietnamese and National Liberation Front (NLF) representatives in Czechoslovakia. SDS leader Tom Hayden attended and was quoted afterward: "Now we're all Viet Cong."[4]

Up to this point, aside from an occasional rhetorical outburst, the president had weathered the domestic storm over the war, generally avoiding the temptation to succumb to Hoover's siren song (with the exception of Martin Luther King).[5] But the antics of would-be revolutionaries, especially in Washington, DC, a city he loved, threatened to push him over the edge. A week after fifty thousand protesters tried to shut down the Pentagon in the fall of 1967, he burst out, "I'm not going to let the Communists take this government and they're doing it right now." He told his advisers that he had been protecting civil liberties "since he was nine years old," but "I told the Attorney General that I am not going to let two-hundred-thousand of these people ruin everything for the 200 million Americans. I've got my belly full of seeing these people put on a Communist plane and shipped all over this country."[6] Johnson instructed the CIA to place under surveillance leaders of the SDS, SANE, and Yippies (Youth International Party), Mothers against the War, and other antiwar groups and to do everything possible to gather evidence that they were communist-controlled, even operating on orders from foreign governments. This program, later institutionalized as Operation CHAOS, violated the CIA's charter, which prohibited domestic spying.

The war against the peace movement soon shifted from surveillance to harassment and disruption. Dr. Benjamin Spock, an American pediatrician and antiwar advocate, among others, was indicted for counseling draft resistance. Agents provocateur penetrated various organizations, encouraging division, sabotaging demonstrations, and gathering evidence of illegal activities. Not surprisingly, the FBI got into the act. Shortly after Vietnam Veterans against the War was formed in April 1967, Hoover's men infiltrated the organization, encouraging activities that they hoped would discredit the movement.[7]

VIRTUALLY EVERYONE IN THE WORLD ASSUMED THAT LYNDON JOHN-son would run for another full term as president in 1968. The president's chief political advisers—Arthur Krim, Abe Fortas, James Rowe, and Clark Clifford—urged LBJ to employ a strategy similar to that used by Harry Truman in 1948. LBJ's campaign advisers assigned the task of playing J. Strom Thurmond—the 1948 Dixiecrat nominee—to Alabama governor George Wallace. Unlike Thurmond, however, the Johnson campaign team expected Wallace to attract much more media attention and perform better in nonsouthern states, especially in midwestern industrial areas. The LBJ camp anticipated that an antiwar presidential candidate on the left—analogous to Henry Wallace in 1948—would challenge him for the Democratic nomination and, perhaps like Wallace, form a third party. Bobby Kennedy's announcement at a Democratic dinner in 1967 that he supported LBJ for reelection in 1968 reassured Johnson's advisers that Kennedy had decided to wait until 1972. "Forget (not forgive) the whole Kennedy caper," White House aide John Roche advised the president. "The point has been made to Bobby that if we go down, he goes with us. . . . He has nowhere else to go and your victory is imperative to his plans for 1972."[8]

Voters had been decidedly unenthusiastic about Truman in 1948, but they had voted for him as a means to avoid the extremism of both Left and Right. The Johnson camp assumed that the same would be true for their man in 1968. Fred Panzer, a White House aide influenced by several Lou

Harris polls, told the president, "Your greatest strength is to overtly run against Wallace in the South and the peace party in the North. . . . It would also insure national coverage so that Negroes in the North would know of your attacks on George Wallace, and farmers, small towners, and southerners would know of your attacks on the peace wing."[9] No matter who the GOP nominated—Nixon, Rockefeller, or Romney—Johnson's centrism would force the GOP to embrace either the Wallaceites or the peaceniks—or if they avoided this, to conduct an empty campaign. Among other things, this analysis underestimated the degree to which the antiwar movement and the white backlash had come to include the "Vital Center" Arthur Schlesinger had identified as crucial to any Democratic presidential victory.

RFK's disavowals notwithstanding, an organization calling itself Citizens for Kennedy/Fulbright began soliciting pledges of support in the fall of 1967. Most outspoken of the dissidents was Allard Lowenstein, who seemed determined to merge the Democratic Party with the New Left. In October he announced a conference for all those interested in dumping LBJ.[10] But taking on an incumbent president, especially if that incumbent was Lyndon Johnson, was a daunting prospect, and Bobby refused to throw his hat in the ring. Desperate for a rallying point for the Stop LBJ movement, dissident Democrats persuaded Senator Eugene McCarthy, a Minnesota Democrat, to make himself available. Best known for his eloquent speech nominating Adlai Stevenson at the Democratic convention in 1960, McCarthy was described by *Newsweek* as "a scholarly, witty, somewhat lazy man who writes books, reads poetry and laces his lectures with dollops of theology."[11]

It was clear that George Wallace was going to make another run for the presidency, if not as a Democrat then as an Independent. But Johnson's advisers were divided as to whether the Wallace candidacy would hurt or help. If the Republicans nominated a neo-Goldwaterite like Governor Ronald Reagan of California, Wallace would drain away from the GOP segregationist and superhawk votes in the South and the working-class neighborhoods of the North, but if the Republicans nominated a moderate like Romney, the Wallace challenge would hurt the Democrats.[12]

In November, LBJ briefly hit the campaign trail and delivered a series of speeches lauding the accomplishments of the Great Society and the bravery of America's fighting men. At a White House press conference, he lambasted the Vietnam naysayers in Congress. To a pro-union crowd he called for passage of the tax surcharge. In a ceremony swearing in newly elected members of the Washington, DC, city council, he declared war on "crime in the streets." He denounced the GOP for its social irresponsibility. "Some have called the passage of this act [an appropriations bill for HUD] a legislative victory," he remarked at the signing ceremony. "It might better be called a legislative miracle." He added, "Ninety-three percent of the House Republicans voted to recommit and kill rent supplements. Eighty percent voted to . . . delete all funds for model cities."[13] In December, he flew to Bar Harbor, Florida, to address the twelve hundred delegates to the AFL–CIO Convention, which had just voted to endorse him.

When LBJ had lashed his aides and congressional allies mercilessly in 1965, saying, "We have so little time, we have so little time," they had wondered why.[14] He had won in a landslide. Liberal majorities in both houses waited to do his bidding; the country was then in the midst of an incredible economic boom. But Johnson had been right. Reform is rare and difficult in the United States, a deeply conservative country. And political unity is not its natural state. Now, as the calendar turned to 1968, time was almost up. Dissension was high. Urban riots, the white backlash, and the black power movement were whipsawing the country. The Vietnam conflict was corroding the public spirit.

Yet Johnson would not give up. He wanted to raise taxes and to spend more money, not just to fight crime but to build affordable housing and to fund jobs. As he prepared for the 1968 State of the Union address, he took John Roche and Harry McPherson's advice to heart: "We have to utilize 'conservative' tactics to protect the substance of liberalism—'liberalism', as enacted over the past three years, has to become *the* status quo."[15] Standing before Congress, the president spoke quietly, conversationally. He renewed his request for a 10 percent income tax surcharge and presented a $186 billion budget, an increase of $10 billion over the previous fiscal year.

Joe Califano had wanted the president to go at Wilbur Mills head-on. The Arkansan, he told his boss, "wants either (or both) (1) to force . . . you to your knees or (2) to dismantle great hunks of the Great Society."[16] Johnson agreed. "I warn the Congress and the Nation tonight that this failure to act on the tax bill will sweep us into an accelerating spiral of price increases, a slump in homebuilding, and a continuing erosion of the American dollar," he said. He asked Congress for $455 million in new job program funds, most of it to initiate a public-private three-year plan to train and employ five hundred thousand of the least qualified jobless. He proposed $1 billion for Model Cities and $2.2 billion for the War on Poverty. To rousing applause, LBJ told the joint session that in his safe streets and crime control bill, he was doubling the money he had originally asked for, but he also renewed his call for gun control: "Those who preach disorder and those who preach violence must know that local authorities are able to resist them swiftly, to resist them sternly, and to resist them decisively."[17]

AS 1968 OPENED, LYNDON JOHNSON WAS MORE WORRIED ABOUT THE prospect of a race war in the United States than he was about losing the war in Vietnam. In the fall of 1967, novelist William Styron's *The Confessions of Nat Turner* had been published. The book, an immediate best seller, was a fictionalized account of a black slave revolt that took place in the tidewater country of southern Virginia in 1831. An educated black slave and preacher with apocalyptic vision, Nat Turner had led the uprising. For two days, Turner's band of seventy-five runaways rampaged through the countryside, slaughtering fifty-five white men, women, and children before being over-come by a hastily formed white militia. Those slaves who were not killed immediately were summarily executed. James Baldwin, who read the book in manuscript, declared it historically accurate and socially relevant. Less sympathetic observers also drew contemporary parallels. Throughout 1967 and 1968, as riots erupted in Detroit; Washington, DC; Newark; and Mem-phis, the white backlash continued to gain momentum, especially north of the Mason-Dixon line. In primarily Catholic, blue-collar, white south Boston, segregationist Louise Day Hicks declared her candidacy for mayor.[18]

As his and the nation's troubles mounted, the president spent what little spare time he had reading the speeches of Abraham Lincoln. He ran across an antislavery address that his predecessor had delivered at Edwardsville, Illinois, in 1858. "Now when by all these means," Lincoln had said to the nation in the wake of the Dred Scott decision (in which the Supreme Court ruled that whether slave or free, African Americans could not be US citi-zens), "you have succeeded in dehumanizing the Negro; when you have put him down and made it forever impossible for him to be but as the beasts of the field; when you have extinguished his soul and placed him where the ray of hope is blown out in darkness like that which broods over the spirits of the damned; are you quite sure the demon which you have roused will not turn and rend you?"[19]

Johnson's strategy through early 1968 was to try to placate blacks by distancing the administration from the Moynihan report and by focusing on jobs and housing, while trying to appease whites with tough law-and-order rhetoric.[20] The White House reintroduced legislation outlawing discrimination in the sale, renting, and leasing of housing, the touchiest of all subjects among white urban dwellers. Opposition to a similar bill had helped Ronald Reagan defeat California governor Pat Brown in 1966. Yet Johnson was determined.

The second order of business was jobs. Sargent Shriver suggested public works, but Johnson felt they would take too long and were unaffordable. The key was the private sector. LBJ wanted to "get some ghetto grime under those highly polished executive fingernails."[21] He succeeded in enlisting Henry Ford to chair the National Alliance of Businessmen (NAB), a voluntary organization committed to persuading the nation's corporations to hire and train the chronically unemployed. The federal government would pay for most of the training, including health care and literacy instruction. On January 27, LBJ hosted the first executive committee meeting of the NAB. In addition to Ford, the chief executive officers of Mobil Oil, Safeway Stores, ITT, and Alcoa were in attendance. "We're faced with the hardcore unemployed," Johnson told them. "You all are going to have to teach them how to wash and stay clean, how to read, how to write. All the things everyone around this table got from their mommies and daddies. Only these people don't have mommies and daddies who give a damn about them. Or if they do, those mommies and daddies can't read or don't know how to help them." One of the executives said, "This is a tough job, Mr. President." LBJ turned to him and said, "I didn't invite you here to tell me how tough a job this is. I invited you here to get the job done. . . . This economy has been so good to you that you can afford to give a little back."[22] In late January LBJ sent a special message to Congress entitled "To Earn a Living: The Right of Every American." Among other things he asked the House and Senate to fund a $2.1 billion manpower-training program.[23] By the end of 1968, the NAB had succeeded in seeing a hundred thousand of the poorest, most disadvantaged Americans trained and put to work. The subsequent retention rate was almost 75 percent.[24]

With the law-and-order forces demanding raw meat, Johnson saw no reason why Stokely Carmichael should not be offered up. Had he not, after all, preached violent resistance to authority, particularly to the draft, using Havana as his pulpit, no less? LBJ and the White House wanted the black power advocate prosecuted under the Logan Act, an eighteenth-century statute prohibiting private citizens from attempting to influence diplomatic relations between the United States and a foreign government. The problem was, Attorney General Ramsey Clark pointed out, most of the evidence against alleged subversives like Carmichael had been gathered by illegal wiretap.[25] The Justice Department had a better chance of making a case against George Romney than Stokely Carmichael, he told presidential aide Larry Temple. Clark was much more interested in going after the South Carolina State Police after they fired shotgun blasts into the ranks of peaceful protestors at the all-black State College at Orangeburg. Three were killed and thirty wounded.[26] Johnson made no secret of his irritation with his attorney general. He ranted to Senators Russell and Dirksen, denouncing Clark in their private conversations, but in the end, typically, he listened to reason. As Clark pointed out, what the vast majority of urban-dwelling blacks wanted was law and order, protection from looting and violence, safety for their children. To stretch or even violate the law to satisfy vigilante groups was to start down a dangerous, slippery slope. Moreover, as Clark argued, "I think that the notion that you can control dissent by convicting a few of the most outspoken radicals is absurdly naïve. If there's nothing to it but the charisma of a few leaders fanning flames, why, it's not a very serious problem."[27]

In mid-March the Kerner Commission announced that the riots of 1967 had social and not conspiratorial roots. The commission's report emphasized the existence of a pervasive white racism and warned that more violence would ensue if cities, states, and the federal government did not move massively and rapidly to improve living conditions in urban ghettoes. "What white Americans have never fully understood—but what the Negro can never forget—is that white society is deeply implicated in the ghetto," declared the introduction. "White institutions created it, white institutions maintain it, and white society condones it."[28] The Kerner report in essence endorsed the notion of a Marshall Plan for the poor; increased taxes and economic growth would, it claimed, provide $30 billion for the creation of one million new jobs in the public sector, the construction of six hundred

thousand low- and moderate-income housing units in the next year (part
of six million new units over the next five years), the extension of welfare
assistance, and the expansion of the Model Cities program.[29] Ramsey Clark
was delighted with the report. The selection of Kerner was, he would claim,
one of "my recommendations, my rather ardent recommendations."[30] Conservatives were predictably outraged. Presidential candidate Richard Nixon
condemned the report because it "in effect blames everybody for the riots
except the perpetrators."[31] Law-and-order advocates declared it to be another blueprint for rewarding rioters. Wilbur Mills and his ilk decried the
Kerner recommendations as a permanent path to an unbalanced budget.

"To me," Joseph Califano would later write, "the commission had the
potential to be a political Frankenstein's monster and it was almost inevitable that Lyndon Johnson would sour on his hasty creation."[32] Indeed, for
six agonizing days the president kept silent on the report. What chance was
there now to keep working- and middle-class whites on board the ship of
reform? Couldn't Kerner and his colleagues read? He was calling for a tax
surcharge, and Congress was calling for deep budget cuts. This was clearly
the work of Bobby Kennedy and the ongoing need of liberals to make a
statement rather than a record. The president found himself in the end—as
Califano had feared—in the worst of all possible political worlds, taking
blame from conservatives for proposing the commission and from liberals
for not endorsing its conclusions. Warning that the report was becoming
the "Bible of the liberals," Harry McPherson advised the president that his
continued hostility would "turn the politics of long-term riot prevention
over to Bobby Kennedy as a 'responsible politician who cares,' one who is
'willing to carry out the Kerner Commission's recommendations to save
our cities.'"[33] Eventually, LBJ relented, telling a group of black newspaper
editors the Kerner report was "the most important report made to me since
I have been President." He asked all cabinet officers to come up with plans
to remedy the inequities identified.[34] Harry McPherson later explained why
Johnson was so conflicted about the commission's findings:

> The only thing that held any hope for the Negro was the continua-
> tion of the coalition between labor, Negroes, intellectuals, . . . big city
> bosses and political machines, and some of the white urban poor. . . .
> In other words it required keeping the Polacks who work on the line
> at River Rouge [Ford Auto Plant in Michigan] in the ball park and

supporting Walter Reuther and the government as they try to spend a lot of money for the blacks. That's the only way they'll ever make it, because the people [in office buildings] don't give a damn about them. They're scared of them, always have been; they're middle-class whites. . . . Then a presidential commission is formed and goes out and comes back and what does it say? Who's responsible for the riots? "The other members of the coalition. They did it. Those racists." And thereupon the coalition says, you know, a four-letter word, and "we'll go find ourselves a guy like George Wallace, or Richard Nixon."[35]

In early February 1968, with Ralph Nader's image splashed across the front pages of America's newspapers and magazines, LBJ sent to Congress another special message entitled "To Protect the Consumer Interest." It called for sweeping new legislation to outlaw deceptive advertising, investigate the auto insurance industry, ensure quality control in fish and poultry processing, strengthen auto safety standards, and appoint a government ombudsman to represent the consuming public. Nader, a lanky, sallow-faced young lawyer, had converted a one-man crusade for consumer protection into a national movement. Working eighteen-hour days, he had directed his controlled outrage at the likes of Henry Ford II and Harvey Firestone over auto safety issues, and then spread out to diseased fish, unnecessary dental X-rays, and deceptive labeling. Public opinion polls indicated that federal action in these areas had almost universal approval.[36] Finally, proclaiming education to be "the Fifth Freedom," Johnson asked Congress to increase annual appropriations for the Head Start program from $340 million to $380 million, for a new Stay in School program at $30 million, and for adult education at $50 million.[37]

THROUGHOUT LATE 1967 AND EARLY 1968, JOHNSON'S POLITICAL advisers had urged him to commit to the upcoming presidential campaign. They noted that he responded with avoidance behavior or intense anxiety. "The president is a tortured and confused man," Senator George McGovern (D-SD) noted following a stag dinner for Democratic leaders. "He seemed to be almost begging for political advice; yet, when we would try to interject, he would immediately break in [on an unrelated matter]. I think one time . . . he went on for 45 minutes without interruption. You almost want to put your hand on his shoulder and say, 'Now Lyndon, calm down, back away a little and take a cooler look.'"[38] Harry McPherson, LBJ's friend and adviser, wanted him to run but could not lie to him. Circumstances were forcing Johnson, reformer extraordinaire, to pose as a preserver of the status quo, a status quo with which an increasing number of Americans were extremely dissatisfied:

> You represent things as they are—the course we are following, the policies and programs we have chosen. Therefore you are the most conservative [candidate} . . . the man who is not calling for change but resisting it. That is a tough position today. When you say, "stick with it in Vietnam", i.e., stick with the policy of the past three years . . . you are saying, stick with a rough situation that shows signs of growing worse. When you say, "persevere at home," you are saying keep the HEW appropriations growing and the new programs proliferating, although the Negros, for whom we adopted these programs, rioted last summer and will probably riot again. When you say, "prepare for austerity," you are saying to the businessman and taxpayer, "get set for a shock; meanwhile, I'm going to continue the programs—particularly Vietnam—that cause the shock."[39]

As 1967 turned into 1968, Johnson was increasingly inclined toward not running for another term. In early January, he asked Horace Busby to draft a withdrawal statement. John Connally, who was privy to the decision, had suggested that the State of the Union address would be an excellent venue for the sure-to-be-dramatic announcement. "The longer he waited," Connally observed, the more it would help Bobby Kennedy, who "was free to operate while others were not."[40] But Johnson decided that the time was not right. It was too soon. He still had some blows to strike, and he did not want to become a lame duck yet. And, in truth, he was still on the fence.[41]

In January and February, the president had several remarkable conversations with HEW secretary John Gardner. As Gardner later recalled:

> I had become increasingly concerned about the state of the country, about the war, about the riots, about the course of events as I saw them. . . . We were discussing what could be done to ensure the

reelection of President Johnson. . . . And I found to my consternation sometime in early January that I did not think that the president should run for reelection. . . . I wrote a letter of resignation [to Johnson], took it in and handed it to him, and he read it and laid it on the table and asked me why I did it. . . . And I said, "Well, I just don't believe that you can unite the country. I just think that we're in a terrible passage in our history and that you cannot do what needs to be done, with the best will in the world. I just think that is not in the cards for you. . . . " And he said, "Well I've had the same thought myself many times."[42]

March 1968 proved one of the most tumultuous months in American political history. As the spring primary season approached, LBJ's political advisers again urged him to give some attention to the forthcoming campaign. Polls showed Eugene McCarthy lagging far behind the president, but Bobby was waiting in the wings. "I am sure that B K is sponsoring a 'War of Liberation' against you and your administration," John Roche observed to LBJ.[43] Orville Freeman and other party luminaries had pressed Johnson to give them the go-ahead to organize the reelection campaign. In early January, he had, but in an almost off-handed way, and with a few exceptions, turned away requests to meet with party leaders. Jim Rowe agreed to head a volunteer effort to generate grassroots support, but LBJ took little notice.[44] Intimates and close observers murmured that electoral politics seemed to have lost its interest for the president.

Defections from the ranks of Johnson's Democratic supporters became a weekly and even daily affair. Jesse Unruh, the powerful speaker of the California Assembly, was reportedly ready to jump ship, as was Walter Reuther. From every corner of the country, Democratic governors warned the president's men that if matters did not take a dramatic new course in Vietnam, they would all go down to defeat in November.[45]

By 1968 liberals had divided into a pro-war faction typified by Henry Jackson and Hubert Humphrey and an antiwar segment led by Bobby Kennedy, Frank Church, and George McGovern. To the delight of conservatives, antiwar liberals seemed to be willing to go to any lengths to stop the war and get rid of LBJ, even to the point of sacrificing Democratic rule. With another wave of rioting looming as summer approached, urban ethnic

Democrats were rallying to Wallace, a southerner, a populist, and a law-and-order segregationist. Southern Democrats were breaking away from the Great Society consensus and joining with the GOP to block further initiatives in the areas of health, civil rights, public works, and social security. This, in turn, would further embitter the disadvantaged, and the country would be plunged into an endless cycle of black rage and white reaction.

Perhaps, LBJ believed, if he could remove himself from the picture, this disaster could be avoided. Perhaps the fanaticism of the anti-Johnson liberals would cool, and the New South could once again join hands with the northern liberal-labor coalition. Moreover, out of contention, the president could work for an "honorable peace" in Vietnam. It was a long shot, but worth a try. Thus, though he was at times ambivalent, reluctant to give up, hungering for more approval at the polls, desirous of revenge against his enemies, LBJ was tempted not to run for the very reasons John Gardner had laid out. He could do more for his country—and his reputation—politically dead than alive. Johnson ordered his speechwriters to prepare a major address on Vietnam to be delivered the evening of March 31.

On March 12 Eugene McCarthy and his "Children's Campaign" shocked the nation. Predicted to win no more than 11 or 12 percent of the vote in the New Hampshire primary, the Minnesotan captured 42.4 percent compared to LBJ's 49.5 percent (the president, who was technically still exploring his candidacy, was on the ballot as a write-in candidate). "Dove bites Hawk," a journalist quipped. Exit polls indicated that most of McCarthy's support came from those disenchanted with the war, both hawks and doves. With the exception of speechwriter Richard Goodwin, who had left the Johnson White House over the war and other issues, students directed the entire McCarthy effort. McCarthy's success, and Johnson's distress, were more than Robert Kennedy could bear. On March 14, using Clark Clifford as an intermediary, Bobby proposed a deal to the White House. If LBJ would appoint a national commission to investigate the war effort in Vietnam, headed presumably by him or brother Ted, and to make recommendations, presumably binding, he would not jump into the race. All he wanted, Bobby said, was peace in Vietnam.[46] LBJ told Clifford to tell RFK that he and his views on Vietnam were always welcome at the White House, but that the deal being proposed would alienate everyone if it became public knowledge, which it surely would.[47] Two days later, RFK threw his hat into the ring.

Johnson hardly seemed devastated by McCarthy's showing. Speaking to a Veterans of Foreign Wars (VFW) group the night of the New Hampshire primary, he observed that he had had an early report on the voting—of the first twenty-five votes cast, he had not received one. "I said to Mrs. Johnson, 'What do you think about that?' She had answered, 'I think the day is bound to get better, Lyndon.'"[48]

A few days after Kennedy's announcement, Orville Freeman saw the president during a cabinet meeting. "As usual he was a half hour late. . . . Finally about 8:00 he drifted in, in an exceptionally good humor. It was really quite impressive. Actually, I don't think he could have put it on."[49] But Freeman found the president's nonchalance unsettling. "Mr. President," he said, "what we really need now is someone that's calling the signals on this [campaign]." Johnson remarked that he thought Georgia governor Terry Sanford was coming in to do that. "All in all," Freeman observed, "what comes through loud and clear is at this point, this is almost like a big ship without a rudder."[50]

ALL OF THIS TRANSPIRED IN THE MIDST OF THE TET OFFENSIVE, IN which the Vietcong, supported by elements of the North Vietnamese Army (NVA), attacked 36 of 64 provincial capitals, 5 of 6 major cities, 64 district capitals, and 50 hamlets. Initially caught off guard, Army of the Republic of Viet Nam (ARVN) and US forces quickly recovered and took the initiative. Seeing the opportunity for a knockout blow, General Westmoreland had asked for an additional 205,000 troops and permission to strike across the demilitarized zone into North Vietnam and at communist sanctuaries in neighboring Cambodia.

On March 22, LBJ formally rejected Westmoreland's massive troop request. He then summoned a group of so-called Wise Men to a meeting at the White House on March 26. Prior to the gathering, the commander in chief had his briefers paint as bleak a picture of the military and fiscal situation as possible. The contingent—former Secretary of State Dean Acheson, former Undersecretary of State George Ball, former Assistant Secretary of War John J. McCloy, former National Security Adviser McGeorge Bundy, Deputy Secretary of Defense Cyrus Vance, Army Generals Matthew Ridgway and Maxwell Taylor, former Ambassadors Robert Murphy and

Henry Cabot Lodge, Abe Fortas, and UN Ambassador Arthur Goldberg—
were appropriately gloomy. A minority advocated holding the line and even
widening the war if necessary, but the majority favored immediate steps to
deescalate. Acheson spoke for all when he said that "the United States could
no longer do the job we set out to do in the time we have left and we must
begin to take steps to disengage."

Johnson was reportedly furious: "The establishment bastards have bailed
out," he is said to have remarked after the meeting.[51] He was playing to the
galleries. The "establishment bastards" were doing just what he wanted them
to do. Indeed, that same day, in a tense meeting with Joint Chiefs of Staff
Chairman General Earl Wheeler and General Creighton Abrams, who had
been tapped to become Westmoreland's successor, Johnson pled with the
military to support his peace overtures, which consisted primarily of feelers
extended to the North Vietnamese through third parties. He lamented the
deteriorating fiscal situation, divisions at home, and his own "overwhelming
disapproval" in the press.[52]

On March 28, LBJ met with Califano and McPherson over lunch to
discuss his forthcoming speech on Vietnam. They mulled over the bombing pause and tax surcharge, and then the president suddenly asked, "What
do you think about my not running for reelection?" McPherson said that,
personally, he would not run if he were the president, but both he and Califano insisted that Johnson had to win another term. Otherwise, the country
would become hopelessly deadlocked. It is already deadlocked, Johnson
observed. "Others can get things done," he said. "The Congress and I are
like an old married couple. We've lived together so long and we've been
rubbing against each other night after night so often and we've asked so
much of each other over the years we're tired of each other."[53] Later, alone
with Califano, LBJ asked, "If I don't run, who do you think will get the
nomination?" Bobby Kennedy, Califano said.

"What about Hubert?"

"I don't think he can beat Kennedy."

"What's wrong with Bobby?" Johnson replied. "He's made some nasty
speeches about me, but he's never had to sit here. . . . Bobby would keep
fighting for the Great Society programs. And when he sat in this chair he
might have a different view on the war. His major problem would be with
appropriations. He doesn't know how to deal with people on the Hill and
a lot of them don't like him. But he'll try. . . . Whether Kennedy or Nixon

won, at least the leadership would support them in the first year or so. . . . And that might provide the necessary time to heal the wounds now separating the country."[54]

Meanwhile, Horace Busby had been working secretly on an addendum to the March 31 "peace with honor" speech on Vietnam.[55] Early Sunday morning, the 31st, found the president surrounded by his staff, fine-tuning the text of his address scheduled for that night. Only Busby had the addendum paragraphs, and he kept them close to his chest. Lady Bird was allowed to see the portions on Vietnam, of which she very much approved, but not the abdication material.

At seven o'clock the Johnsons' daughter Lynda had returned from California, where she had said goodbye to her husband, Marine Captain Charles Robb, at Camp Pendleton. He would leave in a fortnight for his thirteen-month tour of duty in Vietnam. She was pregnant with her first child. Lady Bird recalled being stunned by her appearance. Looking like a "wraith from another world," Lynda stared directly at her father and asked, "Why do we have to go to Vietnam?" Her father just stared at her, and Lady Bird later wrote that she had not seen such pain in his eyes since his mother had died.[56]

Around ten o'clock in the morning, LBJ gathered up aide Jim Jones and his other daughter Luci and drove to Saint Dominic's, a Catholic chapel in suburban Washington, to attend mass. During the service, he instructed Jones to get the Secret Service to fetch the draft of the speech, including the Busby material, from his bedroom and to call Vice President Humphrey and tell him that they were coming over. When the speech and LBJ arrived at the Humphreys' apartment, the second couple was preparing to fly to Mexico City for a state visit. "At the Vice President's apartment in southwestern Washington," Jones later wrote, "Mrs. Humphrey and Luci visited while the President gave Humphrey the speech. When he got to the final paragraph, the Vice President's face flushed, his eyes watered and he protested that Mr. Johnson could not step down. 'Don't mention this to anyone until Jim calls you in Mexico tonight. But you'd better start now planning your campaign for President.' Humphrey's face went slack, his shoulder hunched. 'There's no way I can beat the Kennedys,' he said."[57]

Back at the White House, the president continued to fiddle with the wording of the Vietnam sections of the speech. He glanced at the newspapers, which included a just-released Gallup poll showing his approval ratings at an all-time low: only 36 percent endorsed his overall job performance, and 26 percent his handling of the war in Vietnam.[58] Late in the afternoon, LBJ had his press secretary, George Christian, call John Connally and ask him if he thought withdrawal was the right thing to do. Connally said yes. The president should have done it in the State of the Union, and if he was going to step down, he must wait no longer. He owed it to the party and to the country.[59]

Just after six o'clock Johnson met with Soviet Ambassador Anatoly Dobrynin and told him he was going to send an additional 13,500 troops to Vietnam but that he would couple it with an announcement that the United States would cease bombing above the twentieth parallel for an indefinite period. Washington was prepared to go 90 percent of the way toward peace; now it was time for Moscow to get the North Vietnamese to go the remaining 10 percent of the way. It was up to the United States and the USSR to end the war soon and prevent hostilities from spreading.[60]

The address was scheduled for nine fifteen in the evening. At eight fifteen, Jim Jones took the last two pages over and had them put on the teleprompter. The president rattled off a series of names of people that Jones and Christian should call—cabinet members, party leaders, and lifelong friends—once the speech had started to give them advance warning about its punch line. Both Lynda and Luci were in tears. Lynda was particularly distraught. How could her father think of not running? What would happen to Chuck and the other soldiers in Vietnam? "Now I'll be free to work for them full time," her father told her.[61]

A somber, somewhat haggard president went on national television to announce that henceforward the bombing of North Vietnam would be limited to the area just north of the demilitarized zone below the twentieth parallel. The United States, he declared, was ready for comprehensive peace talks anywhere, anytime, and he announced that veteran diplomat W. Averill Harriman would represent the administration should such talks materialize. The nation, he said, had done its very best to keep faith with the words spoken by John F. Kennedy, to "pay any price, bear any burden, meet any hardship, support any friend, oppose any foe to assure the survival and the success of liberty." But without "the unity of our people," the United States could do nothing. "There is division in the American house now. There is divisiveness among us all tonight. And holding the trust that is mine, as President of all the people, I cannot disregard the peril to the progress of the American people and the hope and the prospect of peace for all peoples."[62]

Lyndon Johnson and the republic to which he was committed had come to a crossroads. They had embarked on their nation-building enterprise believing that freedom was indivisible, that historically, intellectually, and morally the United States was bound to combat communist totalitarianism on every front. But they had discovered that there were limits to American power, that in its pursuit of liberty for the Vietnamese the nation was verging on forfeiting its own freedoms. The moral imperatives that Lyndon Johnson invoked to justify the Second Reconstruction and the conflict in Southeast Asia were not equivalent. The sins of racial injustice were America's own; the sins of communist totalitarianism, of Sino-Soviet imperialism belonged to others. For the first, the nation could and should risk self-immolation, but not for the second. The most America could do in a dangerous world was protect itself and protect only those others who were vital to the nation's survival. For a variety of reasons, Johnson could not simply withdraw from Vietnam. Historical errors are not that easily corrected. But he could sacrifice himself. The Texan then dropped his bombshell. "I shall not seek, and I will not accept, the nomination of my party for another term as president," he told a stunned nation.[63]

In the wake of the dramatic announcement, friends and cabinet members gathered in the West Wing. LBJ appeared relaxed, increasingly confident that he had done the right thing. Johnson loved surprises. And he had just pulled off one of the great surprises of twentieth-century political life. Given his personality, of course, the Texan found the notion of self-sacrifice deeply satisfying. "[He was] telling stories and jokes and laughing," Vicky McCammon remembered, while staff and guests huddled in knots, talking in hushed tones.[64] LBJ stayed up until well after midnight taking calls from well-wishers, telling his Texas friends to polish up on their dominoes, remarking several times that he was looking forward to spending more time with his grandson, Patrick Lyndon Nugent.[65]

Johnson's decision not to run produced a collective sigh of relief. Perhaps the president's politically selfless act could in fact bring the country together, stem the urban rioting that seemed to have gotten a life of its own, and end the seemingly endless conflict in Vietnam. The respite was to be short-lived, however, the nation's hopefulness delusional.

CHAPTER 18

AMERICAN DYSTOPIA

AT 7:30 P.M. ON APRIL 4, 1968, AS LBJ WAS PREPARING TO DEPART the White House to attend a Democratic fund-raiser for Vice President Humphrey, he was informed that Martin Luther King had been shot in Memphis. Earlier in the day, a white petty crook, James Earl Ray, had told his brother that he was going to "get the big nigger."[1] That evening, he did just that, shooting King while he stood on the balcony of the Lorraine Motel. At 8:20 George Christian informed LBJ that King was dead. "Everything we've gained in the last few days we're going to lose tonight," he remarked dejectedly to Joe Califano.[2]

As news of King's death went out over radio and television, new waves of rioting racked the nation. "When white America killed Dr. King," declared Stokely Carmichael, "she declared war on us." In Washington, DC, over seven hundred fires turned night into day, and smoke from them completely obscured the Capitol. LBJ instructed his aides to convene a meeting of congressional leaders and prominent black activists the following morning. Among those invited were Whitney Young, A. Philip Randolph, Roy Wilkins, Bayard Rustin, Mayor Carl Stokes of Cleveland, and NAACP field director Charles Evers of Jackson, Mississippi. Johnson asked King's father to attend, but his doctors would not allow him to travel. Told that the president's prayers were with him, the elder King replied, "Oh no, my prayers are with the President."[3]

The meeting got under way at eleven the next morning. Johnson paid tribute to King and promised to continue to work day and night to realize his dream. The real question was what his murder would mean to America. "Let us be frank about it," he said. "It can mean that those—of both races—who believe that violence is the best means of settling racial problems in America, will have had their belief confirmed." Black Americans must recommit to nonviolence and white Americans to "root out every trace of racism from their hearts."[4] The black leaders were generally receptive, but they warned that time was short. "The large majority of Negroes were not in favor of violence, but we need something to fight back with," declared Reverend Leon Sullivan. "Otherwise we will be caught with nothing."[5] From the White House the president and his guests motored to the National Cathedral to attend a memorial service for King. Back at the Rose Garden, LBJ, flanked by prominent blacks and congressional leaders, issued a proclamation declaring Sunday, April 7, a day of national mourning for the fallen civil rights leader. He dashed off a note to Coretta Scott King: "My thoughts have been with you and your children throughout this long and anguished day. . . . Since early morning, I have devoted all my hours and energy to honoring your good husband in the manner he would most approve. I have sought—by word, deed and official act—to unite this sorrowing and troubled nation against further and wider violence."[6]

From the Situation Room the president received hourly reports: "As of 8:00 P.M., 6 deaths, 533 arrests and 209 injuries treated at hospitals [in Washington, DC]; 8:55 P.M., confirmed report of four men with rifles on top of the Hawk and Dove Restaurant in the 300 block of Pennsylvania Avenue, SE."[7] General Westmoreland, in town for a meeting with LBJ and Secretary of Defense Clark Clifford, recalled that the capital "looked worse than Saigon did at the height of the Tet offensive." He quipped that in 1814 the British had burned Washington, but this time we were doing it ourselves.[8] From Chicago, Mayor Daley advised that he was probably going to have to request federal troops to quell postassassination disturbances. Burnings and shootings were reported from Detroit, Cleveland, and Houston.[9] Somehow, Johnson managed to keep a sense of humor. Upon hearing rumors that Stokely Carmichael was organizing a group at 14th and U Streets Northwest to march on Georgetown and burn it down, the president smiled and said, "Goddamn! I've waited thirty-five years for this day!"[10]

By late Saturday night the White House had received reports of rioting and looting in more than a hundred American cities. The first contingents of nearly fourteen thousand regular Army, Marine, and National Guard troops began to deploy in Washington. Roadblocks were set up around the White House, and soldiers took up positions at the southwest gate. Johnson was determined that the world would not be treated to scenes of Americans shooting Americans, as he put it, in the nation's capital. He ordered troop commanders and police to use the absolute minimum force necessary to maintain order. Senator Russell called Johnson to complain that Marines guarding the Capitol grounds had not been issued live ammunition. Senator Robert Byrd of West Virginia phoned to ask why martial law had not been proclaimed and to insist that adult looters be shot on sight.[11] The president stuck to his unloaded guns.

The next day, April 6, was Palm Sunday. LBJ gathered up Luci, White House secretary Marie Fehmer, Jim Jones, and Joe Califano and left to attend mass at Saint Dominic's. On Monday reports of sporadic violence continued to trickle in, but black anger seemed to have crested. The president had every intention of attending King's funeral scheduled for that day in Atlanta, but by that morning, the Secret Service and FBI were reporting several threats on Johnson's life.[12] From New York, UN Ambassador Arthur Goldberg called: "The President should not . . . leave Washington and should stay right in the White House. This could be very explosive. His presence in the White House is a stabilizing influence."[13] LBJ dispatched Air Force One with Vice President Humphrey and top black officials, including Thurgood Marshall and Robert Weaver. One of Richard Nixon's aides called the White House to suggest that Nixon, McCarthy, and Kennedy be invited to fly with the official party to show national solidarity, but Johnson demurred, so they traveled on their own. Bobby, who the day before had walked the streets of a burned-out neighborhood in northwest Washington, was cheered. Nixon was booed. McCarthy was ignored.[14]

KING'S MURDER COINCIDED WITH THE CLIMAX OF THE LATEST BAT-tle over fair housing legislation. Undeterred by Congress's rejection of the Civil Rights Act of 1966, which included an open housing provision, LBJ had in February 1967 submitted a successor measure. It called for adoption of a national policy against discrimination in housing, the strengthening of existing federal laws against interference with voting, legislation to further guard against discrimination in jury selection in both federal and state courts, authorization for the Equal Employment Opportunity Commission (EEOC) to issue judicially enforceable cease-and-desist orders, and a five-year extension of the United States Commission on Civil Rights.[15] Virtually everyone in Johnson's inner circle had advised the president not to proceed. Like Nicholas Katzenbach before him, Attorney General Clark warned the president that fair housing had no chance of passing. The urban riots of the three previous years had intensified the determination of northern whites to resist opening their neighborhoods to blacks. The violent white resistance to King's efforts to integrate Chicago's white neighborhoods had thoroughly spooked northern congressmen. Johnson remained undeterred.[16] On February 6, 1968, Senators Walter Mondale (D–MN) and Edward Brooke (R–MA) added a fair housing proviso to a pending bill making it a federal crime to interfere with or injure civil rights workers. Predictably, the conservative coalition filibustered. On February 20, a cloture vote failed by a vote of 55 for to 37 against. Republicans split 18 to 18, with Dirksen opposing both cloture and open housing.[17]

In a reprise of the drama surrounding passage of the 1964 civil rights bill, LBJ began working on Dirksen. Was he or was he not the chief representative of the party of Lincoln? Did the GOP want to be responsible for more urban rioting? Signaling that he was ready to bend to the president's will, the minority leader began to bargain for his support. After a climactic meeting with Dirksen, Johnson told several of his aides, "We are going to get the Civil Rights bill! Dirksen is going to come out in support . . . and don't ask me what I had to give him."[18] On March 4, by a vote of 65 to 32, cloture was invoked for the third time in the Johnson presidency. On March 11, the Senate version of HR 2516, amended to include the open housing provision, passed on a 71 to 20 vote.[19] Attention now focused on the House.

On March 27, 1968, LBJ signed into law the Jury Selection and Service Act, banning racial discrimination in federal jury selection. He used the ceremony to blast the House for its refusal to enact fair housing legislation. "I am shocked to even think that the boys I put on a plane at the 82nd Airborne—most of whom were Negro boys going back to Vietnam the second time to protect the flag and to preserve our freedom—that they can't live near the base where they have to train in this country," he declared.

"They must drive 15, 20, or 30 miles sometimes to get to their homes. . . . I think the conscience of America calls on the Congress to quit fiddling and piddling and take action on this civil rights bill. The time for excuses has ended."[20] Though Johnson had not been simpatico with King and resented particularly King's outspoken opposition to the war, he was more than ready to use the man's martyrdom to get the fair housing bill passed. In the days following the assassination, LBJ never missed an opportunity to invoke King's name and to brandish his "dream" before Congress and the public. On April 10, the House passed the fair housing bill by a wide margin and sent it to the president for his signature.[21]

Johnson had no doubt seduced Dirksen by promising to place his candidates on federal regulatory boards and guaranteeing minimal Democratic opposition to the minority leader's 1968 reelection bid. But he had also conceded to a major weakening to the open housing bill. Although it forbade discrimination in the rent, sale, or lease of housing by race, creed, national origin, or sex, Title VIII left it to private individuals or advocacy groups to file suit against owners, real estate agents, and others who might discriminate. The burden of proof, expensive and time consuming, would be on the victims.[22]

EVEN MORE IMPORTANT THAN HOUSING, TO THE PRESIDENT'S MIND, was the pending tax surcharge bill. Perhaps the time was right. "It seems to me," White House aide Harold "Barefoot" Sanders observed, "that the President's decision not to run and the assassination of King may have created a climate in Congress for a dramatic new approach to the financial crisis. That new approach should not emphasize appropriations cuts, but, rather, the need for new revenues."[23] Unfortunately, Wilbur Mills, from his chokehold position as chair of the House Ways and Means Committee, seemed totally unmoved by the events in Memphis and the March 31 abdication speech. Joe Califano argued that more was at stake than just the tax increase. "For the past month we have been moving with increased power and ability to get things done," he wrote LBJ, "as you are doing whatever you do without any ax to grind and only because it is right. This has all resulted from your pulling out of the race. But this remarkable assertion of power in a lame duck status could deteriorate rapidly if Wilbur Mills rolls over us on the tax legislation."[24]

By the close of April 1968, LBJ had persuaded liberals in his administration and organized labor that the best that could be gotten from Congress was a tax surcharge bill that would require $5 billion in spending cuts for fiscal year 1969. In conversations at the White House, Johnson told Mills, "If I could appoint you president, I would take Ways and Means and [you could] do what you think about it. . . . My God, I have given all I have got. I have given my life—my political life. . . . I don't want to see this country go down the drain. . . . And I think I know more about it than you do. I don't think you see what is happening. . . . And I think that there has got to be a position somewhere in between what you want in the way of a tax bill and what we want."[25] Mills told Johnson that he believed the nation could "get by" with the $5 billion figure.

Then, on May 2, the chair of Ways and Means announced that the president not only would have to agree to a $6 billion cut in his budget but also would have to give up an additional $14 billion in new obligational authority.[26] At his news conference on May 3, LBJ came out swinging. "I want to make it perfectly clear to the American people," he told the assembled reporters, "that I think we are courting danger by this continued procrastination, this continued delay. . . . I proposed a budget. If they [members of Congress] don't like that budget, then stand up like men and answer the roll call and cut what they think ought to be cut. Then the president will exercise his responsibility of approving it or rejecting it and vetoing it."[27] That night he recalled to Joe Califano Senator Alvin Wirtz's statement to him some thirty years earlier, that one could tell another man to go to hell, but making him go was another matter. "Well, I just told someone to go to hell," he chuckled to his domestic policy adviser.[28] Over the next six weeks the president called scores of members of Congress, warning liberals that if the tax surcharge were not enacted, runaway inflation would gobble up the monies available to finance programs of social justice, and warning conservatives that the soundness of the dollar and the stability of the international economy depend on passage.[29]

WHILE LBJ TWISTED CONGRESSIONAL ARMS, MINDS, AND CON-sciences in an effort to pass his housing and tax bills, some three thousand "poor people" trekked to the nation's capital by rail, bus, mule train, and

automobile. During the last two weeks in May 1968, they threw up a shantytown made of plywood and canvas huts on the Washington Mall near the
Reflecting Pool; they named their encampment "Resurrection City."

The Poor People's Campaign had been the brainchild of Martin Luther
King. Ghetto uprisings were continuing to whip up a white backlash that
promised to make further reform impossible. But the violence was sure to
continue if the lives of African Americans living in the nation's cities did
not improve. The 1966 freedom budget—which had called for job creation
programs, a guaranteed annual income for poor families, and increased federal spending to eradicate slums, improve schools, and build public works—
had died aborning with the conservative resurgence in the 1966 midterm
elections. It would have to be revived. The key, King had believed, was
to focus on poverty across racial lines, to realize the dream reformers had
dreamed since the late nineteenth century: the creation of a political coalition in which blacks, poor whites, Mexican Americans, and Native Americans would seek to transform the nation's political and economic landscape.
To launch the campaign, King had envisioned a Poor People's March on
Washington that would be nonviolent but more radical and disruptive than
the orderly marches of Selma and Birmingham. Something more along the
lines of the antiwar demonstrations that had threatened to shut down the
Pentagon.

In February 1968, King had traveled to Washington to meet with local
activists and to gather the resources necessary to support the campaign.
Convening a press conference, King announced plans for a Poor People's
March on Washington to dramatize the campaign's objectives: $30 billion for
antipoverty programs, full employment, guaranteed income, and the annual
construction of five hundred thousand affordable residences. The SCLC
subsequently recruited marshals, who first attended a training workshop
in Atlanta in March and then returned home to recruit participants, raise
funds, and solicit organizational support. Participants were required to sign
an agreement to stick to nonviolence and to obey the marshals.[30]

Following the riots of 1967, LBJ had authorized the creation of a massive intelligence-gathering network in the nation's inner cities. Led by the
FBI, this web of spies included the Justice Department, CIA, Department
of Defense, the intelligence arms of each of the military services, and local
law enforcement officials. The goal was to gather information concerning

potential ghetto rioters in order to foretell and prevent violent outbreaks before they began. The FBI recruited three thousand inner-city informants in the Ghetto Informant Program (GIP). The forthcoming Poor People's March provided the first major opportunity for the FBI to test its network. The bureau's plan, code-named POCAM, was launched on January 4, 1968.[31] The administration's program of spying and spoiling would give a new meaning to the War on Poverty.

King's April trip to Memphis had been designed both to highlight a sanitation strike and to launch the march on Washington. In mid-March, the Reverend James Lawson, a pioneering civil rights activist and old friend of King's, had called and urged him to come to Memphis to support the garbage workers' strike then in progress. Lawson's Community on the Move for Equality (COME) had stepped forward to convert what began as a wildcat walkout into a full-fledged civil rights battle in which COME backed the workers' demands for a union, decent working conditions, and a living wage. Memphis city officials fired the striking workers, nearly all of whom were black, en masse, and refused to negotiate. Six thousand marchers, including black high school students, trooped up Beal Street, past the statue of blues great W. C. Handy. When some of the protesters began smashing store windows, organizers attempted to turn the group around. But by that time the police had massed, and they charged the demonstrators, clubs swinging. On March 18, King had addressed a rally of fifteen thousand strike supporters at the huge Masonic Temple in downtown Memphis. Caught up in the tumult, he promised to return later in the month to lead a one-day strike.[32] King had flown back to Memphis on April 3 and was murdered on the 4th.

Following King's assassination, his successor as head of the SCLC, Ralph David Abernathy, took up the gauntlet and assumed leadership of the Poor People's March. "It isn't going to be a Sunday-school picnic like the '63 march on Washington," said Andrew Young, one of Abernathy's aides. "Something is going to change or we'll all be in jail. This is do or die—not just for nonviolence but for the nation."[33] After the Poor People's Campaign applied for a permit to camp on the Washington Mall,[34] White House officials met with Abernathy and an advance party of some sixty people to try to establish ground rules for what promised to be a prolonged and perhaps inflammatory demonstration.[35]

On April 29, the Committee of 100, the campaign's steering body, began lobbying members of Congress. On Sunday, May 12, Mother's Day, Coretta

Scott King came to Washington to agitate for an economic Bill of Rights. Five thousand people marched to protest 1967 cuts to Head Start funding and a legislatively mandated freeze on welfare payments; during the debate over the freeze, Senator Russell Long of Louisiana had described mothers on welfare as "brood mares."[36] "I want you to listen very closely and sympathetically to their appeals," Johnson told his cabinet. "See if there is anything that your departments may have left undone that would help them."[37] From that directive came dozens of proposals, including a summer school program for the nation's one hundred largest cities and one hundred poorest counties. Selected schools would be kept open "morning, noon, and night, seven days a week, to conduct work-study, athletic, and training programs," in the words of the scheme's authors.[38]

Upon hearing of the planned "occupation" of the mall, law-and-order advocates took up their cudgels. Senator Long called for the censure of members of Congress whom he accused of "bending the knee" to the campaign. "When that bunch of marchers comes here," the Louisianan declared, "they can just burn the whole place down and we can just move the capital to some place where they will enforce the law."[39]

Throughout May, nine large caravans of poor people set out for Washington. On Tuesday, May 21, participants set up a shantytown on the National Mall—Resurrection City. In return for a permit to camp on the most famous strip of grass in the United States, campaign leaders agreed to limit the population to three thousand and the duration to thirty-six days.[40] SCLC leaders led small groups of residents on marches and attempts to meet with members of Congress, excursions that were mostly uneventful. The inhabitants of Resurrection City never conducted the large-scale civil disobedience operations in Washington that King had envisioned. There were reports of discipline problems, and Abernathy was criticized for living in a hotel. Continuous rain turned the tent city into a sea of mud.[41]

"I'm sitting here waiting for the delegation from the Poor People's March to appear," Orville Freeman wrote in his diary on May 21. "What a comedy of uncertainty and errors this performance is. They've got this town standing on its head. The problem of course is one of uncertainty. In the first place they can't control their own people, although they are doing much better than I would have dreamed possible. They already have sent home by bus some gangs from various cities and groups that make trouble. This morning an off-shoot group went to the hill and when Mills wouldn't see them began to picket and sing in a restricted area."[42] On the anniversary of Malcolm X's birthday, Black Nationalists marched, distributed leaflets, and forced black merchants to close for the day, but true to King's philosophy, the Poor People's March remained peaceful.[43]

LBJ's immediate concern was to see that the inevitable friction between the capital police and the residents of Resurrection City did not get out of hand. He told journalist Ken Crawford that he had been in Washington during the World War I veterans' Bonus March and did not want a repetition of that sorry episode.[44] But pressure was mounting on the administration to act. The conservative senior senator from Arkansas, John McClellan, had opened hearings on urban unrest and its causes. His staff managed to round up some gang members from Chicago who testified that they received OEO money that they used to stock weapons and plan riot and revolution.[45] On Thursday, June 20, police fired several canisters of tear gas into the encampment—reportedly after members of the Milwaukee NAACP provoked them by throwing rocks. By this time, life in the camp had become increasingly chaotic. Reports circulated of vandalism perpetrated by escaped mental patients. As of late Friday the population of Resurrection City had dwindled to five hundred. "The poor whites from the Appalachian area left today in buses and the Mexican-Americans have indicated that they do not intend to go to the encampment," Joe Califano reported to the president. Still, the police would have to tread lightly "since some of the people in Resurrection City have guns and some mean and mentally deficient individuals will be there."[46] When the Campaign's National Park Service permit expired on Sunday the 23rd, assorted members of the House called for immediate removal. The next day a thousand police officers arrived and arrested those who would not leave voluntarily, a total of 288, including Reverend Abernathy.[47]

The summer of 1968 saw the African American civil rights movement in disarray. Ideologically and politically splintered, its leadership had lost its way. Martin Luther King's power had stemmed from his success in holding up the nation's Judeo-Christen ethic before its collective face and demanding that it adhere to its principles. That, coupled with nonviolent disobedience, proved dramatically effective in the South, less so in the North. In the wake of the awarding of the Nobel Peace Prize in 1964, King had suffered from a bout of mission overreach. Astride his new international stage and confronted with the dynamics of a civil rights movement whose focus had shifted to the North and Midwest, the SCLC chief had increasingly embraced the New Left critique of capitalism and the military–industrial complex. In attacking the war in Vietnam and calling for systemic changes in the economic and political life of the country, King played into the hands of law-and-order advocates who were working to link the civil rights and antiwar movements with the forcers of international communism. The Poor People's Campaign, another attempt to mobilize the nation's poor across ethnic and demographic lines, was doomed to failure, undone by the long-standing racism and job insecurity of the white working class and, to a degree, by the prosperity generated by the Great Society. Black power had little to offer in terms of overcoming chronic poverty. Its rejection of integration and emphasis on cultural nationalism did not help either. The African American community lacked the capital, infrastructure, and training for economic self-sufficiency. NAACP director William Rutherford, Roy Wilkins, and others of the civil rights old guard recognized this and spoke out, but all they were left with was New Deal–Great Society liberalism, and that was under attack on virtually all fronts.

Abernathy, out on bail, addressed fifty thousand people at the Lincoln Memorial and blasted the administration and Congress, calling the Great Society's record on social justice and civil rights a series of "broken promises." For Johnson, this was the last straw. He complained to Orville Freeman that "the very people we are seeking to help in Medicare and education and welfare and Food Stamps are protesting louder and louder and giving no recognition or allowance for what's been done. Our efforts seem to have resulted only in anarchy. . . . The women no longer bother to get married, they just keep breeding. The men go their way and the women get relief— why should they work?"[48] Why didn't people pay attention to the positives? The number of individuals living below the poverty line had dropped by eight million. Overall spending for health, education, and welfare had increased from $23 billion to $46.7 billion during the Johnson presidency.[49] On June 19 the director of the budget reported that summer jobs would increase by 285,000 over 1967 through the efforts of the National Alliance of Businessmen.[50] LBJ remarked to presidential aide Tom Johnson that he had learned from reading Alexis de Tocqueville that the leaders of revolutions often become their victims.[51]

Johnson claimed to see Bobby Kennedy's fine hand behind the Poor People's Campaign. And, in fact, in the wake of the King assassination, RFK had met publicly with Abernathy, who subsequently declared to reporters, "In it, white America does have someone who cares." Indeed, as several of RFK's aides later admitted, the King assassination had given their man's candidacy new life. Bobby had jumped into the presidential race after McCarthy's strong showing in the New Hampshire primary. If the election was to be about LBJ, Bobby would be the perfect challenger, heir to the programs and vision that the Texan was allegedly betraying. But then Bobby's great foil had withdrawn. Then, with King's assassination, RFK could pose as champion of the Negro, the Hispanic, and the downtrodden in general.[52]

Bobby had found Abe Ribicoff's hearings on neglect of the cities most useful in building his reputation as a modern-day Populist. He found another in Pennsylvania Democrat Joseph Clark's Senate hearings on hunger, which began on March 13, 1968. The liberal Clark, one of Kennedy's few good friends in the Senate, was running for reelection in 1968. His subcommittee had scheduled field hearings across the nation in the spring of 1967, and the first place on its itinerary was the Mississippi Delta. Kennedy was in attendance as locals told stories of intense suffering from inadequate diets; one spokesperson estimated that 95 percent of the children in the Delta were malnourished. Upon his return to New York, RFK exclaimed melodramatically to an aide, "You don't know what I saw! I have done nothing in my life! Everything I have done was a waste!"[53]

The Clark subcommittee reconvened and summoned Secretary of Agriculture Orville Freeman. Senator Jacob Javits (D-NY) accused his department of ignoring the problem of malnutrition in America. When Freeman angrily rejected the charge, RFK waved a photo of a wide-eyed black girl with a swollen abdomen and ulcerated skin. "While we sit here arguing about whether hunger exists or not," he proclaimed, "children are going to die!"[54] The problem of hunger in rural areas of the South and Appalachia was real and acute, but the administration was getting whipsawed. "Both he [RFK] and Clark refused to say what we should do, refused to consider the need to replace the local authorities if we're really going to get anything done," Freeman complained to his diary. "Yet, they make their demands and now additional hearings are being held by the Committee. . . . Jamie Whitten [Democratic congressman from Mississippi] and Governor [Paul]

Johnson keep insisting that there really aren't hungry people and anyone who really wants food can get it through relief, work, or some way."[55]

Then, on May 21, as the Poor People's Campaign was picking up steam, CBS aired a heart-wrenching documentary entitled *Hunger in America,* depicting black, female-headed, inner-city families and white Appalachian and southern families, all of them with malnourished infants and toddlers, some of them suffering from tuberculosis and influenza. Abernathy and other campaign leaders had made hunger a major issue in their demand for a guaranteed income. Southern Democrats such as Senator Ernest F. "Fritz" Hollings of South Carolina had begun seizing on the issue as they confronted the political problem of appeasing newly enfranchised blacks without further accelerating the white backlash. There was no threat to the white power structure in feeding the hungry.[56] The Clark committee charged that the administration was "permitting" fourteen million Americans to go hungry every day. Freeman denounced the CBS report as a pack of lies and demanded equal time.[57] The network responded by re-airing its program.

A task force led by Joe Califano and including Freeman put forward a proposal "to guarantee to every American an adequate diet for the first time in the history of our country." It would increase funding for the Food Stamp program from $225 million to $445 million and expand other programs for needy school children by $56 million and for preschool children by $32 million.[58] The president was initially unreceptive. Congress was scheduled to vote on the surtax bill within a week, and the administration had just finished cutting $6 billion from the federal budget. In the short run, all he could think of was that the hunger program was just another attempt by liberals to ambush him. "He told me," Freeman wrote in his diary, "that most of this was pure emotion rather than hungry people. Joe Califano told me later that the President doesn't really believe there are hungry people and has on occasion said this is a good year, the rains have been good, anyone can grow a garden."[59] True to form, however, Johnson relented and approved a request for $250 million to $300 million in additional funds to feed the hungry.[60]

LBJ and his aides were, of course, afraid that the Poor People's Campaign, *Hunger in America,* violence on college campuses, and RFK's machinations would create a white middle-and working-class reaction that would make passage of the fair housing bill and the tax surcharge impossible. "It's a real challenge as to how we handle this and keep them [protesters, demonstrators, marchers] active and participating and making progress without permitting them to become destructive of the functioning of Government and our society and without creating the resentments and apprehensions that will result in a middle class white backlash," Freeman observed.[61] But things did hold together. Congress passed the housing bill and in the last week in June enacted a 10 percent tax surcharge; LBJ had to agree in principle to a $6 billion spending reduction for the coming fiscal year, but he intended not to take the initiative, suspecting that when it came down to it, Congress would not have the will to make specific program reductions. He was proved right. Congress was unable to cut even $4 billion in pending expenditures. Fiscal year 1969 ended with a $3.2 billion surplus and with most of the Great Society programs intact.[62]

FROM THE EVENING OF MARCH 31, WHEN HE ANNOUNCED HE WAS not going to run, LBJ's overriding objective was to keep himself and the presidency above politics so that he could preserve as much of the Great Society as possible and secure what he believed would be an honorable peace in Vietnam, two goals he saw as inextricably intertwined. During a congressional leadership breakfast on April 2, several of those present asked whether they could talk politics briefly. Johnson refused. He said that he was "tired of begging anyone for anything. I had a partnership with Jack Kennedy and when he died I felt it was my duty to look after the family and stockholders and employees of my partner. . . . [Now], the divisions are so deep within the party that I could not reconcile them."[63] Later, he promised both Bobby Kennedy and Hubert Humphrey that he would stay out of the campaign.

Through Joe Califano, LBJ let his cabinet officers and agency heads know that he did not want them participating in the presidential race either. If they felt the need, they should resign, like Postmaster General Larry O'Brien, who had departed to work for Bobby. Though he knew that Freeman, Labor Secretary Willard Wirtz, newly named HEW secretary Wilbur Cohen, and others wanted to attend Humphrey's announcement luncheon on April 27, he would not let them. Freeman, especially, was incensed. He was a fellow Minnesotan and would undoubtedly be asked to participate in and even manage the Humphrey campaign, he told the president. Johnson would not budge.[64]

Of course, LBJ did not want Richard Nixon to be president. He detested the man, believing him to be devoid of principle, the ultimate political opportunist. But he also thought that Nixon would be hardest to beat. Johnson felt fairly confident that he could defeat the Californian, but he was not sure either Humphrey or Bobby Kennedy could. As a result, for six weeks in the spring of 1968 the president did everything in his power to persuade Nelson Rockefeller to run for president and touted him to Republicans who had voted for LBJ in 1964. The two men had long expressed mutual regard for each other. In 1962 Rockefeller had drawn the ire of Catholics and conservative Protestants when he divorced his first wife, Mary Todhunter Clark, and then a year later married Margaretta (Happy) Murphy. Johnson told friends that he felt "Nelson took a terrible beating in the press for marrying Happy" and repeatedly invited the couple to White House dinners to "put a stamp of approval on that marriage."[65] In April, LBJ and Lady Bird hosted a private dinner at the White House during which the first couple worked to persuade Rockefeller and his wife that the country needed them.[66]

By May, Bobby Kennedy's well-financed campaign was in high gear. That month he defeated a favorite son candidate who was running as a Humphrey stand-in in the Indiana primary. Instead of focusing on organizing and fund-raising, the Humphrey campaign wallowed in self-pity.[67] When Eugene McCarthy triumphed in Oregon, he and Kennedy prepared for a showdown in California, a state whose large electoral vote made it crucial to any presidential campaign. McCarthy's young supporters stuck by him, but he was no match for the handsome, charismatic RFK. A bland speaker who seemed to lecture his audiences, the Minnesota senator sounded like "the dean of the finest English department in the land," as Norman Mailer put it.[68] The grinning Bobby, hair flopping, hand perpetually extended, blitzed the state and called in all of his family's political debts. Shrieking young women vied with large contingents of Mexican farm workers for a glimpse of the candidate. On June 4 Kennedy won with 46 percent of the vote to McCarthy's 42 percent. He was well on his way to the nomination.

At midnight Bobby collected Ethel and headed downstairs to address campaign workers in the ballroom of the Embassy Hotel in Los Angeles. Exhausted by the grueling primary campaign, he had spent the morning at Malibu bodysurfing with six of his ten children. He appeared fresh and exhilarated, and he addressed his worshipful audience with characteristic humor, self-effacement, and inspiration. At the last minute his aides had agreed to a press conference following the speech. Led by the NFL football great Roosevelt Grier and Olympic decathlon champion Rafer Johnson, Kennedy took a shortcut through the hotel pantry. Waiting for him there was a short, dark Palestinian American named Sirhan Sirhan. As Bobby approached, Sirhan pulled a .22-caliber pistol and shot him twice, once in the head and once in the armpit. As bodyguards struggled to subdue the assailant, the heir-apparent to the Kennedy dynasty lay motionless, his eyes open, staring blankly.[69] Finally, an ambulance arrived and whisked him off to the hospital, where he hovered between life and death.

At 3:31 A.M. on the morning of June 5, Walt Rostow wakened LBJ to give him the news. "Too horrible for words," Johnson responded. It was too horrible for words on many levels. If RFK should die, as his doctors privately predicted he would, the nation would be treated to yet another violent death and was bound to sink once again into a slew of despondency and self-questioning. Whatever momentum toward peace and reconciliation that had begun with the March 31 speech would be lost. And LBJ's hopes of being remembered as one of the nation's most effective and dedicated presidents would evaporate. The bookends to his administration would be the two Kennedy assassinations, he being reduced to a cipher and they elevated in the public imagination to the level of political demigods embodying the youth, vigor, and idealism of the nation.

The president had scheduled a ten o'clock broadcast to the nation, and he worked feverishly with his aides to come up with the proper words:

> A young leader of uncommon energy and dedication, who has served his country tirelessly and well, and whose voice and example have touched millions throughout the entire world, has been senselessly and horribly stricken. . . . We pray to God that He will spare Robert Kennedy. . . . It would be wrong, it would be self-deceptive, to ignore the connection between . . . lawlessness and hatred and this act of violence. It would be just as wrong, and just as self-deceptive, to conclude from this act that our country itself is sick, that it has lost its balance, that it has lost its sense of direction, even its common decency. Two

hundred million Americans did not strike down Robert Kennedy last night any more than they struck down President John F. Kennedy in 1963 or Dr. Martin Luther King.[70]

At 5:01 A.M. the next morning, LBJ was informed that Senator Kennedy had died. "It seems impossible," Orville Freeman wrote in his diary. "That strange, moody, intense, combative, competitive but really gentle and sensitive human being is gone like the brother before him."[71]

Once again Johnson moved to take advantage of a fallen hero's martyrdom. He had been pressing Congress for gun control legislation since John Kennedy's death, but to no avail. On the day of Bobby's funeral on June 8, the White House taped and aired a gun control message. Two days later, LBJ met with the members of the National Commission on the Causes and Prevention of Violence. He pointed out that one in every five presidents since 1865 had been assassinated, and one in three had been the target of attempted assassinations. The crescendo of shootings associated with attempts to suppress the civil rights movement and with urban rioting had been made immeasurably worse by the ready availability of firearms. He asked the blue ribbon panel to draft a sweeping justification for gun control. Shortly thereafter, the president called on Congress to ban all mail-order and out-of-state sales of handguns, rifles, and shotguns; halt the sale of firearms to minors; and require the national registration of all guns. After a brutal behind-the-scenes battle, the administration's bill was defeated. Congress did present the White House with a gun control measure, but it said nothing about registration and licensing. LBJ signed the measure but lashed out at the National Rifle Association. "The voices that blocked these safeguards," he declared, "were the voices of a powerful lobby, a gun lobby, that has prevailed for the moment in an election year. . . . We have been through a great deal of anguish these last few months and these last few years—too much anguish to forget so quickly."[72]

Congress reacted to RFK's death not with effective gun control legislation but with a revised Safe Streets Act that posed a clear threat to the Fourth Amendment prohibiting unreasonable searches and seizures. In the wake of the riots in Newark and Detroit, LBJ, then still a potential presidential candidate, had been whipsawed between the War on Poverty and the War on Crime. Presidential aide Harry McPherson had urged the president to take a strong stand on the issue of future riots. "Make no speeches about Constitutional inhibition," urged McPherson, a moderate whose hardline advice thus carried extra weight. "Back up law and order in a hurry; be seen to be more concerned with securing the peace than with protracted legal discussions or political advantage."[73] In his 1968 State of the Union address, LBJ strongly denounced criminal violence and once again called for a Safe Streets Act—the only sections of the speech to draw sustained applause.[74]

On February 7, in a special message to Congress, Johnson proposed the Omnibus Crime Control and Safe Streets Act.[75] As originally conceived, the administration bill would have provided federal grants to police departments for equipment, training, and pilot programs. The preferred method was through categorical grants to municipalities with specific priorities rather than through block grants to states with vague federal mandates. In mid-February, the House approved a bill opting for block grants and adding $25 million specifically for riot control. The Senate Judiciary Committee followed the House's lead. Conservatives favored block grants to state planning agencies that would be responsive to governors and local authorities. Most offensive to the administration were Titles II and III of the bill. A direct assault on the Supreme Court's *Miranda* decision, Title II held that in federal cases, a confession was admissible so long as the judge deemed it voluntary. It also stated that a delay in pressing charges, whether caused by holding the suspect incommunicado or questioning him at length, was not in itself grounds for disallowing a confession. It took away the Supreme Court's authority to review federal and state criminal cases in which a voluntary confession was ruled admissible. The preeminent champion of Title II, Senator Sam Ervin (D–NC), wrote a colleague: "Those who are in favor of self-confessed murderers and rapists going free should vote against Title II."[76]

Title II was bad, but Title III "may do more to turn the country into a police state than any law we have ever enacted," an aide to Joe Califano advised him.[77] A federal assistant attorney general, state district attorney, or local district attorney with the appropriate judicial approval could plant a bug or tap a phone if the crime or potential crime in question was punishable by a prison sentence of at least one year.[78] Despite his authorization of bugging at the 1964 Democratic National Convention and his approval of the FBI's wiretapping of Martin Luther King, Johnson was by this time a fanatical opponent of electronic eavesdropping. "It barely resembles the Safe

Streets Bill we sent the Congress with such high hopes and ardent pleas," Deputy Attorney General Warren Christopher observed to the president. "The bill is far more a reflection of the fears, frustration, and politics of the times than an intelligent carefully tailored measure."[79]

The administration's only real success came in the area of gun control. Title IV, which the White House supported, imposed strict limits on the purchase of handguns and marked the liberal shift from social programs to gun control as the primary response to violent crime and urban unrest. On April 4, Senator Thomas Dodd (D–CT) attempted to amend the Omnibus Crime Bill to empower the federal government to regulate the sale, distribution, and importation of all firearms. His proposal initially failed, but then word of King's assassination arrived, and Washington erupted in rioting the next day. Polls taken at the close of the month indicated that the public supported more restrictive gun control by a margin of 71 percent to 23 percent. The day RFK died the House voted by a vote of 368 to 17 to accept the Senate bill, which included Dodd's proposed amendment.[80]

Because of Titles II and III, LBJ was tempted to veto the Safe Streets Act, but even Attorney General Clark advised against it. "From a practical standpoint," he told Johnson, "the result might be a worse bill. . . . If the Congress acted again it might . . . limit the jurisdiction and habeas corpus powers of the federal courts. This would be disastrous."[81] The president clenched his teeth, held his tongue, and signed the bill into law. Five years later, Congress would be forced to investigate abusive wiretapping by the FBI, and state surveillance programs such as Mississippi's would become national scandals.[82]

AS LYNDON JOHNSON WATCHED THE CONSERVATIVE COALITION ONCE again assert itself, he moved to erect a judicial barrier around his Great Society programs. Like FDR in 1937, LBJ in 1968 was worried that a conservative court, sure to emerge if a Republican such as Richard Nixon won the presidency, would issue decisions dismantling Medicare, the various civil rights measures passed during his administration, and federal aid to education. On June 13, Chief Justice Earl Warren informed the president that he intended to retire "effective at your pleasure." Warren admired Johnson and hated Nixon. If he could give LBJ a chance to appoint a new chief justice, he believed, it would be worth an early retirement.[83] Johnson had long since decided that if Warren stepped down, he would nominate Associate Justice Abe Fortas, his longtime friend, confidant, and personal lawyer, to be chief justice.

From the outset he knew that it would be a tough fight. Fortas's credentials as a liberal jurist had made him persona non grata among conservatives. While a student at Yale and editor of the *Yale Law Journal,* Fortas was deeply influenced by legal realism, the school's dominant approach to jurisprudence. Yale was the center of a rebellion against the traditional case method, against "conceptualists" who insisted that law could be reduced to a few fundamental rules and principles derived from the study of individual cases. Conceptualists believed that a judge's decisions should not reflect his or her own particular views, the specific circumstances of the case, or the greater good. Instead of "making" law, the ideal magistrate would discover concepts, rules, and principles that had been revealed in previous decisions and apply them. The conceptualists were descendants of Thomas Jefferson and the first Republican Party's "strict constructionist" approach to constitutional interpretation.

Legal realism was part of a "revolt against formalism" that swept the intellectual world during the first half of the twentieth century. Philosophy, psychology, anthropology, linguistics, history, economics, and sociology questioned all received truths and abstractions, moving away from the study of structure to a concern with operations. Legal realism traced its historical roots back to Hamilton and the Federalist Party's call for a broad interpretation of the Constitution, paving the way for an activist federal government with the power to promote the nation's economic well-being.

Harvard was the bastion of conceptualism and thus the enemy. "Harvard people tended to look upon us as unsound maniacs, and we in turn looked upon them as sort of antiques whose time had passed by," Fortas observed.[84] As a teacher, practitioner, and justice, he had worked to perpetuate Justice Brandeis's philosophy that jurists must adjudicate not only according to precedent but also in response to social and economic conditions that changed over time. He was an activist who, in interpreting the law, would not defer to Congress as often as most justices. In 1950 he had defended Owen Lattimore against the red-baiting assaults of Senator Joe McCarthy. Nor was he inclined to defer to the states. Fortas was an original New Dealer who defended Roosevelt's decision to use the federal government to achieve a degree of economic justice. In *Gideon v. Wainwright,* which established the right of an indigent to publicly funded defense counsel, he had defended Clarence Gideon on appeal.[85] Fortas had proved a staunch advocate for laws furthering the Second Reconstruction, and he was a known intimate of Lyndon Johnson, either of which alone was sufficient to raise the hackles of conservatives.

By the time the White House submitted Fortas's nomination to the Senate to become chief justice, legal realism had become the order of the day. The Supreme Court, presided over by Chief Justice Earl Warren since 1953, was unquestionably an activist tribunal, an agency in service to the liberalism of the 1960s.[86] Warren, generally supported by Justices Hugo Black, William O. Douglas, and William Brennan, engineered nothing less than a constitutional revolution in his application of the Bill of Rights to the states; in his generous interpretation of specific constitutional provisions of criminal justice safeguards for the individual; in the broad application and interpretation of both the letter and the spirit of the Civil War amendments; in rendering any executive or legislative classification by race or nationality constitutionally suspect; in the liberalization of the right to vote; and in an expansive definition of freedom of expression.

Among the Warren Court's most famous and controversial decisions were the *Brown* decision outlawing segregated schools; *Miranda,* which protected criminal defendants against self-incrimination; *Engle v. Vitale,* which outlawed the recitation of state-prepared and prescribed prayers in public schools; and *Reynolds v. Sims,* in which the court ruled that both houses of state legislatures must be apportioned on a one-person, one-vote basis. In the latter decision, the chief justice declared that "legislators are elected by voters, not farms or cities or economic interest."[87] Unlike Franklin Roosevelt, who saw his National Industrial Recovery Act and Agricultural Adjustment Act declared unconstitutional, with the Warren Court ascendant, LBJ did not have to worry that the Supreme Court would strike down major pieces of Great Society legislation. Installing Fortas as chief justice, he believed, would extend that protection for the foreseeable future

By the mid-1960s the Warren Court had become the bête noir of the conservative coalition. It was perceived to be a principal instrumentality of the welfare state that LBJ was building. Law-and-order advocates were appalled at the protections extended to defendants in criminal cases. Under

Warren and his acolyte Fortas, they believed, the High Court had coddled criminals and encouraged the ghetto riots and violent antiwar protests that were threatening to destroy America. All of this was pleasing in the collective eyes of Moscow and Beijing, they declared.

Republicans were not about to stand idly by and see Johnson have his way with the high court. They resented the fact that the president had hedged his bets. In his response to Warren's letter of resignation, LBJ had declared, "With your agreement, I will accept your decision to retire effective at such time as a successor is qualified."[88] If the Fortas nomination were to fail, LBJ wanted Warren still on the court. Yet the presidential election was only five months away. Dirksen and other GOP stalwarts believed that Nixon had an excellent chance of winning and that the victor ought to have the right to nominate Warren's successor.[89]

Freshman senator Robert Griffin (R–MI) took it upon himself to lead the opposition. As a matter of principle, he would never support a Supreme Court nominee made by a lame-duck president, he announced. If necessary, he would lead a filibuster. Democrats Robert Byrd, Russell Long, and Sam Ervin let it be known that they would vote no. John McClellan of Arkansas told Jim Eastland that he was looking forward to having "that SOB formally submitted to the Senate" so that he could fight his nomination. Eastland, chair of the Senate Judiciary Committee, told Mike Manatos, White House congressional liaison, that he "had never seen so much feeling against a man as against Fortas."[90] Eastland himself was under tremendous pressure from his white constituents in Mississippi. The state's racist governor, John Bell Williams, was then blaming the chair of the Senate Judiciary Committee for permitting confirmation of justices who had struck down various "freedom of choice" school plans. Indeed, Williams was threatening to run for the Senate himself in the next election.[91]

From July 16 to 19, Fortas testified before the Senate Judiciary Committee, the first nominee for chief justice and the first sitting justice to do so. He successfully turned aside questions concerning his liberal voting record, citing separation of powers and the need to respect the court's independence. But he did agree to address himself to charges that he had had an inappropriately close relationship with President Johnson while he was on the court. He denied that he had violated the separation of powers or given advice improperly to LBJ. Yet Fortas had been a regular at White

House meetings on everything from Vietnam to labor disputes. He had helped draft Johnson's 1966 State of the Union address. All of this he denied. Asked whether he had written the president's statement on sending troops into Detroit during the 1967 riots, he said no. It was another lie. "Fortas' testimony was so misleading and deceptive," Joe Califano later wrote, "that those of us who were aware of his relationship with Johnson winced with each news report."[92]

LBJ was still hopeful. With August approaching, Congress would have to adjourn for the presidential nominating conventions. Just as the Senate Judiciary Committee appeared to be winding down its hearings, Senator Strom Thurmond of South Carolina, now a Republican, raised a new issue. Both as private counsel and as a Supreme Court justice, Fortas had given aid and comfort to pornographers. Thurmond cited especially a case in which the New York courts had found that the film *Flaming Creatures* had violated that state's obscenity laws. Fortas had stood alone among his colleagues in voting to reverse the conviction.[93] Dirksen began to waver. Sam Ervin declared that he could not vote on Fortas's nomination because no vacancy had occurred. Warren should either resign or not resign. Thurmond promised to show the Judiciary Committee every salacious film on which Fortas had ruled. Behind the scenes, Nixon pressured Dirksen to rise above his friendship with LBJ and help block the Fortas nomination.[94]

The White House fought back. Spokesmen pointed out that never in the history of the Supreme Court nominations had one failed due to filibuster. Johnson, who by this time had come to regard the fight over Fortas as a personal battle between him and his reactionary enemies, lashed his subordinates to renewed effort. "We're a bunch of dupes down here," he told Califano and White House aide Larry Temple. "They've got all the wisdom . . . they're smarter than we are. We're a bunch of ignorant, immature kids who don't know anything about this. . . . We've got to do something."[95] He had one of his aides draft two papers, one depicting Fortas as a liberal activist and the other as a strict constructionist. When the aide suggested that the White House might be criticized for sending out contradictory signals, LBJ reminded him of the story of the young man who was interviewing for a teaching job in a rural Texas district. The climax of the interview came when the redneck chairman of the school board asked the extremely stressed candidate, "Do you teach that the world is flat or do you teach that the world is round?" The young man hesitated and then replied, "I can teach it either way."[96] The object of the exercise, LBJ reminded his staffer, was to have Fortas named chief justice.

After the August recess, shortly before the committee reconvened on September 13, the White House learned that Griffin had come into possession of more damning evidence. Paul Porter, Fortas's former law partner, had raised $30,000 from past and present clients to pay Fortas to teach a series of seminars at American University Law School. Some of the contributors could expect to be parties to cases that would reach the high court. Fortas had already been paid $15,000. At the time, that was a significant sum of money, greatly increasing Fortas's income through an arrangement that risked creating conflicts of interest. Though no actual conflicts were claimed, it was a far more damaging scandal that any pornography decision or White House conversation. The Fortas nomination was dead.[97] Thus did LBJ botch his effort to leave the Supreme Court in liberal hands. Richard Nixon would make three appointments to the high court.

WAS THERE ANY HOPE FOR A DEMOCRATIC WHITE HOUSE AFTER Johnson's abdication and RFK's assassination, pundits asked? If the void were to be filled it would have to be by Hubert Humphrey. Johnson wanted his vice president to win, but he doubted whether Humphrey could or even should be president. Above all, LBJ believed, his liberal protégé would have to sit tight on Vietnam. Meaningful negotiations to end American involvement were crucial to Humphrey's successful candidacy. In order to ensure negotiations that would give Vietnamization a chance, and a settlement that would not enrage conservatives, the North Vietnamese Army and the Vietcong first would have to be beaten bloody and then convinced that the best deal they could get from their enemy would be sooner rather than later. If Humphrey in his quest to attract Kennedy-McCarthy supporters prematurely called for de-escalation, a bombing halt, and even unilateral withdrawal, all would be lost—on the political battlefield at home and on the military battlefield in Vietnam. In the White House's view, Humphrey's best bet was for LBJ's plan to work: for there to be a period of all-out war in Vietnam followed by meaningful negotiations that would give the nation a glimpse of peace with honor and thus vindicate the foreign policy with which Johnson had so long been identified. But the vice president would have to hold his water.

Shortly after LBJ's abdication speech, negotiations between US and North Vietnamese representatives had begun in Paris. (At the secret urging of the Nixon camp, the South Vietnamese government was boycotting the talks.) Throughout June and July, LBJ labored to persuade the leading presidential candidates not to take positions on the war and the conversations in Paris that would tie his hands. As he told Richard Nixon—by then the frontrunner for the GOP nomination—at the White House on June 26, if he were the Democratic nominee and Nixon were president, he would issue a statement to the effect that he (Johnson) was not responsible for the country until he became president. He had similar conversations with Rockefeller, Humphrey, and Wallace. But not McCarthy; the other candidate from Minnesota was hopeless, Johnson believed. The contenders duly agreed to do everything possible not to interfere or narrow the president's options.

But because he was vice president, Humphrey's silence would link him irrevocably to Johnson's policies. There were dangers for Nixon as well. Privately and publicly, he had indicated support for the war in Vietnam, for the assumptions that lay behind it, and for the notion of military victory. His criticism had been that the administration had been too timid, had placed too many restraints on the military. If Nixon continued this hawkish support for LBJ and his policies, and nothing changed, all would be well; but what if sometime during the fall and before the election, the administration initiated a bombing halt, and the talks in Paris began to move toward a settlement? Nixon would be left hanging, twisting in the wind, to anticipate a phrase.

IF 1968 HAD NOT ALREADY PROVEN ITSELF TO BE A DISASTROUS YEAR, through two assassinations, more urban rioting, and continued agony in Vietnam, events at the close of August were about to remove any doubt of it. The Democratic National Convention in Chicago, which met from August 26 through August 29, would be one of the most memorable in American history. The meeting itself was an angry, bitter affair in which the delegates quickly polarized into antiwar and pro-war factions. McCarthy managed to attract some of Kennedy's delegates, and he consistently led Humphrey in the polls. Nonetheless, the vice president easily captured the nomination on the first ballot. Most professional politicians distrusted McCarthy and had heaped ridicule on his "Children's Crusade." Without winning one state primary, Humphrey had worked behind the scenes to line up almost fifteen hundred delegates. He had also made it clear that he supported "Johnson's war." "Nothing would bring the real peaceniks back to our side," confided an aide to a reporter, "unless Hubert urinated on a portrait of Lyndon Johnson in Times Square before television—and then they'd say to him, why didn't you do it before."[98] As his running mate, the Happy Warrior chose the environmentalist and moderately liberal Senator Edmund Muskie of Maine.

On the floor of the convention, black delegates from the Northeast sneered at white southerners, calling them racists, while antiwar delegates and administration supporters traded insults. Mayor Daley's beefy security men were everywhere. As the nation watched, CBS reporter Dan Rather was knocked to the floor while covering the ejection of a regular Georgia delegate. Watching from his anchor booth, Walter Cronkite was incensed. "I think we've got a bunch of thugs down there," he said, his voice quivering.[99]

Unbeknownst to the media, the delegates, and the American public, the chief challenger to Hubert Humphrey's nomination at Chicago was Lyndon Johnson. In June, presidential aide Tom Johnson had reported to LBJ on a conversation he had had with Richard Moose, a former member of the National Security Council staff: "Dick said he is of the opinion that the President should be prepared to accept the nomination of the Democratic Party. He said he had talked with many young people . . . who are convinced that the President is the only man who can keep the country on the move after January. He doesn't think Humphrey can beat Nixon, and unless the President runs, Nixon will be President."[100] LBJ was hearing the same thing from other contacts.

From the outset, Johnson labored to ensure that nothing transpired at the 1968 Democratic National Convention in Chicago without his knowledge or approval. His chief lieutenant in this effort was John Criswell, the treasurer of the Democratic National Committee and chairman of the convention. Criswell, a longtime friend of the Johnsons, headed a team that included Marvin Watson, presidential aides Jim Jones and Larry Temple, and Arthur Krim, another LBJ friend and financial supporter, among others.[101] According to a plan developed by the Criswell team, Daley, in behalf of the Arrangements Committee, would issue a secret, open-ended invitation to the President to attend. No mention would be made in the program of LBJ's visit. Johnson had expressed concern about being caught up in and embarrassed by antiwar demonstrations that were sure to occur. This would not be a problem, Criswell reported to the White House. "On Tuesday morning—we could make firm recommendations and we would not even need to know the decision until take-off from the Ranch. We would be flexible enough with the program so that it could be broken at whatever point for the President."[102] Ideally, LBJ would fly to Chicago and address the convention after the showing of a film tribute to the Great Society narrated by Gregory Peck. He would then attend a gala birthday celebration, replete with fireworks, on Michigan Avenue.

Shortly after he arrived in Chicago to attend the convention, Humphrey had learned that Johnson was exploring the possibility of a draft. Working through Jones, the president had John Connally survey southern governors to see how an LBJ candidacy would go down with them.[103] He also instructed Arthur Krim to have a quick poll run to see how he would stack up against Nixon. On Sunday, LBJ's lieutenants relayed bad news: "Nixon 42; LBJ 34; Wallace, 17; undecided 7." Connally reported that he had found absolutely no support in the South at this stage for an LBJ candidacy. Finally, according to Krim, Daley was balking: "He said, 'the President has got to announce or do something to show that he wants it. Otherwise there's nothing I can do.'" At this point, Johnson told all concerned to go full bore for Humphrey.[104]

As the Democratic delegates jousted in Chicago's cavernous amphitheater, a wrenching spectacle was unfolding on the streets outside. An army of antiwar protestors, anti-establishment crusaders, and counterculture figures had descended on the city. Tom Hayden told reporters, "We are coming to Chicago to vomit on the 'politics of joy,'" a reference to Humphrey's campaign slogan. "We are coming . . . to expose the secret decisions, upset the night club orgies, and face the Democratic Party with its illegitimacy and criminality."[105] The nihilistic Yippies spread rumors that they were going to put LSD in Chicago's water supply and use female members to seduce Humphrey delegates.

Mayor Daley ordered an army of twelve thousand police officers to cordon off and control the demonstrators. He persuaded the governor to station some six thousand Illinois National Guard members armed with rifles, flame throwers, grenade launchers, and bazookas outside the city as backup.

He also ordered his plainclothes police to infiltrate protest organizations and prevailed on the federal government to dispatch a thousand agents to Chicago. For every six demonstrators active during the convention, there was one undercover agent. The *Chicago Tribune* published a series of revelations concerning "plans by Communists and left-wing agitators to disrupt the city." When some of the Yippies and SDS members began hurling bags of urine and screaming obscenities, the police went berserk. For three days, a national television audience watched as Daley's men beat not only the demonstrators but some innocent bystanders as well. As journalist Nicholas von Hoffman noted, the police had "taken off their badges, their name plates, even the unit patches on their shoulders to become a mob of identical, unidentifiable club swingers."[106]

Meanwhile, the Republicans had gathered in Miami Beach in early August and nominated Nixon on the first ballot. To be his running mate, he selected Spiro T. Agnew, the Maryland governor who had attracted national attention by his explicit, public denunciation of urban rioting in which he declared all involved to be criminals who should be incarcerated. In his acceptance speech, Nixon proclaimed that a "new voice" was being heard across America, not "the voices of hatred, the voices of dissension, the voices of riot and revolution."[107] He represented, he said, those who did not break the law, "people who pay their taxes and go to work, people who send their children to school, who go to their churches, people who are not haters, people who love this country."[108] The party platform was no surprise. It called for a national war against crime, reform of the welfare system to encourage a maximum number of poor to work, and a stronger national defense. The GOP program did not, however, call for abolition of Medicare, an end to federal aid to education, or repeal of the various civil rights acts. Although Republicans called for less government regulation of the private sector, they did not denounce the clean air, clean water, wilderness, or consumer protection acts. There was no call to restore national origin quotas to American immigration policy. On Vietnam, the platform promised simultaneously to "de-Americanize the war" and not to accept a "camouflaged surrender."

Nixon's advisers were perhaps more concerned about the candidacy of George Wallace than that of Hubert Humphrey. Following a brief run at the Democratic nomination, Wallace had founded the American Independent

Party. Appealing to the worst in the American people, he blamed urban rioting on black power advocates and their "socialist" white allies. He none too subtly hinted that integration ought to remain a personal choice. He blamed the federal government and especially the Supreme Court for encouraging racial unrest and for coddling criminals and tolerating welfare cheats. His campaign would not be limited to the South, he assured his supporters: "the people of Cleveland and Chicago and Gary and St. Louis will be so goddamned sick and tired of Federal interference in their local schools, they'll be ready to vote for Wallace." To the delight of large, raucous crowds, he blamed the nation's problems on "briefcase totin' bureaucrats, ivory-tower guideline writers . . . and pointy-headed professors" who did not know how to "park a bicycle straight."[109] Selecting retired Air Force General Curtis E. LeMay, the former commander of America's nuclear strike force, to be his running mate, the Alabama governor promised total victory in Vietnam.

Wallace's candidacy constituted the cutting edge of the law-and-order movement. He embodied the hopes and fears of whites on the lower rungs of the middle class, a former core constituency for Democrats. His coalition comprised Goldwater voters in the South and union members in the North. The southern bloc was made up of rural white Protestants. The northern wing consisted of urban ethnic Catholics. Almost three-quarters of Wallace supporters wanted to halt the civil rights movement, and almost 70 percent expressed anxiety about urban riots and street crime. To those whites most proximate to urban lawlessness, the Alabama governor offered a more aggressive form of law and order than Nixon—rollback versus containment, in the words of one historian. Wallace countenanced the calculated use of massive force against rioters and protesters. If as president he were confronted by a riot, he would, he vowed, halt it by shooting arsonists and looters first, and asking questions later. There was also the usual rhetoric about permissiveness, welfare dependency, and rewarding the rioters.[110] Ridiculed by black revolutionaries and white liberals alike, Wallace had turned on the establishment with a vengeance. Indeed, for him and his followers, the establishment was the liberal establishment. Wallace affirmed his supporters' belief in the existence of a conspiracy by the media, the federal government, blacks, and communists to take what was theirs, especially their sense of worth and patriotism. Political prognosticators watched in amazement as the Alabama governor's ratings in the polls climbed from 9 percent in May 1968 to 16 percent in June and, in September, just after the Democratic Convention, to 21 percent.

In the ensuing campaign, Nixon managed to seize the political middle, with Wallace on his right and antiwar liberals on his left, while subtly appealing to the same fears that Wallace was exploiting. The "new Nixon" appeared relaxed and self-confident, posing successfully as a harmonizer, an antidote to the angry and divided Democrats, and a conservative alternative to the race-baiting Wallace.

Nevertheless, Humphrey was a skilled, experienced campaigner. On September 30, the "Happy Warrior" established some distance between himself and President Johnson. "I would stop the bombing of North Vietnam as an acceptable risk for peace," he told a Salt Lake City audience, "because I believe it could lead to success in the negotiations and thereby shorten the war."[111]

Johnson was furious. Orville Freeman saw the president shortly after Humphrey's Vietnam speech. "He called him a coward. He charged him with having been with this Administration, this was his family . . . and now he's trying to back off from his own family." LBJ insisted that the vice president was undermining his last-ditch effort to arrange a truce in Vietnam, to wit, bloody North Vietnam once again and then summon them to the negotiating table. But then at the close of his tirade, he told Freeman, "'Now don't tell Humphrey anything about this. After all he's the candidate, its hard going, I know he's discouraged . . . let's see if we can't help him."[112]

As October progressed, some of Wallace's labor supporters began to return to the Democratic fold, as did antiwar liberals who were more afraid of Nixon and "the bombsy twins," as Humphrey dubbed Wallace and LeMay, than they were repelled by the Johnson foreign policy. When on November 1 Johnson announced a total halt in the bombing of North Vietnam, Humphrey drew virtually abreast of Nixon in the polls. Going on the attack, the Democratic nominee challenged his opponent to a debate. When the Republicans refused, Humphrey dubbed Nixon "Richard the Chickenhearted." A week before the election, McCarthy endorsed his party's selection: "I'm voting for Humphrey, and I think you should suffer with me," he told the American people.[113]

When the final tallies were counted on election Tuesday, however, Richard Nixon had won a narrow victory. The Republican ticket polled 31.7

million votes, 43.4 percent of the total, while Humphrey and Muskie rolled up 31.2 million, and 41.7 percent of the whole. Wallace trailed far behind with 9.9 million, which amounted to 13.5 percent of the electorate. The Independent Party candidate carried 5 states (all southern), while Humphrey ran ahead in 13 and Nixon carried 32. In a sense, the election was close, but in another sense it amounted, as journalist Theodore White observed, to a "negative landslide" of gigantic proportions.

Since 1965 the Democrats had squandered a plurality of more than sixteen million votes. The solid consensus that Johnson had stitched together had been ripped apart by Vietnam, inflation, urban rioting, and the white backlash. The Democrats experienced defections from nearly every component of the New Deal coalition—labor, the South, urban ethnics, liberal intellectuals, and farmers. Humphrey won a mere 38 percent of the white vote; only massive majorities among blacks and Jews kept him in contention. Even the reliable black vote had fallen 11 percent from 1964. "What a year," declared *Time* in one of its patented essays, "one tragic, surprising and perplexing thing after another."[114]

CONCLUSION

FOR THE PAST FIFTY YEARS, CONSERVATIVES FROM RICHARD NIXON TO Ronald Reagan to William F. Buckley have derided the "failed" welfare policies and social experiments of the 1960s. When pressed to cite specific examples of those failures, they point to the Community Action Program, burgeoning welfare rolls, excessive government regulation, and a massive growth in the size of the federal bureaucracy. A few have attacked Medicare, but not those with aging parents or college-age children. Neither Pat Buchanan nor Newt Gingrich seriously advocated (at least publicly) ending medical insurance for the aged and disabled, federal aid to education, voting rights for blacks, public television, Head Start, or the Great Society amendments to Social Security. Those on the right railed at the excesses of the National Endowment for the Arts and whittled away at the power of various regulatory agencies, but the substance of their conservatism has had more to do with social issues—prayer in the schools, flag burning, abortion, gay marriage—than with the reforms and initiatives of the Great Society. On one issue, critics of the Johnson reforms have been correct: the reforms constituted a massive expansion of the federal power, unprecedented encroachment on the private sphere, and extensive interference with state and local government.

In general, however, conservatives have misrepresented the phenomenon. The reforms of the 1960s did not represent "creeping socialism." There was no assault on capitalism, and America certainly did not undergo a transformation to a European-style welfare state. Like Populism, Progressivism, and the New Deal, the Great Society was an effort to update and preserve liberal capitalism. "I remember being given the unwelcome task of combing the 'Economic Report of the President' to make sure that the words 'Great Society' never appeared in the same sentence with the words 'welfare' or 'income transfer payment,'" recalled Lester Thurow, a Council of Economic Advisers (CEA) staffer in 1964 and 1965. "President Johnson insisted that the Great Society had nothing to do with welfare programs. It was an education and training program designed to equip everyone to earn a decent living on their own in the private economy."[1] Or making "tax payers out of tax eaters," as LBJ famously told Richard Russell. And, in truth, the Great Society accelerated the trend from welfare to workfare. All of the War on Poverty and public assistance plans—most notably Aid to Families with Dependent Children—privileged work in the marketplace, not only for males but single mothers as well. The National Welfare Rights Organization, which had as its mission expanding rather than contracting welfare rolls, was a glaring unintended consequence.

In terms of its stated objectives, the Great Society was an unquestioned success. Between 1963 and 1969, when Lyndon Johnson left office, the portion of Americans living below the poverty line dropped from 22.2 percent to 12.6 percent. The Elementary and Secondary Education Act established a lasting mandate for the federal government to extend aid to America's public schools, in the process, not coincidentally, creating an instrument to eliminate segregation and discrimination in public education. Costly though it has proven to be, Medicare since 1969 has provided health care to seventy-nine million Americans who would otherwise not have received it, and in the process desegregated southern health facilities. The immigration bill, coupled with affirmative action, reversed the discriminatory trend that began in the 1920s and had the effect of making America as diverse at the beginning of the twenty-first century as it had been at the outset of the twentieth. And what would have become of the nation, particularly the American South, without the civil rights acts of the 1960s? Failure to provide African Americans with full citizenship and some degree of opportunity would have led to a national crisis that might have made Vietnam and Watergate pale by comparison.

The Great Society was but another chapter in the story of reform in twentieth-century America. The liberal philosophies and policies of the 1960s were rooted in Populism, Progressivism, and the New Deal. Johnson readily admitted that his father had been a Populist, and as a congressman representing the Tenth Congressional District in Texas, he had championed public power and farm aid during the 1930s and 1940s. The Great Society's determination to use the federal power to right social and economic wrongs echoed the People's Party platform of 1892, which called on Congress, the executive, and the federal judiciary to act in both the public and private spheres to promote social and economic justice.

Johnson agreed with advanced Progressives like Theodore Roosevelt that in a modern, industrial democracy it was necessary to use Hamiltonian means to achieve Jeffersonian ends—that is, to use the national power to protect and empower the individual. The rights of the common man and woman, both positive and negative, could only be secured through an activist federal government. Echoing Progressivism, the Great Society was very much about individual regeneration through job training, health care, and general education—all of which were supposed to enable Americans to better compete in the existing system; it never envisioned a major overhaul of that system. The Great Society was one with the Progressive movement in its belief that society could be reengineered by impartial experts acting on scientific principles. In the 1950s, with the renaissance of the social sciences, the secular forces driving social justice became a phenomenon to be reckoned with and remained so throughout the 1960s. In a very real sense, the technocrats and social engineers that emerged from the nation's universities in the post–World War II period and that populated Lyndon Johnson's task forces were descendants of Jane Addams and the settlement house movement.

Progressivism drew strength from a powerful current of environmentalist thought flowing through turn-of-the-century America. LBJ was certainly an environmentalist in both the natural and social senses. The Clean Air, Clean Water, and Wilderness Acts aimed at conserving natural resources and preserving areas of natural beauty. The Economic Opportunity Act of 1964, the Job Corps, Model Cities, HUD, Area Redevelopment, ESEA, and Medicare were part of the same cloth with antipollution and wilderness preservation laws. They were all environmental measures, some focused on poverty and crime, some on education both for the underclass and the middle class, some on public health, and some on nature refuges for members of the Greatest Generation and their children.

The architects of the Great Society faced a dilemma common to utopian reformers. Excessive social engineering threatened, ironically, to extinguish the individual, bringing forth a reform regime that was dangerously totalitarian in nature. In its concern for the poor and disadvantaged, the architects of the Great Society were forced to consider restructuring the black family, but they were daunted. Historian James McGregor Burns speculated on the limits of liberalism in its effort to bring social and economic justice to America's ghetto dwellers. "Poverty is many things," he observed:

> Poverty is not just lack of money . . . not just lack of food, housing, clothing, crucial though those elements are, but a poverty of knowledge, aspiration, of self-esteem, of motivation. And by adopting these multiple approaches . . . the Johnson administration, I think, took what had to be the correct approach. . . . But there was an Achilles heel. . . . The problem was that not only were there multiple causes of poverty, but these causes were self-reinforcing and other-reinforcing . . . to deal with it—a structure of poverty, the pathology of poverty—called for not only an amazingly comprehensive set of programs . . . because you were working on one individual, one three-year-old black child somewhere and he is not separate things—health and knowledge and motivation—he is a bundle of these things and he is a bundle of possibilities and he is a bundle of frustrated possibilities . . . because this effort, if you really took seriously this concept, would mean such early intervention and such comprehensive intervention . . . as to call for the kind of . . . government in this country that we have never seen.[2]

Historians and political scientists have most often linked the Great Society to the New Deal; there is no doubt that LBJ was committed to expanding the Rooseveltian reform structure, a phenomenon that he saw as organic rather than static. As he remarked in a March 1937 radio address: "If the administration program [the New Deal] were a temporary thing the situation would be different. But it is not for a day or for a year, but for an age. It must be worked out through time, and long after Roosevelt leaves the White House, it will still be developing, expanding. . . . The man who goes to Congress this year, or next year, must be prepared to meet this condition. He must be capable of growing and progressing with it."[3] In truth, the Great Society marked the culmination of the effort by liberals to use the concept of positive rights (the right to a decent education, a good job, adequate health care) as opposed to negative rights (freedom of religion, freedom of speech, the right to vote) to achieve social and economic justice.

But, ardent New Dealer though Johnson may have been, he realized that the 1960s were dramatically different from the 1930s. If the New Deal was about security and disengagement from the labor force through such devices as retirement pensions, unemployment compensation, and pensions for the worthy poor, the Great Society, in contrast, was about opportunity and labor force participation. The New Deal supported hard-pressed Americans at a time of economic catastrophe; the Great Society invested in people at the margins of the labor force at a time of economic opportunity. The New Deal was pessimistic, the Great Society optimistic.[4] FDR wanted in the end to create a larger pie, but above all he wanted to ensure that the pieces of whatever pie that existed were more equitably distributed. Assured of an ever-growing pastry by postwar prosperity in general and by the Kennedy tax cut specifically, Johnson was more about political and educational empowerment of the poor and disadvantaged so that they could better compete. He did not on the whole support government-driven redistribution of wealth. He exhibited strong opposition to both guaranteed income measures and public works, favoring instead programs of social rehabilitation and affirmative action.

An "us against them" motif ran through each of the three great reform movements that preceded the Great Society. The Populists railed against bankers, middle men, and railroad magnates. The Progressives decried the threat posed to middle-class society by robber baron capitalists and ignorant, rootless immigrants. In his 1936 acceptance speech, FDR denounced "economic royalists" who were laboring to replace American democracy with an American plutocracy. Lyndon Johnson was determined to rule through consensus, to avoid pitting one group against another. Not only was this a personal inclination, but the stratagems developed for dealing with the civil rights crisis seemed to demand it, and the prevailing prosperity promised to permit it. LBJ made the enemy—the "them"—abstract. Poverty, ignorance, ill health were not the fault of a class or group—they were boils on the body politic. These things were not the result of evil intent or greed on the part of groups or individuals, but seemingly free radicals that everyone hoped to see eliminated from the environment.

The Great Society's most glaring departure from Populism, Progressivism, and New Deal liberalism was its frontal assault on Jim Crow laws in the South. Despite their idealism, the reformers that preceded Johnson proved unwilling or unable to confront the issue of full citizenship and equality of opportunity for African Americans. In many respects, the interests of black Americans had been sacrificed in the drive by Populists, Progressives, and New Dealers to secure economic and social justice for male-dominated, white, working-class families. Even before he became president, LBJ decided that civil rights for black Americans was an issue that could not wait. If the United States was to retain its fundamental characteristics—individual freedom and democracy coupled with equality under the law and equal opportunity—the nation would have to turn its back on racism in both the public and private spheres. The Great Society would do what previous reform regimes had not dared attempt and in so doing move the nation forward in its ongoing effort to resolve the greatest American dilemma of them all.

The Great Society's efforts to defeat Jim Crow in the South were largely successful. In uneasy partnership with Martin Luther King, Johnson exploited the SCLC and SNCC protests and demonstrations and the violent opposition they elicited to pass the Civil Rights Acts of 1964 and 1965. The Elementary and Secondary Education Act and Medicare were converted into antidiscrimination weapons, and new HEW guidelines began to make school integration a reality. As of 1980, only 7 percent fewer blacks proportionately than whites were on the nation's voting rolls.

Neither Lyndon Johnson nor Martin Luther King, both southerners, were prepared for the northern, urban phase of the Second Reconstruction, however. Its goals were different, its participants were different, and its dynamic was different. From Chicago to New York to Detroit, few activists saw the battle to end segregation as an end in itself but rather as part of a larger struggle to eliminate discrimination in the workplace, to open housing markets, to provide quality education, to promote the economic development of impoverished communities, and to ensure full access to consumer marketplaces. Beginning in 1963, observers noted a shift away from the conciliatory rhetoric of Roy Wilkins and toward the apocalyptic visions of James Baldwin. Unlike the SCLC's campaign against Jim Crow in the South, the civil rights movement in the North would place less emphasis on racial reconciliation and more on rights—through coercion, harassment, intimidation of the white and black power structures if necessary. The Johnson administration wielded the War on Poverty, Model Cities, HUD, the Fair Housing Act, and other programs to battle inner-city blight and urban unrest, but unemployment, inferior services, high crime rates, broken homes, and black frustration persisted. The riots of the 1960s subsided, but their root causes remained, as recent outbursts in St. Louis, Baltimore, and Charleston have demonstrated.

Fundamental to Johnson's political philosophy was the belief that individual citizens, even the humblest, were able to perceive and act in their own self-interest. Enfranchisement and opportunity were the keys to stability and progress. But he and his advisers recognized that despite the promises of the Declaration of Independence and the Constitution, citizenship had been granted in degrees to some and denied completely to others. Discrimination against African Americans was most obvious, but women, Native Americans, and certain classes of immigrants had been denied the full fruits of citizenship as well. The Social Security Act and Fair Labor Standards Act embodied the notion of "positive rights," but privileged working white males. The minimum wage excluded jobs overwhelmingly held by women and nonwhites. And though old-age and unemployment assistance were not means tested, Aid to Families with Dependent Children (AFDC) was. So, there was still much to do when LBJ took office.

What the Great Society was about was expanding the definition of citizenship and extending full citizenship to as many individuals as possible. Expanded Social Security, the Elementary and Secondary Education Act, the War on Poverty, Model Cities, clean air and clean water legislation, and Medicare/Medicaid were collectively an effort to realize the positive rights that FDR had articulated during the New Deal—the right to adequate health care, to a basic education, to a decent-paying job, to a secure old age, to a safe environment. But also at the heart of these initiatives as well as of the Civil Rights Acts of 1964, 1965, and 1968 was a strong equity rationale; the federal government was promising first to expand the benefits of citizenship and then to extend them to those previously excluded.

Johnson's fervent belief that individuals, left to their own devices, would always act politically in their own interests and those of society as a whole seems to have been mistaken. The achievements of the Great Society, with a few notable exceptions, were not the result of a popular, grassroots movement. In general, except for the Civil Rights Act of 1964, a suprapartisan, centrist consensus favoring liberal programs for the poor, powerless, neglected segments of the American population did not seem to exist. In a May 12, 1965, poll, a plurality of nonsouthern whites claimed that LBJ was "pushing integration too fast," while only 8 percent said that his backing was not strong enough. Only 35 percent of poll respondents supported the enactment of a fair housing law. By contrast, two of the Big Four domestic policy goals of the Great Society, the income tax cut and Medicare, enjoyed consistent, widespread public support in the opinion surveys. Opposition to tax increases remained strong even if for the purposes of reducing inflation and avoiding a budget deficit.[5]

The Great Society was not a purely domestic phenomenon. The "other war" in Vietnam, focusing as it did on counterinsurgency and pacification, drew heavily on the philosophies and programs of the Great Society, especially the War on Poverty. America's experiment in nation building was far less successful in the international than the domestic sphere, however. By the end of 1970, more than a thousand civilians and five thousand American military personnel were spread across the villages and hamlets of South Vietnam building schools and infirmaries, introducing new crops such as miracle rice, constructing power grids, opening roads, and organizing local communities to battle communist terrorism. By the close of the Johnson administration, the percentage of the population controlled by the Vietcong nationwide had dropped to 13.3 percent. In the end, it did not matter; the government in Saigon remained as corrupt and distrustful of the peasantry as ever. Unless the rice-roots revolution manifested itself at the national political level in South Vietnam, lasting reform would be impossible. And the United States proved unwilling to overthrow an avowedly anticommunist regime no matter how rotten.

Whereas World War II vastly strengthened Roosevelt's moral authority, Vietnam greatly weakened Johnson's. Moreover, the war in Southeast Asia along with urban rioting helped undermine the consensus that LBJ had conjured up in behalf of the Great Society. The moral imperative that Lyndon Johnson, Martin Luther King, and others had invoked to persuade white, middle-class America to support the drive for racial equality had reinforced and been reinforced by the liberal internationalist notion that the United States had an obligation to help the nonwhite peoples of the Third World resist communist domination. Johnson's talk of internationalizing the Great Society and of transforming the Mekong Delta into another Tennessee Valley Authority had woven the connecting fabric tighter and tighter. But as the black power advocates co-opted the civil rights movement and intimidated white liberals, and as a new wave of urban rioting swept the nation's cities, a white backlash erupted that threatened not only the Great Society—especially the Second Reconstruction—but the war in Vietnam as well. Liberals who surrendered to the New Left and who joined with Tom Hayden and Stokely Carmichael in indicting American institutions and political processes played their part in eroding the Vietnam consensus, but it was the growing doubts among the average American that the Judeo-Christian ethic could or should be applied to social problems at home and abroad that did the real damage.

The initiatives of the Johnson years would have profound consequences for American politics. As part of the Mississippi Freedom Democratic Party dustup at the Democratic National Convention in 1964, the president had backed a fundamental reform of convention rules that would change the face of the party. Previously, state parties possessed sole authority to establish delegate selection procedures. The result had been completely white, mostly male, generally over-forty delegations, particularly from the South. Henceforth, the DNC and other national party bureaucracies would decide not only how many votes each state delegation could cast at the national convention but also enforce uniform rules on what kinds of persons could be selected. Beginning in 1972, Democratic conventions became younger and more diverse. At the same time, however, the Great Society's civil rights initiatives together with major demographic changes ensured that the South would become a stronghold of the Republican Party. The post–Great Society white majorities that ruled Dixie accepted the black vote but gerrymandered state and federal congressional districts to ensure their continued dominance.

The reforms of the 1960s unquestionably advanced the cause of social and economic justice in America, but many achievements were limited and ambiguous. The Great Society marked the beginning and not the end of the ongoing debate over the appropriate goals and techniques of federally subsidized education. What it did do was to make education a national priority alongside defense and economic growth. The Higher Education Act helped make US colleges and universities the envy of the world, but colleges and universities remained inaccessible to many poor and minority Americans. Medicare and Medicaid made subsidized health care available to the poor and elderly for the first time in American history, but these programs fell far short of establishing a system of national health insurance. Nevertheless, Medicare lifted a huge economic burden from the backs of middle-class families. Affirmative action coupled with Title VII of the 1964 Civil Rights Act, and measures designed to protect and empower individuals in their workplace, led to a rights revolution that would make state and federal courts the primary cockpits of grievance resolution. Reformers of the 1960s did not, however, resolve the ongoing debate as to whether social and economic justice were best realized through a guarantee of equal rights and equal opportunity or through special treatment. Perhaps most significant, the War on Poverty, especially its Community Action Program, left in its wake more than a thousand local nonprofit agencies that would apply for and receive hundreds of millions of dollars in grants from federal and state governments and private foundations that would do much to improve the quality of life for the poor and disadvantaged.

The Immigration Act Amendments of 1965 abolished the national origins system, the nativist cornerstone of US immigration policy since the 1920s. Henceforward, admission would be based on preferences and quotas having nothing to do with country of birth. As it was designed to do, the Immigration Act ensured that America remained a melting pot, a nation of diversity in which citizenship was defined by a set of political principles rather than by blood and soil. The 1965 act did not address the problem of illegal immigrants—the right of the undocumented to enter the country and their treatment when and if they did.

By 1967 the Great Society was under siege. Urban rioting and the white backlash that ensued created an opening for conservatives to equate civil disobedience with arson and looting. They declared that the War on Poverty was responsible for urban unrest in that it encouraged a sense of entitlement and undermined individual responsibility. The War on Crime, then, was in no small part a war on the Great Society. At the same time, Dixiecrats and professional anticommunists—who had long sought to equate liberalism with socialism and socialism with communism—depicted urban unrest as part of an international communist conspiracy. Meanwhile, prominent liberals, spooked by the black power movement, seduced by the New Left, or lured by the opportunity for political gain, denounced the Great Society for not doing enough to empower the poor, feed the hungry, rebuild America's inner cities, and combat institutional racism. Of course, what delivered the coup de grace to the Johnsonian consensus were classical economics and the American public's aversion to higher taxes. When LBJ was forced to ask Congress for a 10 percent surcharge on corporate and individual income taxes to pay for his domestic reform programs and the war in Vietnam, Congress, corporate America, and the white middle class lost whatever appetite they had had for reform.

Perhaps the darkest legacy of Lyndon Johnson and the Great Society—aside from urban rioting—was a string of civil liberties violations. Determined to secure election in his own right in 1964 and then to preserve the consensus that underpinned both the Great Society and the war in Vietnam, LBJ authorized widespread and illegal programs of domestic intelligence gathering. He ordered J. Edgar Hoover and the FBI to spy on both the Mississippi Freedom Democratic Party (MFDP) and the Kennedys at the Atlantic City Convention. In 1967, he directed the CIA to put leaders of various antiwar groups under surveillance and to exert every effort to gather evidence that they were communist controlled. That initiative would morph into the infamous Operation CHAOS. Finally, in an effort to thwart further urban unrest, Johnson had the FBI put together an interagency Ghetto Informant Program that penetrated and spied on virtually every civil rights and black power organization.

The fires of the 1960s may have burned the liberals' house to the ground, but when the smoke had cleared, its foundation—the Great Society—remained and remains intact.

ACKNOWLEDGMENTS

I HAVE BEEN CONSIDERING THIS PROJECT OFF AND ON FOR THE PAST twenty years. I have had conversations and consultations with colleagues too numerous to mention. Especially important, however, has been the staff of the LBJ Library, including Claudia Anderson, Barbara Cline, Shannon Jarett, John Wilson, and Allen Fisher. A special thanks to Mark Updegrove, library director and Johnson scholar, and to Larry Temple, a leading member of the Johnson official family and power behind the LBJ Foundation.

As usual, my in-house editor, Rhoda Woods, proved invaluable. John Milton Cooper, Mitch Lerner, Patrick Williams, Michael Pierce, and Jeff Woods read the book in manuscript and were gratifyingly honest and insightful in the comments. I spent the fall of 2013 as a visiting fellow at the Rothermere American Institute at Oxford University, where I passed many a valuable hour discussing LBJ and his legacy with Nigel Bowles, Gareth Davies, Jay Sexton, and Ursula Hackett. Thanks also to the Cambridge University American history duo of Tony Badger and Andrew Preston for organizing a very enlightening conference on The Age of Lyndon Johnson.

My agent, Geri Thoma, provided wise counsel throughout. An author could not ask for a better publishing team than that put together and supervised by Lara Heimert at Basic Books. It is rare in today's world when a publisher contributes intellectually and editorially to a project, but Lara did that in spades. Special thanks to Roger Labrie, the text editor, and to Melissa Veronesi, Leah Stecher, and Christina Yeager. Melinda Marie Adams was my media/technical guru.

NOTES

ABBREVIATIONS

FRUS	*Foreign Relations of the United States*
JFKL	John F. Kennedy Library
LBJL	Lyndon B. Johnson Library
NSF	National Security Files
OF	Office Files
OH	Oral History
PP	Personal Papers
SOF	Senate Office Files
TCC	Transcripts of Telephone Conversations
VP	Vice Presidential
WH	White House
WHCF	White House Central File

INTRODUCTION: THE PARADOX OF REFORM

1. "Remarks in Cadillac Square, Detroit," September 7, 1964, in *Public Papers of the Presidents: LBJ, 1963–1964,* vol. II (Washington, DC, 1965), 1051–1052.

2. Sidney Milkis, "Franklin D. Roosevelt, the Economic Constitutional Order, and the New Politics of Presidential Leadership," in *The New Deal and the Triumph of Liberalism,* ed. Sidney M. Milkis and Jerome M. Mileur (Amherst, MA, 2002), 32.

3. Quoted in Richard J. Ellis, *American Political Cultures* (New York, 1993), 24.

4. "Remarks at a Reception for Members of the American Society of Newspaper Editors," April 17, 1964, in *Public Papers: LBJ, 1963–1964,* vol. I, 485.

5. Sidney M. Milkis, "Lyndon Johnson, the Great Society, and the Modern Presidency," in *The Great Society and the High Tide of Liberalism,* ed. Sidney M. Milkis and Jerome M. Mileur (Amherst, MA, 2005), 5.

6. Thomas F. Jackson, *From Civil Rights to Human Rights: Martin Luther King, Jr., and the Struggle for Economic Justice* (Philadelphia, 2007), 137.

7. Ibid., 68–69.

8. See Jeff Woods, *Black Struggle, Red Scare: Segregation and Anti-Communism in the South, 1948–1968* (Baton Rouge, 2003).

CHAPTER 1: "I AM A ROOSEVELT NEW DEALER": LIBERALISM ASCENDANT

1. Randall Bennett Woods, *Quest for Identity: America Since 1945* (New York, 2005), 185.

2. See Wayne Fields, *Union of Words: A History of Presidential Eloquence* (New York, 1996), 215–216.

3. Text of President's Off-the-Record Remarks to Governors, November 11, 1963, Diary Backup, Box 1, LBJL.

4. Robert Dallek, *Flawed Giant: Lyndon B. Johnson and His Times, 1961–1973* (New York, 1998), 67; see Eric F. Goldman, *The Tragedy of Lyndon Johnson* (New York, 1969).

5. LBJ and George Reedy Conversation, January 25, 1964, TCC, Box 1, LBJL.

6. Goldman, *Tragedy of Lyndon Johnson,* 124–125.

7. Ibid., 106–107.

8. Ibid., 107.

9. Ibid., 115–117; James Jones interview with author.

10. Goldman, *Tragedy of Lyndon Johnson,* 109.

11. See ibid., 108–111.

12. Harry McPherson OH, VI, May 16, 1985, LBJL; James Rowe OH, II, September 16, 1969, LBJL.

13. See Clark Clifford OH, II, July 2, 1969, LBJL.

14. Laura Kalman, *Abe Fortas: A Biography* (New Haven, 1990), 28–29.

15. Ibid., 3, 15–16.

16. Diary Backup, November 23, 1963, Johnson Papers, LBJL.

17. Abe Fortas, "Portrait of a Friend," in *The Johnson Presidency: Twenty Intimate Perspectives of Lyndon B. Johnson,* ed. Kenneth W. Thompson, vol. 5, *Portraits of American Presidents* (Lanham, MD, 1986), 7.

18. Jack Valenti OH, October 18, 1969, LBJL.

19. Merle Miller, *Lyndon: An Oral Autobiography* (New York, 1980), 338.

20. Ibid., 338–339.

21. "Address Before a Joint Session of the Congress," November 27, 1963, in *Public Papers of the Presidents: LBJ, 1963–1964,* vol. I (Washington, DC, 1965), 8–10; Miller, *Lyndon,* 338–339.

22. "Address Before a Joint Session of the Congress," 9.

23. "Remarks at the State Capitol in Austin, Texas," November 2, 1964, in *Public Papers: LBJ, 1963–1964,* vol. I, 1579–1580.

24. "Remarks to Members of the Southern Baptist Leadership Seminar," March 15, 1964, in *Public Papers: LBJ, 1963–1964,* vol. I, 420.

25. Robert C. McMath, "The History of the Present," in *The Ongoing Burden of Southern History: Politics and Identity in the Twenty-First-Century South,* ed. Angie Maxwell, Todd Shields, and Jeannie Whayne (Baton Rouge, 2012), 90–91.

26. Sidney Milkis, "Roosevelt and the New Politics of Presidential Leadership," in *The New Deal and the Triumph of Liberalism,* ed. Sidney M. Milkis and Jerome M. Mileur (Amherst, MA, 2002), 37, 39.

27. Quoted in Milkis and Mileur, eds., *New Deal,* 3.

28. Milkis, "Roosevelt and the New Politics of Presidential Leadership," 40.

29. Ibid., 56–57.

30. Suzanne Mettler, "Social Citizens of Separate Sovereignties: Governance in the New Deal Welfare State," in *New Deal,* ed. Milkis and Mileur, 243, 246.

31. Ibid., 248.

32. Jytte Klausen, "Did World War II End the New Deal? A Comparative Perspective on Postwar Planning Initiatives," in *New Deal,* ed. Milkis and Mileur, 197. The per capita gross national product declined from $722 to $718 from 1930 to 1935. In 1940, it was $916, and in 1945, $1,293. Growth was also more evenly distributed during the war than before. The top 5 percent of the population saw their share of all income decrease from 30 percent in 1929 to 21.3 percent in 1946. Income distribution stabilized after the war, with the top 5 percent taking 20 percent of all incomes throughout the 1950s. War mobilization also allowed corporate profits to bounce back, but with matching increases in wages and farm incomes. Corporate net profits, after taxes, peaked at $12,181 million in 1942, three times what they had been in 1935. Average annual earnings per full-time employee in manufacturing rose from $1,432 in 1940 to $2,517 in 1945.

33. Ibid., 199. In 1930 the national public debt was $131 per capita. In 1940 it was still only $325, despite the New Deal's use of deficit spending as a remedial tool. The war changed that: in 1945 per capita national public debt was $1,848. The debt remained stable after the war, however, as the country simply outgrew it.

34. Michael McGerr, *A Fierce Discontent: The Rise and Fall of the Progressive Movement in America* (New York, 2003), 183.

35. Terry H. Anderson, *The Pursuit of Fairness: A History of Affirmative Action* (New York, 2004), 73.

36. Mel Stuart Interview with LBJ, April 27, 1968, Marilyn Conkle to Jim Jones, April 30, 1968, Diary Backup, Box 97, LBJL.

37. Seth Jacobs, "'Our System Demands the Supreme Being': The U.S. Religious Revival and the 'Diem Experiment,' 1954–55," *Diplomatic History* 25, no. 4 (Fall 2001): 600.

38. Woods, *Quest for Identity,* 141.

39. "Remarks to a Group of Civil Rights Leaders," April 29, 1964, in *Public Papers: LBJ, 1963–1964,* vol. I, 588–589.

40. "Remarks at the 12th Annual Presidential Prayer Breakfast," February 5, 1964, in *Public Papers: LBJ, 1963–1964,* vol. I, 172.

41. Sidney M. Milkis, "Lyndon Johnson, the Great Society, and the Modern Presidency," in *The Great Society and the High Tide of Liberalism,* ed. Sidney M. Milkis and Jerome M. Mileur (Amherst, MA, 2005), 2.

42. Robert C. McMath, "History of the Present," in *The Ongoing Burden of Southern History: Politics and Identity in the Twenty-First Century South,* ed. Angie Maxwell, Jeannie Whayne, and Todd Shields (Baton Rouge, 2012), 92.

43. Quoted in Sean J. Savage, *JFK, LBJ, and the Democratic Party* (Albany, 2004), 263.

44. Ibid., 262.

45. See Diaries of Orville Freeman, July 22, 1964, PP/Orville Freeman, #9, Diary vol. 4, LBJL.

46. Richard J. Ellis, *American Political Cultures* (New York, 1996), 74–76.

47. Bill Moyers, "Setting the Stage," in *The Johnson Years: The Difference He Made,* ed. Robert L. Hardesty (Austin, 1993), 65.

48. President and Isabelle Shelton Conversation, March 21, 1965, Telephone Transcripts, WH Tapes, LBJL.

49. Presidential Notes on Conversation with Roy Wilkins, November 4, 1965, 9105–07, TCC, Papers of LBJ, LBJL.

50. Mel Stuart Interview with LBJ, April 27, 1968, Marilyn Conkle to Jim Jones, April 30, 1968, Diary Backup, Box 97, LBJL.

51. Marc Landy, "Presidential Party Leadership and Party Realignment: FDR and the Making of the New Deal Democratic Party," in *New Deal,* ed. Milkis and Mileur, 73–75.

52. Busby to LBJ, June 1964, OF/H. Busby, Box 52, LBJL.

53. Savage, *JFK, LBJ, and the Democratic Party,* 118.

54. LBJ and Ford Conversation, January 22, 1965, Tape WG6501.03, Presidential Tape Recordings, LBJL.

55. Savage, *JFK, LBJ, and the Democratic Party,* 160.

56. Ibid., 158.

57. Doris Kearns Goodwin, *Lyndon Johnson and the American Dream* (New York, 1991), 226.

58. Dallek, *Flawed Giant,* 64.

59. Ibid., 65.

CHAPTER 2: FUNDING THE GREAT SOCIETY AND THE WAR ON POVERTY

1. Iwan Morgan, "Promoting Prosperity: JFK and the New Economics," unpublished paper delivered to British Library Conference, "John F. Kennedy's Presidential Heritage," November 4, 2013, 2.

2. Randall Bennett Woods, *A Changing of the Guard: Anglo-American Relations, 1941–1946* (Chapel Hill, 1990), 25–27.

3. Jytte Klausen, "Did World War II End the New Deal? A Comparative Perspective on Postwar Planning Initiatives," in *The New Deal and the Triumph of Liberalism,* ed. Sidney M. Milkis and Jerome M. Mileur (Amherst, MA, 2002), 199.

4. Iwan Morgan, "Promoting Prosperity," 3.

5. Ibid., 5.

6. Irving Bernstein, *Guns or Butter: The Presidency of Lyndon Johnson* (New York, 1996), 31.

7. Ibid.

8. Notes of Troika Meeting, Diary Backup, Box 1, Presidential Papers of LBJ, LBJL.

9. Diaries of Orville Freeman, January 1, 1964, PP/Orville Freeman, Box 9, LBJL.

10. John McCone Memos, Meetings with President, January 17, 1964, Box 1, LBJL.

11. LBJ and Robt. Anderson Conversation, January 7, 1964, TCC, LBJL.

12. Bernstein, *Guns or Butter*, 33.

13. Jack Valenti OH, October 18, 1969.

14. Robert Dallek, *Flawed Giant: Lyndon B. Johnson and His Times, 1961–1973* (New York, 1998), 73; LBJ and Byrd Conversation, January 8, 1964, TCC, LBJL.

15. LBJ and Richard Russell Conversation, WH Tapes, WH6401.15, LBJL.

16. Bernstein, *Guns or Butter*, 34.

17. LBJ and George Brown Conversation, January 8, 1964, TCC, LBJL.

18. Kim McQuaid, *Big Business and Presidential Power: From FDR to Reagan* (New York, 1982), 224.

19. Ibid., 226.

20. Diaries of Orville Freeman, December 10, 1963, PP/Orville Freeman, Box 9, LBJL.

21. "Johnson Impresses the Nation," May 1, 1964, LBJ Handwriting File, Box 3, LBJL.

22. McQuaid, *Big Business*, 227.

23. "Secrets of Success," *Dallas Morning News*, May 3, 1964.

24. Report to the President on the Economic Situation by the CEA, April 20, 1965, Cabinet Papers, Box 2, LBJL.

25. See Robert L. Heilbroner, "Capitalism Without Tears," *New York Review of Books*, June 29, 1967.

26. Charles M. Haar, "The Bold Dreamer," in *The Johnson Years: The Difference He Made*, ed. Robert L. Hardesty (Austin, 1993), 61.

27. Walter Lippmann, "The Principle of the Great Society," *Newsweek*, January 18, 1965.

28. LBJ and Lippmann Conversation, December 1, 1963, in Michael R. Beschloss, ed., *Taking Charge: The Johnson White House Tapes, 1963–1964* (New York, 1997), 80.

29. Bill Moyers, "Setting the Stage," in *Johnson Years*, ed. Hardesty, 66.

30. Eric F. Goldman, *Tragedy of Lyndon Johnson* (New York, 1969), 112.

31. Quoted in Dallek, *Flawed Giant*, 80–81.

32. Goldman, *Tragedy of Lyndon Johnson*, 6–7.

33. Jack Valenti OH, July 12, 1972, V, LBJL.

34. Sean J. Savage, *JFK, LBJ, and the Democratic Party* (Albany, 2004), 124.

35. Richard N. Goodwin, *Remembering America: A Voice from the Sixties* (New York, 1989), 272.

36. Jerome M. Mileur, "The Great Society and the Demise of the New Deal Liberalism," in *The Great Society and the High Tide of Liberalism*, ed. Sidney M. Milkis and Jerome M. Mileur (Amherst, MA, 2005), 427.

37. Sidney M. Milkis, "Lyndon Johnson, the Great Society, and the Modern Presidency," in *Great Society*, ed. Milkis and Mileur, 40.

38. Buzz to President, May 27, 1964, Box 107, Papers of LBJ, LBJL.

39. Memorandum for the President, May 18, 1964, WH Central Files, SP, LBJL.

40. "Remarks at the University of Michigan, May 22, 1964," in *Public Papers of the Presidents: LBJ, 1963–1964,* vol. I (Washington, DC, 1965), 704–706.

41. Dallek, *Flawed Giant,* 83.

42. Merle Miller, *Lyndon: An Oral Autobiography* (New York, 1980), 377.

43. UPI, April 2, 1965, OF/Bill Moyers, Box 7, LBJL.

44. LBJ and Sidey Conversation, June 11, 1964, in Beschloss, *Taking Charge,* 404.

45. Milkis, "Lyndon Johnson, the Great Society, and the Modern Presidency," 11.

46. Bernstein, *Guns or Butter,* 82–90; David Burner, *Making Peace with the 60s* (Princeton, 1996), 169–170; Douglas Cater, "The Politics of Poverty," *The Reporter,* February 13, 1964, 15–20.

47. Carl M. Brauer, "Kennedy, Johnson, and the War on Poverty," *Journal of American History* 69, no. 1 (June 1, 1982): 103.

48. Bernstein, *Guns or Butter,* 91–93.

49. Edward R. Schmitt, "The War on Poverty," in *A Companion to Lyndon B. Johnson,* ed. Mitchell B. Lerner (Malden, 2012), 94.

50. Michael W. Flamm, *Law and Order: Street Crime, Civil Unrest, and the Crisis of Liberalism in the 1960s* (New York, 2005), 24.

51. Ibid., 28.

52. Nick Kotz, *Judgment Days: Lyndon Baines Johnson, Martin Luther King Jr., and the Laws That Changed America* (Boston, 2005), 27.

53. R. Sargent Shriver Jr., "The War on Poverty," in *The Great Society: A Twenty Year Critique,* ed. Barbara Jordan and Elspeth Rostow (Austin, 1986), 40.

54. Miller, *Lyndon,* 362.

55. Ibid.

56. Terry H. Anderson, *The Pursuit of Fairness: A History of Affirmative Action* (New York, 2004), 105.

57. "Annual Message to the Congress on the State of the Union," January 8, 1964, in *Public Papers of the Presidents: LBJ, 1963–1964,* vol. I (Washington, DC, 1965), 91–92.

58. Burner, *Making Peace,* 166–70.

59. Brauer, "Kennedy, Johnson, and the War on Poverty," 101.

60. LBJ and J. K. Galbraith Conversation, January 29, 1964, TCC, LBJL.

61. Bernstein, *Guns or Butter,* 99.

62. Dallek, *Flawed Giant,* 76.

63. LBJ and Shriver Conversation, February 1, 1964, TCC, LBJL.

64. Dallek, *Flawed Giant,* 79.

65. LBJ and Carl Albert Conversation, May 26, 1964, in Beschloss, *Taking Charge,* 360.

66. "Remarks upon Signing the Economic Opportunity Act," August 20, 1964, in *Public Papers: LBJ, 1963–1964,* vol. II, 989.

67. Diary Backup, November 29, 1963, Box 1, LBJL; Moyers, "Setting the Stage," 36–37.

68. Bernstein, *Guns or Butter,* 104.

69. Goldman, *Tragedy of Lyndon Johnson,* 187.

70. LBJ and Shriver Conversation, March 26, 1964, TCC, Box 3, LBJL.

71. Wickenden to Walter Jenkins, May 4, 1964, OF/Bill Moyers, Box 39, LBJL.

72. Bernstein, *Guns or Butter,* 105.

73. LBJ and Daley Conversation, January 20, 1964, in Beschloss, *Taking Charge,* 168.

74. LBJ and Moyers, Conversation, August 8, 1964, TCC, Box 5, LBJL.

75. Diaries of Orville Freeman, February 22, 1964, PP/Orville Freeman, Box 9, LBJL.

76. Bernstein, *Guns or Butter,* 105.

77. Dallek, *Flawed Giant,* 108.

78. LBJ and Shriver Conversation, April 30, 1964, TCC, Box 4, LBJL.

79. Brauer, "Kennedy, Johnson, and the War on Poverty," 112.

80. Vicky and Simon McHugh OH, June 9, 1975, LBJL; "Remarks in the City Hall, Rocky Mount, North Carolina," May 7, 1964, in *Public Papers: LBJ, 1963–1964,* vol. I, 638–639.

81. Ibid.

82. "Remarks at the 20th Washington Conf. of the Advertising Council," May 6, 1964, in *Public Papers: LBJ, 1963–1964,* vol. I, 611.

83. "Remarks to Leaders of Organizations Concerned with the Problems of Senior Citizens," January 15, 1964, in *Public Papers: LBJ, 1963–1964,* vol. I, 134.

84. Diaries of Orville Freeman, May 18, 1964, PP/Orville Freeman, Box 9, LBJL.

85. Moyers, "Setting the Stage," 36.

86. LBJ and O'Brien Conversation, May 11, 1964, WH Tapes, WH6405.03, LBJL.

87. LBJ and McCormack Conversation, May 11, 1964, TCC, Box 4, LBJL.

88. LBJ and Shriver Conversation, May 13, 1964, in Beschloss, *Taking Charge,* 347.

89. LBJ and McCormack Conversation, May 11, 1964, TCC, Box 4, LBJL.

90. LBJ and Shriver Conversation, May 13, 1964, TCC, Box 4, LBJL.

91. LBJ and O'Brien Conversation, August 7, 1964, TCC, Box 5, LBJL.

92. LBJ and McCormack Conversation, August 6, 1964, TCC, Box 5, LBJL.

93. Quoted in Bernstein, *Guns or Butter,* 110–111.

94. LBJ and Jenkins, Moyers Conversation, August 8, 1964, WH Tapes WH6408.13, LBJL.

95. Dallek, *Flawed Giant,* 110.

CHAPTER 3: THE SECOND RECONSTRUCTION

1. Irving Bernstein, *Guns or Butter: The Presidency of Lyndon Johnson* (New York, 1996), 44; on the importance of a community relations service, see Ted Kheel to George Reedy, June 10, 1963, VP Papers of G. Reedy, Box 8, LBJL.

2. Bernstein, *Guns or Butter,* 47.

3. Charles Whalen, "Johnson and the Civil Rights Act of 1964," in *The Johnson Presidency: Twenty Intimate Perspectives of Lyndon B. Johnson,* ed. Kenneth W. Thompson, vol. 5, *Portraits of American Presidents* (Lanham, MD, 1986), 63.

4. Lawrence O'Brien OH, September 1985, ff., LBJL.

5. Reedy to LBJ, May 21, 1963, Willie Day Taylor Files, Box 434, LBJL.

6. Ibid.

7. Robert Dallek, *Flawed Giant: Lyndon B. Johnson and His Times, 1961–1973* (New York, 1998), 114.

8. Quoted in Thomas F. Jackson, *From Civil Rights to Human Rights: Martin Luther King, Jr., and the Struggle for Economic Justice* (Philadelphia, 2006), 168–169.

9. Anthony Lewis, "Civil Rights Issue: Administration Will Be Judged to Large Degree by Fate of This Bill," *New York Times,* December 8, 1963.

10. George Reedy to Vice-President, June 10, 1963, Willie Day Taylor Files, Box 434, LBJL.

11. Louis Martin OH, May 14, 1969, LBJL.

12. Bernstein, *Guns or Butter,* 44.

13. Ibid.

14. H. McPherson OH, VI, May 16, 1985, LBJL.

15. LBJ and Whitney Young Conversation, November 24, 1963, in Michael R. Beschloss, ed., *Taking Charge: The Johnson White House Tapes, 1963–1964* (New York, 1997), 27.

16. Roy Wilkins Appointment, November 29, 1963, Diary Backup, Box 1, Presidential Papers of LBJ, LBJL.

17. LBJ and Randolph Conversation, November 29, 1963, TCC, Box 4, LBJL.

18. "Over 300 Attended the SNCC Conference," *Student Voice,* December 9, 1963; LBJ and King Conversation, November 25, 1963, in Beschloss, *Taking Charge,* 37–38; James Farmer OH, October 1969, LBJL.

19. LBJ and Robt. Anderson Conversation, November 30, 1963, TCC, LBJL.

20. LBJ, "Remarks to New Participants in 'Plans for Progress,'" January 16, 1964, in *Public Papers of the Presidents: LBJ, 1963–1964,* vol. I (Washington, DC, 1965), 140.

21. LBJ and Robt. Anderson Conversation, November 30, 1963, TCC, LBJL.

22. Bernstein, *Guns or Butter,* 44, 49.

23. Charles Whalen and Barbara Whalen, *The Longest Debate: A Legislative History of the 1964 Civil Rights Act* (New York, 1986), 65.

24. Ibid.

25. Terry H. Anderson, *The Pursuit of Fairness: A History of Affirmative Action* (New York, 2004), 75.

26. Ibid., 77.

27. Ibid.

28. Ibid., 78.

29. Ibid., 81.

30. Bernstein, *Guns or Butter,* 53–55.

31. Jake Pickle OH, March 2, 1972, LBJL.

32. Dallek, *Flawed Giant,* 115.

33. Ibid.

34. Transcript of Telephone Conversation, April 10, 1964, TCC, LBJL.

35. LBJ and Rauh Conversation, January 7, 1964, TCC, Box 1, LBJL.

36. Bill Moyers, "Civil Rights," in *The Great Society: A Twenty Year Critique,* ed. Barbara Jordan and Elspeth Rostow (Austin, 1986), 78.

37. Ernest "Tex" Goldstein OH, LBJL; Merle Miller, *Lyndon: An Oral Autobiography* (New York, 1980), 366.

38. Jack Valenti OH, LBJL; Robert Dallek, *Nixon and Kissinger: Partners in Power* (London, 2008), 112.

39. LBJ, *The Vantage Point: Perspectives of the Presidency, 1963–1969* (New York, 1971), 158–159.

40. Whalen, "Johnson and the Civil Rights Act of 1964," 68.

41. Nicholas Katzenbach, "The Bold Dreamer," in *The Johnson Years: The Difference He Made,* ed. Robert L. Hardesty (Austin, 1993), 80–81.

42. Whalen, "Johnson and the Civil Rights Act of 1964," 70; Miller, *Lyndon,* 368.

43. Richard J. Piper, *Ideologies and Institutions: American Conservative and Liberal Governance Prescriptions Since 1933* (Lanham, MD, 1997), 114.

44. Bernstein, *Guns or Butter,* 67.

45. Harry McPherson, *A Political Education: A Washington Memoir* (Austin, 1994), 72.

46. Byron C. Hulsey, *Everett Dirksen and His Presidents: How a Senate Giant Shaped American Politics* (Lawrence, KS, 2000), 8.

47. Ibid., 9.

48. Bernstein, *Guns or Butter,* 61.

49. Miller, *Lyndon,* 368–369; see Hubert H. Humphrey, *The Education of a Public Man: My Life and Politics,* ed. Norman Sherman (New York, 1976), 274–283.

50. Whalen, "Johnson and the Civil Rights Act of 1964," 70.

51. Pres. Notes on Telephone Conversation with Bill Moyers, April 28, 1964, Transcripts of White House Telephone Conversations, Box 4, LBJL.

52. Fields observes of the difference between Jeffersonian and Lincolnesque language: "The former dedicated propositions, the latter cemeteries." Wayne Fields, *Union of Words: A History of Presidential Eloquence* (New York, 1996), 291.

53. LBJ, "Remarks to New Participants in 'Plans for Progress,'" January 16, 1964, 141–142.

54. "The President's Sermon," *Fort Worth Star-Telegram,* May 4, 1964.

55. Doris Kearns Goodwin, *Lyndon Johnson and the American Dream* (New York, 1991), 321.

56. David Burner, *Making Peace with the 60s* (Princeton, NJ, 1996), 17.

57. "Remarks in Atlanta at a Breakfast of the Georgia Legislature," May 8, 1964, in *Public Papers: LBJ, 1963–1964,* vol. I, 648.

58. Beschloss, *Taking Charge,* 341.

59. "LBJ Given Tumultuous Welcome," *Dallas Herald,* May 8, 1964.

60. Nick Kotz, *Judgment Days: Lyndon Baines Johnson, Martin Luther King Jr., and the Laws That Changed America* (Boston, 2005), 120.

61. Hoover to Jenkins, April 14, 1964, OF/Mildred Stegall, Box 32, Presidential Papers of LBJ, LBJL.

62. Kotz, *Judgment Days,* 146.

63. Ibid., 122–123.

64. Beschloss, *Taking Charge,* 331.

65. Ibid., LBJ and Mansfield Conversation, April 29, 1964.

66. See Bernstein, *Guns or Butter,* 69; Whalen, "Johnson and the Civil Rights Act of 1964," 71.

67. Hulsey, *Dirksen and His Presidents,* 13–18.

68. LBJ and Dirksen Conversation, May 13, 1964, in Beschloss, *Taking Charge,* 350.

69. Diaries of Orville Freeman, December 10, 1963, PP/Orville Freeman, Box 8, LBJL.

70. Miller, *Lyndon,* 369.

71. Bernstein, *Guns or Butter,* 71.

72. LBJ and HHH Conversation, February 25, 1964, TCC, Box 1, LBJL.

73. LBJ and Russell Conversation, April 9, 1964, in Beschloss, *Taking Charge,* 312.

74. LBJ and Kermit Gordon Conversation, April 29, 1964, TCC, Box 1, LBJL.

75. Dallek, *Flawed Giant,* 119.

76. Humphrey, *Education of Public Man,* 283.

77. Kotz, *Judgment Days,* 134–135.

78. Ibid., 231. Many civil rights activists were not as enthusiastic as LBJ. They had pressed for a jury trial provision that would either prohibit discrimination in jury selection or make judges rather than juries the final arbiter in civil rights cases. Johnson told King and his colleagues that such an amendment would be a deal breaker, but on November 19, after his landslide victory in the 1964 presidential election, LBJ met with civil rights leaders on another matter. After the meeting, he pulled Jack Greenberg, head of the NAACP Legal Defense Fund, aside. "And what can I do for you?" the president asked. Greenberg replied that civil rights lawyers' greatest problem in the South was trying to cope with the segregationist federal judges appointed by President Kennedy. Johnson promised that henceforth he would clear all judicial appointments in the South with Greenberg and other civil rights leaders. He was as good as his word. On December 10, he called MLK to get his views on an appointment to the US circuit court in the South.

79. Quoted in Randall Bennett Woods, *Quest for Identity: America Since 1945* (New York, 2005), 189.

80. Ibid.

81. Kotz, *Judgment Days,* 164–165.

82. Quoted in Woods, *Quest for Identity,* 190.

83. Dallek, *Flawed Giant,* 120.

84. LeRoy Collins OH, November 15, 1972, LBJL.

85. LBJ and Eastland Conversation, June 23, 1964, in Beschloss, *Taking Charge,* 433.

86. LBJ and Hodges Conversation, June 23, 1964, TCC, Box 4, LBJL.

87. Quoted in Sidney M. Milkis, *The President and the Parties: The Transformation of the American Party System since the New Deal* (New York, 1993), 197.

88. Miller, *Lyndon,* 371.

89. LBJ and Connally Conversation, July 3, 1964, WH Tapes, WH6407.03, LBJL.

90. Lee White Memorandum, July 2, 1964, Diary Backup, Box 7, LBJL.

91. LBJ and W. Young Conversation, June 19, 1964, WH Tapes WH6406.11, LBJL.

92. Dallek, *Flawed Giant,* 120.

CHAPTER 4: THE MANDATE: THE ELECTION OF 1964

1. Diaries of Orville Freeman, May 4, 1964, PP/Orville Freeman, Box 9, LBJL.

2. Diaries of Orville Freeman, May 16, 1964, PP/Orville Freeman, Box 9, LBJL.

3. Robert Dallek, *Flawed Giant: Lyndon B. Johnson and His Times, 1961–1973* (New York, 1998), 124.

4. Murray Kempton, "The People's Choice," *New York Review of Books,* November 5, 1964.

5. Ed Weisl OH, October 24, 1968, I, LBJL.

6. Dallek, *Flawed Giant,* 124.

7. "The Democratic Party and the Presidency in the Twentieth Century," Busby to LBJ, July 1964, OF/H. Busby, Box 52, LBJL.

8. Busby to LBJ, June 1964, OF/H. Busby, Box 52, LBJL.

9. "Image Assessment and Suggested Activities," Busby to LBJ, May 1964, OF/H. Busby, Box 52, LBJL.

10. Goldman to the President, September 24, 1964, OF/Bill Moyers, Box 53, LBJL.

11. Lloyd C. Gardner, *Pay Any Price: Lyndon Johnson and the Wars for Vietnam* (Chicago, 1995), 106.

12. Cater to LBJ, June 3, 1964, OF/Bill Moyers, Box 53, LBJL.

13. LBJ and Wirtz Conversation, February 27, 1964, WH Tapes WH6402.22, LBJL.

14. LBJ and McNeil Conversation, April 10, 1964, TCC, Box 4, LBJL.

15. Ibid.

16. Quoted in Eric F. Goldman, *The Tragedy of Lyndon Johnson* (New York, 1969), 88.

17. Unpublished Diary of Lady Bird Johnson, April 21, 1964, LBJL.

18. LBJ and Wirtz Conversation, April 17, 1964, TCC, LBJ and Kennedy Conversation, April 22, 1964, TCC, Box 4, LBJL.

19. Michael R. Beschloss, *Reaching for Glory: Lyndon Johnson's Secret White House Tapes, 1964–1965* (New York, 2001), 323.

20. Quoted in *The Record* (South Bend, Indiana), May 1, 1964.

21. Dallek, *Flawed Giant,* 128.

22. "LBJ Called Strong in the Deep South," *Houston Post,* January 26, 1964.

23. LBJ and Luther Hodges Conversation, July 7, 1964, WH Tapes, WH6407.05, LBJL.

24. LBJ and G. Smathers Conversation, August 1, 1964, WH Tapes, WH6408.01, LBJL.

25. LBJ and Connally Conversation, July 3, 1964, WH Tapes, WH6407.03, LBJL.

26. Quoted in Randall Bennett Woods, *Quest for Identity: America Since 1945* (New York, 2005), 187.

27. LBJ and Harte Conversation, June 4, 1964, in Beschloss, *Reaching for Glory.*

28. Diaries of Orville Freeman, July 22, 1964, PP/Orville Freeman, Box 9, LBJL.

29. I. F. Stone, "The Collected Works of Barry Goldwater," *New York Review of Books,* August 13, 1964, 3.

30. Dan T. Carter, *The Politics of Rage: George Wallace, the Origins of the New Conservatism and the Transformation of American Politics* (Baton Rouge, 1995), 163.

31. Ibid., 156.

32. Quoted in ibid., 135.

33. "FBI Agents Probe Riot in Harlem," *Houston Post,* July 23, 1964.

34. Valenti to President, August 4, 1964, LBJ Handwriting File, Box 3, LBJL.

35. Cater to LBJ, June 3, 1964, OF/Bill Moyers, Box 53, LBJL; see also Busby to LBJ, June 1964, OF/H. Busby, Box 52, LBJL

36. Dallek, *Flawed Giant,* 135.

37. Clark Clifford OH, July 2, 1969, II, LBJL.

38. LBJ and Clifford Conversation, July 29, 1964, WH Tapes, WH6407.18, LBJL.

39. "Memo Cites LBJ Order for Wiretaps," *Dallas Times Herald,* January 26, 1975; see also Kenneth O'Reilly, *Racial Matter: The FBI's Secret File on Black America, 1960–1972* (New York, 1991), 185–190.

40. James Hilty, *Robert Kennedy: Brother Protector* (Philadelphia, 1997), 223–225; Richard Gid Powers, *Secrecy and Power: The Life of J. Edgar Hoover* (New York, 1988), 382–390.

41. Anthony Summers, *Official and Confidential: The Secret Life of J. Edgar Hoover* (New York, 1993), 312.

42. C. Deloach OH, January 11, 1991, I, LBJL.

43. Powers, *Secrecy and Power,* 393–399.

44. LBJ and Hoover Conversation, February 28, 1964, WH Tapes, WH6402.22, LBJL.

45. Quoted in Ronald Radosh, *Divided They Fell: The Demise of the Democratic Party, 1964–1996* (New York, 1996), 2.

46. John Dittmer, *Local People: The Struggle for Civil Rights in Mississippi* (Urbana, 1994), 239.

47. Ibid., 281; Joseph Rauh OH, III, August 8, 1969, LBJL.

48. LBJ and Connally Conversation, July 23, 1964, in Michael R. Beschloss, ed., *Taking Charge: The Johnson White House Tapes, 1963–1964* (New York, 1997), 467.

49. LBJ and McCormack Conversation, July 14, 1964, TCC, Box 5, LBJL.

50. LBJ and Roy Wilkins Conversation, August 15, 1964, in Beschloss, *Taking Charge,* 517.

51. White to Spottswood, July 17, 1964, LBJ Handwriting File, Box 3, LBJL. Article IV, Section 4 provides that "The United States shall guarantee to every state in this Union a republican form of government and shall protect each of them against invasion, and on application of the legislature, or of the executive, against domestic violence."

52. White to President, August 19, 1964, Diary Backup, Box 8, LBJL.

53. Nick Kotz, *Judgment Days: Lyndon Baines Johnson, Martin Luther King Jr., and the Laws That Changed America* (Boston, 2005), 185.

54. Quoted in Dittmer, *Local People,* 290.

55. LBJ and HHH Conversation, August 14, 1964, WH Tapes, WH6408.18, LBJL.

56. Quoted in Adam Cohen and Elizabeth Taylor, *American Pharaoh: Mayor Richard J. Daley: His Battle for Chicago and the Nation* (Boston, 2000), 321.

57. Quoted in Dittmer, *Local People,* 288.

58. P. Johnson OH, September 8, 1970, LBJL.

59. Kotz, *Judgment Days,* 199.

60. Ibid.

61. Ibid., 200.

62. Ibid., 196. Rauh, cofounder of the Americans for Democratic Action and general counsel to the United Auto Workers, was one of the nation's most prominent liberals.

63. Ibid.

64. Ibid., 209.

65. Beschloss, *Taking Charge,* 527.

66. LBJ and George Reedy Conversation, August 25, 1964, in ibid., 527–532.

67. Kotz, *Judgment Days,* 213.

68. Quoted in Dittmer, *Local People,* 92.

69. Ibid., 287–302; Joseph Rauh OH; Radosh, *Divided They Fell,* 1–15.

70. Quoted in Dittmer, *Local People,* 30.

71. Sidney M. Milkis, "Lyndon Johnson, the Great Society, and the Modern Presidency," in *The Great Society and the High Tide of Liberalism,* ed. Sidney M. Milkis and Jerome M. Mileur (Amherst, MA, 2005), 24–25.

72. Diaries of Orville Freeman, August 27, 1964, PP/Orville Freeman, Box 9, LBJL.

73. Quoted in Dallek, *Flawed Giant,* 169.

74. Ibid., 170.

75. Joe English to Bill Moyers, September 28, 1964, OF/Bill Moyers, Box 53, LBJL.

76. The Campaign, Busby to LBJ, ND 1964, OF/H. Busby, Box 52, LBJL.

77. Dutton to Moyers, September 26, 1964, OF/Bill Moyers, Box 53, LBJL.

78. Busby to the President, September 28, 1964, OF/H. Busby, Box 52, LBJL.

79. LBJ and Sanders Conversation, August 1, 1964, TCC, Box 5, LBJL.

80. LBJ and Connally Conversation, August 9, 1964, WH Tapes, WH6408.15, LBJL.

81. LBJ and Sparkman Conversation, 1964, WH Tapes 5635, LBJL.

82. E. Carpenter OH, December 3, 1968, LBJL.

83. Ibid.

84. Buford Ellington OH, October 2, 1970, I, LBJL; E. Carpenter OH, December 3, 1968, LBJL.

85. Quoted in Jan Jarboe Russell, *Lady Bird: A Biography of Mrs. Johnson* (New York, 1999), 263.

86. "Remarks at a Fund-Raising Dinner in New Orleans," October 9, 1964, in *Public Papers of the Presidents: LBJ, 1963–1964,* vol. II (Washington, DC, 1965), 1283–1286. The official transcript of the speech reads "Negro, Negro Negro!" but numerous first-hand witnesses testify that he used the pejorative term.

87. Busby to the President, ND 1964, OF/Bill Moyers, Box 10, LBJL.

88. Quoted in Jeff Woods, "The Changing South," in *A Companion to Lyndon B. Johnson,* ed. Mitchell B. Lerner (Malden, 2012), 15.

89. "Remarks at City Hall, Macon, Georgia," October 26, 1964, in *Public Papers of the Presidents: LBJ, 1963–1964,* vol. II (Washington, DC, 1965), 1446.

90. LBJ and Rusk Conversation, October 2, 1964, WH Tapes, WH6401.01, LBJL.

91. LBJ and Charles Guy Conversation, October 11, 1964, WH Tapes, WH6410.08, LBJL.

92. Rogers M. Smith, *Civic Ideals: Conflicting Visions of Citizenship in U.S. History* (New Haven, 1997), 33.

93. "Communist Influence in Racial Matters," Jones and King Conversation, July 27, 1964, Files of Mildred Steagal, Box 71A, Presidential Papers of LBJ, LBJL.

94. Hoover to Moyers, October 22, 1964, Files of Mildred Stegall, Box 32, Presidential Papers of LBJ, LBJL.

95. Hoover to Moyers, October 20, 1964, Files of Mildred Stegall, Box 32, Presidential Papers of LBJ, LBJL. King also observed that many whites were confusing demonstrations with riots, and the civil rights leadership must be careful to protect the image of nonviolent civil disobedience.

96. Dallek, *Flawed Giant,* 183–184.

97. Jeff Woods, "The Changing South," 18.

98. Merle Miller, *Lyndon: An Oral Autobiography* (New York, 1980), 402.

99. Quoted in Byron C. Hulsey, *Everett Dirksen and His Presidents: How a Senate Giant Shaped American Politics* (Lawrence, KS, 2000), 38.

100. LBJ and Scotty Reston Conversation, January 8, 1964, WH Tapes, WH6401.09, LBJL.

CHAPTER 5: LIBERAL NATIONALISM VERSUS
THE AMERICAN CREED: THE GREAT SOCIETY
FROM SCHOOLROOM TO HOSPITAL

1. "The State of the Union," *Newsweek,* January 11, 1965, 18.

2. William E. Leuchtenberg, "The Genesis of the Great Society," *The Reporter* 34 (April 21, 1966): 39.

3. Sean J. Savage, *JFK, LBJ, and the Democratic Party* (Albany, 2004), 248.

4. "The State of the Union," 17.

5. "Annual Message to the Congress on the State of the Union," January 4, 1965, in *Public Papers of the Presidents: LBJ, 1965,* vol. I (Washington, DC, 1966), 9.

6. Richard J. Ellis, *American Political Cultures* (New York, 1993), 74–76.

7. Henry Fairlie, "The Hidden Meaning of 'Consensus,'" *New Republic,* January 1, 1966, 15–19.

8. John D. Morrissa, "Johnson's Way with Congress," *New York Times,* January 17, 1965.

9. Eric F. Goldman, *The Tragedy of Lyndon Johnson* (New York, 1969), 259.

10. Cater to the President, January 12, 1966, LBJ Handwriting File, Box 11, LBJL.

11. "Annual Message to the Congress on the State of the Union," January 4, 1965, 1.

12. "LBJ and His Congress: Made for Each Other," *Newsweek,* January 18, 1965, 17.

13. Wilbur Cohen OH, I, December 8, 1968, LBJL.

14. "Annual Message to the Congress on the State of the Union," January 4, 1965, 1.

15. D. B. Hardeman OH, February 15, 1965, LBJL.

16. Quoted in Doris Kearns Goodwin, *Lyndon Johnson and the American Dream* (New York, 1991), 238.

17. LBJ and Walter Reuther Conversation, November 24, 1964, WH Tapes, WH6411.29, LBJL.

18. Robert Dallek, *Flawed Giant: Lyndon B. Johnson and His Times, 1961–1973* (New York, 1998), 194.

19. C. Albert OH, III, August 13, 1969, LBJL.

20. LBJ and McCormack Conversation, WH Tapes, WH6411.08, LBJL.

21. "The 89th: LBJ's Do-Plenty Congress," *Newsweek,* February 15, 1965, 21.

22. "Remarks Before the National Connference on Educational Legislation," March 1, 1965, in *Public Papers of the Presidents: LBJ, 1965,* vol. I, 227.

23. Martin E. Marty, *The One and the Many: America's Struggle for the Common Good* (Cambridge, MA, 1997), 51.

24. Ibid., 56–57.

25. "Senators Not in Accord on U.S. Aid to Education," *Dallas Morning News,* May 8, 1949.

26. Quoted in Patrick McGuinn and Frederick Hess, "The Great Society and the Evolution of the Elementary and Secondary Education Act of 1965," in *The Great Society and the High Tide of Liberalism,* ed. Sidney M. Milkis and Jerome M. Mileur (Amherst, MA, 2005), 293–294.

27. Ibid., 291–292.

28. Ibid., 292.

29. Goldman, *Tragedy of Lyndon Johnson,* 304.

30. Irving Bernstein, *Guns or Butter: The Presidency of Lyndon Johnson* (New York, 1996), 187.

31. Savage, *JFK, LBJ, and the Democratic Party,* 125.

32. Goldman, *Tragedy of Lyndon Johnson,* 36–37.

33. Bernstein, *Guns or Butter,* 184; Goldman, *Tragedy of Lyndon Johnson,* 297.

34. Lawrence F. O'Brien OH, September 18, 1985, LBJL.

35. Bernstein, *Guns or Butter,* 186–188.

36. Ibid., 188–189.

37. D. Cater OH, I, April 29, 1969, LBJL; Goldman, *Tragedy of Lyndon Johnson,* 300.

38. D. Cater OH; Bernstein, *Guns or Butter,* 191.

39. McGuinn and Hess, "Great Society and the Evolution of Education," 304. A 1966 amendment to the ESEA created a new title (Title VI) to provide grants to programs for "handicapped" children. This new program continued to expand over time as the definition of "handicapped" was broadened to cover more and more students.

40. Dallek, *Flawed Giant,* 196.

41. Goldman, *Tragedy of Lyndon Johnson,* 300.

42. Louis Martin OH, June 12, 1986, II, LBJL.

43. Lawrence F. O'Brien OH, September 18, 1985; Goldman, *Tragedy of Lyndon Johnson,* 302.

44. LBJ and Ralph Dungan Conversation, April 10, 1964, Box 4, LBJL.

45. Goldman, *Tragedy of Lyndon Johnson,* 301.

46. Douglass Cater to President, March 10, 1968, LBJ Handwriting File, Box 6, LBJL.

47. LBJ and HHH Conversation, March 6, 1965, in Michael R. Beschloss, *Reaching for Glory: Lyndon Johnson's Secret White House Tapes, 1964–1965* (New York, 2001), 169.

48. Savage, *JFK, LBJ, and the Democratic Party,* 126–127.

49. Goldman, *Tragedy of Lyndon Johnson,* 306.

50. Savage, *JFK, LBJ, and the Democratic Party,* 126–127.

51. "Remarks in Johnson City, Texas, upon Signing the Elementary and Secondary Education Bill," April 11, 1965, in *Public Papers: LBJ, 1965,* vol. I, 413.

52. "Remarks to Members of Congress at a Reception Marking the Enactment of the Education Bill," April 13, 1965, in *Public Papers of the Presidents: LBJ, 1965,* vol. I, 416.

53. Dallek, *Flawed Giant,* 201.

54. "Remarks Before the National Conference on Educational Legislation," March 1, 1965, in *Public Papers of the Presidents: LBJ, 1965,* vol. I, 227.

55. Stephen C. Halpern, *On the Limits of the Law: The Ironic Legacy of Title VI of the 1964 Civil Rights Act* (Baltimore, 1995), 43.

56. Ibid., 45.

57. Ronald Story, "The New Deal and Higher Education," in *The New Deal and the Triumph of Liberalism,* ed. Sidney M. Milkis and Jerome M. Mileur (Amherst, MA, 2002), 272.

58. Ibid., 276.

59. Ibid., 274.

60. Bernstein, *Guns or Butter,* 204–210.

61. LBJ and HHH Conversation, March 6, 1965, in Beschloss, *Reaching for Glory,* 209.

62. See Allen J. Matusow, *The Unraveling of America: A History of Liberalism in the 1960s* (Athens, 1984), 224.

63. Dallek, *Flawed Giant,* 202.

64. Quoted in McGuinn and Hess, "Great Society and the Evolution of Education," 297.

65. Quoted in ibid., 298.

66. Bernstein, *Guns or Butter,* 157.

67. Reedy to Senator Johnson, ND 1959, SOF/G. Reedy, Box 429, LBJL.

68. Larry DeWitt and Edward D. Berkowitz, "Health Care," in *A Companion to Lyndon B. Johnson,* ed. Mitchell B. Lerner (Malden, 2012), 163–164.

69. Ibid., 164.

70. Ibid., 165–166.

71. Notes of an Interview with LBJ During Preparation of Exhibits for LBJ Library, n.d., OF/Harry Middleton, "Exhibits," Box 64, LBJL.

72. Dallek, *Flawed Giant,* 205.

73. Wilbur Mills OH, II, LBJL.

74. Julian E. Zelizer, *Taxing America: Wilbur D. Millis, Congress, and the American State, 1945–1975* (New York, 2000), 216–217.

75. LBJ and L. O'Brien Conversation, May 18, 1964, TCC, Box 4, LBJL.

76. LBJ and Wilbur Mills Conversation, June 9, 1964, WH Tapes, WH6406.03, LBJL.

77. Zelizer, *Taxing America,* 221.

78. LBJ and L. O'Brien Conversation, June 22, 1964, WH Tapes, WH6406.12, LBJL.

79. LBJ and L. O'Brien Conversation, August 14, 1964, WH Tapes, WH6408.19, LBJL.

80. LBJ and Carl Albert Conversation, September 3, 1964, WH Tapes, WH6409.05, LBJL.

81. Zelizer, *Taxing America,* 231.

82. Bernstein, *Guns or Butter,* 171.

83. Quoted in Zelizer, *Taxing America,* 241.

84. Bernstein, *Guns or Butter,* 173.

85. Merle Miller, *Lyndon: An Oral Autobiography* (New York, 1980), 410–411.

86. Dallek, *Flawed Giant,* 209.

87. Bernstein, *Guns or Butter,* 176.

88. "Biggest Change Since the New Deal," *Newsweek,* April 12, 1965.

89. LBJ and L. O'Brien Conversation, April 9, 1965, in Beschloss, *Reaching for Glory,* 277.

90. Dallek, *Flawed Giant,* 298–210.

91. Bernstein, *Guns or Butter,* 179.

92. Dallek, *Flawed Giant,* 210.

93. Bernstein, *Guns or Butter,* 177–178.

94. Ibid.

95. Edward Berkowitz, "The Great Society's Enduring National Health Insurance Program," in *The Great Society and the High Tide of Liberalism,* ed. Sidney M. Milkis and Jerome M. Mileur (Amherst, MA, 2005), 121–122.

96. DeWitt and Berkowitz, "Health Care," 172.

97. Ibid., 173.

98. Wilbur Cohen OH, II, LBJL.

99. DeWitt and Berkowitz, "Health Care," 173–174.

100. Miller, *Lyndon,* 412.

101. Berkowitz, "Great Society's Enduring National Health Insurance Program," 327.

102. DeWitt and Berkowitz, "Health Care," 174.

103. Bernstein, *Guns or Butter,* 180–181; Dallek, *Flawed Giant,* 211.

CHAPTER 6: MARCH TO FREEDOM:
SELMA AND THE VOTING RIGHTS ACT

1. Irving Bernstein, *Guns or Butter: The Presidency of Lyndon Johnson* (New York, 1996), 223.

2. William H. Chafe, *The Unfinished Journey: America Since World War II* (New York, 2003), 311.

3. Robert Dallek, *Flawed Giant: Lyndon B. Johnson and His Times, 1961–1973* (New York, 1998), 212.

4. LBJ and Roy Wilkins Conversation, November 4, 1965, WH Tapes, WH6511.01, LBJL.

5. LBJ and Roy Wilkins Conversation, October 30, 1965, WH Tapes, WH6510.03, LBJL.

6. Dallek, *Flawed Giant,* 212.

7. George Reedy to President, November 29, 1963, Diary Backup, Box 1, LBJL.

8. David Burner, *Making Peace with the 60s* (Princeton, 1996), 18.

9. LBJ and Richard Russell Conversation, November 11, 1964, White House Tapes of Telephone Conversations, WH6411.15, LBJL.

10. Burner, *Making Peace,* 5.

11. Nick Kotz, *Judgment Days: Lyndon Baines Johnson, Martin Luther King Jr., and the Laws That Changed America* (Boston, 2005), 66–67.

12. Ibid., 51.

13. Taylor Branch, *Pillar of Fire: America in the King Years 1963–65* (New York, 1998), 28.

14. Ibid., 150; Kent B. Germany, "African-American Civil Rights," in *A Companion to Lyndon B. Johnson,* ed. Mitchell B. Lerner (Malden, 2012), 121. In *The FBI and Martin Luther King, Jr.: From "Solo" to Memphis* (New York, 1981), David Garrow breaks down the FBI's surveillance and investigation of King into three distinct periods. The bureau's early focus was on Stanley Levison, the King adviser known in the FBI as "Solo" who allegedly had close ties to the Communist Party USA (CPUSA). Its second phase began in late 1963 with an assault on King's personal life. The final period concerned King's politics prior to his assassination, his calls for a social and economic revolution, and his support for the anti–Vietnam War movement.

15. Hoover to Jenkins, March 9, 1964, OF/Mildred Stegall, Box 32, Presidential Papers of LBJ, LBJL.

16. Branch, *Pillar of Fire,* 207.

17. Bernstein, *Guns or Butter,* 216.

18. James Farmer OH, II, July 20, 1971, LBJL.

19. J. Edgar Hoover to the President, November 30, 1964, OF/Mildred Stegall, Presidential Papers of LBJ, LBJL.

20. J. Edgar Hoover to the President, December 31, 1964, OF/Mildred Stegall, Box 32, Presidential Papers of LBJ, LBJL.

21. Kotz, *Judgment Days,* 235–236.

22. Lee White to the President, December 18, 1964, Diary Backup, Box 12, LBJL.

23. Quoted in Kotz, *Judgment Days,* 234–244.

24. Quoted in ibid., 245.

25. Quoted in Branch, *Pillar of Fire,* 555.

26. LBJ and Edward Clark Conversation, November 7, 1964, WH Tapes, WH6411.12, LBJL.

27. Buford Ellington OH, I, October 2, 1970, LBJL.

28. Bernstein, *Guns or Butter,* 215.

29. Ibid., 219–220.

30. Michael R. Beschloss, *Reaching for Glory: Lyndon Johnson's Secret White House Tapes, 1964–1965* (New York, 2001), 171.

31. See LBJ and Katzenbach Conversation, February 5, 1965, in ibid.

32. Lee White to President and Points That Dr. King Might Make upon Leaving the White House, February 5, 1965, Diary Backup, Box 13, LBJL.

33. Dallek, *Flawed Giant,* 214.

34. Quoted in Kotz, *Judgment Days,* 265.

35. Carter, *Politics of Rage,* 125.

36. Bernstein, *Guns or Butter,* 227.

37. "An American Tragedy," *Newsweek,* March 22, 1965, 18–20.

38. LBJ and L. Hill Conversation, March 8, 1965, in Beschloss, *Reaching for Glory,* 219.

39. LBJ and Katzenbach Conversation, March 10, 1965, in ibid., 224.

40. N. Katzenbach OH, I, November 11, 1968, LBJL.

41. Kotz, *Judgment Days,* 303.

42. Cater to the President, March 1965, Diary Backup, Box 15, LBJL.

43. Quoted in Dan T. Carter, *The Politics of Rage: George Wallace, the Origins of the New Conservatism and the Transformation of American Politics* (Baton Rouge, 1995), 252.

44. Robert Dallek, *Nixon and Kissinger: Partners in Power* (London, 2008), 216–217; Bernstein, *Guns or Butter,* 230–231; Katzenbach to President, March 13, 1965, Katzenbach Papers, JFK Library. The points that LBJ made with Wallace were carefully worked out in advance with Nick Katzenbach.

45. "Remarks Delivered to a Press Conference in the Rose Garden," March 13, 1965, in *Public Papers of the Presidents: LBJ, 1965,* vol. I (Washington, DC, 1966), 276.

46. McPherson to President, March 12, 1965, Diary Backup, Box 15, LBJL.

47. LBJ, *The Vantage Point: Perspectives of the Presidency, 1963–1969* (New York, 1971), 164.

48. Dallek, *Flawed Giant,* 218.

49. "Special Message to the Congress: The American Promise," March 15, 1965, in *Public Papers: LBJ, 1965,* vol. I, 281–287.

50. Quoted in Eric F. Goldman, *The Tragedy of Lyndon Johnson* (New York, 1969), 322.

51. LBJ, Wallace, Ellington, and Katzenbach Conversation, March 18, 1965, in Beschloss, *Reaching for Glory,* 231–232.

52. LBJ and Ellington Conversation, March 18, 1965, in ibid., 235.

53. "Statement by the President in Response to a Telegram from the Governor of Alabama," March 18, 1965, in *Public Papers: LBJ, 1965,* vol. I, 296–297.

54. "Forces in Position," March 1965, Diary Backup, Box 15, LBJL.

55. Valenti Notes on Meeting in President's Office, March 18, 1965, Diary Backup, Box 15, LBJL.

56. LeRoy Collins to the President, March 24, 1965, OF/Harry McPherson, Box 1, LBJL.

57. See Ramsey Clark OH, February 11, 1969, LBJL.

58. Cyrus Vance to President, March 20, 1965, Diary Backup, Box 15, LBJL; Bernstein, *Guns or Butter,* 235.

59. Kenneth O'Reilly, *Nixon's Piano: Presidents and Racial Politics from Washington to Clinton* (New York, 1995), 255.

60. Ibid.

61. LBJ and Katzenbach Conversation, March 26, 1965, in Beschloss, *Reaching for Glory,* 247.

62. "Road from Selma: Hope—and Death," *Newsweek,* April 5, 1965.

63. LBJ and Katzenbach Conversation, August 17, 1965, WH Tapes, WH6508.05, LBJL.

64. Ramsey Clark OH, II, February 11, 1969, LBJL.

65. Busby to Moyers and White, February 27, 1965, OF/Bill Moyers, Box 6, LBJL.

66. Katzenbach to Moyers and White, March 1, 1965, OF/Bill Moyers, Box 6, LBJL.

67. Quoted in Kotz, *Judgment Days,* 313.

68. Ibid., 315.

69. Bernstein, *Guns or Butter,* 236–237.

70. Busby to Moyers and White, February 27, 1965, and Moyers and White to Katzenbach, March 1, 1965, OF/Bill Moyers, Box 6, LBJL; Meeting in Cabinet Room of Bipartisan Congressional Leaders, March 14, 1965, Diary Backup, Box 15, LBJL; LBJ and Vance Hartke Conversation, May 7, 1965, TCC, Box 6, LBJL.

71. LBJ and Birch Bayh Conversation, May 7, 1965, 7603–04, LBJL.

72. Bernstein, *Guns or Butter,* 241.

73. LBJ and Roy Wilkins Conversation, November 4, 1965, WH Tapes, WH6511.01, LBJL. See also LBJ and Katzenbach Conversation, August 17, 1965, WH Tapes, WH 6508.04, LBJL. LBJ was also very mindful of the favorable impact the Voting Rights Act and subsequent mass voter registration would have on the nonwhite peoples of the rest of the world.

74. President Johnson's Notes on Conversation with Thurgood Marshall, January 3, 1966, Transcripts of White House Telephone Conversations, 9403, LBJL.

75. Bernstein, *Guns or Butter,* 241–242.

76. Dallek, *Flawed Giant,* 220–221.

CHAPTER 7: CULTURES OF POVERTY

1. "New Crisis: The Negro Family," *Newsweek,* August 9, 1965, 32.

2. Ibid.

3. Moynihan to McPherson, September 22, 1966, OF/H. McPherson, Box 22, LBJL.

4. Harry McPherson OH, III, LBJL.

5. Dona Cooper Hamilton and Charles V. Hamilton, *The Dual Agenda* (New York, 1998), 129–130.

6. Though he was heavily influenced by Moynihan's report on the black family, he could not bring himself to trust its author. Moynihan was a self-made New York Irish intellectual who had been much too close to the Kennedys for Johnson's taste. Harry McPherson, who was a close friend and admirer of Moynihan, did his best to persuade LBJ to bring him into the presidential inner circle, but to no avail. See Douglas Cater to President, July 7, 1965, LBJH Handwriting File, Box 8 and McPherson to President, June 24, 1965, OF/H. McPherson, Box 52, LBJL.

7. "Commencement Address at Howard University: 'To Fulfill These Rights,'" June 4, 1965, in *Public Papers of the Presidents: LBJ, 1965,* vol. II (Washington, DC, 1966), 635–640.

8. Moynihan to McPherson, September 22, 1966, OF/H. McPherson, Box 22, LBJL.

9. Hamilton and Hamilton, *Dual Agenda,* 132.

10. George Reedy, "Affirmative Action Forgets Its Roots," *USA Today,* July 19, 1995, 11A.

11. "South LA was a circumscribed realm of diminishing opportunity," Gerald Horne has written. Gerald Horne, *Fire This Time: The Watts Uprising and the 1960s* (Charlottesville, VA, 1995), 52.

12. "Los Angeles: The Fire This Time," *Newsweek,* August 23, 1965, 15–16.

13. See Terry H. Anderson, *The Movement and the Sixties: Protest in America from Greensboro to Wounded Knee,* 5th ed. (Oxford, 1995), 132.

14. Quoted in Randall Bennett Woods, *Quest for Identity: American Since 1945* (New York, 2005), 250.

15. Stokely Carmichael, "What We Want," *New York Review of Books,* September 22, 1966, 5.

16. See Fred Dutton to Attorney General, July 17, 1964, OF/Bill Moyers, Box 53, LBJL.

17. Joseph A. Califano, *The Triumph and Tragedy of Lyndon Johnson: The White House Years* (College Station, 2003), 59–63.

18. LBJ and Califano Conversation, August 14, 1965, WH Tapes, WH6508.04, LBJL.

19. Ramsey Clark OH, II, February 11, 1969, LBJL.

20. Ramsey Clark OH, III, March 21, 1969, LBJL.

21. Reedy to President, August 22, 1965, OF/H. McPherson, Box 21, LBJL.

22. President Johnson's Notes on Conversation with A. G. Katzenbach, August 17, 1965, 8544, TCC, LBJL.

23. "'Tough Years Ahead,'" *Newsweek,* August 30, 1965, 19.

24. He would get Shriver on it the next day, Johnson said, but it would be much easier to get pending social programs through Congress and funding for existing ones if King would stop opposing the White House on Vietnam. President and Martin Luther King Conversation, August 19, 1965, Diary Backup, Box 21, LBJL.

25. Nick Kotz, *Judgment Days: Lyndon Baines Johnson, Martin Luther King Jr., and the Laws That Changed America* (Boston, 2005), 342–343.

26. Attorney General to President, August 6, 1964, OF/H. Busby, Box 52, LBJL.

27. Ramsey Clark OH, II, February 11, 1969, LBJL.

28. Califano, *Triumph and Tragedy,* 59–63.

29. LBJ and John McCone Conversation, August 18, 1965, WH Tapes, WH6508.05, LBJL.

30. LBJ and J. McClellan Conversation, March 23, 1965, in Michael R. Beschloss, *Reaching for Glory: Lyndon Johnson's Secret White House Tapes, 1964–1965* (New York, 2001), 237.

31. In the beginning the architects and managers of the War on Poverty had gone to great lengths to prove that the initiative was color-blind. It never was, and it became increasingly difficult to conceal the truth. The budget for fiscal year 1966 for the Appalachian program was cut by 44 percent, causing John Sweeney of the Appalachian Regional Commission to warn LBJ that he faced a revolt from the region's governors. John L. Sweeny to The President, December 132, 1965, OF/H. McPherson, Box 50, LBJL.

32. "Remarks at the White House Conference on Equal Employment Opportunities," August 20, 1965, in *Public Papers: LBJ, 1965,* vol. II, 898.

33. Quoted in Woods, *Quest for Identity,* 227.

34. Southerners such as Russell and Allen Ellender (D-LA) were privately advising the president against becoming more deeply involved in Vietnam, but they would not have spoken out in his defense if and when the communists overran the South.

35. "Address at Johns Hopkins University: 'Peace without Conquest,'" April 7, 1965, in *Public Papers: LBJ, 1965,* vol. I, 396.

CHAPTER 8: PROGRESSIVISM REDUX: THE CHALLENGES OF SOCIAL ENGINEERING

1. See Robert Dallek, *Flawed Giant: Lyndon B. Johnson and His Times, 1961–1973* (New York, 1998), 226–227.

2. LBJ and Abraham Ribicoff Conversation, August 19, 1965, TCC, 8573 and 8574, LBJL.

3. Moyers to LBJ, August 12, 1964, Diary Backup, Box 8, Presidential Papers of LBJ, LBJL.

4. Nelson Lichtenstein, "Pluralism, Postwar Intellectuals, and the Demise of the Union Idea," in *The Great Society and the High Tide of Liberalism,* ed. Sidney M. Milkis and Jerome M. Mileur (Amherst, MA, 2005), 87.

5. See ibid., 97.

6. "Preface," in Milkis and Mileur, eds., *Great Society,* xiv–xv.

7. Sidney M. Milkis, "Lyndon Johnson, the Great Society, and the Modern Presidency," in *Great Society,* ed. Milkis and Mileur, 3.

8. Ibid., 5.

9. Thomas J. Sugrue, *Sweet Land of Liberty: The Forgotten Struggle for Civil Rights in the North* (New York, 2009), 367–371.

10. "Shriver and the War on Poverty," *Newsweek,* September 13, 1965.

11. Quoted in Adam Cohen and Elizabeth Taylor, *American Pharaoh: Mayor Richard J. Daley: His Battle for Chicago and the Nation* (Boston, 2000), 343.

12. LBJ and Abe Ribicoff Conversation, September 1, 1965, WH6509.01, LBJL.

13. President's Notes on Conversation with Bill Moyers, August 8, 1964, Transcripts of Telephone Tapes, Box 5, LBJL.

14. See Moyers to President, August 12, 1964, Diary Backup, Box 8, LBJL; Moyers to President, April 5, 1965, OF/Bill Moyers, Box 11, LBJL; "Poverty War: Birth Pains," *Newsweek,* March 29, 1965; and "War within a War," *Newsweek,* December 20, 1965.

15. Eileen Boris, "Contested Rights: The Great Society between Home and Work," in *Great Society,* ed. Milkis and Mileur, 121.

16. Valenti to President, August 20, 1965, Diary Backup, Box 21, LBJL.

17. Boris, "Contested Rights," 127–128.

18. "Can Bobby Kennedy [who with his wife Ethel was hewing to the Biblical dictum 'to be fruitful and multiply'] benefit from this program?" McPherson to Moyers, March 16, 1965, OF/H. McPherson, Box 51, LBJL.

19. See also Cater to President, March 30, 1965, LBJ Handwriting File, Box 6 and McPherson to Moyers, December 13, 1965, OF/H. McPherson, Box 51, LBJL; and "Shriver and the War on Poverty," *Newsweek,* 26. Gallup polls taken at the time showed a huge majority supporting programs that offered family planning advice and services on a voluntary basis. Even 55 percent of the Catholics interviewed backed such

programs. But the Vatican and the American Catholic hierarchy remained adamantly and publicly opposed. McPherson to the President, May 10, 1966, OF/H. McPherson, Box 52, LBJL.

20. Laura Kalman, *Abe Fortas: A Biography* (New Haven, 1990), 244–245.

21. LBJ and Abe Fortas Conversation, July 29, 1965, in Michael R. Beschloss, *Reaching for Glory: Lyndon Johnson's Secret White House Tapes, 1964–1965* (New York, 2001), 413.

22. Kalman, *Abe Fortas,* 240–245; LBJ and Katzenbach Conversation, July 29, 1965, in Beschloss, *Reaching for Glory,* 415–416.

23. See LBJ and Gov. Grant Sawyer Conversation, August 17, 1965, TCC, 8547, LBJL.

24. Moyers and LBJ Conversation, August 1, 1964, White House Telephone Tapes, WS6407.06, LBJL.

25. Quoted in Nick Kotz, *Judgment Days: Lyndon Baines Johnson, Martin Luther King Jr., and the Laws That Changed America* (Boston, 2005), 181.

26. President's Notes on Telephone Conversation with George Mahon, July 29, 1964, 4407, TCC, LBJL.

27. Quoted in Kotz, *Judgment Days,* 181–183.

28. Ibid., 344.

29. "Shriver and the War on Poverty," *Newsweek,* 26.

30. "Statement by the President Upon Announcing a Program of Assistance to Los Angeles," August 26, 1965, in *Public Papers of the Presidents: LBJ, 1965,* vol. II (Washington, DC, 1966), 933–934.

31. LBJ and Abe Ribicoff Conversation, September 1, 1965, WH Tapes, WH 6509.01, LBJL.

32. Califano to President, September 16, 1965, Diary Backup, Box 22, LBJL.

33. He confided to an aide that whenever he sat across from Reuther in the Oval Office, "I'm sitting in my rocker, smiling and thinking all the time, 'How can I get that hand out of his pocket [Reuther had been maimed by a would-be assassin's bullet] so I can cut his balls off!'" Quoted in Dallek, *Flawed Giant,* 224–225.

34. LBJ and Al Friendly Conversation, August 28, 1965, WH Tapes WH6508.13, LBJL.

35. Quoted in Beschloss, *Reaching for Glory,* 418.

36. Quoted in Sean J. Savage, *JFK, LBJ, and the Democratic Party* (Albany, 2004), 135.

37. LBJ and Roy Wilkins Conversation, September 13, 1965, White House Telephone Tapes, WH6509.03, LBJL.

38. LBJ and Katzenbach Conversation, November 29, 1965, WH Tapes, WH6511.09, LBJL.

39. LBJ and Roy Wilkins Conversation, October 30, 1965, TCC, 9048 and 9049, LBJL.

40. LBJ and Roy Wilkins Conversation, November 4, 1965, TCC, 9105–07, LBJL.

41. Dallek, *Flawed Giant,* 229.

42. "Haynesville Justice," *Newsweek,* October 11, 1965, 36.

43. Reedy to President, October 2, 1965, LBJ Handwriting, Box 10, LBJL.

44. "Opening a Second Front," *Newsweek,* November 8, 1965, 33.

45. "What to Do Next?" *Newsweek,* November 29, 1965, 27.

46. Harry McPherson OH, III, LBJL.

47. Kim McQuaid, *Big Business and Presidential Power: From FDR to Reagan* (New York, 1982), 238–239.

48. Joseph A. Califano, *The Triumph and Tragedy of Lyndon Johnson: The White House Years* (College Station, TX, 2003), 86–87.

49. Breakfast Meeting about Steel Strike, August 30, 1965, Diary Backup, Box 21, LBJL.

50. "Steel Answers—and Real Questions," *Newsweek,* September 13, 1965, 19–20.

51. Dallek, *Flawed Giant,* 305.

52. LBJ and Katzenbach Conversation, September 2, 1965, WH Tapes, WH6509.01, LBJL.

53. Heller to President, September 5, 1965, Diary Backup, Box 21, LBJL.

54. Connor and Fowler and LBJ Conversation, January 7, 1966, White House Telephone Tapes, 6601.05, LBJL.

55. Milton Friedman, "Social Responsibility: A Subversive Doctrine," *National Review,* August 24, 1965, 721–723.

56. "What Happens to Bargaining Now?" *Newsweek,* September 20, 1965, 73–75.

57. Ibid.

58. Quoted in Dallek, *Flawed Giant,* 307.

59. Lichtenstein, "Pluralism," 83–85.

60. Ibid., 104–105.

61. Ibid., 104.

62. Ibid., 105.

63. "Remarks at the White House Festival of the Arts," June 14, 1965, in *Public Papers: LBJ, 1965,* vol. II, 659.

64. Irving Bernstein, *Guns or Butter: The Presidency of Lyndon Johnson* (New York, 1996), 443.

65. McPherson to President, December 1, 1965, OF/H. McPherson, Box 52, LBJL.

CHAPTER 9: NATIVISM AT BAY:
IMMIGRATION AND THE LATINO MOVEMENT

1. Rogers M. Smith, *Civic Ideals: Conflicting Visions of Citizenship in U.S. History* (New Haven, 1997), 14–15.

2. Ibid., 16.

3. Roger Daniels, *Guarding the Golden Door: American Immigration Policy and Immigrants Since 1882* (New York, 2004), 6.

4. Quoted in ibid., 7–8.

5. Ibid., 11.

6. Irving Bernstein, *Guns or Butter: The Presidency of Lyndon Johnson* (New York, 1996), 245–247.

7. Ibid., 59.

8. Ibid., 131–132.

9. Ibid., 133.

10. "Remarks at the Signing of the Immigration Bill," Liberty Island, New York, October 3, 1965, in *Public Papers of the Presidents: LBJ, 1963–1964,* vol. II (Washington, DC, 1965), 1038.

11. Daniels, *Guarding the Golden Door,* 135.

12. Bernstein, *Guns or Butter,* 258–259.

13. Daniels, *Guarding the Golden Door,* 139.

14. Randall Bennett Woods, *Quest for Identity: America Since 1945* (New York, 2005), 372.

15. Lorena Oropeza, "Mexican Americans," in *A Companion to Lyndon B. Johnson,* ed. Mitchell B. Lerner (Malden, MA, 2012), 134.

16. Quoted in Nick Kotz, *Judgment Days: Lyndon Baines Johnson, Martin Luther King Jr., and the Laws That Changed America* (Boston, 2005), 95.

17. Lorena Oropeza, "Mexican Americans," 140.

18. Ibid., 144–145.

19. Woods, *Quest for Identity,* 373.

20. Aside from the War on Poverty and especially community action, the Kennedy and Johnson administrations did not have a major impact on the lives of Native Americans. The forced termination policies of the 1950s had come and gone by the time Kennedy assumed office. Washington's approach to Native American affairs, spearheaded by Secretary of the Interior Stewart Udall, was political and economic assimilation coupled with measures to preserve ethnic and cultural identity. See Thomas Clarkin, *Federal Indian Policy in the Kennedy and Johnson Administrations, 1961–1969* (Albuquerque, 2001).

CHAPTER 10: THE NEW CONSERVATION

1. Quoted in Michael McGerr, *A Fierce Discontent: The Rise and Fall of the Progressive Movement in America* (New York, 2003), 167.

2. Ibid., 168–169.

3. Martin V. Melosi, "Environmental Policy," in *A Companion to Lyndon B. Johnson,* ed. Mitchell B. Lerner (Malden, MA, 2012), 196.

4. Ibid., 196.

5. Sarah T. Phillips, *This Land, This Nation: Conservation, Rural America, and the New Deal* (New York, 2007), 150–151.

6. Ibid., 152.

7. Ibid., 153.

8. Melosi, "Environmental Policy," 192–193.

9. Ibid., 190.

10. Ibid., 192.

11. LBJ and Orville Freeman Conversation, July 7, 1964, WH Tapes, WH6407.05, LBJL.

12. "Remarks at the Signing of the Water Quality Act of 1965," October 2, 1965, in *Public Papers of the Presidents: LBJ, 1965,* vol. II (Washington, DC, 1966), 1035.

13. Lee White, "The Bold Dreamer," in *The Johnson Years: The Difference He Made,* ed. Robert L. Hardesty (Austin, 1993), 85.

14. "Remarks at a Meeting of the Water Emergency Conference," August 11, 1965, in *Public Papers: LBJ, 1965,* vol. II, 868.

15. Jan Jarboe Russell, *Lady Bird: A Biography of Mrs. Johnson* (New York, 1999), 279.

16. See Elizabeth Carpenter OH, II, April 4, 1969 LBJL; Joe Frantz OH, September 7, 1972, I, LBJL; James Rowe OH, September 16, 1969, II, LBJL; Bobby Baker OH, VII, October 11, 1984, LBJL; Goodwin to President, July 29, 1964, Diary Backup, Box 7,

LBJL; LBJ to Udall, January 21, 1965, LBJ Handwriting File, Box 5, LBJL; Paul South-wick to Make Manatos, September 7, 1965, Diary Backup, Box 232, LBJL; and "Re-marks at a Meeting of the Water Emergency Conference," August 11, 1965, in *Public Papers: LBJ, 1965,* vol. II, 868.

17. Melosi, "Environmental Policy," 188.

18. Irving Bernstein, *Guns or Butter: The Presidency of Lyndon Johnson* (New York, 1996), 259. John Vrevelli asserts that Johnson was "not generally recognized as a conser-vationist" but might have come close to being "the greatest conservation president." In part his reputation suffered because of a feud with Udall that occurred late in LBJ's presidency. Johnson chose to sign a bill designating 300,000 acres as new parkland in-stead of the 78 million Udall had wanted. Melosi, "Environmental Policy," 192–193. Johnson believed Udall had overreached and suspected that at heart the Interior secre-tary was loyal to Bobby Kennedy rather than him.

19. "LBJ and the Fabulous 89th Go Home," *Newsweek,* November 1, 1965, 21–22.

20. Ibid.

21. See Emmet John Hughes, "The Two Presidents," *Newsweek*, September 6, 1965, 13.

22. "I thought of this opening as a way of being ingratiating since I had some doubt whether this Congress really was as important as those early in the New Deal," the historian wrote of his encounter with the president.

23. William E. Leuchtenburg, "A Visit with LBJ," *American Heritage*, May/June 1990, 47–64.

24. Diaries of Orville Freeman, September 30, 1965, PP/Orville Freeman, Box 10, LBJL.

25. LBJ and Ford and Boggs Conversation, October 22, 1965, TCC, 9045, LBJL.

CHAPTER 11: GUNS AND BUTTER

1. J. K. Galbraith to President, October 19, 1965, LBJ Handwriting File, Box 10, LBJL.

2. Robert C. Wood, *Whatever Possessed the President? Academic Experts and Presidential Policy, 1960–1988* (Amherst, MA, 1993), 77–78.

3. Report to President and Cabinet on the Economic Situation by the CEA, April 20, 1965, Cabinet Papers, Box 2, LBJL; Gardner Ackley to President, June 19, 1965, LBJ Handwriting File, Box 8, LBJL; Troika Staff Memorandum, September 10, 1964, Diary Backup, Box 9, LBJL.

4. LBJ and McNamara Conversation, December 2, 1965, TCC, 9305, LBJL.

5. Gardner Ackley to President, December 17, 1965, LBJ Handwriting File, Box 11, LBJL.

6. LBJ and M. Bundy Conversation, December 3, 1965, WH Tapes WH6512.01, LBJL.

7. John L. Sweeny to President, December 13, 1965, OF/H. McPherson, Box 50, LBJL.

8. Stewart Alsop, "The McNamara Equation," *Saturday Evening Post,* May 16, 1964, 12.

9. LBJ and McCormack Conversation, August 23, 1965, WH Tapes, WH 6508.10, 8620, LBJL.

10. Ibid.

11. LBJ and R. Clark Conversation, August 20, 1965, WH Tapes, WH6508.08, LBJL.

12. LBJ and McCormack and Rovers Conversation, August 23, 1965, WH Tapes, WH6508.10, 8621, LBJL.

13. Deborah Shapley, *Promise and Power: The Life and Times of Robert McNamara* (Boston, 1993), 384.

14. Moynihan to McPherson, July 16, 1965, OF/H. McPherson, Box 21, LBJL; McNamara Interview with Rostow, January 8, 1975, Reference File, LBJL.

15. Daniel P. Moynihan, "Who Gets in the Army?" *New Republic,* November 5, 1966, 20–21.

16. Shapley, *Promise and Power,* 385; David Sanford, "McNamara's Salvation Army," *New Republic,* September 10, 1966, 14.

17. Minutes of Cabinet Meeting, November 1, 1967, LBJ Handwriting file, Box 11, LBJL.

18. McNamara Interview with Rostow, January 8, 1975, Reference File, LBJL.

19. Moynihan to McPherson, July 16, 1965, OF/H. McPherson, Box 21, LBJL.

20. LBJ and McNamara Conversation, December 22, 1967, WH6512.04, LBJL.

21. LBJ and Moyers Conversation, December 31, 1965, TCC, 9349, LBJL.

22. Shapley, *Promise and Power,* 384.

23. LBJ and McNamara Conversation, November 14, 1964, White House Telephone Tapes, WH6411.20, LBJL.

24. Moyers to Bob Kinter, May 5, 1966, OF/Bill Moyers, Box 12, LBJL.

25. Valenti OH, July 12, 1972, LBJL.

26. Harry McPherson OH, May 16, 1985, LBJL.

27. Ibid.

28. See Joseph A. Califano Jr., *Inside: A Public and Private Life* (New York, 2004), 3–45.

29. McPherson OH, LBJL.

30. Eric F. Goldman, *The Tragedy of Lyndon Johnson* (New York, 1969), 266–267.

31. Quoted in Joseph A. Califano, *The Triumph and Tragedy of Lyndon Johnson: The White House Years* (College Station, 2003), 114–115.

32. Robert Dallek, *Flawed Giant: Lyndon B. Johnson and His Times, 1961–1973* (New York, 1998), 299.

33. Schultz to President, November 7, 1966 Diary Backup, Box 49, LBJL.

34. Califano, *Triumph and Tragedy,* 51.

35. From the President's Pocket, March 8, 1966, LBJ Handwriting File, Box 13, LBJL.

36. "Remarks in Baltimore at the Celebration of the Bicentennial of American Methodism," April 22, 1966, in *Public Papers of the Presidents: LBJ, 1966,* vol. I (Washington, DC, 1967), 447.

37. Califano, *Triumph and Tragedy,* 115.

38. Dallek, *Flawed Giant,* 302.

39. "Annual Message to the Congress on the State of the Union," January 12, 1966, in *Public Papers: LBJ, 1966,* vol. I, 3–6.

40. Ibid.; "U.S. Can Continue the 'Great Society' and Fight in Vietnam . . . LBJ Hands Congress Massive Work Load," read a *Washington Post* headline. Quoted in Dallek, *Flawed Giant,* 300.

41. See Minutes of the Meeting between the President and the Bi-Partisan Leaders of the House and Senate, July 18, 1966, Diary Backup, Box 39, LBJL.

42. Diaries of Orville Freeman, April 4, 1966, PP/Orville Freeman, Box 10, LBJL.

43. Ackley to Califano, June 16, 1966, LBJ Handwriting, Box 24, LBJL; see also Fowler to President, January 7, 1966, LBJ Handwriting File, Box 11, LBJL.

44. Califano to President, February 9, 1966, LBJ Handwriting File, Box 12, LBJL.

45. LBJ and Meany Conversation, February 22, 1966, WH Tapes, TCC, February 1966, LBJL.

46. Martin to President, March 15, 1966, LBJ Handwriting File, Box 13, LBJL; and Califano to President, June 14, 1966, Diary Backup, Box 37, LBJL.

47. See Middleton Notes of an Interview with LBJ During Research and Writing of *The Vantage Point,* OF/Harry Middleton, Box 79, LBJL.

48. Califano to President, June 22, 1966, Diary Backup, Box 38, LBJL.

49. "Rising Prices: How Long, How High?" *Newsweek,* September 5, 1966, 69.

50. Redmon to Moyers, August 31, 1966, OF/Bill Moyers, Box 12, LBJL.

51. Congressional Briefing, September 6, 1966, Congressional Briefings, Box 1, LBJL.

52. mjdr to President, September 12, 1966, LBJ Handwriting File, Box 31, LBJL.

53. "Special Message to the Congress on Transportation," March 2, 1966, in *Public Papers: LBJ, 1966,* vol. I, 250–258.

54. Quoted in Califano, *Triumph and Tragedy,* 125.

55. Quoted in ibid., 126.

56. Fifteen years later, Congress placed the shipping industry in the Department of Transportation.

57. Quoted in Califano, *Triumph and Tragedy,* 131.

58. Irving Bernstein, *Guns or Butter: The Presidency of Lyndon Johnson* (New York, 1996), 462–463.

59. See Milton P. Semer to President, June 10, 1966, LBJ Handwriting File, Box 15, LBJL.

60. Quoted in Califano, *Triumph and Tragedy,* 132.

61. Bernstein, *Guns or Butter,* 465.

62. Gareth Davies, *From Opportunity to Entitlement: The Transformation and Decline of Great Society Liberalism* (Lawrence, KS, 1996), 137–138.

63. Califano, *Triumph and Tragedy,* 135.

64. LBJ, *The Vantage Point: Perspectives of the Presidency, 1963–1969* (New York, 1971), 330.

65. Bernstein, *Guns or Butter,* 469.

66. Davies, *From Opportunity to Entitlement,* 137.

CHAPTER 12: THE SEARCH FOR A NEW KIND OF FREEDOM

1. "Remarks to the Delegates to the White House Conference 'To Fulfill These Rights,'" June 1, 1966, in *Public Papers of the Presidents: LBJ, 1963–1964,* vol. I (Washington, DC, 1965), 573.

2. "Crisis of Color '66," *Newsweek,* August 22, 1966, 20–26; Robert Dallek, *Flawed Giant: Lyndon B. Johnson and His Times, 1961–1973* (New York, 1998), 323.

3. Fortas to Valenti, January 17, 1966, LBJ Handwriting File, Box 11, LBJL.

4. Ibid.

5. Dewey W. Grantham, *The South in Modern America: A Region at Odds* (New York, 1994), 255.

6. Thomas J. Sugrue, *Sweet Land of Liberty: The Forgotten Struggle for Civil Rights in the North* (New York, 2009), xiii.

7. This had been historically true of labor forces as economies made the transformation from agricultural to industrial bases.

8. Christopher Lasch, "The Trouble with Black Power," *New York Review of Books,* February 29, 1968, 4–14.

9. Sugrue, *Sweet Land of Liberty,* xv.

10. Ibid., 361.

11. Terry H. Anderson, *The Pursuit of Fairness: A History of Affirmative Action* (New York, 2004), 83.

12. Carl Holman to Lee White, December 16, 1965, OF/H. McPherson, Box 21, LBJL.

13. Ibid.

14. Sugrue, *Sweet Land of Liberty,* 401–402.

15. Quoted in Thomas F. Jackson, *From Civil Rights to Human Rights: Martin Luther King, Jr., and the Struggle for Economic Justice* (Philadelphia, 2007), 2.

16. Ibid., 189.

17. Ibid., 204.

18. Ibid., 20–21.

19. Ibid.

20. Notes on Meredith March, June 25, 1966, OF/H. McPherson, Box 22, LBJL.

21. "The March Meredith Began," *Newsweek,* June 20, 1966, 28–29.

22. John Dittmer, *Local People: The Struggle for Civil Rights in Mississippi* (Urbana, IL, 1994), 396. See also Stokely Carmichael, "What We Want," *New York Review of Books,* September 22, 1966, 5–6.

23. "Crisis of Color '66," *Newsweek,* August 22, 1966, 34.

24. Harry McPherson OH, V, April 9, 1969, LBJL.

25. Jackson, *Civil Rights to Human Rights,* 137.

26. Quoted in Doris Kearns Goodwin, *Lyndon Johnson and the American Dream* (New York, 1991), 320.

27. "Remarks to Members of the Bishops' Council, African Methodist Episcopal Church," September 27, 1966, in *Public Papers of the Presidents: LBJ, 1966,* vol. II (Washington, DC, 1967), 945; "Remarks at a Reception for Members of the American Society of Newspaper Editors," April 17, 1964, in *Public Papers: LBJ, 1963–1964,* vol. I (Washington, DC, 1965), 1072–1073.

28. Adam Cohen and Elizabeth Taylor, *American Pharaoh: Mayor Richard J. Daley: His Battle for Chicago and the Nation* (Boston, 2000), 335. See also Cater to President, March 25, 1966, LBJ Handwriting File, Box 13, LBJL.

29. Stephen C. Halpern, *On the Limits of the Law: The Ironic Legacy of Title VI of the 1964 Civil Rights Act* (Baltimore, 1995), 45–52. See also McPherson to President, May 12, 1966, OF/H. McPherson, Box 52, LBJL.

30. "What Grenadans Are Like," *Newsweek,* September 26, 1966, 33–34.

31. Cohen and Taylor, *American Pharaoh,* 161.

32. See Ed Weisl OH, October 30, 1968, LBJL.

33. Cater to President, May 19, 1966, LBJ Handwriting File, Box 14, LBJL.

34. Cohen and Taylor, *American Pharaoh,* 351–353; Cater to President, October 4, 1965, Box 23, LBJL; W. Wilbur Cohen OH, December 8, 1968, I, LBJL; "Leaning on HEW," *Newsweek,* October 18, 1966, 98.

35. On Thanksgiving Day 1962, JFK had signed a fair housing order prohibiting the Federal Housing Authority (FHA) from insuring any mortgages benefiting discriminatory home builders. But the FHA insured only 20 percent of newly constructed homes, so FHA director Robert Weaver urged Kennedy to extend the prohibition to all financial institutions. Pressured by big-city Democratic legislators, the president exempted banks, savings and loans, and two million federally insured housing units already under construction. Jackson, *Civil Rights to Human Rights,* 128–129.

36. Henry Wilson to President, March 11, 1966, and Katzenbach to President, March 15, 1966, LBJ Handwriting File, Box 13, LBJL.

37. Byron C. Hulsey, *Everett Dirksen and His Presidents: How a Senate Giant Shaped American Politics* (Lawrence, KS, 2000), 68–69.

38. Dallek, *Flawed Giant,* 324. Johnson was then under increasing pressure from black leaders who had embraced the concept of a multi-billion-dollar "Marshall Plan" for African Americans. And this at a time when Congress was pressing for a $6 billion cut in domestic spending. Housing was an area where Johnson could do something for civil rights that would not cost any money.

39. Ramsey Clark OH, IV, April 16, 1969, LBJL.

40. McPherson to President, September 12, 1966, Katzenbach Papers, Box 15, JFKL.

41. "Special Message to the Congress Proposing Further Legislation to Strengthen Civil Rights," April 28, 1966, in *Public Papers: LBJ, 1966,* vol. I, 461–468.

42. Katzenbach to Wilson, March 15, 1966, LBJ Handwriting File, Box 13, and Katzenbach to President, March 17, 196, Diary Backup, Box 37, LBJL.

43. "Remarks of the President at the Olive Medal of Honor Ceremony," March 21, 1966, Diary Backup, Box 33, LBJL; see also Sparks and Hardesty to Valenti, April 1, 1966, Diary Backup, Box 33, LBJL.

44. Sugrue, *Sweet Land of Liberty,* 416–417.

45. "The Touchiest Target," *Newsweek,* August 15, 1966, 29.

46. "Colorful Campaign," *Newsweek,* October 17, 1966, 29.

47. McPherson to Katzenbach, September 20, 1966, Katzenbach Papers, Box 15, JFKL.

48. Moynihan to McPherson, September 22, 1966, OF/H. McPherson, Box 22, LBJL.

49. Andrew Kopkind, "Soul Power," *New York Review of Books,* August 24, 1967, 3.

50. Roche to President, February 16, 1967, LBJ Handwriting File, Box 20, LBJL.

51. McPherson to President, December 19, 1966, and Moynihan to McPherson, September 22, 1966, OF/H. McPherson, Box 22, LBJL.

52. Bernstein, *Guns or Butter: The Presidency of Lyndon Johnson* (New York, 1996), 439.

53. McPherson to President, April 14, 1966, OF/H. McPherson, Box 52, LBJL.

54. "Statement by the President Upon Signing Bill Providing for the Joseph H. Hirshhorn Museum and Sculpture Garden," November 7, 1966, in *Public Papers: LBJ, 1966,* vol. II, 1345.

55. Irving Bernstein, *Guns or Butter,* 440–441, 444–457.

56. Quoted in ibid., 273.

57. "Remarks to Members of the National Recreation and Park Association," October 13, 1966, in *Public Papers: LBJ, 1966,* vol. II, 1174.

58. Bernstein, *Guns or Butter,* 278–279.

59. "Remarks to Members of the National Recreation and Park Association," October 13, 1966, in *Public Papers: LBJ, 1966,* vol. II, 1176.

CHAPTER 13: THE IMP OF THE PERVERSE: COMMUNITY ACTION AND WELFARE RIGHTS

1. Quoted in Jim Wright, *Balance of Power: Presidents and Congress from the Era of McCarthy to the Age of Gingrich* (Atlanta, 1996), 41.

2. Califano Commencement Address at Mercy College, Califano to LBJ, June 4, 1968, OF/Joe Califano, Box 17, LBJL.

3. Robert Dallek, *Flawed Giant: Lyndon B. Johnson and His Times, 1961–1973* (New York, 1998), 330.

4. Califano Commencement Address at Mercy College, Califano to LBJ, June 4; Dallek, *Flawed Giant,* 330.

5. See Gareth Davies, *From Opportunity to Entitlement: The Transformation and Decline of Great Society Liberalism* (Lawrence, KS, 1996), 89.

6. Sidney M. Milkis, *President and the Parties: The Transformation of the American Party System since the New Deal* (New York, 1993), 182.

7. "Bill Moyers Talks about LBJ, Power, Poverty, War and the Young," *The Atlantic* 22, no. 1 (July 1968): 22.

8. Davies, *From Opportunity to Entitlement,* 91.

9. Dallek, *Flawed Giant,* 331.

10. Theda Skocpol, *Protecting Soldiers and Mothers: The Political Origins of Social Policy in United States* (Cambridge, MA, 1992), 1.

11. Michael McGerr, *A Fierce Discontent: The Rise and Fall of the Progressive Movement in America* (New York, 2003), 11.

12. Ibid.

13. Skocpol, *Soldiers and Mothers,* 5.

14. Michael B. Katz, *In the Shadow of the Poorhouse: A Social History of Welfare in America, Tenth Anniversary Edition* (New York, 1996), ix–x.

15. Eileen Boris, "Contested Rights: The Great Society between Home and Work," in *The Great Society and the High Tide of Liberalism,* ed. Sidney M. Milkis and Jerome M. Mileur (Amherst, MA, 2005), 130–131.

16. Suzanne Mettler, "Social Citizens of Separate Sovereignties: Governance in the New Deal Welfare State," in *The New Deal and the Triumph of Liberalism,* ed. Sidney M. Milkis and Jerome M. Mileur (Amherst, MA, 2002), 246.

17. Frances Fox Piven and Richard A. Cloward, "The Politics of the Great Society," in *Great Society,* ed. Milkis and Mileur, 261–62.

18. Boris, "Contested Rights," 116.

19. Ibid., 188–189.

20. Ibid., 131.

21. LBJ and Elmer Staats Conversation, January 25, 1964, White House Telephone Tapes, WH6401.22, LBJL.

22. Thomas J. Sugrue, *Sweet Land of Liberty: The Forgotten Struggle for Civil Rights in the North* (New York, 2009), 383–385.

23. See Davies, *From Opportunity to Entitlement,* 115–118.

24. Piven and Cloward, "Politics of the Great Society," 261–262.

25. Edward D. Berkowitz, *Creating the Welfare State: The Political Economy of Twentieth Century Reform* (Lawrence, KS, 1992), 117–119.

26. Quoted in Sugrue, *Sweet Land of Liberty,* 375.

27. "War on Poverty: Present Danger," *Newsweek,* August 8, 1966.

28. Edward R. Schmitt, "The War on Poverty," in *A Companion to Lyndon B. Johnson,* ed. Mitchell B. Lerner (Malden, MA, 2012), 96–97.

29. J. Roche OH, I, July 16, 1970, LBJL.

30. Quoted in Jeff Shesol, *Mutual Contempt: Lyndon Johnson, Robert Kennedy, and the Feud That Defined a Decade* (New York, 1998), 172.

31. McPherson to LBJ, June 24, 1965, OF/H. McPherson, Box 21, LBJL.

32. "The Bobby Phenomenon," *Newsweek,* October 24, 1966, 30–31.

33. See, for example, "Robert Kennedy Tops Johnson in California Test," *Los Angeles Times,* June 29, 1966, and "The President's News Conference of August 24, 1966," *Public Papers of the Presidents: LBJ, 1966,* vol. II (Washington, DC, 1967), 880.

34. LBJ and Daley Conversation, July 19, 1966, WH Tapes, WH660702, LBJL.

35. Wilbur Cohen OH, December 8, 1968, LBJL.

36. McPherson to President, June 24, 1965, OF/H. McPherson, Box 21, LBJL.

37. Califano to LBJ, June 4, 1968, OF/ Joe Califano, Box 17, LBJL.

CHAPTER 14: REFORM UNDER SIEGE

1. "Fulbright Fears Y. S. Eliminating Chance for Peace," *Arkansas Gazette,* February 11, 1966.

2. Quoted in "The Late, Great Society," *New Republic,* April 9, 1966.

3. Ronald Steel, "A Visit to Washington," *New York Review of Books,* October 6, 1966, 5–6.

4. Hans J. Morgenthau, "Truth and Power," *New Republic,* November 26, 1966, 8–11.

5. Hans J. Morgenthau, "The Colossus of Johnson City," *New York Review of Books,* March 31, 1966.

6. See Redmon to Moyers, July 27, 1966, OF/Bill Moyers, Box 12, LBJL.

7. LBJ and George Brown Conversation, June 13, 1966, WH Tapes, WH6605.04, LBJL.

8. Gardner Ackley to LBJ, February 27, 1967, LBJ Handwriting File, Box 20, Presidential Papers of LBJ, LBJL.

9. Diaries of Orville Freeman, September 21, 1966, PP/Orville Freeman, Box 11, LBJL.

10. Douglass Cater to the President, January 12, 1967, LBJ Handwriting File, Box 11, Presidential Papers of LBJ, LBJL.

11. Sean J. Savage, *JFK, LBJ, and the Democratic Party* (Albany, 2004), 139.

12. Quoted in Sidney M. Milkis, *The President and the Parties: The Transformation of the American Party System since the New Deal* (New York, 1993), 189.

13. James Rowe OH, II, September 16, 1969, LBJL.

14. "Nixon and the GOP Comeback," *Newsweek,* October 10, 1966, 30–33.

15. "Martin Luther King, Jr. and Stokely Carmichael, FBI Confidential Report," October 4, 1966, OF/Mildred Stegall, Box 32, LBJL.

16. "The [Republican] resurgence is a welcome antidote to the flagrant abuses of unchallenged power which we have suffered since January 1965." Walter Lippmann, "The War and the Election," *Newsweek,* December 5, 1966, 23.

17. Quoted in Jeff Shesol, *Mutual Contempt: Lyndon Johnson, Robert Kennedy, and the Feud That Defined a Decade* (New York, 1998), 347. See also "T.R.B. from Washington," *New Republic,* June 27, 1966.

18. UPI 10, December 1, 1966, Diary Backup, Box 49, LBJL.

19. See LBJ to Nelson Rockefeller, November 18, 1966, LBJL Handwriting File, Box 18, LBJL.

20. Quoted in Robert Dallek, *Flawed Giant: Lyndon B. Johnson and His Times, 1961–1973* (New York, 1998), 294.

21. Quoted in Joseph A. Califano, *The Triumph and Tragedy of Lyndon Johnson: The White House Years* (College Station, 2003), 178–179.

22. Ibid., 179–180.

23. Quoted in ibid., 182–183.

24. Lady Bird Johnson, *A White House Diary* (New York, 1970), 471. A House investigation had found Powell guilty of misusing public funds.

25. See Robert Kintner to President, January 11 and 13, 1967, LBJ Handwriting File, Box 19, LBJL.

26. James Reston, "Johnson and the Age of Reform," *New York Times,* January 15, 1967.

27. "Annual Message to Congress on the State of the Union," January 10, 1967, *Public Papers of the Presidents: LBJ, 1967,* vol. I (Washington, DC, 1968), 2–14.

28. "'Help Party, Don't Run' Dissenters Tell Johnson," *Washington Evening Star,* July 31, 1967.

29. Ibid.

30. McPherson to President, February 2, 1967, OF/H. McPherson, Box 53, LBJL.

31. "Remarks at a Ceremony at the Lincoln Memorial," February 12, 1967, *Public Papers: LBJ, 1967,* vol. I, 176–178.

32. "Commencement Address at Catholic University," June 6, 1965, *Public Papers: LBJ, 1963–1964,* vol. II, 641–642.

33. Nick Kotz, *Judgment Days: Lyndon Baines Johnson, Martin Luther King Jr., and the Laws That Changed America* (Boston, 2005), 354.

34. Ibid., 346.

35. Watson to the President, September 15, 1965, OF/Mildred Stegall, Box 31A, LBJL.

36. Charles DeBenedetti, *An American Ordeal: The Antiwar Movement of the Vietnam Era* (Syracuse, 1990), 172–173.

37. Quoted in Kotz, *Judgment Days,* 375.

38. McPherson to President, April 4, 1967, OF/H. McPherson, Box 53, LBJL.

39. Kotz, *Judgment Days,* 377.

40. McPherson to President, April 4, 1967, OF/H. McPherson, Box 53, LBJL.

41. Marvin to the President, September 15, 1965, and September 26, 1967, OF/Mildred Stegall, Box 31A, LBJL.

42. Actually, Levison had been urging MLK to tone down his antiwar statements, and the FBI knew it. Kotz, *Judgment Days,* 354.

43. James Farmer OH, II, July 20, 1971, LBJL.

44. Califano to President, July 25, 1966, and Lodge to M. Bundy, July 26, 1966, Diary Backup, Box 40, LBJL.

45. Clifford Alexander to President, April 18, 1967, Diary Backup, Box 62, LBJL.

46. Califano to President, June 28, 1967, LBJ Handwriting File, Box 23, LBJL; "Negro Casualties in Vietnam," 1961–1965, n.d., OF/H. J. McPherson, Box 22, LBJL.

47. Wilson to LBJ, February 4, 1966, WHCF, Box 322, LBJL.

CHAPTER 15: WHIPLASH: URBAN RIOTING AND THE WAR ON CRIME

1. See Robert V. Spike, "Fissures in the Civil Rights Movement," *Christianity and Crisis,* February 21, 1967, 18–20. See also Moynihan to McPherson, April 15, 1966, OF/H. McPherson, Box 21, LBJL.

2. McPherson to President, January 19, 1967, OF/H. McPherson, Box 53, LBJL.

3. "Special Message to the Congress on Equal Justice," February 15, 1967, *Public Papers of the Presidents: LBJ, 1967,* vol. I (Washington, DC, 1968), 188–189. See also Califano to President, February 10, 1967, LBJ Handwriting File, Box 20, LBJL.

4. "Something Borrowed," *Newsweek,* July 24, 1967, 28.

5. See "Newark Boils Over," *Newsweek,* July 24, 1967, 21–22.

6. Quoted in Joseph A. Califano, *The Triumph and Tragedy of Lyndon Johnson: The White House Years* (College Station, 2003), 210.

7. "You Can't Run Away," *Newsweek,* July 31, 1967, 17.

8. Califano, *Triumph and Tragedy,* 212–213.

9. Ibid.

10. Thomas J. Sugrue, *Sweet Land of Liberty: The Forgotten Struggle for Civil Rights in the North* (New York, 2009), 290.

11. Ibid., 319–321.

12. Ibid., 343.

13. Ibid., 344–345.

14. "An American Tragedy, 1967," *Newsweek,* August 7, 1967, 19.

15. Ramsey Clark OH, IV, April 16, 1969, LBJL.

16. Quoted in Califano, *Triumph and Tragedy,* 214.

17. Notes of the President's Activities During the Detroit Crisis, July 24, 1967, Diary Backup, Box 71, LBJL.

18. Ibid.

19. Quoted in Califano, *Triumph and Tragedy,* 217.

20. See the Detroit Riots Chronology, July 23–25, 1967, and AP208 ff., July 24, 1967, Diary Backup, Box 71, LBJL. In truth, the situation improved dramatically after regular Army troops arrived. Under the command of General John Throckmorton, a veteran of World War II, Korea, Vietnam, and Mississippi, the paratroopers from the 101st and 82nd Airborne, some of whom had protected black children at Central High and James Meredith at Ole Miss, soon restored relative peace with minimal force. Michael W. Flamm, *Law and Order: Street Crime, Civil Unrest, and the Crisis of Liberalism in the 1960s* (New York, 2005), 92–93.

21. "An American Tragedy, 1967," *Newsweek,* 18.

22. Flamm, *Law and Order,* 125–127.

23. Ibid., 99.

24. Ibid.

25. Ibid., 84–85.

26. Ibid., 111.

27. "Havana: Fanning the Guerrilla Flames," *Newsweek,* August 14, 1967.

28. "SNCC and the Jews," *Newsweek,* August 28, 1967, 22; "What Has Become of the Treason Laws?" *Congressional Record,* April 12, 1967, LBJ Handwriting File, Box 21, LBJL.

29. "There have been no indications in the clandestine operations field that Cuba or Red China have engaged in promoting rioting or mass violence in the United States," Langley reported to the White House. Castro had infiltrated some intelligence agents into the country, but their primary task was to gather information on Cuban exiles plotting to overthrow the communist regime in Havana. *Cuba/Red China Involvement in Promoting Violence in the United States,* CIA Report, July 26, 1967, NSF Memos, Box 20, Rostow, LBJL.

30. Edward Schmitt, *President of the Other America: Robert Kennedy and the Politics of Poverty* (Amherst, MA, 2010), 120–121.

31. Ibid., 140.

32. Ibid., 184–185.

33. Ibid., 170.

34. See Larry Levinson, Memo for the Record, July 31, 1967, Diary Backup, Box 72, LBJL; Emmet John Hughes, "The Great Disgrace," *Newsweek,* August 7, 1967.

35. See Summary of the President's Meeting with HUD's Urban Development Advisory Committee, July 31, 1967, Diary Backup, Box 72, LBJL.

36. Emmet John Hughes, "A Curse of Confusion," *Newsweek,* May 1, 1967, 17.

37. Quoted in Califano, *Triumph and Tragedy,* 220. See also the President's Meeting with the National Advisory Commission on Civil Disorders, July 29, 1967, Diary Backup, Box 72, LBJL.

38. Sidney M. Milkis, "Lyndon Johnson, the Great Society, and the Modern Presidency," in *The Great Society and the High Tide of Liberalism,* ed. Sidney M. Milkis and Jerome M. Mileur (Amherst, MA, 2005), 26.

39. McPherson to Johnson, July 29, 1967, Diary Backup, Box 72, LBJL.

40. "After the Riots: A Survey," *Newsweek,* August 27, 1967, 18.

41. Diaries of Orville Freeman, May 6, 1967, PP/Orville Freeman, Box 11, LBJL.

42. "LBJ at Low Ebb," *Newsweek,* August 21, 1967, 15.

43. Sugrue, *Sweet Land of Liberty,* 341.

44. Milkis, "Lyndon Johnson, the Great Society, and the Modern Presidency," 27.

45. Ibid.

46. "Too Much Good News Is Bad," *Newsweek,* April 29, 1968.

47. Minutes of a Cabinet Meeting, November 20, 1967, Cabinet Papers, Box 11, LBJL.

48. "LBJ's War Budget—and Its New Math," *Newsweek,* February 6, 1967, 30–31.

49. Jytte Klausen, "Did World War II End the New Deal? A Comparative Perspective on Postwar Planning Initiatives," in *The New Deal and the Triumph of Liberalism,* ed. Sidney M. Milkis and Jerome M. Mileur (Amherst, MA, 2002), 197.

50. Gardner Ackley to the President, September 21, 1967, LBJ Handwriting File, Box 2, LBJL.

51. McPherson to Califano, OF/H. McPherson, Box 50, LBJL.

52. See Emmet John Hughes, "The Great Disgrace," *Newsweek,* August 7, 1967.

53. Diaries of Orville Freeman, December 8, 1967, PP/Orville Freeman, Box 4,Vol. 8, LBJL.

54. Califano, *Triumph and Tragedy,* 242.

55. Diaries of Orville Freeman, June 10, 1967, PP/Orville Freeman, Box 11, LBJL.

56. Barefoot Sanders to the President, July 20, 1967, Diary Backup, Box 72, Presidential Papers of LBJ, LBJL.

57. Califano, *Triumph and Tragedy,* 244.

58. Notes on Meeting of the President with Joseph Kraft, September 27, 1967, White House Aides, George Christian, Box 1, LBJL.

59. Quoted in Califano, *Triumph and Tragedy,* 245.

60. Ibid., 245–246.

CHAPTER 16: A "RICE-ROOTS REVOLUTION": THE GREAT SOCIETY IN VIETNAM

1. The Selective Service and Training Act, first passed in 1917 and renewed in 1940, 1947, and 1967, required all American males between the ages of eighteen and thirty-five years to register for military service. Full-time students in colleges and training programs were exempt as long as they stayed in school. During the Kennedy administration, married men were exempt, but that deferment was canceled by President Johnson. Permanent health conditions or injuries were also grounds of deferment.

2. Quoted in Randall Bennett Woods, *Quest for Identity: America Since 1945* (New York, 2005), 258.

3. David Ekbladh, *The Great American Mission: Modernization and the Construction of an American World Order* (Princeton, NJ, 2010), 4–5.

4. Ekbladh, *American Mission,* 190.

5. Quoted in ibid., 191.

6. Ibid., 193.

7. Ibid., 195.

8. Ibid., 207.

9. Quoted in ibid., 209.

10. Richard Helms, with William Hood, *A Look over My Shoulder: A Life in the Central Intelligence Agency* (New York: 2003), 321; author interview with Frank Scotton, October 12–14, 2007.

11. Randall B. Woods, *Shadow Warrior: William Egan Colby and the CIA* (New York, 2013), 207–208.

12. Tran Ngoc Chau, "Hawks, Doves and the Dragon" (unpublished memoir in the possession of author), 364.

13. Neil Sheehan, *A Bright Shining Lie: John Paul Vann and America in Vietnam* (New York, 1988), 538.

14. Quoted in Randall B. Woods, *LBJ: Architect of American Ambition* (New York, 2006), 436.

15. Ibid., 608.

16. Ibid., 719.

17. Robert Komer to LBJ, May 9, 1966, NSF, Komer Files, Box 4, LBJL; Robert Komer to LBJ, April 19, 1966, NSF, Komer Files, Box 2, LBJL; Robert Komer to Colonel Robert I. Channon, June 20, 1974, Box 22, Colby Papers, Texas Tech University.

18. William Colby, *Lost Victory: A Firsthand Account of America's Sixteen-Year Involvement in Vietnam* (Chicago, 1989), 206; Thomas L. Ahern Jr., *CIA and Rural Pacification in South Vietnam* (Washington, DC, Center for the Study of Intelligence, August 2001), 205. Available at National Security Archive: http://nsarchive.gwu.edu/NSAEBB/NSAEBB284/3-CIA_AND_RURAL_PACIFICATION.pdf.

19. Chau, "Hawks, Doves and Dragons," 368, 374.

20. Quoted in Ahern, *CIA and Rural Pacification,* 244.

21. Author interview with Mike Hacker, October 13, 2007.

22. Author interview with Mike Hacker, October 23, 2007; author interview with Louis Jankowski, November 7, 2007; author interview with Bruce Kinsey, September 20, 2007.

23. As Colby would later admit, the PRUs contained some of South Vietnam's most unsavory citizens—criminals, soldiers of fortune, turncoat VC, henchmen of local warlords. In some provinces the PRUs fought with valor against the VC; in others they acted as extortionists and bagmen for corrupt officials.

24. William E. Colby to Michael Forrestal, November 16, 1964, CREST, National Archives II.

25. Rostow to President Johnson, July 31, 1967, National Security File Memos, Box 20, Vol. 36, Presidential Papers of LBJ, LBJL.

26. Ed Lansdale to Ellsworth Bunker, June 7, 1968, NSF Memos to President, Rostow, Box 35, LBJL; author interview with James Nach, September 2, 2008. See also Douglas Blaufarb to William E. Colby, December 1, 1989, Box 6, F20, Colby Papers, Texas Tech University. Blaufarb lamented "the failure of the Thieu government to develop a popular political base, choosing instead to rely on the officer corps as its base. That led to the massive corruption within the military and the assignment and promotion of unqualified leaders. . . . It also led to an immense gap between the provincial and district governments and the peasant population."

CHAPTER 17: ABDICATION

1. Edward R. Schmitt, "The War on Poverty," in *A Companion to Lyndon B. Johnson,* ed. Mitchell B. Lerner (Malden, MA, 2012), 96–97.

2. B. Baker OH, II.

3. Quoted in Charles DeBenedetti, *An American Ordeal: The Antiwar Movement of the Vietnam Era* (Syracuse, 1990), 192.

4. Ibid.

5. Diaries of Orville Freeman, August 10, 1967, PP/Orville Freeman, Box 11, LBJL.

6. Jones to President, November 4, 1967, *FRUS,* 1964–1968, V, 917.

7. Randall B. Woods, *Fulbright: A Biography* (New York, 1995), 464.

8. Sean J. Savage, *JFK, LBJ, and the Democratic Party* (Albany, 2004), 162.

9. Ibid., 163.

10. "Dump LBJ?" *Newsweek,* October 9, 1967, 25.

11. "The Move to 'Dump' Johnson," *Newsweek,* November 27, 1967, 25.

12. Roche to President, March 15 and June 6, 1967, LBJ Handwriting File, Boxes 21 and 22, LBJL.

13. "Meet Candidate Lyndon Johnson," *Newsweek,* November 13, 1967, 31.

14. James Reston, "Johnson's Theme of 'Little Time' Puzzles Friends," *New York Times,* November 30, 1966.

15. Roche to President, July 6, 1967, LBJ Handwriting File, Box 23, LBJL.

16. Quoted in Joseph A. Califano, *The Triumph and Tragedy of Lyndon Johnson: The White House Years* (College Station, 2003), 254.

17. "Annual Message to Congress on the State of the Union," January 17, 1968, *Public Papers of the Presidents: LBJ, 1968–1969,* vol. I (Washington, DC, 1970), 31.

18. "Backlash in Boston—and across the U.S.," *Newsweek,* November 6, 1967.

19. Quoted in Theodore H. White, *The Making of the President 1964* (New York, 1965), 259.

20. See Cater to President, October 11, 1967, Cabinet Papers, Box 11, LBJL.

21. Califano, *Triumph and Tragedy,* 223.

22. Ibid., 225–226.

23. "Special Message to the Congress: 'To Earn a Living: The Right of Every American.'" January 23, 1968, *Public Papers: LBJ, 1968,* vol. I, 46–47.

24. Califano, *Triumph and Tragedy,* 225–226. See also Califano to President, March 11, 1968, OF/Joe Califano, Box 16, LBJL; "Remarks at a Meeting of the National Alliance of Businessmen," March 16, 1968, *Public Papers: LBJ, 1968,* vol. I, 402–405.

25. Temple to President, January 19, 1968, LBJ Handwriting File, Box 27, LBJL.

26. Clark to President, February 12, 1968, PP/W. Christopher, Box 1, LBJL.

27. Ramsey Clark OH, V, June 3, 1968, LBJL.

28. Michael W. Flamm, *Law and Order: Street Crime, Civil Unrest, and the Crisis of Liberalism in the 1960s* (New York, 2005), 106.

29. Ibid., 109.

30. Ramsey Clark OH, IV, April 16, 1969, LBJL.

31. "Guilty or Not?" *Newsweek,* March 18, 1968, 46.

32. Flamm, *Law and Order,* 105.

33. Ibid., 109–110.

34. Notes on Meeting with Negro Editors and Publishers, March 15, 1968, Diary Backup, Box 93, LBJL. See also Califano to President, March 2, 1968, OF/Joe Califano, Box 16, LBJL.

35. Harry McPherson OH, IV, March 24, 1969, LBJL.

36. "Special Message to the Congress: 'To Protect the Consumer Interest,'" February 6, 1968, *Public Papers: LBJ, 1968–1969,* vol. I, 174; "Meet Ralph Nader," *Newsweek,* January 22, 1968, 65.

37. "Special Message to the Congress: 'The Fifth Freedom,'" February 5, 1968, *Public Papers: LBJ, 1968–1969,* vol. I, 165–167.

38. Informal Stag Dinner, HHH, Mansfield, Long, Hayden, Clark, Church et al., September 21, 1967, Papers of George McGovern, Box 1A, Mudd Library, Princeton.

39. McPherson to the President, March 18, 1968, OF/H. McPherson, Memos to the President, Box 53, LBJL.

40. Robert Dallek, *Flawed Giant: Lyndon B. Johnson and His Times, 1961–1973* (New York, 1998), 24–25.

41. Ibid.

42. John Gardner OH, II, December 20, 1971, LBJL.

43. Roche to LBJ, December 4, 1967, PP/A. Schlesinger, Box W59, JFKL.

44. Diaries of Orville Freeman, March 22, 1968, PP/Orville Freeman, LBJL.

45. See Weisl to President, January 26, 1968, LBJ Handwriting File, Box 27, LBJL; Rostow to LBJ, February 22, 1968, NSF Country File, Vietnam Box 102, LBJL.

46. C. Clifford OH, III, July 14, 1969, LBJL. According to Richard Daley's biographers, the idea had come from him. "Rather than go through the divisiveness of a primary challenge to a sitting president, Kennedy should get Johnson to agree to submit the future of the Vietnam War to binding arbitration. It must have seemed odd to Kennedy that his presidential candidacy, viewed by his supporters as a moral crusade, was being reduced to the level of a truckers' strike." Adam Cohen and Elizabeth Taylor, *American Pharaoh: Mayor Richard J. Daley: His Battle for Chicago and the Nation* (Boston, 2000), 450.

47. Notes Taken at Meeting, March 14, 1968, PP/C. Clifford, Box 1, LBJL.

48. "Remarks at a Dinner of the Veterans of Foreign Wars," March 12, 1968, *Public Papers: LBJ, 1968–1969*, vol. I, 381. Johnson and his lieutenants had long held McCarthy in mild contempt. "Around 1960–61," Harry McPherson said, "I began to realize that he [McCarthy] was spending all of his time down in the Senate Restaurant making bon mots for the press and no time on the floor helping with legislation or in committee. He was a master of what Hermann Hesse called feuilleton, extraneous information." McPherson OH, III.

49. Diaries of Orville Freeman, March 22, 1968, PP/Orville Freeman, Box 11, LBJL.

50. Ibid.

51. George C. Herring, *America's Longest War: The United States and Vietnam, 1950–1975* (New York, 1996), 225–226; Summary of Meeting, March 26, 1968, Meeting Notes File, Box 2, LBJL.

52. Herring, *Longest War,* 225.

53. Quoted in Califano, *Triumph and Tragedy,* 268. See also Joe Califano, Memo of Conversation, July 25, 1971, PP/A. Schlesinger, Box W59, JFKL.

54. Ibid.

55. Buzz to President, March 29, 1968, LBJ Handwriting File, Box 29, LBJL.

56. Jan Jarboe Russell, *Lady Bird: A Biography of Mrs. Johnson* (New York, 1999), 300.

57. James Jones, "LBJ's Decision Not to Run in '68," *New York Times,* April 16, 1988.

58. George Gallup, "Johnson's War and Job Ratings Sink," *Washington Post,* March 31, 1968.

59. Christian to President, March 31, 1968, Diary Backup, Box 94, LBJL.

60. Rostow Memorandum for the Record, March 31, 1968, NSF Memos, Box 31, LBJL.

61. Arthur Krim OH, IV, November 9, 1982, LBJL; Marie Fehmer Notes, July 30, 1968, Diary Backup, Box 94, LBJL. See also Clark Clifford OH, August 7, 1969, LBJL.

62. "The President's Address to the Nation Announcing Steps to Limit the War in Vietnam and Reporting His Decision Not to Seek Reelection," March 31, 1968, *Public Papers: LBJ, 1968–1969,* vol. I, 469–476.

63. Ibid.

64. Simon and Vickie McHugh OH, June 9, 1975, LBJL.

65. Marie Fehmer to Dorothy, July 30, 1968, Diary Backup, Box 94, LBJL.

CHAPTER 18: AMERICAN DYSTOPIA

1. Quoted in Randall Bennett Woods, *Quest for Identity: America Since 1945* (New York, 2005), 273.

2. Joseph A. Califano, *The Triumph and Tragedy of Lyndon Johnson: The White House Years* (College Station, TX, 2003), 274.

3. McPherson and Califano to President, April 5, 1968, Diary Backup, Box 95, LBJL.

4. Talking Points for Civil Rights Meeting, April 5, 1968, OF/Joe Califano, Box 17, LBJL.

5. Quoted in Califano, *Triumph and Tragedy*, 275.

6. LBJ to Mrs. King, April 5, 1968, OF/Joe Califano, Box 17, LBJL.

7. Situation Room Information Memorandum, April 5, 1968, Diary Backup, Box 95, LBJL.

8. Visits to Washington, January 28, 1973, Box 30, PP/W. Westmoreland, LBJL.

9. Situation Room Information Memorandum, April 6, 1968, Diary Backup, Box 95, LBJL.

10. Quoted in Califano, *Triumph and Tragedy*, 279.

11. Adm. S. D. Cramer Memo for the Record, April 5, 1968, Diary Backup, Box 95, LBJL. See also Califano, *Triumph and Tragedy*, 279–280.

12. Situation Room Information Memorandum, April 6, 1968, Diary Backup, Box 95, LBJL; Califano, *Triumph and Tragedy*, 281–282.

13. Jim Jones to President, April 5, 1968, Diary Backup, Box 96, LBJL.

14. Califano, *Triumph and Tragedy*, 282; UPI 030A, April 7, 1968, Diary Backup, Box 95, LBJL.

15. "Special Message to the Congress on Equal Justice," February 15, 1967, *Public Papers of the Presidents: LBJ, 1967,* vol. I (Washington, DC, 1968), 188–189.

16. Increasingly, nonwhites were being concentrated in the central cities, but employment opportunities were growing only in outlying sections and suburbia where nonwhites were denied access to accommodations. Despite the growing number of nonwhite central city residents, jobs actually declined in Philadelphia and St. Louis central city areas. In Baltimore and San Francisco, only 11,000 jobs were added in the ghettoes, while the nonwhite population in these areas had grown by 150,000 during the previous ten years. In all four cities, plus New York City, suburban jobs increased in excess of one million. McPherson to the President, April 3, 1968, OF/H. McPherson, Box 53, LBJL.

17. Nick Kotz, *Judgment Days: Lyndon Baines Johnson, Martin Luther King Jr., and the Laws That Changed America* (Boston, 2005), 390.

18. Quoted in ibid.

19. Ibid., 392.

20. Quoted in ibid., 396.

21. Califano to President, April 10, 1968, LBJ Handwriting File, Box 29, LBJL; Barefoot Sanders to President, April 5, 1968, Diary Backup, Box 95, LBJL; Harold "Barefoot" Sanders OH, November 3, 1969, LBJL.

22. Thomas J. Sugrue, *Sweet Land of Liberty: The Forgotten Struggle for Civil Rights in the North* (New York, 2009), 423.

23. Barefoot Sanders to President, April 5, 1968, Diary Backup, Box 95, LBJL.

24. Califano to President, May 2, 1968, OF/Joe Califano, Box 17, LBJL.

25. Notes of meeting, April 11, 1968, *FRUS, 1964–68, VI,* 568.

26. Califano to President, May 2, 1968, OF/Joe Califano, Box 17, LBJL.

27. "The President's News Conference of May 3, 1968," *Public Papers: LBJ, 1968– 1969,* vol. I, 561.

28. Quoted in Califano, *Triumph and Tragedy*, 286.

29. See LBJ, *The Vantage Point: Perspectives of the Presidency, 1963–1969* (New York, 1971), 453–456. See also Okun to President, April 27 and May 13, 1968, Diary Backup, Box 97, LBJL.

30. Amy Nathan Wright, "Civil Rights 'Unfinished Business': Poverty, Race, and the Poor People's Campaign" (PhD diss., University of Texas at Austin, 2007), 240.

31. Kotz, *Judgment Days,* 387.

32. Ibid., 401.

33. Quoted in "Do or Die," *Newsweek,* May 6, 1968, 30.

34. Gerald McKnight, *The Last Crusade: Martin Luther King, Jr., the FBI, and the Poor People's Campaign* (Boulder, CO, 1998), 107–108, 111–112.

35. Warren Christopher to Califano, April 27, 1968, LBJ Handwriting File, Box 29, LBJL.

36. McKnight, *Last Crusade,* 89.

37. Minutes of the Meeting, May 1, 1968, Cabinet Papers, Box 13, LBJL.

38. Cater to President, May 2, 1968, LBJ Handwriting File, Box 29, LBJL.

39. "Russell Long Hits March of the Poor," *New York Times,* April 26, 1968.

40. Wright, "Civil Rights 'Unfinished Business'," 357–361.

41. Kotz, *Judgment Days,* 422.

42. Diaries of Orville Freeman, May 21, 1968, PP/Orville Freeman, Box 12, LBJL.

43. Califano to President, May 17, 1968, OF/Joe Califano, Box 17, LBJL.

44. Christian Notes on President's Meeting with Ken Crawford, May 23, 1968, WH Aides, George Christian, Box 1, LBJL.

45. A Minnesota poll taken on the 18th revealed that 60 percent of the people questioned opposed the Poor People's March and the whole concept of Resurrection City. This from one of the most liberal states in the Union. Diaries of Orville Freeman, June 22, 1968, PP/Orville Freeman, Box 12, Vol. 9, LBJL.

46. Califano to the President, June 22, 1968, OF/Joe Califano, Box 18, LBJL.

47. McKnight, *Last Crusade,* 357–361.

48. Diaries of Orville Freeman, May 21, 1968, PP/Orville Freeman, Box 12, LBJL.

49. Minutes of the Meeting, May 1, 1968, Cabinet Papers, Box 13, Presidential Papers of LBJ, LBJL.

50. Charles Zwick to the President, June 19, 1968, LBJ Handwriting File, Box 30, Presidential Papers of LBJ, Box 30, LBJL.

51. Kotz, *Judgment Days,* 395.

52. Green and Gwirtzman Conversation, April 4, 1972, and Hackman and Edelman Conversation, July 29, 1965, Box F59, PP/A. Schlesinger, JFKL.

53. Quoted in Edward Schmitt, *President of the Other America: Robert Kennedy and the Politics of Poverty* (Amherst, MA, 2010), 177–179.

54. "Poverty: 'Lord, I'm Hungry,'" *Newsweek,* July 24, 1967.

55. Diaries of Orville Freeman, June 19, 1967, PP/Orville Freeman, Box 11, Vol. 8, LBJL.

56. David T. Ballantyne, "Ernest F. Hollings and the Transformation of South Carolina Politics, 1948–1975" (PhD diss., Cambridge University, 2013), 160–190.

57. Diaries of Orville Freeman, June 12, 1968, PP/Orville Freeman, Box 12, Vol. 9, LBJL.

58. Joe Califano to the President, June 25, 1968, OF/Joe Califano, Box 18, LBJL.

59. Diaries of Orville Freeman, July 11, 1968, PP/Orville Freeman, Box 12, Vol. 9, LBJL.

60. Ibid., June 26, 1968.

61. Diaries of Orville Freeman, May 2, 1968, PP/Orville Freeman, Box 12, LBJL.

62. Califano, *Triumph and Tragedy,* 288.

63. Congressional Leadership Breakfast, April 2, 1968, Meeting Notes File, Box 2, LBJL.

64. Diaries of Orville Freeman, April 24 and 26, 1968, PP/Orville Freeman, Box 12, LBJL.

65. Quoted in Califano, *Triumph and Tragedy,* 289.

66. MR to Marie, April 23, 1968, Diary Backup, Box 97, LBJL.

67. Diaries of Orville Freeman, May 26, 1968, PP/Orville Freeman, Box 11, LBJL.

68. Quoted in Woods, *Quest for Identity,* 274.

69. "Bobby's Last, Longest Day," *Newsweek,* June 17, 1968, 22.

70. "Address to the Nation Following the Attack on Senator Kennedy," June 5, 1968, *Public Papers: LBJ, 1968–1969,* vol. I, 692.

71. Diaries of Orville Freeman, June 5, 1968, PP/Orville Freeman, Box 12, LBJL.

72. Califano, *Triumph and Tragedy,* 304. See also Christian to President, June 10, 1968, LBJL Handwriting File, Box 30, LBJL.

73. Quoted in Michael W. Flamm, *Law and Order: Street Crime, Civil Unrest, and the Crisis of Liberalism in the 1960s* (New York, 2005), 145.

74. Ibid., 135.

75. "Special Message to the Congress on Crime and Law Enforcement: 'to Insure the Public Safety,'" February 7, 1968, *Public Papers: LBJ, 1968–1969,* vol. I, 183.

76. Quoted in Flamm, *Law and Order,* 135. Conviction rates had actually remained steady in the wake of *Miranda.*

77. Ibid., 136.

78. Ibid.

79. Christopher to the President, June 14, 1968, PP/W. Christopher, Box 1, LBJL.

80. Flamm, *Law and Order,* 138.

81. Ramsey Clark to President, June 14, 1968, PP/W. Christopher, Box 1, LBJL.

82. As Michael Flamm has observed, all of the law-and-order activity had little impact on the commission of crimes. Police interrogations without the *Miranda* warning were unlikely to lead to more convictions based on confessions. Phone taps were not going to prevent the commission of most street crimes, and restrictions on the sale of guns were unlikely to prevent career criminals from acquiring firearms. Flamm, *Law and Order,* 199.

83. See "LBJL Picks a New Chief Justice," *Newsweek,* July 8, 1968, 18.

84. Laura Kalman, *Abe Fortas: A Biography* (New Haven, 1990), 15–16.

85. Califano, *Tragedy and Triumph,* 308.

86. Henry J. Abraham, "Justices and Justice: Reflections on the Warren Court's Legacy," in *The Great Society and the High Tide of Liberalism,* ed. Sidney M. Milkis and Jerome M. Mileur (Amherst, MA, 2005), 352.

87. Ibid., 353–355.

88. Christopher to Temple, December 20, 1968, PP/W. Christopher, Box 3, LBJL.

89. See George Christian OH, IV, June 30, 1970, LBJL.

90. Christopher to Temple, December 20, 1968, PP/W. Christopher, Box 3, LBJL.

91. McPherson to Manatos, OF/H. McPherson, Box 51, LBJL.

92. Quoted in Califano, *Triumph and Tragedy,* 312.

93. Christopher to Temple, December 20, 1968, PP/W. Christopher, Box 3, LBJL.

94. Eugene Rostow to Walt Rostow, October 29, 1968, NSF Memos to President, Rostow, Box 41, LBJL.

95. Quoted in Califano, *Triumph and Tragedy,* 311.

96. Ibid.

97. Christopher to Temple, December 20, 1968, PP/W. Christopher, Box 3, LBJL.

98. Ibid., 276.

99. "Mule Teams at Work," *Newsweek,* September 9, 1968.

100. Tom Johnson to the President, June 11, 1968, WHCF, Box 89, Presidential Papers of LBJ, LBJL.

101. See Hubert H. Humphrey, *The Education of a Public Man: My Life and Politics,* ed. Norman Sherman (New York, 1976), 396.

102. "Drafting Lyndon Johnson: The President's Secret Role in the 1968 Democratic Convention" (unpublished manuscript, LBJL).

103. John B. Connally with Mickey Herskowitz, *In History's Shadow: An American Odyssey* (New York, 1993), 203.

104. Arthur Krim OH, November 9, 1982, LBJL.

105. Quoted in Ronald Radosh, *Divided They Fell: The Demise of the Democratic Party, 1964–1996* (New York, 1996), 121.

106. Quoted in Woods, *Quest for Identity,* 276.

107. Quoted in ibid., 277.

108. Ibid.

109. Quoted in ibid., 278.

110. Flamm, *Law and Order,* 163–164.

111. Woods, *Quest for Identity,* 279.

112. Diaries of Orville Freeman, September 11, 1968, PP/Orville Freeman, Box 12, Vol. 9, LBJL.

113. Quoted in Woods, *Quest for Identity,* 279.

114. Quoted in ibid., 280.

CONCLUSION

1. Lester Thurow, "A Liberal Look at Income Distribution," *New York Times,* February 7, 2007.

2. James McGregor Burns, "What Worked? What Failed? Why?" in *The Great Society: A Twenty Year Critique,* ed. Barbara Jordan and Elspeth Rostow (Austin, 1986), 137.

3. Sidney M. Milkis, "Lyndon Johnson, the Great Society, and the Modern Presidency," in *The Great Society and the High Tide of Liberalism,* ed. Sidney M. Milkis and Jerome M. Mileur (Amherst, MA, 2005), 2.

4. Edward Berkowitz, "The Great Society's Enduring National Health Insurance Program," in *Great Society,* ed. Milkis and Mileur, 322–323.

5. Sean J. Savage, *JFK, LBJ, and the Democratic Party* (Albany, 2004), 139.

INDEX

Randall B. Woods is John A. Cooper Distinguished Professor of History at the University of Arkansas. The author of *Shadow Warrior* and award-winning biographies of Lyndon B. Johnson and William Fulbright, Woods lives in Fayetteville, Arkansas.